Advertising Research:

The Internet,
Consumer Behavior,
and Strategy

Advertising Research:

The Internet, Consumer Behavior, and Strategy

George Zinkhan, Editor

AMERICAN MARKETING ASSOCIATION

Chicago, Illinois

Contents

Preface

The articles that appear in this volume were originally presented at American Marketing Association meetings—held at both Winter and Summer Educators' Conferences—over a five-year period. These meetings, sponsored by the Advertising Special Interest Group (SIG), took place on the Saturday prior to the start of the main conference. In some cases, authors presented complete papers that stimulated lively discussions. In others, authors presented "works in progress" that, following constructive feedback from the audience, have been expanded into the articles published here.

The members of the Advertising SIG favor a broad description of advertising that includes promotional activities, new media such as the Internet, topics that cross-fertilize with other business disciplines (e.g., business strategy), and related subjects (e.g., how consumers respond to specific advertising appeals). These broad perspectives are reflected by the articles in this volume.

Although the majority of the authors in this book have academic appointments, a few are employed in industry. As such, the articles are written in a style that should be accessible to both marketing managers and social scientists. Following the themes of the AMA conferences, the articles are intended to stimulate fresh insights and provide even seasoned readers with a new perspective on traditional topics.

At this point, I want to extend my gratitude to Francesca Van Gorp Cooley, who encouraged this project since its inception five years ago. Thanks to Stan Madden of Baylor University for his vision regarding the SIGs and what they could become. Thanks also to Dean Krugman, Margy Conchar, and Hyokjin Kwak (University of Georgia) for their stimulating approach to advertising and to Tom Leigh (University of Georgia) for his perceptive feedback on the sessions that were scheduled at the AMA conferences. Finally, I thank my family for their patience as I devoted time to this enjoyable but expansive project.

George M. Zinkhan
University of Georgia

Introduction to Advertising Research

George M. Zinkhan
University of Georgia

Marketing and advertising are dynamic disciplines, in terms of both practice and academic writing. For example, the television commercials that appear in the year 2000 have little in common with those from the 1960s. Specifically, advertisements from this earlier period used a "hard sell" technique and were primarily informative. They appear somewhat unsophisticated to a twenty-first-century eye, which is more familiar with image-oriented television commercials that are generally much shorter than the commercials that appeared in the 1960s. Although hard-sell, informative advertisements still appear in twenty-first century television, there is no denying that advertising styles have evolved over the 40-year period. Similarly, advertising research styles have evolved and advanced, partly through the influence of improved technology and access to advanced theories and methods.

Organization of this Book

Just as advertising practice has been transformed in the past 40 years, styles in academic marketing have evolved as well. This volume contains 19 articles, divided into seven main sections, that describe emerging trends in advertising research. The first section contains this introductory chapter. The main topic areas explored in the remaining sections include (1) the Internet as a new advertising medium, (2) consumer behavior and behavioral responses to advertising, (3) advertising appeals (e.g., sex appeals, negative appeals such as attack advertisements in the political arena), (4) strategic issues, and (5) ethical issues in advertising. The book concludes with an article that looks ahead to the new millennium and forecasts advertising (and societal) trends in this era.

Each of the main themes is highlighted subsequently. Note that the Internet, as an emerging technology, has the potential to transform advertising research and practice. This certainly is not a topic that would have appeared in a 1960 book on advertising. In contrast, the remaining four themes might have appeared in an earlier book on advertising; but, similar to the practice of advertising, these topics have broadened and evolved. For example, today's concept of strategic thinking is certainly different than it was in 1960.

A New Medium: The Internet

By most estimates, approximately half of all U.S. households are online. Spending on Internet-related advertising is increasing in two ways. First, as shown in Figure 1, advertising that appears on the Internet is expected to increase from $3.3 billion in 1999 to $33 billion in the year 2004. Second, Internet-related organizations (i.e., "dot-com" companies) are beginning to advertise heavily in traditional media, as indicated by the amount of money that dot-com firms spent on advertisements that aired during the 2000 Super Bowl.

To date, the Internet has more significantly affected business-to-business marketing than consumer marketing. However, in both arenas, the Internet has the potential to transform communication patterns. For example, business partners now have an opportunity to establish an "extranet," a close electronic connection between two firms, that enables them to share data electronically (Watson et al. 2000). In one such case, Dell Computer created a "Premium" Web page for key clients. By going to this site, a purchaser at Ford Motor Company is able to order Dell products online at prices that are especially designed for Ford. The Premium page can be established so that any personal computer (PC) ordered for Ford comes with certain built-in specifications (e.g., a certain minimum speed). Beyond these basic specifications, decision makers in the client firm may have some leeway in determining the exact attributes that will be built into the products. As another benefit to the client, the Premier page can enable electronic forms to be automatically distributed to relevant actors within Ford. Thus, an ordering scenario might take on the following sequence or pattern:

(1) A design engineer selects a PC from Ford's Premier page.
(2) The order is transmitted to that engineer's manager for electronic approval.
(3) The order is transmitted electronically to a purchasing agent for approval.
(4) The order is electronically submitted to the accounting department for record keeping.

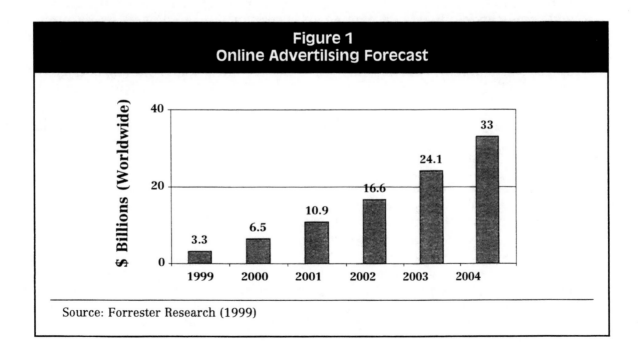

Figure 1
Online Advertilsing Forecast

Source: Forrester Research (1999)

(5) The approved order is transmitted to Dell, which builds the computer upon receipt.

(6) Dell ships the computer within a guaranteed time period for the Premier customer.

Two or more firms can create an extranet by "walling off" a portion of the Internet (in a secure way) that enables the partners to share confidential information (Watson et al. 2000). Notice that this extranet transforms the communication process. If orders can be generated and processed so quickly online, what is the role of a sales force? Dell's Web site (including the Premier pages, which are uniquely designed for specific clients) contains information that previously appeared in business-to-business print advertisements. In the same way, the Web site can take on many of the communication functions that were formerly performed by the sales force.

Approximately 75% of Dell's sales are generated online. The sales force is not the kind of profit center that it was before dot-coms were prevalent. As such, Dell has changed the way the sales force is compensated so that most of the sales force compensation comes from salary, rather than commission. That is, there is a decoupling of the sales person from the revenue stream of fresh orders (from both established and new customers). As a result, the function of the sales force changes within the organization. Communication patterns change. The sales force focuses more on strategic issues and less on day-to-day interactions with customers. Promotion and advertising practices are radically altered by the success of Dell's "Direct Business Model."

"First we make our tools, and then our tools make us" (Meyer and Hovde 1999). This famous quotation provides an interesting way to view the potential impact of the Internet on advertising and society as a whole. The Internet is a new tool that is just beginning to have an impact on humankind. But, the Internet is not really a single tool. Rather, it is a series of related tools. The extranet is one kind of broad tool. The Intranet (electronic communications within a firm) is a related kind of broad tool (Watson et al. 2000). The Premier page is a tool that represents a specific application of the extranet. Thus, the Internet is really a package of related tools (some broad and some narrow) that is developing and evolving at a rapid pace. At the same time, this new set of tools is beginning to have pervasive effects on business, society, the academy, and advertising practice. In this sense, the articles on the Internet that appear in this book examine this emerging technology and how it is beginning to "make us."

Consumer Behavior and Behavioral Responses to Advertising

A basic principle of advertising practice is that promotional messages are targeted to a specific audience. As such, the audience's response to advertising messages has long been a key topic in advertising research. In this volume, Brown, Homer, and Inman summarize the emotional reactions that advertising generates. Throughout the 1970s, academic advertising researchers concentrated on the audience's cognitive reactions to advertising. In the 1980s, this pattern began to change; there was an increased interest in monitoring consumers' emotional reactions. However, measuring consumer responses to advertising has proved challenging because, in an experimental or survey setting, there is a tendency to operationalize emotional reactions by having respondents circle a number on a questionnaire. A number on a questionnaire would, on the face of it, seem to have very little to do with human emotional reactions. Thus, qualitative research methods must play an important role if researchers are interested in understanding the emotional world of advertising response.

Also in this volume, Taylor and Stamps investigate the issues associated with appealing to minority consumers. This is another traditional topic in advertising research—understanding and appealing to small or neglected audiences. As media technology advances, advertisers find that they have the capability of designing promotional messages for an audience of one. That is, one-to-one marketing provides an opportunity for the ultimate segmentation approach, in which each individual customer is a segment. Consider a World Wide Web site that is truly interactive. When consumers access a site, they can be asked to indicate their preferences through a series of relatively simple questions. Then, the site can deliver promotional information (over time) that is specifically tailored to the preferences of each of these Web visitors. Database marketing provides another avenue for targeting detailed messages to individual consumers.

Advertising Appeals

When advertisers understand who their customers are, the next step is to design a particular advertising appeal. Traditionally, academic advertising research classifies these advertising appeals into groups, such as "fear" appeal, product benefit appeal, sex appeal, personality appeal, and many others. In this volume, the authors concentrate on three basic kinds of appeals—sex appeals, green advertising, and negative advertisements (e.g., advertisements that attack the competition). The appeal must somehow match the sentiments of the target audience. At the same time, advertisers must take the competition's advertising into account. Hensel and James consider this issue when they examine the effect of negative advertisements, which specifically argue against a competitor's position. According to their analysis, this kind of attack advertising is more likely to work for political advertising than for consumer product advertising.

Strategic Issues in Advertising

Strategy underlies all of business practice. Marketing strategy is a subset of the "strategic management perspective." In the same way, advertising strategy can be viewed as a subset of general marketing strategy.

In this book, five different articles are devoted to strategic issues. Two of these chapters are highlighted here. First, Angela Patton—an Art Professor—discusses advertising from a strategic design perspective. Design is a key concept in marketing (Zinkhan 1993); products are designed, advertisements are designed, promotional campaigns are designed, and an overall marketing strategy is designed. In general, marketing academics do not have much exposure to the highly advanced design literature that has emerged in recent years. Professor Patton outlines some design principles that might inform our understanding of merchandising, consuming, and ownership.

Second, Dr. Ritchie is a sociologist currently employed by Bank of America in Charlotte, N.C. In her article, she reports the results of a longitudinal study that investigates the effectiveness of marketing and advertising activities in the health care industry. In general, she reports evidence that advertising works. This finding is important, because it is often difficult to separate the effects of advertising from all of the noise that exists in the environment (e.g., competitive actions, economic climate, societal trends). Are advertising expenses justified? Some advertising agencies have begun to argue that, in some industries, advertising is a cost of doing business, in the same way that maintaining an accounting department is an unavoidable cost of doing business. For example, if a firm such as McDonald's reduces advertising spending in the final quarter of 2000, it might lose market share that is very difficult to regain in any future quarter. Dr. Ritchie presents some interesting evidence that advertising expenditures are a good investment.

Ethical Issues in Advertising

Just about every business college now offers one or more required courses in business ethics. There is always a major challenge associated with teaching or researching in this important macromarketing (or macroadvertising) area. What are the appropriate standards by which to judge the ethical actions of business organizations? Many approaches are possible, including a legal approach, a philosophical approach, a logic-based approach, a human conscience approach (e.g., can the decision maker sleep soundly at night?), a religious approach, an economics approach (e.g., a cost and benefit approach), an industry approach (e.g., developing industry standards), an organizational approach (e.g., developing an organizationwide ethics code), and many others. There are well-known problems with each of these approaches.

A relatively new approach has been proposed by French and Granrose (1995), and this application has proven quite popular in Europe and other areas. Following Socrates, French and Granrose argue that an ethical person is a reasoning person. That is, if the focus of ethics is on resolving conflicts, then such resolution "is more likely to occur through careful reasoning than through reliance on either tradition or mere emotion" (p. 62). These authors argue that ethical conflicts can be resolved by strategic communication and through a process of negotiation. In this way, they cleverly resolve the normative question: What is the standard for determining whether or not a specific (advertising) practice is ethical?

In this volume, Denise DeLorme—a professor for a communications college—describes the potential ethical issues associated with qualitative research that is conducted in cyberspace. As advertising researchers take advantage of new comminations media, new ethical challenges may emerge. DeLorme identifies these challenges and makes some progress toward developing an ethical code to address these challenges. Mike Hyman proposes to identify the full range of ethical dilemmas that might confront advertisers and their agencies.

Conclusion

Advertising is a dynamic and exciting field. From an academic perspective, there are many ways to approach it. In this volume, Misty Richie approaches the topic as a sociologist. Denise DeLorme approaches it from a communications research perspective. Angela Patton approaches it as a professor of art and design. Because this volume is sponsored by the American Marketing Association, the remaining authors largely assume a marketing perspective. Many challenges remain for future scholars and managers, regardless of the perspective they adopt. This volume identifies and discusses current issues in advertising research and proposes perspectives for understanding future problems and opportunities.

References

Forrester Research (1999), Forrester home page, (accessed August 1999), [available at http://www.forrester.com].

French, Warren A. and John Granrose (1995), *Practical Business Ethics*. Englewood Cliffs, NJ: Prentice Hall.

Meyer, Muffie and Ellen Hovde (1999), "American Photography," Public Broadcasting System, (October 13).

Watson, Richard T., Pierre Berthon, Leyland F. Pitt, and George M. Zinkhan (2000), *Electronic Commerce: The Strategic Perspective*. Fort Worth, TX: The Dryden Press.

Zinkhan, George M. (1993), "Advertising, Design, and Corporate Identity," *Journal of Advertising*, 22 (4), 1–3.

A New Medium: The Internet

1

Conducting Advertising and Marketing Research on the World Wide Web

Vanitha Swaminathan
University of Massachusetts

This article investigates the influence of customer characteristics on brand switching behavior in online versus offline shopping environments. A comparison is made of online shopping and offline shopping across a sample of consumers. Customer characteristics such as variety seeking, information seeking, enjoyment afforded by Internet use, and planned shopping behavior are posited to have an impact on brand switching behavior in online versus offline environments. Results of this study are based on a survey of consumers using online and offline services and scanner panel data on these same consumers in the context of an online grocery store. The results support some of the hypothesized relationships. Implications for theory and practice are discussed.

Online shopping is gaining popularity. Analysts predict that online shopping revenues will grow from $11 billion in 1999 to $41 billion in 2002 (National Retail Federation 1999). The U.S. Department of Commerce (1999), citing a study by Forrester Research, suggests that online retail trade, which ranged from $7 billion to $15 billion in 1998, will reach anywhere from $40 billion to $80 billion by 2002. The growth of online shopping in recent years has given rise to interest among academic researchers in investigating the impact of online shopping on various aspects of consumer choice behavior.

Various researchers have begun to examine the effect of computer-mediated environments on patterns of consumer choice and shopping behavior (e.g., Alba et al. 1997; Degeratu, Rangaswamy, and Wu 1999; Shankar, Rangaswamy, and Pusateri 1999; Swaminathan, Lepkowska-White, and Rao 1999; Watson et al. 2000). Much of this research has focused on examining the role of online or computer-mediated environments in influencing the impact of brand name, price, and other search attributes (Degeratu, Rangaswamy, and Wu 1999); the impact of the online medium on price sensitivity of consumers (Shankar, Rangaswamy, and Pusateri 1999); the factors that have an impact on shopping online versus offline (Swaminathan, Lepkowska-White, and Rao 1999); and an analysis of interactive home shopping (Alba et al. 1997). The results from these studies suggest the following: (1) The online medium can enhance the value of a brand name in those categories in which less information about attributes is available (Degeratu, Rangaswamy, and Wu 1999); (2) the online medium does not increase price importance but increases the value of undertaking a search (Shankar, Rangaswamy, and Pusateri 1999); and (3) shopping motivations (e.g., convenience) dominate other aspects such as privacy, security concerns, and vendor characteristics in the decision to shop online (Swaminathan, Lepkowska-White, and Rao 1999).

Previous research has focused on examining the impact of the online medium on choice behavior and likelihood of shopping online, however scant research focuses on characteristics of customers that may influence their shopping behavior in the online environment. In other words, although researchers in the past have focused their attention on the overall impact of the online medium on brand choice behavior, it is possible that the influence of online shopping on brand switching or brand choice varies across different segments of consumers. Thus, whereas some consumers may exhibit greater brand switching in the online environment, others may exhibit less switching. Accordingly, the objectives of this article are to examine (1) the role of customer characteristics such as variety seeking, enjoyment from Internet use, convenience, and planned shopping on differences in shopping online versus offline and (2) characteristics of customer segments based on their shopping behavior with respect to four frequently purchased items, liquid detergents, powder detergents, dish soaps, and paper towels. Data for this study come from the scanner panel data of an online grocery store. In addition, a sample of consumers who shop at this store was surveyed to capture data on customer characteristics. The scanner data were merged with the survey data for purposes of this study.

The rest of the article is organized as follows: In the next section, the hypotheses are developed. Following that, the data collection method is outlined. Next, the data are analyzed. In the last section, the results, conclusions, and implications for further research are presented.

Hypotheses

Variety-Seeking Behavior

Prior research has examined situational and customer characteristics that influence consumers' variety-seeking behavior. *Variety-seeking behavior* is defined as the tendency for a consumer to switch away from the item consumed previously (Givon 1984; Kahn, Kalwani, and Morrison 1986). Variety seeking has been identified as one of the factors that influences brand switching (Bawa 1990). Menon and Kahn (1995) suggest that one of the reasons consumers seek variety is to satisfy a need for stimulation. They base their argument on the premise that consumers often find themselves in choice situations that differ in the degree of novelty, change, uncertainty, conflict, or complexity. Because most consumers prefer intermediate levels of stimulation to either very high or very low levels, the stimulation provided by these choice situations often needs to be counterbalanced. One balancing mechanism is the reduction in variety-seeking behavior. Menon and Kahn also suggest that changes in the retail environment might provide a basis for stimulation. Given this argument, it is expected that when consumers switch from an offline shopping environment to an online environment, the stimulation offered by shopping in the new Internet environment will serve to depress or reduce the amount of variety seeking in a given product category, at least initially. In other words, the stimulation offered by the new retail environment is counterbalanced by routinization of brand choices. In summary, high variety seekers will exhibit lower brand switching in the online environment.[1] In the offline environment, high variety seekers will exhibit greater brand switching behavior.

H_1: The greater the variety-seeking behavior of a consumer, the lower the brand-switching behavior in online (versus offline) environments.

Enjoyment from Internet Use

Menon and Kahn (1995) suggest that if a choice situation induces positive affect, then it might enhance consumers' awareness of the differences among items and their expectations of the purchase experience, thereby increasing the potential enjoyable stimulation offered by each item. This serves to enhance brand-switching behavior. This argument can be extended to apply to those situations in which the positive affect may be induced by the retail environment as well. Some consumers are not only familiar with Internet technology but also derive enjoyment from using it (Hoffman and Novak 1996). Hoffman and Novak refer to this enjoyment as "flow." If consumers enjoy using the Internet, they might be induced to explore the capabilities afforded by the technology. This enhances the enjoyment afforded by the Internet experience. For example, one feature of the Internet is the ability to search and compare across brands and items. This search capability, in addition to the enjoyment afforded by Internet usage, might serve as an incentive to consumers to explore different alternative brands in the various categories shopped. Thus, it is expected that consumers who enjoy Internet use are more likely to exhibit brand-switching behavior on the Internet than those who enjoy it less. Enjoyment derived from Internet use has a direct impact on brand-switching behavior in online environments. Therefore, the following is proposed:

H_2: The greater the enjoyment derived from Internet use, the greater is the brand-switching behavior in online environments.

Information-Seeking Behavior

Various studies have focused on shopping motivations. Stephenson and Willett (1969) grouped consumers into recreational, convenience, and price-oriented shoppers. Bellenger and Kargaonkar (1980) distinguish between convenience and recreational shoppers. They suggest that the recreational shopper is motivated by the social aspects of shopping as well as the ability to gather information. The Internet offers consumers the ability to gather information on products and brands by sorting various product categories by unit price, brand, and description. These sorting capabilities make the online medium ideal for search and comparison across brands and products and are therefore likely to appeal to those shoppers who are motivated by information seeking. Information seeking is likely to lead to greater brand switching behavior in online versus offline environments because of a reduction in search

---

[1]It is acknowledged that when consumers become familiar with the new Internet environment, the novelty will wear off. This will reduce the stimulation offered by the retail environment and encourage variety seekers to increase their brand switching. However, given that the online retail environment is in its early stages, especially during the time period in which this study is conducted, it is likely to be a new environment for consumers and therefore a source of stimulation.

costs offered by sorting capabilities. Among low information seekers, there is unlikely to be a significant difference in brand switching behavior in online and offline environments. This leads to the following hypothesis:

H_3: The more a consumer is motivated by information seeking, the greater is the brand-switching behavior in online (versus offline) environments.

Planned Shopping Behavior

There is a vast literature in marketing on consumers who are impulse versus planned shoppers (Beatty and Ferrell 1998; Rook 1987). Whereas impulse buying has been defined as purchases occurring spontaneously without previous intention (Beatty and Ferrell 1998), planned shopping may be viewed as purchases occurring on the basis of decisions made prior to entering the store. The online store offers the capability of storing previous purchases through the use of personalized shopping lists. Consumers can gain access to their previous purchases by using this shopping list. This shopping list may enhance the ability to plan shopping and reduce the level of impulse purchases. Indeed, previous research has pointed to the possibility that when consumers add a product to their personal list, they tend to repeat purchase at a higher rate (Degeratu, Rangaswamy, and Wu 1999). Therefore, the online medium may discourage brand switching especially among those consumers who are prone to planning their shopping more than offline environments will because of the additional convenience offered by the use of personalized shopping lists. The following, based on these factors, is proposed:

H_4: The more the consumer is a planned shopper, the lower is the brand-switching behavior in online (versus offline) environments.

A summary of the hypotheses outlined previously are presented graphically in Figure 1.

Measures

The measures for the various constructs in this study are outlined subsequently. These measures have been chosen on the basis of previous research. A summary of these, along with means and standard deviations, is presented in Table 1. The survey items were measured using seven-point agree/disagree scales.

Brand-Switching Behavior

To measure the brand-switching behavior of consumers, the average number of brands bought in a category by a household over a one-year period was used.

Variety-Seeking Behavior

Variety-seeking behavior is measured using four scale items: (1) I enjoy exploring several different alternatives of stores when shopping; (2) Investigating new types of stores is generally a waste of time; (3) I like to try out new products and brands for fun; and (4) I like to buy the same brand name every time I shop. The reliability of this four-item scale was moderate ($\alpha = .60$).

Enjoyment Derived from Internet Use

The enjoyment derived from Internet use is measured using responses to the following scale items: (1) Shopping over the Internet is a pleasant experience; (2) I enjoy

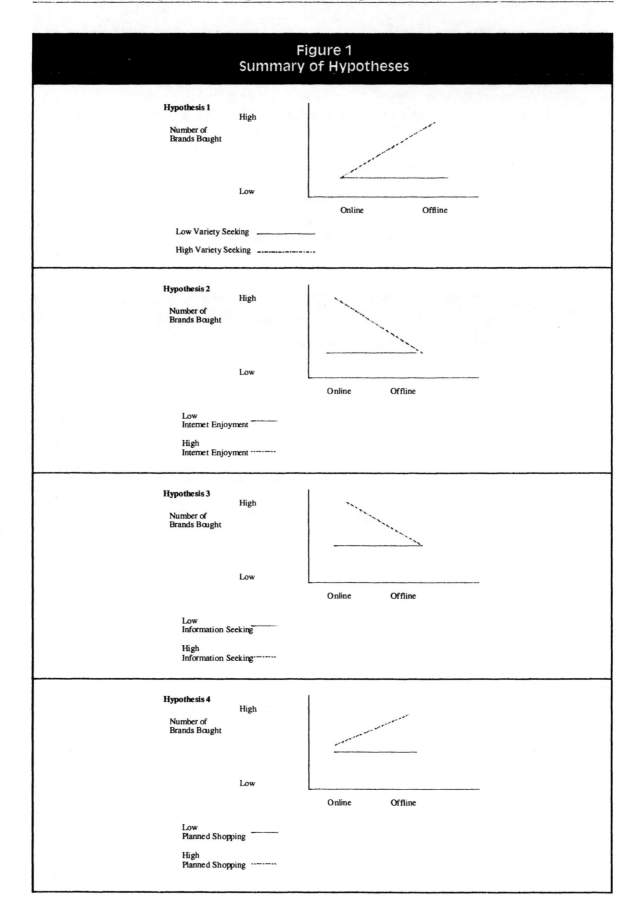

Figure 1
Summary of Hypotheses

shopping over the Internet; and (3) For me, the Internet is often frustrating or confusing. The reliability of this three-item scale is also moderate (α = .63).

Information-Seeking Behavior

Information seeking as a shopping motivation is measured by responses to the following scale items: (1) I always compare prices for similar products among various grocery stores; and (2) I like to have a great deal of information before I buy. The correlation between these items is moderate at .38.

Impulse Versus Planned Shopping Behavior

The level of impulse versus planned shopping behavior for an individual consumer was measured on the basis of responses to the following items: (1) I carefully

---

Table 1
Scale Items, Means, and Standard Deviations

Scale Items	Means and Standard Deviations (seven-point Likert Scale where 1 = strongly disagree and 7 = strongly agree)
Variety Seeking	
I enjoy exploring several different alternatives of stores when shopping.	4.201 (1.532)
Investigating new types of stores is generally a waste of time.	4.828 (1.367)*
I like to try out new products and brands for fun.	4.757 (1.351)
I like to buy the same brand name every time I shop.	3.649 (1.403)*
Enjoyment Derived from Internet Usage	
Shopping over the Internet is a pleasant experience.	5.004 (1.582)
I enjoy shopping over the Internet.	5.070 (1.537)
For me, the Internet is often frustrating or confusing.	4.961 (4.884)*
Information Seeking	
I always compare prices for similar products among various grocery stores.	3.451 (1.657)
I like to have a great deal of information before I buy.	4.214 (1.505)
Planned Shopping Behavior	
I carefully plan most of my purchases.	5.090 (1.440)
I use a shopping list every time I shop for groceries.	4.760 (1.880)

*Items have been reverse-coded.

plan most of my purchases, and (2) I use a shopping list every time I shop for groceries. The correlation coefficient between these items is .59. The continuous scales in this study were recoded so that respondents could be classified as either high or low on any one dimension. Although there was some loss of information associated with this, it enabled me to summarize the information and simplify the analysis of interaction effects. Therefore, respondents that scored five or higher on any dimension (e.g., information seeking, enjoyment, planned shopping behavior, variety seeking) were classified as high on the given dimension, and those that scored lower than five were classified as low on the given dimension.

Method

The data for this study come from a survey of online grocery shoppers. Scanner data on these same shoppers were also collected. The purchase data on these shoppers were collected over a two-year period. The online grocery store also offers customers the option of placing orders by telephone based on catalogs sent by mail. Ideally, to test the hypotheses regarding online and offline shopping behavior, the same sample of consumers must be observed making purchases in both the online and offline shopping environments. Although some data on consumers shopping in both online and offline media were available, the sample sizes were too small to allow any meaningful test of the hypotheses proposed previously.

An alternative method for testing the previous hypotheses might be using an experiment. In an experimental design, a sample of consumers can be assigned randomly to online and offline shopping, and their responses can be measured. Randomization accounts for sample selection biases that are likely to limit the generalizability of research findings. Randomization also enables researchers to neutralize differences in study respondents across treatments. However, an experiment also creates an artificial environment and has the limitation of being unrealistic. A natural experiment conducted in a field setting enables researchers to capture the complexities extant in the real world and thereby enhance the external validity of the research.

In this study, the hypotheses were tested using a field experiment. To contrast choice behavior in online and offline samples, a matched sample of consumers shopping online and offline was created. For the purpose of this study, a consumer was classified as an online shopper if more than 70% of their purchases were made on the Web. Conversely, a consumer was classified as an offline shopper if more than 70% of their purchases were made by catalog. Further analyses were restricted to purchases made in one medium (either Web or catalog) only. The online and offline samples were matched on the basis of age and education. The creation of matched samples based on age and education to contrast online and offline shopping has been a feature of previous research in this area (Degeratu, Rangaswamy, and Wu 1999; Schlosser, Shavitt, and Kanfer 1999). To justify the use of matched samples, I analyzed the dependent variable, that is, the number of brands bought in four product categories, for both the matched sample (Table 2) and the sample of consumers that switched from offline to online purchases. The analysis suggests that the pattern of purchases are similar in both samples, with the number of brands bought typically being lower in the online environment than in the offline environment. Given the similar pattern of results, the use of the matched sample in further analyses is justified.

Table 2
T-Tests of Differences in Means in Number of Brands Bought By Matched Online and Offline Samples

Category Description	Means and Standard Deviations (Online and Offline Samples)	Sample Size	T-Test
Liquid detergents	Online: 3.051 (2.827)	39	−2.565 ($p < .01$)
	Offline: 6.000 (6.034)	20	
Paper towels	Online: 5.529 (5.555)	34	−1.773 ($p < .10$)
	Offline: 9.391 (9.394)	23	
Dish soaps	Online: 2.286 (1.840)	35	−1.891 ($p < .01$)
	Offline: 4.950 (6.143)	20	
Powder detergents	Online: 2.857 (2.013)	35	−.011 (ns)
	Offline: 2.867 (3.335)	20	

Contrasting Web and catalog shoppers enables me to capture the impact of the unique aspects of Internet shopping such as search-and-comparison capabilities and the use of personalized shopping lists. Because catalog purchases offer benefits of asynchrony and convenience similar to those associated with ordering over the Web, contrasting catalog and Web shopping is more meaningful than a contrast involving Web shoppers and bricks-and-mortar shoppers.

To test the hypotheses, various restrictions were imposed on the sample. First, only those respondents that had placed at least six orders within a one-year period were included. This is essential to establish sufficient purchase histories. Second, respondents were classified as online or offline shoppers on the basis of the medium in which more than 70% of their orders were placed. To create a contrast, the online and offline samples were matched on the basis of age and education. Respondents in the 30–49 age group were selected from both samples. Only those with at least a college degree were retained for further analyses. As a result of these restrictions, approximately 30 respondents were retained in each of the two matched online and offline samples.

Data Analysis and Results

A test of the hypotheses in this study can be accomplished through analysis of variance. A summary of cell means for the various conditions is presented for the paper towel category in the study (see Table 3).

An examination of the cell means shows that for many of the conditions, the dependent measure varies in the expected direction. For example, the difference between high variety seekers and low variety seekers is less pronounced in the Web environment than is the difference between high variety seekers and low variety seekers in the catalog environment, though a strict test of the hypothesis requires that the high variety seekers have a lower average number of brands bought than the low variety seekers. Similarly, the average number of brands bought is higher for information-seeking Web shoppers than for those who do not seek information. The small sample size in the case of the information-seeking catalog shoppers makes it

	Means (Category = paper towels)
Conditions	
High variety-seeking Web shoppers	6.1
Low variety-seeking Web shoppers	5.1
High variety-seeking catalog shoppers	16
Low variety-seeking catalog shoppers	7
High information-seeking Web shoppers	6.3
Low information-seeking Web shoppers	5.04
High information-seeking catalog shoppers	19.5*
Low information-seeking catalog shoppers	8.43
High enjoyment Web shoppers	5.42
Low enjoyment Web shoppers	5.25*
High enjoyment catalog shoppers	9.6
Low enjoyment catalog shoppers	9.23*
Planned Web shoppers	6.2
Unplanned Web shoppers	3.4
Planned catalog shoppers	10.25
Unplanned catalog shoppers	8.45

Table 3
Summary of Cell Means for Dependent Variable (Number of Brands Bought)

* Sample size less than five.

difficult to contrast Web and catalog shoppers on this characteristic. A similar issue with sample sizes makes it difficult to draw conclusions regarding enjoyment derived from Internet usage. In the case of planned shopping behavior, there is a larger difference between planned shoppers and unplanned shoppers in the number of brands bought in the case of Web shoppers than in the case of catalog shoppers. However, the differences are not in the expected direction. The differences suggest that planned shoppers buy more brands on average than unplanned shoppers in both the Web and catalog samples. Although the differences are not significant, this finding is intriguing.

To test further the hypotheses, an analysis of variance was conducted on the data. The results of this are summarized in Table 4.

As can be seen in Table 4, there is a significant effect of the medium (Web versus catalog) in influencing the number of brands bought in three of four cases. Only in the case of powder detergents is the main effect of medium not significant. The main effect of customer characteristics is significant in two of three cases. The enjoyment derived from Internet use ($p < .01$) and variety seeking ($p < .10$) were each significant in one of the four cases. The interaction between medium and customer characteristics was significant in three of four cases. The interaction between information seeking and medium was significant in the case of liquid detergents ($p < .01$) and paper towels ($p < .10$). The interaction between variety seeking and medium was significant in the case of paper towels ($p < .10$). The interaction between Internet enjoyment and medium was significant in the case of powder detergents ($p < .05$). These results suggest some support for the hypothesized relationships.

Table 4
Analysis of Variance Summary of Results Matched Online and Offline Samples

Category	F-Value	p Value	Main Effect Medium	Main Effect Customer Characteristic	Interaction Between Medium and Customer Characteristic
Liquid Detergents					
Variety seeking	2.81	p < .05	p < .05	ns	ns
Information seeking	5.22	p < .01	p < .05	ns	p < .01
Internet enjoyment	4.99	p < .01	p < .01	p < .01	ns
Planned shopping	2.47	p < .01	p < .01	ns	ns
Paper Towels					
Variety seeking	3.72	p < .05	p < .05	p < .10	p < .10
Information seeking	2.99	p < .05	p < .05	ns	p < .10
Internet enjoyment	.27	ns	p < .05	ns	ns
Planned shopping	1.35	ns	p < .05	ns	ns
Dish Soaps					
Variety seeking	1.88	ns	p < .10	ns	ns
Information seeking	2.01	ns	p < .10	ns	ns
Internet enjoyment	2.38	p < .10	p < .05	ns	ns
Planned shopping	3.21	p < .05	p < .01	ns	ns
Powder Detergents					
Variety seeking	.27	ns	ns	ns	ns
Information seeking	.25	ns	ns	ns	ns
Internet enjoyment	2.60	p < .10	ns	ns	p < .05
Planned shopping	.37	ns	ns	ns	ns

Summary and Limitations

This study examines the role of customer characteristics in influencing brand-switching behavior in online environments. This research uses a combination of survey data and scanner data to examine the effect of medium and customer characteristics on the average number of brands bought in four frequently purchased categories. The data are based on actual choices made by consumers in online and offline environments. This enhances the validity of the study.

The findings suggest that the choice of Web or catalog medium has a significant impact on the number of brands bought in various categories. In addition, information seeking and variety seeking have a significant impact on number of brands bought. The interaction between medium and information seeking and medium and enjoyment derived from Internet use also is significant. There is no conclusive evidence of the role of planned purchases in influencing the number of brands bought in online versus offline environments. Although it was hypothesized that the number of brands bought would be lower, on average, among consumers who plan their purchases, and particularly among those who purchase on the Web, this was not significant. In addition, some of the cell means for planned and unplanned purchasing were not in the expected direction. Further research investigating the impact of planned purchasing among a larger sample of consumers will help shed further light on this issue.

This study has a few limitations. First, the results are based on small sample sizes. Given the nature of the questions posed in this study, the results might be viewed as providing initial insights into the nature of brand-switching behavior in online environments. Further research must enhance the sample size and conduct further exploration to confirm the findings in this study. Given that the Internet and its role in marketing has been the subject of considerable interest in academia, the results of this exploratory study are worth reporting and will serve to spur further research on this topic. A second limitation may be the use of matched online and offline samples. Although matching decreases the problems associated with selection biases, it does not completely eliminate the sample selection bias. In providing results from both the matched sample and the sample of consumers that shopped both online and offline, this study overcomes that limitation to some extent. Further research incorporating this approach and testing the hypotheses on a larger sample of respondents will help extend knowledge further.

References

Alba, Joseph, John Lynch, Barton Weitz, Chris Janiszewski, Richard Lutz, Alan Sawyer, and Stacy Wood (1997), "Interactive Home Shopping: Consumer, Retailer, and Manufacturer Incentives to Participate in Electronic Marketplaces," *Journal of Marketing*, 61 (3), 38–54.

Bawa, Kapil (1990), "Modeling Inertia and Variety Seeking Tendencies in Brand Choice Behavior," *Marketing Science*, 9 (Summer), 263–78.

Beatty, Sharon E. and M. Elizabeth Ferrell (1998), "Impulse Buying: Modeling Its Precursors," *Journal of Retailing*, 74 (2), 169–91.

Bellenger, Danny N. and Pradeep K. Kargaonkar (1980), "Profiling the Recreational Shopper," *Journal of Retailing*, 56 (3), 77–82.

Degeratu, Alexandru, Arvind Rangaswamy, and Jianan Wu (1999), "Consumer Choice Behavior in Online and Traditional Supermarkets: The Effects of Brand Name, Price and other Search Attributes," working paper, Pennsylvania State University.

Givon, Moshe (1984), "Variety-Seeking Through Brand Switching," *Marketing Science*, 3 (Winter), 1–22.

Hoffman, Donna and Thomas P. Novak (1996), "Marketing in Hypermedia Computer-Mediated Environments: Conceptual Foundations," *Journal of Marketing*, 60 (3), 50–68.

Kahn, Barbara, Manohar U. Kalwani, and Donald G. Morrison (1986), "Measuring Variety-Seeking and Reinforcement Behaviors Using Panel Data," *Journal of Marketing Research*, 23 (May), 89–100.

Menon, Satya and Barbara E. Kahn (1995), "The Impact of Context on Variety Seeking in Product Choices," *Journal of Consumer Research*, 22 (3), 285–96.

National Retail Federation (1999), "1998 Holiday Sales Data," (accessed May 15, 1999), [http://www.nrf.com/hot/holiday/dec98].

Rook, Dennis W. (1987), "The Buying Impulse," *Journal of Consumer Research*, 14 (September), 189–99.

Schlosser Ann E., Sharon Shavitt, and Alaina Kanfer (1999), "Survey of Internet Users' Attitudes Toward Internet Advertising," *Journal of Interactive Marketing*, 13 (3), 34–54.

Shankar, Venkatesh, Arvind Rangaswamy, and Michael Pusateri (1999), "Customer Price Sensitivity and the Online Medium," working paper, University of Maryland.

Stephenson, Ronald P. and Ronald P. Willett (1969), "Analysis of Consumers' Retail Patronage Strategies," in *Marketing Involvement in Society and Economy*, Philip R. McDonald, ed. Chicago: American Marketing Association, 316–22.

Swaminathan, Vanitha, Ela Lepkowska-White, and Bharat P. Rao (1999), "Browsers or Buyers in Cyberspace? An Investigation of Factors Influencing Electronic Exchange," (accessed January 30, 2000), [available at http://www.ascusc.org/jcmc/vol5/issue2/swaminathan].

U.S. Department of Commerce (1999), "The Emerging Digital Economy II," (accessed January 30, 2000), [available at http://www.ecommerce.gov/ede/].

Watson, Richard T., Leyland Pitt, Pierre Berthon, and George M. Zinkhan (2000), *Electronic Commerce: The Strategic Perspective*. Fort Worth, TX: Dryden Press.

2

The Theory of Flow: Applications to Advertising and Consumers' Internet Experiences

Margy P. Conchar
The University of North Carolina, Charlotte

George M. Zinkhan
The University of Georgia

Marketing is concerned with "creating exchanges that satisfy individual and organizational goals" (Bennett 1995, p. 166). Marketers engage in an ongoing process of identifying unmet consumer needs or wants and then creating products and/or services that attempt to satisfy those needs/wants. Thus, the marketing manager is charged with the responsibility of facilitating the exchange of goods and services to optimize value for all parties participating in marketplace exchanges. In a very general sense then, marketing involves making people happy with their marketplace exchanges. A rich tradition of marketing research considers consumer satisfaction with purchases, service encounters, and consumption experiences.

From a macro perspective, satisfaction with specific consumption events could, on aggregate, contribute to a more global sense of satisfaction with life, general well-being, or happiness. Aristotelian philosophy maintains that happiness is the only goal sought in and of itself: every other goal we set in the course of our lives aims toward the achievement of happiness (Csikszentmihalyi 1990). Taking this view of consumer motivation, we expect that products and services that contribute to the fulfillment of the overriding goal of happiness would be sought out by consumers. In contrast, we expect that consumers would resist products and services that block the achievement of happiness.

According to this position, marketing would best serve its constituencies (marketers and consumers) by identifying approaches to facilitate exchanges that contribute to happiness for consumers. These approaches could encompass a range of elements of the marketing mix, such as the inherent nature of the product or service (e.g., pleasing music on a compact disc), the nature of the distribution process (an enjoyable music shopping experience on the Internet or in a music store), the advertising message (video clips on television or a Web site), and a price that signals value for money. Consumers will be drawn toward offerings they perceive as enhancing their level of happiness, and they will avoid marketplace offerings that reduce their overall sense of happiness.

The difficulty in defining and measuring happiness has limited the direct application of this philosophy to marketing theory. Psychologists have struggled to identify material correlates of happiness. Studies that measure self-reports of happiness find that people's assessments of their levels of well-being differ less than would be expected across such variables as occupation, sex, age, and education (Inglehart and Rabier 1986). One interpretation of the concept of happiness is "optimal experience" or "flow," which is "an almost effortless, yet highly focused state of consciousness" (Csikszentmihalyi 1997b, p. 9). This construct has been measured in a way that successfully differentiates certain types of human experience as optimal.

Here, we discuss some ways marketing contributes toward the achievement of happiness. Specifically, we adopt Csikszentmihalyi's flow construct and suggest that consumers may experience flow while engaging in a range of consumption behaviors, from search activity (on the Web or in a more traditional retail environment) to the consumption experience itself (e.g., playing a video game). We propose that advertising serves as one component of a product or service and, as such, is one element of the mix that might, in and of itself, contribute to or block flow. The Internet embodies many of the characteristics that enable flow experiences (Hoffman and Novak 1996). We describe some of these flow-enabling characteristics of consumption on the Internet and demonstrate how this new technology provides an excellent example of a consumption experience that might be sought out by consumers for the flow experiences it produces.

The Concept of Flow

The concept of flow was introduced by the influential social scientist Mihaly Csikszentmihalyi. In his best-selling book, *Flow: The Psychology of Optimal Experience*, Csikszentmihalyi (1990, p. 158) describes flow as a kind of peak experience that all humans seek. Such experiences are relatively rare, but they are quite satisfying and pleasurable. Flow is "the state in which people are so involved in an activity that nothing else seems to matter; the experience itself is so enjoyable that people will do it even at great cost, for the sheer sake of doing it." Flow involves a sense of exhilaration, a deep sense of enjoyment that is long cherished and becomes a landmark in memory. It involves challenges that are not necessarily pleasant at the time. Because of the presence of challenges (inherent in the flow experience), consumers find that they are fully caught up in the experience. Being in flow requires total concentration, and yet this type of concentration is somehow pleasurable (in the long run).

When analyzing the responses of subjects who participated in his study, Csikszentmihalyi found that flow coincides with occasions when both skills and challenges are rated at high levels. As such, people engaged in their favorite challenging activities often experience flow. Some examples of situations that might be favorable to the experience of flow include flying a test aircraft (for a pilot), performing surgery (for a doctor), creating a work of art or performing a dance, making social contacts and forging intimate relationships, playing a video game, climbing a mountain, and participating in a professional conference. In all of these activities, skills are involved. People experience flow when they test and hone their skills to overcome obstacles or challenges. The matching of skill and challenge results in flow.

As implied in the description of flow, it is a delicate state that might not necessarily be maintained for a long period of time. It involves peak performance and concentration. As shown in Figure 1, flow activities are often favorite activities. Both control and arousal approach flow experiences, but neither qualifies as a flow activity. An example of arousal is a learning situation in which a person attempts to

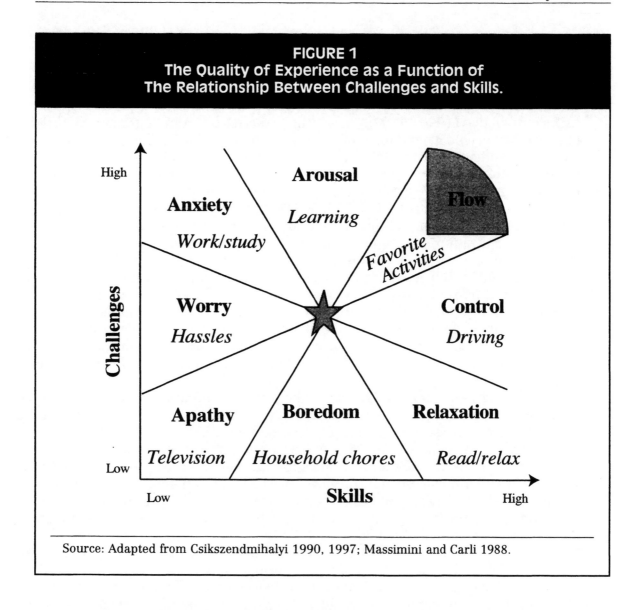

FIGURE 1
The Quality of Experience as a Function of
The Relationship Between Challenges and Skills.

Source: Adapted from Csikszendmihalyi 1990, 1997; Massimini and Carli 1988.

acquire skill. However, for people to experience flow, their skill must already be adequate to meet the challenge at hand.

For a typical person, driving is a control experience. Driving requires skill, but it does not present as much of a challenge as do flow-producing activities. There are individual differences in achievement of flow; what might be flow for one person might not be so for another. For example, driving might be a flow experience for a race car driver but probably is not a flow experience for the majority of the population.

When a task presents little challenge and requires minimal skill, negative human emotions result. For example, people feel apathy when challenges and skills are at their lowest levels. They feel worry when their skills are low and challenges are only moderate. Boredom results when skills are moderate and challenges are low.

In addition to this balance between challenges and skills, other key elements of the flow experience include the presence of clear goals, immediate feedback to actions, intensely focused attention that resists distractions, and the absence of fear of failure or self-consciousness. The activity becomes an end in itself and sense of time becomes distorted as the person becomes completely immersed in the experience.

Measuring Flow

In marketing, the most common approach to measuring people's opinions or feelings is the survey method, in which consumers answer questions directly about the extent and/or intensity of their feelings using multi-item, scaled questions. Csikszentmihalyi (1990, 1997a) uses the experience sampling method (ESM) to observe the specific conditions under which optimal experience is most likely. When using this method, Csikszentmihalyi provides participants in his investigations with a programmable watch that sends off a signal at random times in two-hour segments of the day. Participants are asked to carry a booklet in which they complete information about their location, activity, thoughts, company, and present state of consciousness. They do this by providing ratings on several numerical scales about their levels of happiness, concentration, motivation, self-esteem, and so on. In this way, information is collected over a wide range of times, environments, and types of activities.

Among other things, respondents in Csikszentmihalyi's studies were asked to indicate, on a ten-point scale, how many challenges they faced at a given moment and how many skills they felt they were using. As mentioned previously, Csikszentmihalyi finds that flow coincides with occasions when both skills and challenges are rated at high levels. People are therefore considered in flow every time they mark both the level of challenges and the level of skills above the mean for the week.

Marketing researchers might consider using the ESM approach to obtain feedback on consumer experiences. Alternatively, consumers could be asked to fill out forms similar to those used in the ESM (Csikszentmihalyi and Larson 1987) when they engage in specific consumption experiences. For example, they might be asked to fill out a form each time they visit the supermarket, use the Internet, go to the hairdresser, attend a movie theater, or view specific television shows or advertisements. In this way, descriptions of the circumstances and specific nature of the consumption event and consumers' responses to a set of rating scales about their present state of consciousness could be obtained.

This information would make it possible to measure the quality of experience associated with different consumption activities and thus identify the conditions under which consumption contributes to or blocks flow or happiness. Understanding the nature of these conditions would help marketing managers identify aspects of marketplace experience that might deter or encourage repeat purchases or other target consumption behaviors.

Flow and Consumer Behavior

Flow is a concept that might be useful for understanding certain kinds of consumer behavior. As discussed previously, flow is a way of achieving happiness. In turn, happiness is a motivation that underlies much (but not all) consumer behavior. Flow is a peak experience. Thus, it is not something that is achieved with great frequency, and it cannot explain low-involvement, repetitive behaviors such as eating breakfast. However, at the extremes of consumer behavior, flow seems appropriate for explaining high-risk activities such as mountain climbing, river rafting, bungee jumping, or sky diving. Consumers require a great deal of skill to participate in these activities. At the same time, the challenge of these activities is high.

Consider the book *Into Thin Air*, by John Krakauer. The author describes a tragic climbing season on Mount Everest, during which seven climbers died within a short span of time. Many of the climbers were relative novices, but they had paid as much as $50,000 each to professional guiding companies for the chance to climb the world's highest mountain. Following this accident and the publication of Krakauer's book, there was considerable publicity about the dangers and challenges associated with climbing Mount Everest. A Texas doctor who was on Everest at the same time as Krakauer and lost his nose and all of his fingers to frostbite appeared on morning news programs and described his ordeal. The result of this negative publicity was that more novice climbers than ever wanted to sign up with the professional guiding services. Consumer demand soared. What is the explanation for such a phenomenon? We could repeat the old adage, "There is no such thing as bad publicity." However, the concept of flow provides a good explanation for this sudden surge in demand to climb Mount Everest.

Flow can also describe other kinds of consumer behavior that are not tied to such extreme experiences. For example, playing a video game can present many challenges and can also require much skill.

Flow and Advertising

In the same way that flow can be achieved through consumption, some kinds of advertising approaches can be so engaging or intrinsically enjoyable that they give rise to flow experiences. Even if advertising does not bring about flow in and of itself, the role of advertising in communicating the contribution of products and services toward achieving happiness is key to consumer perceptions of those offerings. In this sense, advertising might be viewed as one component of a product or service that consumers consider in assessing its contribution to their achievement of happiness.

The concept of a supervisory attentional system (SAS) (Baddeley 1990) suggests that people will fix their attention on what they like and avoid what they do not like (du Plessis 1994). This position regarding the tendency of consumers to be more willing to watch commercials they like (Biel 1990) corresponds closely to the proposition that consumers seek advertising that contributes to flow and resist advertising that blocks flow. Indeed, the quest for flow and, in a broader sense, optimal experience, could provide the key to understanding the strong observed correlation between an advertisement's likability and its success. According to du Plessis (1994), advertisement likability can be created by high entertainment value, viewer empathy, or perceived relevant news. In contrast, likability is negatively influenced by familiarity, confusion, or alienation.[1] These likability characteristics of an advertisement could similarly be expected to contribute to or block flow. Thus, the likability construct may represent a proxy for the capacity of the advertisement to promote or deter flow or optimal experience.

Csikszentmihalyi's decision rule for identifying flow experiences might not be directly applicable to the identification of advertising that, in a general sense, promotes or deters happiness. Consumers are not likely to agree that they are highly challenged or require high levels of skill when they watch advertisements. However, they might report that they find some advertising totally engaging and enjoyable. Some of the key elements of flow experiences discussed previously might easily relate to the experience of advertising. For example, advertising that is clear and unconfusing corresponds to the element of flow that calls for the presence of clear goals. Similarly, immediate feedback to actions, another element consistent with flow, is

---

[1]The attributes of advertisements listed here are drawn from the seven dimensions of consumer response to advertising that Schlinger (1979) derives.

conveyed in an advertisement that presents the benefits of product choice (e.g., success in interpersonal relationships, convenience in the completion of household chores). Captivating advertising might result in intensely focused attention, another element present in a flow experience. Some viewers have described their experience of advertisements as follows: "I felt as though I were right there in the commercial experiencing the same thing" (Schlinger 1979, p. 40). This response to advertising reflects the nature of flow experience, in which people become completely immersed in their experience.

These examples demonstrate that though advertising might not meet the criteria of high levels of challenge and skill identified by Csikszentmihalyi, it nevertheless has the capacity to elicit responses that reflect flow experience. In the same way that we have demonstrated advertising's ability to promote flow, it is possible to show that advertising can deter flow. Schlinger (1979, p. 40) identifies negative reactions to advertisement viewing experiences, such as "that commercial irritated me—it was annoying," or "the ad didn't have anything to do with me or my needs."

The nature and quality of the experience advertisements produce could also be measured by methods similar to the ESM approach. Thus, advertisements could be rated on their flow-promoting or flow-deterring qualities. This approach to advertisement testing holds promise for marketing practice. Previous studies have shown that how much an advertisement is liked proved to be the best predictor of commercial success (Haley and Baldinger 1991; Thorsen 1991). The proposition that advertisements are liked because of their flow-promoting qualities and because they contribute in some way to the overarching human goal of the search for happiness offers a theoretical foundation for the understanding of desirable qualities of successful advertisements. The perspective proposed here also provides a backdrop for the formulation of creative development guidelines that are consistent with the position that marketers should aim to facilitate exchanges that contribute to happiness for consumers.

Flow and the Internet

Some kinds of Internet activities might not be conducive to flow experiences. Examples include writing and reading routine e-mail messages or conducting complex searches on the Internet. The Internet has the potential to overwhelm the consumer with data. It is difficult to sort through all the noise and identify those bits of information that are truly useful. Such an environment (in which the number of Web sites is virtually infinite) can create confusion and frustration (not flow).

Nonetheless, some kinds of flow experiences might be possible on the Internet. Web chatting is one example. Some chatters report that they log on for hours. Although hours pass, to some chatters it seems as if time is standing still. Social skills are required to meet new people in a chat room and maintain contact over time ("Do you give good e-mail?"). The Internet provides people with an opportunity to reinvent or misrepresent themselves. For example, a man can pose as a woman in a chat room. A young man can pretend to be older, or an older man can pretend to be young. In some cases, it is difficult for Internet chatters to know exactly to whom they are talking (another kind of skill that is required), which is a potentially negative aspect of the anonymity associated with the Internet. But, at the same time, this fluidity encourages experimentation and allows people to try out new identities online (Zinkhan 2000). A shy person might feel more assertive and social in a virtual rather than face-to-face environment. In situations such as these, consumers not only lose all sense of time as described in Csikszentmihalyi's definition of flow, but they also are able to escape the boundaries of "self" that usually constrain them. This could offer a new way of achieving optimal experience through flow.

As mentioned previously, playing a video game can result in a flow experience. Video games can be played online and the opponents can be humans rather than robots. Human players frequently present more challenges than robot players, because they can be more creative and unpredictable. Playing a video game on a network also allows for many human players, who interact all at once. Such an environment can be both challenging and addictive.

Shopping can result in flow experiences, and online shopping is no exception. The splashy graphics and novel environments created by online retailers might be especially alluring for consumers, particularly in the early days of this experience. Shopping presents a challenge for some as they search endlessly to get the best deal. Skills are certainly involved.

As in previous sections, we must emphasize that flow does not provide an explanation for all of consumers' experiences on the Internet. Nonetheless, flow could prove useful in describing certain kinds of consumer behavior, including behavior on the Web.

Limitations and Further Research

There are potential problems with applying the flow concept to marketing and advertising practice. First, many consumers have an inherent resistance to marketing efforts. Some might find that marketing communications rarely result in pleasure or flow. Even when it is experienced, this form of happiness is somewhat ephemeral. It might be argued that advertisers encourage consumers to seek happiness in the wrong places. For example, video games are heavily promoted by television advertising to children, but playing video games might represent misplaced deployment of psychic energy to critics of this activity.

Some social scientists argue that it is the inherent destiny of humankind to remain unfulfilled. No sooner do people achieve one goal than they adopt another. In this way, it is easy for consumers to be trapped in a never-ending cycle of purchases and rampant materialism. This process leads to distrust of advertising and marketing and thus defeats the original goal of happiness. No single marketing effort will ever be able to satisfy consumers' desire for happiness.

Marketers might err by overpromising. Consumer backlash can be strong if expectations are not fulfilled. Advertising that promises happiness through the consumption of products and services must be able to deliver on these promises. In this regard, it is important to deliver the kind of high-quality product and caring service that consumers have come to expect, almost as a birthright. Here, the World Wide Web provides a useful tool for marketers—to upgrade service and offer online consulting and chat rooms for customers.

The adoption of a suitable instrument for the measurement of flow represents a further challenge for marketers. It is necessary to test the feasibility of the ESM approach and/or rating scales for use in marketing and consumer behavior studies. If this measurement approach cannot be applied directly to marketing situations, empirical means for measuring consumer responses that identify the relationship between marketing activities and flow/optimal experience must be developed and tested in various contexts (e.g., experiences with advertising, service encounters, Internet experiences). When instruments for the measurement of flow-related consumer response have been created, it will be necessary to consider the relationship between the occurrence of flow-producing marketing events or activities and brand or company performance. For marketers to adopt a strategic approach that is driven by the belief that successful marketing contributes to the achievement of happiness, it should be demonstrated that such an approach will deliver superior value to the firm in the long run.

Although many questions still require attention, the concept of flow holds promise for implementation in a marketing context. As such, it might be wise for marketers and advertisers to consider the implications of flow when designing strategies and promotional campaigns, simply because this construct represents such a prime motivator of all human activity.

Summary

In this article, we describe flow and how it might apply to several marketing ideas. In particular, we concentrate on the concepts of consumer behavior, advertising, and marketing on the Internet. Understanding human behavior is always a challenge for social scientists. Some argue that a new theory of human behavior is required with each new generation. The Internet represents a technological revolution. It has the potential to alter radically both business operations and human behavior. For example, advertising might eventually take a different form on the Internet. The term "netvertising" has been coined to describe commercial communications on the Web (Stern 2000). At the same time, consumer behavior might evolve because of the Internet's influence. As described previously, the Internet provides the opportunity for users to create new personae (e.g., in a chat room), which might affect their online consumption behavior. The Internet is a democratic place, where a consumer's Web site (perhaps criticizing a particular airline) can have more visitors than an airline's official Web site. Thus, the balance of power is altered in the marketplace, because one consumer's message competes on equal footing with corporate-sponsored commercial messages.

As social scientists strive to build explanatory models of the kinds of activities they observe in cyberspace, they might want to consider the concept of flow. As discussed here, flow helps explain human experiences when skill levels and challenges are at their peak.

References

Baddeley, Alan (1990), *Human Memory: Theory and Practice*. Boston, MA: Allyn & Bacon.

Bennett, Peter D., ed. (1995), *Dictionary of Marketing Terms*, 2d ed. Lincolnwood, IL: NTC Business Books; Chicago: American Marketing Association.

Biel, Alexander L. and Carol A. Bridgwater (1990), "Attributes of Likable Television Commercials," *Journal of Advertising Research*, 30 (3), 38–44

Csikszentmihalyi, Mihaly (1990), *Flow: The Psychology of Optimal Experience*. New York: HarperCollins Publishers Inc.

———— (1997a), *Finding Flow: The Psychology of Engagement with Everyday Life*. New York: HarperCollins Publishers Inc.

———— (1997b), "Happiness and Creativity," *Futurist*, 31 (September/October), S8–S12.

———— and R. Larson (1987), "Validity and Reliability of the Experience Sampling Method," *Journal of Nervous and Mental Disease*, 175 (9) 526–36.

du Plessis, Erik (1994), "Understanding and Using Likability," *Journal of Advertising Research*, 34 (5), RC3–RC10.

Haley, Russell I. and Allan L. Baldinger (1991), "The ARF Copy Research Validation Project," *Journal of Advertising Research*, 31 (2), 11–32.

Hoffman, Donna L. and Thomas P. Novak (1996), "Marketing in Hypermedia Computer-Mediated Environments: Conceptual Foundations," *Journal of Marketing*, 60 (3), 50–68.

Inglehart, Ronald and Jacques-Rene Rabier (1986), "Aspirations Adapt to Situations—But Why Are the Belgians So Much Happier Than the French?," in *Research on the Quality of Life*, Frank M. Andrews, ed. Ann Arbor, MI: Institute for Social Research, 1–56.

Schlinger, Mary Jane (1979), "A Profile of Responses to Commercials," *Journal of Advertising Research*, 19 (2), 37–46.

Stern, Barbara (2000), "2001 AMA Winter Marketing Educators' Conference Call for Papers," (accessed April 25), [available at http://www.ama.org/events/searchevents.asp?getrecord=81].

Thorsen, Esther (1991), "Likability: 10 Years of Academic Research," paper presented at Eighth Annual ARF Copy Workshop, New York.

Zinkhan, George M. (2000), "New Models of Consumer Behavior for an Emerging Technology," in *Advances in Marketing*. E. Capozzoli, R. Tudor, and D. McKee, eds. San Antonio, TX: Southwest Marketing Association, 248–49.

3

Promoting and Selling on the Internet: The Case of Real Estate

Alex Gray
University of Georgia

George M. Zinkhan
University of Georgia

Ellen Day
University of Georgia

The Internet is a unique phenomenon in human history, especially because of the way it cuts across and transcends existing borders. The network of servers that are interconnected across the globe enables access to a particular resource on the Internet almost completely independent of geography. Given that all of the intervening connections are working, a user in Atlanta can just as easily access a server in Australia or Russia as one located just down the street. With the price of computers and Internet access steadily decreasing, the Internet is becoming more and more democratic as well—the relative ease with which content can be created and distributed allows for a much wider spectrum of users. In theory (though such is not always the case), anyone could make himself or herself known to the world on the Internet simply by learning a few basic computer techniques. The Internet has also gone from being purely text-based (during the days of command-line-only interfaces) to including more and more different types of media, which means that it is potentially more versatile than any other medium of communication. Moreover, because this newer medium is interactive and information is accessed on command, today's consumers are empowered as never before.

The Internet has come to affect almost every facet of daily life, from entertainment to personal communication to education to the way governments and businesses are run. The business world in particular has been quick to find ways to take advantage of the Internet—a medium that can reach almost anywhere, be updated instantly, and attract a sophisticated audience. Although nonexistent a decade ago, e-commerce—business done through or facilitated by the Internet—has blossomed into a rich and diverse field that encompasses the variety of ways that enterprising companies try to take advantage of this totally unprecedented medium. The Internet medium of choice for e-commerce has been the World Wide Web; the flexibility and multimedia appeal of the Web page make it ideally suited for advertising, building a corporate image, or even creating a shopping environment online.

E-commerce and E-Selling

The first e-commerce Web sites were intended merely to give their creators a presence on the Web and thus would be classified most accurately as advertising. They provided information about the company and its products; perhaps something such as a game or online forum to attract visitors; and a telephone number, e-mail address, or other way to get in touch with a company employee who could actually sell to the people brought in by the Web site. Many corporate Web pages remain in this paradigm even now, but e-commerce has moved on from merely drumming up customers for actual transactions that occur face to face through other old-line communication methods. That is, with the development of interactive Web pages and secure transmissions, it has become possible to conduct transactions over the Web itself. However, although the problem of using the Web for something more than one-way mass communication has been solved, moving e-commerce into the realm of online sales to the general public brings its own set of problems.

E-Selling Issues

Among the problems with e-selling, there is the initial public resistance that any true innovation engenders, and Internet shopping is no exception. Many people remain reluctant to send personal information, such as credit-card numbers, over the Internet. The only cure for this sort of problem is time and marketing. E-commerce must simply build a good reputation and make itself more familiar to novices or nonusers.

Similarly, those consumers who do give e-shopping a try may find that it does not measure up to the traditional shopping experience—the unique environment of a store, the ability to browse and inspect products, and the opportunity to interact with store personnel and other customers. There are ways to address these problems online, but the fact remains that buying something online is fundamentally different from buying it in person, and the pros of online shopping must outweigh the cons for a particular person if he or she is to embrace consumer e-commerce.

The biggest problem, though, is simply a matter of product delivery. Transmitting information is the native function of the Web, the purpose for which it was created. Transferring funds over the Web can be done by credit-card numbers or using the services of electronic banks. However, for a sale to take place, a product must change hands or a service must be performed, and some products and services lend themselves better to sale over a wire than others. Those that consist entirely of information, such as music or software, and certain services, such as those provided by stock brokerages or employment agencies, can be delivered entirely over data lines. Many physical products are almost as suitable to being sold electronically; product selection and the transaction itself can be done online, leaving only the actual delivery of the product to the customer. In this case, e-selling is not too different from ordinary mail order. However, some products seem to be entirely incompatible with the concept of e-commerce; a case in point is real estate.

On the face of it real estate seems to be irreconcilable with e-commerce simply as a matter of basic characteristics. Real estate is unique as a category of product or investment because of its immobility, heterogeneity, inseparability from its environment, and the length of commitment and complexity of procedures involved in acquiring, owning, and disposing of it. Any other product can be transmitted or delivered to the customer, but in the case of real estate, the customer must come to the product (unless an unusually trusting investor is willing to base a decision to buy an office building on photographs and third-party testimonials). Land and buildings are as substantial and immovable as products come, at odds even intuitively with the incorporeal, mercurial Internet. However, although a real-estate agent cannot take a home buyer's down payment by e-cash and express him or her the house, enterprising companies have found ways to bring the real-estate industry into the Information Age.

What Can be E-Sold?

To judge a product's fitness for electronic sale, a definition of e-selling fitness is in order. The closer a product comes to being able to be advertised, sold, paid for, and delivered using only Internet facilities (that is, without any reliance on traditional, nononline methods), the better it lends itself to being e-sold (Watson et al. 1999). A product that must be shipped to the customer overnight, or that requires a telephone call during the course of the transaction, is less suited to e-commerce than one that does not.

The products that most readily adapt to e-sale are the ones that can be delivered over the Internet itself. A prime example of this is computer software. Many commercial programs can be downloaded directly from the maker's server in exchange for a payment by credit card or, possibly, electronic money. In many cases, it is possible to acquire software over the Internet without paying for it at all. Long before the first Internet software buyer nervously typed in his or her credit-card number, online cognoscenti have been outfitting their hard drives with shareware—software that can be downloaded for free and used for a limited time but that disables itself or reduces functionality after the trial time has expired or limits its features until the user enters a license number provided by the creator after receipt of payment. Shareware authors collect their fees by checks sent to them by the users of their software; however, it is rare for a shareware product to turn a profit and most shareware is created with this understanding. In most cases, the author merely wishes to provide the online community with something useful or is engaging in software development for his or her own amusement.

The realm of services and entertainment yields even more examples of e-commerce that take place over the Internet. As with software, it is possible for the enterprising browser to find free products such as movie clips and sample songs (and even whole movies and songs if legality is not an issue), but sites such as Emusic (www.emusic.com) have used the MP3 file format (which enables sound recordings of reasonable quality to be sent over the Internet as files only a few megabytes in size) to sell music over the Internet either a song or a whole album at a time.

As for services, one high-profile example of a service delivered entirely over the Internet is online brokerage. Sites such as Ameritrade (www.ameritrade.com) and E*Trade (www.etrade.com) have fueled the astonishing growth of Internet company stocks (and thus, perhaps, the online revolution itself) by allowing people who previously could not afford the time and expense of dealing with traditional stockbrokers to trade securities online in a streamlined, spontaneous fashion. Similarly, employment services have been able to take ample advantage of the Web, collecting a job applicant's résumé and personal data electronically, then allowing employers to search for qualified applicants among those that have been collected. Cases in point include Monster.com and Jobtrak (www.jobtrak.com).

If a product cannot be transmitted over a customer's data line, it can be shipped overnight. There are only a select few tangible products that can be sold over the Internet without the benefit of freight services. However, the model of selling a product online, then shipping it to the customer—essentially an update of mail-order sales—is a versatile one that can be (and has been) applied to almost every product imaginable, including books, clothes, food and wine, flowers and greeting cards, sporting goods, musical instruments, and even major home appliances (see www2sears.com). In addition, Web sites that act as online stores can give customers a great deal of control over their shopping experiences that in many cases more than compensates for the lack of personal contact. Not only can the customer shop any time from any location, but "store" Web sites can allow the customer to select features of the product and essentially have it made to order. Thus, customers are not limited by what is in stock as they would be when shopping at a conventional store. Perhaps the most famous example of this application of consumer e-commerce is Dell Computer (www.dell.com), which custom-builds personal computers as they are ordered by customers. Dell keeps no inventory at all, but builds every personal computer that it sells to order. Clearly the technology fuels the emergent trend toward mass customization.

There is no surefire determinant for success in Internet sales—every product is different, and a gifted salesperson can sell anything to anyone over any medium, the Internet being no exception. However, a dominant factor in predicting the ease with which a product can be sold over the Internet appears to be simply the physical size of the product. Products that exist only as information are the easiest to sell over the Internet; small products such as books and compact discs can be shipped overnight, whereas larger items, particularly those that need to be built to customer specifications, can take more than a month (Watson et al. 1999). In the case of services, the less personalized and interactive a service needs to be, the easier it is to sell online. Performing stock trades is easy, preparing tax returns is somewhat less so, and providing technical support much less so (the long series of e-mails that troubleshooting most problems requires may lead some customers to prefer getting their technical support over the telephone) and it is unlikely that anyone will ever bother to try to sell massages over the Internet.

Also important is the degree to which the product or service can be standardized and systematized; in other words, the less a product needs to be tried before buying or modified before the final sale, the more easily it can be sold by a Web site. Computer parts and shares of stock are uniform, but clothes and food tend to be less so, and some customers might prefer to buy the latter in person to be able to try them on—or at least inspect them—before buying. Products and services consisting of information or data can be tried out right at the Web site. The chief problem in such cases is ensuring that the trials are not abused, particularly with shareware.

Applying the E-Selling Paradigm to Real Estate

With these criteria in place, real estate—too big to be shipped, too expensive to put on a credit card, and too variable to buy off the rack—seems like a sure loser for e-commerce. Customers are not going to buy a house from Ehouse.com the way they would buy music tracks from Emusic.com, but e-commerce is not an all-or-nothing proposition. Even companies that cannot sell directly over the Internet can profit from it, and the real-estate industry has been as quick as any other to take advantage of the possibilities of e-commerce. Attesting to this are new books related to Internet marketing of real estate (e.g., Irwin 1999; Robbins 1999).

A quick visit to the Yahoo search site (www.yahoo.com) yields, within a few clicks, an enormous diversity of sites related to real estate. In addition to the more obvious suspects such as real-estate agents and mortgage lenders, consumers can find appraisers, developers, information resources such as magazines and newsletters, real-estate-related software, reports on local schools, and sites devoted to such specialized areas as retirement communities, golf communities, corporate housing and timeshares. However, most of these sites are merely "ad" sites that give contact information for their respective companies, or they provide their services for free. The actual online selling is left mostly to the real-estate agents and mortgage lenders. That is, the sites are designed to generate sales leads. Nevertheless, using a computer and online services can shorten and simplify the home- or property-buying process (Irwin 1999).

Most real-estate agent sites are centered around a search engine that enables the user to search for homes by price level, amenities, and (in the case of larger companies) geography. A few sites have additional features; for example, Corcoran's NY (www.corcoran.com), which specializes in Manhattan luxury apartments, offers "virtual tours"—each listed apartment can be viewed online using a panoramic-image viewer that shows 360-degree views of interior rooms. On a less flashy note, Owners.com offers a "buyer's handbook" that explains the process of purchasing a home. Many real-estate sites also offer mortgage and loan-qualification calculators. However, at the core, real-estate sites are little more than specialized advertising, a sophisticated version of the real-estate listings in many newspapers or an online version of a listings catalog, such as *The Real Estate Book*. After the visitor to one of these sites has found a home, he or she must still contact the seller and arrange to see the home and complete the transaction in person.

One thing to note about real-estate sites in general is that, except in the case of large organizations such as Coldwell Banker, they tend to focus on a particular geographic area—in fact, they are organized by region in Yahoo's listings. This points, again, to one of the factors standing in the way of the real estate market ever becoming a true e-business—the inseparability of properties from their environments.

Yahoo found 637 mortgage-related sites, and many of them were prepared to determine visitors' loan qualifications and offer them mortgage loans online, usually after a waiting period of a few days. Most of the online lenders show their current best rates for mortgages on their home pages; some of them offer mortgage-payment, loan-eligibility, and other financial-calculation utilities; and many have glossaries or tutorials to help prospective borrowers know their options. The sites can generally be divided into those run by individual banks (such as Apponline.com) and those run by mortgage brokers, which put borrowers in touch with lenders (such as Eloan.com and Lendingtree.com, the latter claiming that it "auctions" loans to lenders, ensuring the best deal for the buyer). The mortgage sites come a lot closer to true online selling than the real-estate sites. Although the real-estate agent will not actually sell the homes online (only advertise them), it is possible to secure a home loan online from any one of many companies, pending a credit check.

As for the vast array of other real-estate-related goods and services that can be purchased over the Internet, it appears that the rule of transmissibility holds—the companies selling books, software, magazines, newsletters, and home-study courses have (in some cases) made their wares available over the Internet directly, whereas those selling appraisals, office space, or relocation services (basically services that organize a real-estate agent, lenders, and movers for a customer wishing to change residences) can do little more than advertise. Indeed, advertising and the dissemination of information seem to be the chief goals among real-estate-related Web sites as a whole. There are sites with every conceivable mix of house, apartment, and office; investment listings sites devoted to particular geographic areas or types of properties; a site (www.gay-home.com) designed to help gays and lesbians find "friendly" real-estate agents, lenders, and neighborhoods; and even search engines that pool information from many different real-estate firms, enabling the user to find a home or an agent on the basis of a variety of criteria. Although the real-estate market has limited abilities to sell over the Web, it has nonetheless found a great many ways to use the Web to sell.

However, at the present time the wealth of information about real estate available from Web sites is not presented in a uniform, standardized format, which exacerbates information-seeking and comparison or even intimidates the cyberneophyte. Moreover, the information needs of the customer often appear to be subjugated to visual razzle-dazzle; that is, the design is not customer-driven (Fisk, Grove, and John 2000). To facilitate information-seeking and the purchase process, advertisers of real estate and related products must understand how potential buyers access online information, what information they deem critical, and what determinant selection criteria are for various real-estate products and services.

The ways e-commerce will affect real-estate agents are not altogether clear. The role of the agent may evolve into something very different because of Internet marketing of real estate. Traditionally, the agent has served as information gatherer, consultant, tour guide, hand-holder, and salesperson. But as potential buyers are empowered to access information heretofore considered proprietary, take virtual three-dimensional tours of properties, evaluate salient characteristics of the neighborhood, and obtain mortgage data and preapproval online, the agent becomes relatively less important in the process. Redefining and refining the role of real-estate agents will be critical to the long-term viability of the profession. Residential home buyers have tended to select an agent, rather than an agency, on the basis of such criteria as perceived integrity, competence, and knowledge of the market (Day and Nourse 1991). These personal attributes are difficult to communicate persuasively through electronic interaction, so agents seeking clients through a Web page link will need to consider not only ways of building credibility and trustworthiness through the new medium, but also ways to convince prospective buyers of the value added by intermediary agents. For example, agents' specialized knowledge of state laws and local ordinances may not be so easily supplanted by the Internet. It may be, contrary to past behavior, that potential buyers will attach more importance to selecting a "branded" agency than choosing a particular agent. Nonetheless, because buying a home is the largest purchase most consumers will make, they may continue to want an expert to guide them through the complex process (Patton 1999), suggesting potential changes in, but not the demise of, residential real-estate agents. Commercial and other types of property purchases may become less dependent on agents, however.

A buyer cannot yet pick the ideal property or dream house and close the deal through the Internet. However, the future of Internet marketing of real estate may dramatically change. Although the entire buying process is not likely to take place online, the process will probably become more streamlined as digital signatures for securely identifying parties, standardized electronic legal papers, and the like become more widely available (Patton 1999).

Conclusion

The Internet is a powerful tool, a medium that can be applied, to some degree, to virtually anything. The distinction to be made is in how much benefit it can bring to a particular application. It is a great boon to personal and mass communication and is similarly beneficial to the business of distributing data and information. The marriage between the Internet and the sale of physical products is an imperfect but still beneficial one; however, the apparent trend is that the more a product or service resembles the native Internet function of transmitting units of data, the more harmonious the marriage can be. The desirable qualities in the perfect Internet sale item, above all, are ease of delivery and standardization. Real estate, being big and heterogeneous and requiring much personal interaction and "soft" information such as is derived from personal inspection of the product, remains perhaps the least e-commerce–compatible product of all. Nonetheless, the Internet is definitely changing the face of business, and though it might not be indispensable to the future of real-estate sales, being able to reach more customers at their own convenience is a good thing regardless.

References

Day, Ellen and Hugh O. Nourse (1991), "Client Selection of a Residential Real Estate Agency or Agent," *Journal of Professional Services Marketing*, 6 (2), 81–95.

Fisk, Raymond P., Stephen J. Grove, and Joby John (2000), *Interactive Services Marketing*. Boston: Houghton Mifflin Company.

Irwin, Robert (1999), *Buying a Home on the Internet*. New York: McGraw-Hill.

Patton, David A. (1999), "The Best Way to House Hunt," *The Wall Street Journal*, (December 6), R43.

Robbins, Curt (1999), *Real Estate Internet Skills*. New York: DDC Publishing.

Watson, Richard T., Pierre Berthon, Leyland F. Pitt, and George M. Zinkhan (1999), *Electronic Commerce: The Strategic Perspective*. Fort Worth, TX: The Dryden Press.

4

An Exploratory Study of the Web's Early Adopters

Traci A. Carte
University of Oklahoma

Barbara H. Wixom
University of Virginia

Richard T. Watson
University of Georgia

The Web has changed today's business environment to an extent not foreseen by most companies. This innovation has been touted as a revolutionary change agent (Jarvenpaa and Ives 1996) and a driving force in changing fundamental business models (Keen 1999). As companies continue to ponder the role the Web will play in their future, it might be interesting to take a look at the Web's beginnings. In this exploratory study, we examine the content of 98 Web sites in the final quarters of 1994 and 1995 and investigate the following questions: How quickly is Web commercial activity growing? What types of businesses are using the Web? How are businesses using the Web? and How is commercial Web activity changing? We analyze the commercial sites using the customer service life cycle (CSLC) model (Ives and Learmonth 1984). The results of the study indicate that Web commercial activity is growing at a quadratic rate, and an increasing number of companies are using the Web to provide product information and support existing customers. The revolution, though, was not yet evident in 1994 and 1995.

A scan of Web sites in 1994 found that businesses ranging from night clubs to motorcycle dealers to information systems providers were advertising on the Internet. The Web use of these businesses ranged from one page of basic product information to sophisticated, multipage offerings with interactive order entry and online newsletters. The popular press suggested that an increasing number of companies was conducting business on the Web (Tetzeli 1994; U.S. News and World Report 1995) and that Web sales revenues were already in the millions (Maddox, Wagner, and Wilder 1995). The Web commerce growth rate was of interest to practitioners and researchers alike.

This study presents the findings of a two-phased analysis of Web commercial activity among early Internet adopters. The data collection took place in the final quarters of 1994 and 1995. Initially, researchers examined 98 companies listed on the *Commercial Sites Index* (*CSI*) by analyzing the content of the companies' Web sites.[1] A year later, the same researchers revisited the sites and recorded changes. Because of a lack of theory and published research studies on Web commerce at the time (Hoffman and Novak 1996), this study was exploratory; it was designed to gain an initial understanding of Web commercial activity.

Research Questions

The research questions that formed the basis of this study are founded in the general interest in Web growth. The questions were as follows:

R_1: What types of businesses are using the Web?
R_2: How are businesses using the Web?
R_3: How quickly is commercial Web activity growing?

The growth in the number of Web sites does not necessarily indicate an increase in sophistication. A better indication of growth is the extent to which sites are evolving and becoming more sophisticated in interacting with the customer and addressing customer needs. Therefore, we also asked the following:

R_4: How is commercial Web activity changing?

Methods

One goal of this research is to report changes over time. To this end, the appropriate research design is a longitudinal, time series design (Menard 1991). Specifically, a Type III longitudinal study, or narrowly focused quantitative study of multiple organizations, is employed to provide insights into how selected variables tend to change over time (Miller and Friesen 1982).

The first phase of this longitudinal study took place in the final quarter of 1994. A sample of 98 companies was selected systematically from the 835 listed on *CSI* on November 4, 1994. The sample was selected by determining a random starting point and then selecting every eighth company from an alphabetical listing. Two researchers visited 49 Web sites each and collected demographic data (e.g., company type, location), site complexity, site content, and customer interaction. To determine company type, one researcher classified the companies by Standard Industrial Code (SIC). The results were reviewed by another researcher, and conflicts were discussed and resolved. These codes were then grouped on the basis of prior research (King 1996) (for a listing of SIC groupings, see Appendix A). To determine customer interaction, each company's Web site was classified according to the phases of the CSLC (Figure 1), a variation on the customer resource life cycle (Ives and Learmonth 1984; Ives and Mason 1990).

The CSLC concentrates on the relationship between the provider of goods and services and the customer. It separates this service relationship between businesses

---

[1]In April 1994, the *CSI* was created at the MIT Lab for Computer Science to provide a central repository of commercial site locations on the Internet. Open Market Inc. began to administer the Web list in August 1994 as a free public service, and the site received attention in the trade press. The *CSI* allowed companies to register a site address free of charge and provide descriptive keywords and categories. Web users could use the *CSI* to locate specific companies or to search for companies that met certain criteria. Because search engines had just begun to mature, this service met an important need for Web customers.

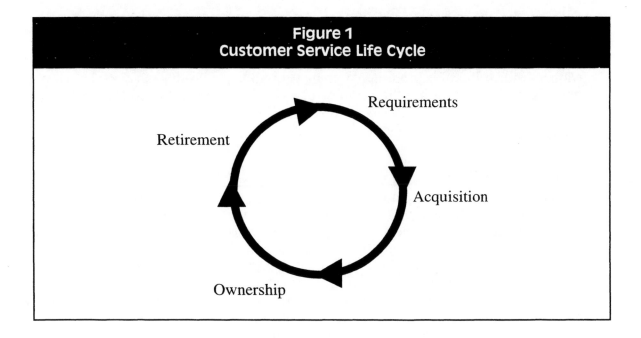

Figure 1
Customer Service Life Cycle

and customers into requirements, acquisition, ownership, and retirement. Each phase represents a different way that a company can relate to its customers. In the requirements phase, the company communicates information about a product or service, and in the acquisition phase, the customer is assisted in acquiring the product or service. During ownership, customers are provided with support for an acquired product or service. Finally, a company helps a customer recycle or dispose of a product or service in the retirement phase. This model is frequently mentioned in information systems research and recently has been used to assess the impact the Web has had on organizational competitiveness (Gonsalves et al. 1999).

For each Web site, the researchers assessed which phases of the CSLC were supported. Examples of how these phases were operationalized for commercial Web activity included

- Requirements: photographs of a product, video presentations, textual descriptions, articles or reviews, sound bytes of speeches or explanations, downloadable demonstration files;
- Acquisition: online order entry, credit card encryption, online services, downloadable product files;
- Ownership: interactive online user groups, online technical support, frequently asked questions, resource libraries, newsletters, online renewal; and
- Retirement: online resale, classified advertisements.

In the final quarter of 1995, we conducted a second analysis of the 98 sample Web sites to identify how the sites had changed. Each site was revisited by the original reviewer, and data about site complexity, site content, and customer interaction were recorded. Ten businesses could not be accessed, and data were collected regarding why the sites were inaccessible.

In both phases of this study, two of the researchers collected descriptive information on half of the sample and used predetermined categories to identify support for CSLC phases. After the initial coding was completed, the researchers categorized the data for the other half of the sample. The results of coding were compared and discussed "to provide a form of analytical triangulation" (Patton 1990, p. 383).

Growth in the number of sites listed on such repositories as the *CSI* would provide an indication of commercial activity growth in the Web's early years. Therefore, the researchers recorded the number of companies listed on the *CSI* each week for the period of September 23, 1994, through February 9, 1996.

Findings

What Types of Businesses Were Using the Web?

Web companies used in this research are listed by industry group in Table 1. The sample included 35 company classifications, varying from hotels/motels to prepackaged software. Many of the sample companies were associated with the information industry, and 24 of the companies were classified as computer integrated systems design. This category includes companies that provide Web services. This is not surprising given that the sample was drawn when the Web was a relatively new phenomenon. Early adopters of this new technology were more likely to be technology-related companies.

The sample Web sites were based throughout the United States and the world. Table 2 illustrates that the southwest and northeast regions of the United States were best represented in this study (for a list of the states represented by each region, see Appendix B). Twenty-five sites were based in California. Five companies did not provide information regarding geographic location.

Table 1
Sample Companies by Industry Group

Industry Group	*CSI* Number of Companies	*CSI* Percentage of Companies
Consumer	7	7.1%
Financial	3	3.1%
Industrial	7	7.1%
Information	58	59.2%
Media	8	8.2%
Service	4	4.1%
Miscellaneous	11	11.2%
Total	98	100.0%

Table 2
Sample Companies by Geographic Location

Geographic Area	Number of Companies
International	12
Southwest United States	34
Northwest United States	4
Southeast United States	10
Northeast United States	33
Geographic Location Not Listed	5
Total	98

How Were Businesses Using the Web?

The results of the 1994 data collection indicated that the sample companies supported different phases of the CSLC and demonstrated different levels of complexity. All of the companies conveyed information about a product or service, exhibiting characteristics of the requirements phase. However, the complexity of the Web sites demonstrating similar life cycle phases varied greatly. For example, The MouseBoard's Web site contained a single page with a product picture and a textual description. Promus, a holding company for multiple hotel chains, presented a complex hierarchy of information that included photographs of hotel rooms, rate listings, press releases, and an employee directory.

Twenty-six percent of the companies demonstrated characteristics of the acquisition phase. This acquisition figure is comparable to similar research: for example, King (1996) finds that 33% of *Fortune* 500 companies conduct sales over the Web. An example of a company demonstrating acquisition characteristics was Lane and Lenge Florists, whose Web site offered customers a mail-order catalog look and feel. The site presented photographs of floral arrangements and textual descriptions, and it offered an order button alongside each product for customers to add a product to an interactive order form. The customer added payment or billing information to complete the order and electronically sent the form to Lane and Lenge to close the deal.

Although none of the companies in 1994 displayed characteristics of the retirement phase, 15% demonstrated ownership, such as electronic newsletters and online user groups. Citicorp, for example, offered an interactive process for reordering checks.

The number of companies that supported each CSLC stage in 1994 is listed by industry group in Table 3. The provision of acquisition support seemed to be related to the industry in which the business competed. All consumer companies in the sample provided acquisition support. This may be due to the ease with which these organizations can provide this support; all but one of these sites conducted electronic versions of mail-order catalog transactions. Only 15% of the information companies provided support for the acquisition stage. However, 8 of the 14 companies that supported the ownership stage were information companies.

Table 3
Number of Sample Companies That Support Each CSLC Stage in 1994 by Industry Group

Category	Requirements	Acquisition	Ownership	Retirement
Consumer	7	7	1	0
Financial	3	1	1	0
Industrial	7	0	1	0
Information	58	9	8	0
Media	8	3	3	0
Service	4	0	0	0
Miscellaneous	11	4	0	0
Totals	98	24	14	0

How Quickly Was Commercial Web Activity Growing?

The number of companies listed on the *CSI* grew steadily, increasing from 466 on September 23, 1994, to 22,500 on February 9, 1996. A square root transformation was applied to the data as recommended for count data (Johnson and Wichern 1982, p. 161), and a linear regression model was developed that provides considerable explanation for the variation in the weekly growth figure ($R^2 = .97$, $p < .0001$, sites $= 28.2 + 23.4x + 4.84x^2$) (see Figure 2).

How Was Commercial Web Activity Changing?

In 1995, the researchers investigated whether companies had changed their level of customer interaction. Ten companies had dropped off the list completely (this phenomenon is discussed subsequently in this article). Table 4 provides a breakdown by industry group of the number of companies that supported each CSLC stage in 1995. All sites remained in the requirements phase, and the number of companies supporting acquisition was approximately the same. This could have been influenced by security concerns. For example, although Lane and Lenge Florist demonstrated acquisition support, the site contained a detailed explanation of the security issues involved in using a credit card number in Web transactions.

Thirty-one percent of the companies displayed ownership characteristics. Lighthouse Design added frequently asked questions (FAQs) indices and online training materials, and Mathworks offered online conference sign-up and online product support. Dell Computer was the only company that displayed retirement characteristics with an online technology replacement program. The majority of companies moving into the ownership support stage were information companies. The number of information companies supporting ownership increased from 14% to 38%.

The attention to service quality in the marketing literature (e.g., Zeithaml, Parasuraman, and Berry 1990) potentially explains why the ownership phase showed the most development over the period of the study. Current marketing prac-

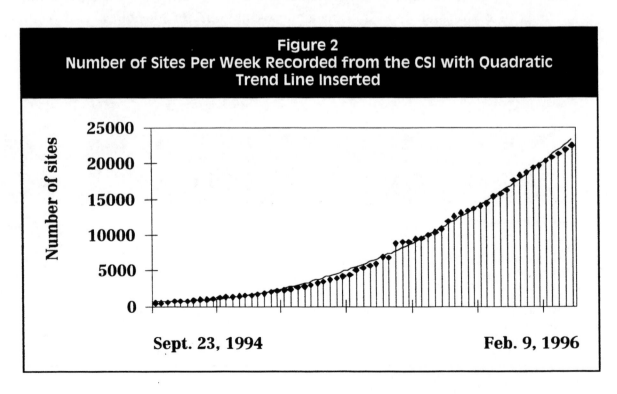

**Figure 2
Number of Sites Per Week Recorded from the CSI with Quadratic Trend Line Inserted**

tice (e.g., Blattberg and Deighton 1991; Peppers and Rogers 1993) stresses the need to address customers individually. A Web site is an effective way of providing services to existing customers (e.g., FAQ, software updates) and is well suited to developing an interactive relationship with the customer. For example, Bank of America's Web site provides a feature called "build your own bank." When Web users access this site, they can customize the site to their individual banking needs. Each time the site is revisited, the customized "bank" is retrieved.

Although many companies had more advanced Web sites in 1995, two companies supported fewer stages of the CSLC. One of these companies, Citicorp, discontinued acquisition phase activities, including the check ordering and automated loan application, citing lack of security as the reason for the decreased service.

The change in complexity of sites was dramatic: 61% of the sites displayed more complexity. Sites were considered more complex if they added features such as context-sensitive maps, online forms, external links, graphics, or surveys over the course of this study. The MouseBoard, for example, no longer had a picture and textual description; the site contained graphical diagrams of the parts that constitute the product, interactive contact forms, and multiple pages of information. Most companies that did not become more complex either started off with highly complex sites or seemed to exist for a single purpose. For example, the National Library of Poetry maintained a site used only in conjunction with its annual poetry contest.

In 1995, we considered ten Web sites from the original sample inaccessible after repeated attempts to reach them failed. We made attempts using multiple browser software packages and two popular search engines, Yahoo and Alta Vista, and tried to contact the company by e-mail and telephone. Five companies could not be located; four companies no longer conducted business on the Web because of lack of sales. One company, the Hyatt Regency in Washington, D.C., discontinued its site when it was included on the corporate Hyatt Web site. Seven of these ten companies supported the acquisition phase in 1994.

Discussion

A broad perspective shows that this time period was one of rapid adoption of the Web by commercial organizations. This is not surprising given that the Web provides a relatively level playing field for all participants (Berthon, Leyland, and Watson 1996; Hoffman and Novak 1996). For example, this study's sample companies

---

Table 4
Number of Sample Companies That Support Each CSLC Stage in 1995 by Industry Group

Category	Requirements	Acquisition	Ownership	Retirement
Consumer	4	4	1	0
Financial	3	1	1	0
Industrial	7	1	3	0
Information	56	12	21	1
Media	6	5	5	0
Service	3	2	0	0
Miscellaneous	9	3	0	0
Totals	88	29	30	0

Appendix A
SIC Groupings

SIC Codes	Code Description	General Code
3911	Jewelers - precious metals	Consumer
5311	Department stores	
5735	Record and prerecorded tape stores	
5947	Gifts, novelties, and souvenir shops	
5961	Catalog and mail-order houses	
5992	Florists	
6021	National commerce banks	Financial
6712	Bank holding company	
2992	Lubricating oils and greases	Industrial
3674	Semiconductors and related devices	
3724	Aircraft engines and engine parts	
3823	Process control instruments	
3861	Photographic equipment and supplies	
5065	Electronic parts and equipment	
3571	Electronic computers	Information
3577	Computer peripheral equipment	
3661	Telephone and telegraph apparatus	
4813	Telephone communications, except radio	
4899	Communications services	
7370	Computer and data processing services	
7371	Computer programming services	
7372	Prepackaged software	
7373	Computer integrated systems design	
7375	Information retrieval service	
2731	Book publishing	Media
7812	Motion picture and video production	
4724	Travel agencies	Services
7011	Hotels/motels	
6411	Insurance agents, brokers, and service	Miscellaneous
6531	Real estate agents	
8111	Legal services	
8231	Libraries	
8299	Schools and educational services	
8733	Noncommercial research organization	
8748	Business consulting services not elsewhere classified	

included organizations ranging in size from one person to more than 300,000 people. Access opportunities were essentially equal for all players, because initial setup costs were so low as to present minimal or nonexistent barriers to entry. Furthermore, there had been so much publicity that the notion of Web commerce diffused rapidly. The conditions were fertile for rapid adoption: high awareness and very low entry barriers.

The second phenomenon that was observed is sophistication creep. Web development was not revolutionary. Organizations built sites to augment current operations and then proceeded by increasing the sophistication and complexity of their sites. There were several possible reasons for this. Software vendors were just starting to release tools to accelerate site development and create more complex sites, plug-ins and helper applications enabled new features to be implemented (e.g., ani-

Appendix B Regions	
Geographic Area	**Countries or States**
International	Australia, Canada, France, Ireland, Norway, South Africa, Sweden, United Kingdom
Southwest United States	Arizona, California, Texas, Utah
Northwest United States	Colorado, Minnesota, Washington
Southeast United States	Florida, North Carolina, Tennessee, Virginia
Northeast United States	Connecticut, District of Columbia, Illinois, Indiana, Maryland, Massachusetts, New York, Pennsylvania

mation), and innovative ideas quickly were diffused (Watson et al. 2000). But revolutionary changes were not yet appearing (or were only appearing in isolation), because back-end applications (e.g., FedEx's parcel tracking service) could not be copied quickly because of long development times. As new Web application development tools appeared on the horizon, the creep of Web development became the seeds of revolution.

Conclusion

This study was intended to explore the activities of early Web pioneers. The research questions were broad because little was known about the real impact the Web would have on organizational practices. We found that all these early adopters were providing support for the requirements phase of the CSLC in 1994. By 1995, the sites were becoming noticeably more sophisticated, and support for the customer relationship was moving into acquisition in some cases and ownership in others. In a more recent study, 472 organizations were surveyed regarding their use of the Web, and similarly, stronger support for the requirements and acquisition phases of the CSLC was found (Gonsalves et al. 1999).

Many articles have been written in recent years about innovative Web sites and changing business practice. The early adopters laid the groundwork for many of these innovative organizations to come. Understanding what limited the accomplishments of the early pioneers may help today's researchers and practitioners identify the stalling points of the current technology. What are today's Web pioneers accomplishing? What tools and technologies will prompt the next revolution?

References

Berthon, P.R., L.F. Leyland, and R.T. Watson (1996), "The World Wide Web as an Advertising Medium: Towards an Understanding of Conversion Efficiency," *Journal of Advertising Research*, 36 (1), 43–54.

Blattberg, R.C. and J. Deighton (1991), "Interactive Marketing: Exploiting the Age of Addressability," *Sloan Management Review*, 33 (Fall), 5–14.

Gonsalves, G.C., A.L. Lederer, R.C. Mahaney, and H.E. Newkirk (1999), "A Customer Resource Lifecycle Interpretation of the Impact of the World Wide Web on Competitive Expectations and Achievements," *International Journal of Electronic Commerce*, 4 (1), 103–120.

Hoffman, D.L. and T.P. Novak (1996), "Marketing in Hypermedia Computer-Mediated Environments: Conceptual Foundations," *Journal of Marketing*, 60 (July), 50–69.

Ives, B. and G.P. Learmonth (1984), "The Information Systems as a Competitive Weapon," *Communications of the ACM*, 27 (12), 1193–1201.

—— and R. Mason (1990), "Can Information Technology Revitalize Your Customer Service?" *Academy of Management Executive*, 4 (4), 52–69.

Jarvenpaa, S.L. and B. Ives (1996), "Introducing Transformational Information Technologies: The Case of the World Wide Web Technology," *International Journal of Electronic Commerce*, 1 (1), 95–126.

Johnson, R.A. and D.W. Wichern (1982), *Applied Multivariate Statistics*. Englewood Cliffs, NJ: Prentice Hall.

Keen, P.G.W. (1999), "Business Re-Model," *Computerworld*, (July 12), 44.

King, D. (1996), "*Fortune* 500 on the Web: The Road to Second Level Effects," in *Proceedings of the 29th Hawaiian International Conference on System Sciences*, Vol. 4, J. Nunamaker Jr. and R. Sprague Jr., eds. Washington, DC: IEEE Computer Society Press, 463–70.

Maddox, K., M. Wagner, and C. Wilder (1995), "Making Money on the Web," *Information Week*, (September 4), 31–40.

Menard, S. (1991), *Longitudinal Research*. Newbury Park, CA: Sage Publications.

Miller, D. and P.H. Friesen (1982), "The Longitudinal Analysis of Organizations: A Methodological Perspective," *Management Science*, 28 (9), 1013–34.

Patton, M.Q. (1990), "Qualitative Analysis and Interpretation," *Qualitative Evaluation and Research Methods*, 2d ed. Newbury Park, CA: Sage Publications, 371–459.

Peppers, D. and M. Rogers (1993), *The One to One Future: Building Relationships One Customer at a Time*. New York: Currency Doubleday.

Tetzeli, R. (1994), "Electronic Storefronts on the Internet," *Fortune*, 130 (11), 191.

U.S. News and World Report (1995), "Gold Rush in Cyberspace," (November 13), 72–80.

Watson, Richard T., Pierre Berthon, Leyland F. Pitt, and George M. Zinkhan (2000), *Electronic Commerce: The Strategic Perspective*. Fort Worth, TX: Dryden Press.

Zeithaml, V., A. Parasuraman, and L.L. Berry (1990), *Delivering Quality Service: Balancing Customer Perceptions and Expectations*. New York: The Free Press.

Consumer Behavior and Behavioral Response to Advertising

5

A Meta-Analysis of Relationships Between Ad-Evoked Feelings and Advertising Responses

Steven P. Brown
Southern Methodist University

Pamela M. Homer
California State University

J. Jeffrey Inman
University of Wisconsin

In recent years, considerable effort has been devoted to understanding how ad-evoked feelings influence advertising responses (e.g., Aaker, Stayman, and Hagerty 1986; Batra and Ray 1986; Burke and Edell 1989; Edell and Burke 1987; Holbrook and Batra 1987).[1] The practical and theoretical importance of these effects has been underscored by a substantial volume of research published in leading journals and by a special Marketing Science Institute-sponsored conference (Yoon 1991). A decade of research has produced a rich body of empirical data, representing a diversity of study designs and advertising stimuli. Results consistently have indicated important effects of ad-evoked feelings on advertising responses (e.g., Batra and Ray 1986; Edell and Burke 1987; Stayman and Aaker 1988). They also have provided useful information regarding the path structure of relationships (e.g., Burke and Edell 1989; MacInnis and Park 1991) and contingency factors that moderate the strength of relationships involving ad-evoked feelings (e.g., Batra and Stephens 1994; Goldberg and Gorn 1987).

Despite these contributions, important theoretical, practical, and methodological questions have not been addressed. For example, prior research has not indicated whether (1) positive and negative feelings are bidimensional or bipolar (i.e., whether they constitute separate constructs or merely opposite poles of the same construct), (2) they have symmetrical or asymmetrical effects, (3) study design characteristics moderate the strength of feeling effects, and (4) they differentially influence the effects of positive and negative feelings. Meta-analysis is useful for addressing these questions because it assesses the generalizability of relationships more objectively, precisely, and conclusively than narrative reviews and can identify relationships and contingency effects that have not been (and could not be) assessed in the context of a single empirical study (Bangert-Downs 1986).

---

[1]We use the terms *feelings* and *emotions* interchangeably.

Several theoretical perspectives drawn from the broader literature on affect make different predictions regarding the absolute and relative strength of positive and negative feeling effects. We use meta-analysis not only to provide a systematic, quantitative analysis of the strength and generalizability of ad-evoked feeling effects, but also to test competing predictions implied by alternative theoretical perspectives using data aggregated across the research stream.

From a practical perspective, the relative strength of positive and negative feeling effects potentially could guide advertisers' decisions regarding executional strategies. For example, if negative (compared with positive) feelings have a greater impact on brand attitudes, advertisers seeking broad market appeal should avoid executions capable of evoking substantial negative affect to minimize potential harm to brand equity. Also, because advertisers often make trade-offs between "breaking through the clutter" and "being liked" (Walker and Dubitsky 1994), decisions regarding repetition, scheduling, and executions could be affected by findings regarding the relative strength of positive and negative feeling effects.

Methodologically, it is important for both industry and academic researchers to understand how study designs influence relationships between ad-evoked feelings and advertising responses. For example, researchers can bias effect sizes by unwittingly creating conditions that influence subjects' cognitive processing sets (Lutz 1985; Madden, Allen, and Twible 1988). Moreover, study design characteristics can influence differentially the effects of positive and negative feelings on advertising responses. Understanding these effects is important for conducting the most informative and precise copy tests, accurately interpreting research data, evaluating alternative theories, and devising the most effective study designs in industry and academic settings.

We also advance meta-analytic methodology by introducing bootstrapping as a way of performing multivariate moderator analyses. Small sample sizes are virtually always a problem in testing moderator effects in meta-analyses (Farley and Lehmann 1986) and often make testing multivariate parametric models of moderator effects infeasible. This typically leads to testing multiple moderators through independent analyses (e.g., t-tests or comparisons of confidence intervals) of one moderator at a time. Unfortunately, this practice does not account for correlations among the moderators or the redundancy of their shared variances with the criterion. The small sample sizes typical of meta-analyses in marketing (and other fields) also lead to limited power to reject the null hypothesis, which leads to high risk of type II errors and erroneous conclusions that "true" (i.e., generalizable) effect sizes have been found. The most likely effect of such conclusions would be to discourage worthwhile research seeking to identify moderator effects (Sacket, Harris, and Orr 1986). Bootstrapping helps overcome these limitations by enabling moderator effects to be tested in multivariate models. Although bootstrapping has been used increasingly in the marketing literature (Bone, Sharma, and Shimp 1989; Inman and McAlister 1993; Van Trijp, Hoyer, and Inman 1996), it has not been applied previously to meta-analysis. However, it has great potential utility for this type of research.

The Research Domain

Research on emotional responses to advertising grew from the extensive research on attitude toward the ad (A_{ad}) and more generally from important developments in the psychology of emotion (e.g., Lazarus 1984; Zajonc 1984). It was motivated by the finding that ad-evoked feelings influence brand attitudes independently of attribute beliefs (e.g., Batra and Ray 1986; Burke and Edell 1989; Mitchell and Olson 1981; Stayman and Aaker 1988). Empirical research on A_{ad} is reviewed by Brown and Stayman (1992). Using covariance structure modeling in conjunction with meta-analysis, they, like MacKenzie, Lutz, and Belch (1986), find support for the dual mediation model, which includes an indirect (as well as a direct) effect of A_{ad} on brand attitude (A_b). (The indirect effect was mediated by brand-related cognitions.) Brown and Stayman (1992) analyze a wide range of relationships involving A_{ad} but do not assess the separate effects of positive and negative feelings. Relationships between ad-evoked feelings and other response variables, such as brand attitudes, are also outside the scope of that study.

Studies of ad-evoked feelings typically have included A_{ad} and brand attitude as dependent variables.[2] The effects of ad-evoked feelings on A_{ad} are considered direct (e.g., Burke and Edell 1989; Stayman and Aaker 1988), whereas the effects of feelings on brand attitude are found to be primarily indirect and mediated by A_{ad} (e.g., Stayman and Aaker 1988). Feelings–A_{ad} and feelings–brand attitude relationships invariably are consistent in direction (i.e., uniformly positive for positive feelings and uniformly negative for negative feelings). Because the feelings–A_{ad} relationship is direct, it tends to be stronger than the indirect relationship between feelings and brand attitude. Feelings–A_{ad} and feelings–brand attitude relationships are found to be contingent on the same moderators, such as involvement and cognitive elaboration, as detailed in the following paragraphs. Thus, our conceptual development is the same for both ad and brand attitudes.

Empirical research on ad-evoked feelings has established that affective responses, as subjective states of the individual, can be distinguished clearly from semantic judgments and evaluations of stimulus advertisements (Aaker, Stayman, and Hagerty 1986; Edell and Burke 1987; Holbrook and Batra 1987). As such, they have substantial effects on ad and brand attitudes, purchase intentions, and actual choice (e.g., Aaker, Stayman, and Hagerty 1986; Batra and Ray 1986; Burke and Edell 1989; Edell and Burke 1987; Holbrook and Batra 1987; MacInnis and Park 1991; Stayman and Aaker 1988; Stayman and Batra 1991). Consistent with the conceptualization described previously, effects of feelings on brand attitudes appear to be primarily indirect and mediated by A_{ad} (Batra and Ray 1986; Edell and Burke 1987; MacInnis and Park 1991), though modest direct effects can occur, especially at low levels of advertising exposure (Stayman and Aaker 1988). In addition to these "online" effects, ad-evoked affect retrieved from memory can increase choice probability for advertised brands (Stayman and Batra 1991).

Research also has investigated the contingencies that moderate the strength of ad-evoked feeling effects on ad and brand attitudes. For example, one research stream identifies program context and placement of target advertisements among other advertisements as moderators of ad-evoked feeling effects. Goldberg and Gorn (1987) find that advertisements placed in happy programs elicit more positive

---

[2]Purchase intentions (PI) also have been considered in several studies. Purchase intentions typically are conceptualized as direct consequences of brand attitude and indirect consequences of A_{ad}. However, an insufficient number of studies exist to conduct meaningful moderator analyses of the feelings–PI relationships. We do report the overall weighted means for the feelings–PI relationships in Table 2.

responses than those placed in sad programs, especially when the advertisements are emotional rather than informational. Aaker, Stayman, and Hagerty (1986) find that warm advertisements are more effective when viewed following contrasting types of executions.

The most reliable contingency effects established to date relate to viewer involvement and the amount of cognitive elaboration of advertisement content. Research has demonstrated that, in general, ad-evoked feelings have relatively weak effects under high involvement and conditions that encourage cognitive elaboration. For example, Batra and Stephens (1994) find that the effects of affective responses on brand attitudes are strongest when motivation to process brand information is low. Madden, Allen, and Twible (1988) find that subjects who receive instructions to evaluate advertisement executions have less affective response than subjects who are not so instructed. Greenwald and Leavitt (1984) suggest that highly involved viewers are likely to engage in greater message elaboration and critical evaluation of advertisements and to experience less affective response. Using data aggregated across the A_{ad} literature, Brown and Stayman (1992) find that experimental conditions favoring greater cognitive elaboration produce a weaker relationship between ad-evoked feelings and A_{ad} than conditions not favoring elaboration.

Similar effects of involvement have been found in research on the influence of positive moods on persuasion. For example, Batra and Stayman (1990) find that a positive mood has a greater effect on brand attitudes for subjects low in need for cognition (i.e., dispositional tendency to elaborate content material cognitively). They also find that positive-mood subjects make less distinction between strong and weak message arguments and produce fewer counterarguments than neutral-mood subjects. Curren and Harich (1994) find that positive mood has a significant effect on brand evaluations when personal relevance is low but not when personal relevance is high. A plausible explanation of these findings is that feelings act as peripheral cues that influence attitudes and intentions when motivation and/or ability to elaborate arguments cognitively are low (Petty and Cacioppo 1986; Schwarz, Bless, and Bohner 1991).

Theoretical Perspectives

We use the aggregated study effects to assess whether the effects of ad-evoked feelings are (1) bidimensional or bipolar and (2) symmetrical or asymmetrical. Furthermore, if asymmetry exists between positive and negative feeling effects, it could be either *generalized* (i.e., invariant across study conditions) or *contingent* (i.e., context specific). Three theoretical perspectives, derived from the broader affect literature, imply different predictions with respect to these questions and possibilities. These perspectives and their predictions are developed in the following sections.

Bipolarity

In recent years, positive and negative affect have come to be viewed as nearly orthogonal independent factors (Diener and Emmons 1984; Isen 1993; Tellegen 1985; Watson, Clark, and Tellegen 1988; Watson and Tellegen 1985; Zevon and Tellegen 1982). However, this view has been challenged strongly by Green, Goldman, and Salovey (1993), who build on previous demonstrations that methodological artifacts tend to suppress negative correlations between positive and negative affect (e.g., Bentler 1969; Russell 1979) to provide strong evidence that low correlations between positive and negative affect result artifactually from random and nonrandom measurement error. They show that correction for random measurement error alone can lead to the conclusion that affect is bipolar rather than bidimensional. For example, averaging across their first two studies, correction for random measurement error causes the negative correlation between positive and negative mood to increase from −.33 to −.89. If positive and negative feelings are polar opposites along a single continuum, their effects on advertising responses are likely to be at least roughly symmetrical.

Generalized Asymmetry

The possibility of generalized asymmetry is illustrated by the finding from decision-making research that negative information generally has greater influence than positive information (e.g., Mizerski 1982; Weinburger, Allen, and Dillon 1981).[3] For example, Weinburger, Allen, and Dillon (1981) found that negative (compared with positive) information has more influence on evaluations of unbranded goods and services. Similarly, Mizerski (1982) finds that negative (compared with positive) information has stronger effects on consumers' ratings of product attributes. A plausible explanation of this generalized negativity bias is grounded in attribution theory. It holds that positive information may be discounted because it is more consistent with social norms than negative information is. Thus, positive information may result from socially desirable responding as well as from veridical responses to stimulus features. In contrast, negative information is more likely to be diagnostic of stimulus characteristics and thus is not discounted (Mizerski 1982). Although it remains unclear whether this negativity bias generalizes to feelings–advertising response relationships, a similar discounting principle potentially could apply. If feelings constitute informational input to ad and brand attitudes as has been proposed in the literature (e.g., Gorn, Goldberg, and Basu 1993; Greenwald and Leavitt 1984; MacInnis and Park 1991), the effects of negative feelings might outweigh those of positive feelings in a manner consistent with the general negativity bias. If so, the conclusion that positive and negative feeling effects are generally asymmetrical would be warranted.

Contingent Asymmetry

In contrast to generalized asymmetry, the persuasion literature offers several conceptual perspectives that predict an interaction between valence of feelings and cognitive elaboration. Three of these (mood as information, mood-congruent recall, and the motivation hypothesis) are consistent in two predictions: (1) that cognitive elaboration is greater when negative rather than positive feelings predominate and (2) that feelings have less impact on ad and brand attitudes when cognitive elaboration is greater (for a review, see Schwarz and Clore 1996). We briefly review these theories, which we classify collectively as the *contingent asymmetry* perspective, in the following sections.

Mood as information. This theory maintains that affective states serve informative functions. It holds that when information is lacking, people evaluate an attitude object simply by asking themselves, "How do I feel about it?" (Schwarz, Bless, and Bohner 1991). The same heuristic comes into play as a simplification strategy when

---

[3]It should be noted that recent research (e.g., Homer and Batra 1994) demonstrates that negative advertising can affect different types of beliefs differently, which suggests that the negativity bias might work selectively.

too much information is available or when ability and/or motivation to process available information is lacking (Schwarz 1990). Positive feelings signal a state of well-being in the person's environment and do not prompt cognitive elaboration. In contrast, negative feelings signal actual or potential problems, prompting effortful, detail-oriented processing to identify and cope with the root cause (Isen 1987; Schwarz 1990). Greater cognitive elaboration in turn leads to less influence of feelings on ad and brand attitudes when feelings are negative.

Mood-congruent recall. A robust empirical finding is that people in good moods are persuaded equally by strong or weak arguments, but people in bad moods are persuaded more by strong arguments (Schwarz and Clore 1996). One possible explanation is that positive mood-congruent material cued from memory is more extensive than negative mood-congruent material and thus occupies a greater proportion of limited processing capacity (Isen et al. 1978; Mackie and Worth 1989, 1991). Mackie and Worth (1989) find that happy subjects elaborate message arguments cognitively when provided ample time (to ease capacity limitations), a finding that they interpret as support for mood-congruent recall. Processing capacity limitations resulting from positive feelings could lead to less elaboration of advertising content and greater impact of feelings than when ad-evoked feelings are negative.

Motivational hypothesis. The motivational hypothesis holds that people in good moods seek to maintain positive feelings, whereas people in bad moods strive to repair negative feelings. Thus, happy people engage in less cognitive processing (e.g., produce fewer counterarguments and overall cognitive responses) because effortful elaboration interrupts their positive feelings (e.g., Batra and Stayman 1990; Batra and Stephens 1994). Conversely, people experiencing negative feelings process information more intensively as a means of identifying and correcting the cause of their feelings (Schwarz and Clore 1996). In turn, more intensive processing leads to weaker effects of negative (compared with positive) feelings on advertising responses.

Potential Moderators

Research on ad-evoked feelings has employed a diversity of study designs, including different types of samples, advertising stimuli, measurement instruments, and exposure conditions. We coded study design characteristics as potential moderators on the basis of a review of ad-evoked feelings research and the methodological literature on meta-analysis. Some coded characteristics ultimately could not be used because insignificant variation existed across studies or because one study characteristic was redundant with another.[4] The study characteristics we analyzed included type of experimental instructions given to subjects (instructed/not instructed to attend to target advertisements), type of cover story (experimenters' interest in reactions to target advertisements was disguised/not disguised), advertising medium (television/print), and type of advertised product (novel/familiar). These are described briefly in the following sections.

---

[4]For example, too few studies used nonstudent samples to estimate a meaningful sample parameter. Also, with the exception of Edell and Burke's (1987) scale, no other measurement scale was used across multiple studies. Whether advertisements were embedded in other content material was correlated too highly with experimental instructions to permit analysis of it as a separate moderator.

Instructions and cover story. Experimental instructions and cover stories are likely to influence subjects' cognitive sets directly upon exposure to target advertisements. Instructions and cover stories that focus attention on target advertisements are conducive to cognitive elaboration of advertising content, whereas those that do not focus attention on target advertisements encourage heuristic processing (Brown and Stayman 1992; Derbaix 1995; Madden, Allen, and Twible 1988). Thus, instructions to attend to advertisements and undisguised cover stories are likely to produce relatively weak feeling effects on ad and brand attitudes. The theories summarized previously as the contingent asymmetry perspective suggest that attentive viewers whose feelings are positive tend to resist cognitive elaboration of advertising material, whereas attentive viewers whose feelings are negative spontaneously engage in elaborated processing. If so, effects of positive feelings are likely to be strong regardless of whether subjects' attention is directed specifically to target advertisements. In contrast, effects of negative feelings are likely to be strong only when attention is not focused specifically on target advertisements. This is the fundamental prediction of the contingent asymmetry perspective.

Medium. Previous research suggests that the advertising medium is a moderator of cognitive and affective responses to advertising (Brown and Stayman 1992; Chaiken and Eagly 1983; Krugman 1965). Comparing print with television, Chaiken and Eagly (1983) find that message information and product cognitions are more important determinants of advertising outcomes for print advertisements, whereas likability of the communicator (a more peripheral cue) is more important for television advertisements. Homer and Yoon (1992) also argue that television advertisements are more complex stimuli than print advertisements and elicit a broader range of emotions. The impact of feelings may be greater for television advertisements than for print advertisements because cognitive elaboration is likely to be less for television (assuming approximately equal attention levels).

Novel/familiar product. Previous research suggests that ad-evoked feeling effects are likely to be stronger for novel brands. Moore and Hutchinson (1983) find that prior brand attitudes can affect advertising responses. It is also likely that attitudes toward established brands are less influenced by ad-evoked feelings than attitudes toward unfamiliar brands (Johnson and Eagly 1989). Consistent with this premise, Brown and Stayman (1992) find stronger relationships between A_{ad} and both brand attitude and purchase intentions for unfamiliar brands but no difference for the feelings–A_{ad} relationship. Derbaix (1995) shows that the effects of ad-evoked feelings on A_{ad} and A_b are stronger for novel brands than for familiar brands.

Implied Theoretical Predictions

In Table 1, we specify the predictions made by the three conceptual perspectives. The bipolarity perspective predicts that the effects of positive and negative feelings on advertising responses are approximately equal in magnitude and that disattenuation for measurement error produces a large negative correlation between positive and negative feelings. The generalized asymmetry perspective predicts a main effect of valence such that the effects of negative feelings are generally greater than those of positive feelings. The contingent asymmetry perspective predicts that valence of feelings interacts with instructions and cover story such that the effects of positive (compared with negative) feelings are greater when instructions and cover story focus attention on target advertisements.

Table 1
Predictions of Conceptual Perspectives

Theoretical Perspective	Main Effect of Valence on A_{ad} and Brand Attitude	Valence × Cognitive Elaboration Interaction (in relation to A_{ad} and Brand Attitude)
Bipolarity	No	No
Generalized Asymmetry	Negative > positive	No
Contingent Asymmetry	No	Positive > negative when attention is directed to target advertisements

Method

Collection of Studies

Studies included in the meta-analyses were located by searching the *Journal of Consumer Research, Advances in Consumer Research, Journal of Marketing, Journal of Marketing Research, Journal of Consumer Psychology, Journal of the Academy of Marketing Science, Journal of Advertising, Journal of Advertising Research, Psychology and Marketing,* and *Journal of Current Issues and Research in Advertising.* The *ABI Inform* and *Psychlit* databases also were searched for additional publications. We contacted authors of published articles and researchers working in the field by mail to request (1) correlation matrices when published articles reported only partialed multivariate statistics, (2) any information necessary for coding study characteristics that was not included in the published reports, and (3) other study reports that met the specifications for inclusion but that we might have overlooked initially. After coding the study characteristics, we contacted authors by mail to ask them to check our codings for accuracy. This resulted in changing only 2 of more than 300 codings.[5]

Our review encompasses all available studies of ad-evoked feelings. We assessed the feasibility of including the smaller number of advertising-related persuasion studies that manipulated mood independently of target advertisements rather than measured the feelings elicited by the advertisements (e.g., Batra and Stayman 1990; Howard and Barry 1994) in the primary analyses. However, a homogeneity test of the positive feelings–brand attitude relationship (the primary area of overlap) indicated substantial differences in mean effect sizes between the two types of studies (corrected $r = .374$, n = 20 for ad-evoked emotion studies; corrected $r = .208$, n = 3 for mood manipulation studies, $t(4) = 1.67$, $p < .10$). This difference was statistically significant at the .10 level despite limited power and a large variance for the ad-

---

[5]A list of studies included in the analysis and their codings is available from Pamela M. Homer.

evoked emotions group.[6] Therefore, the mood manipulation studies were not included in the primary analyses. Including them would have caused a downward bias in a single relationship (i.e., positive feelings–brand attitude) and materially affected conclusions regarding the symmetry or asymmetry of positive and negative feeling effects. Non-advertising-related mood manipulation studies were excluded because their dependent variables were inconsistent with the advertising focus of our study. Also, studies that measured ad-depicted emotions rather than emotions felt by respondents (e.g., Biel and Bridgwater 1990) and those that used the same data as another study (e.g., Stout and Leckenby 1988, which used the same data as Stout and Leckenby 1986) were omitted. These procedures and criteria resulted in a set of 55 studies with independent samples, reported in 46 published articles (dating from 1986 to 1995).

Procedures

We coded discrete ad-evoked feelings as positive or negative. This classification corresponds to the most fundamental conceptual distinction in categorizing emotions (Frijda 1986; Lazarus 1991; Roseman 1991; Smith and Ellsworth 1985). The distinction between positive and negative emotions is acknowledged universally in conceptual models. Watson and Tellegen (1985) find that higher-order positive and negative affect factors account for one-half to three-fourths of the common variance in factor analyses of affect ratings. Bagozzi (1993) also finds that discrete negative emotions load strongly on a higher-order negative emotion construct. The positive/negative distinction provides a conceptually sound and practically meaningful principle for aggregating the study effects. The majority of empirical studies operationalize emotions merely as positive or negative (e.g., Baumgartner, Sujan, and Bettman 1992; MacInnis and Park 1991). In other studies, discrete emotions are classified easily as positive or negative. Thus, the meta-analyses were conducted and are reported separately for positive and negative emotions.

The effect-size metric used in the analyses was r, the Pearson product-moment correlation coefficient. Many studies, however, report only partialed multivariate indices of effect size and not usable pairwise relationships. In these instances, as noted previously, we solicited correlation matrices from the researchers. Bivariate effect-size indices, such as Student's t and F ratios with one degree of freedom in the numerator, were converted to r according to formulas provided by Hunter and Schmidt (1990, p. 272). When multiple effects were reported for a single relationship in a single sample, we analyzed the mean of the reported effects. Thus, we based the analyses on independent observations to the greatest extent possible and only included one effect per relationship per sample (Bangert-Downs 1986). Each correlation was corrected for measurement error (i.e., divided by the product of the square roots of the two reliabilities) and weighted by its sample size relative to the cumulative sample size for that relationship (Hunter and Schmidt 1990, p. 119). For studies that did not report reliabilities, the weighted mean reliability across all studies that did report it was used. We performed moderator analyses on the attenuation-

---

[6]The difference in mean effect sizes is not surprising, because mood manipulation studies typically strive to disassociate mood manipulations from presentation of affectively neutral stimuli, whereas ad-evoked feelings studies overtly measure affective responses to an affectively rich stimulus.

corrected correlations. These represent the best estimates of the strength of relationships between latent constructs in the population (Hunter and Schmidt 1990).

Hunter and Schmidt (1990) maintain that when statistical artifacts such as sampling error, measurement error, and range restriction account for as much as 75% of total between-study variance, the conclusion that no meaningful "true" variance in effect size exists across studies is warranted. Thus, we analyzed the proportion of total variance accounted for by sampling error and measurement error. In addition, a chi-square statistic assessing the significance of between-study variances was computed (Hunter and Schmidt 1990, p. 151). When the ratio of sampling error to total variance around the weighted mean attenuation-corrected correlation was less than 75% and the chi-square statistic was statistically significant, we conducted moderator analyses.

Results

Overall Analyses

In Table 2, we present the mean observed and attenuation-corrected correlations, the ratio of sampling error to total between-study variance, confidence intervals, and credibility intervals[7] for all pairwise relationships with positive and negative feelings that had multiple usable study effects. We also present the chi-square test statistic indicating the statistical significance of the between-study variance in the attenuation-corrected correlations. The results of the overall analysis are noteworthy in three respects: (1) overall, the effects of positive and negative feelings are roughly mirror images, (2) the attenuation-corrected correlation between positive and negative feelings ($r = -.262$) does not approach a level that would suggest bipolarity rather than bidimensionality, and (3) most relationships are not generalizable across study design characteristics.

These findings are inconsistent with both the bipolarity and generalized asymmetry perspectives. The roughly equal overall magnitudes of positive and negative feeling effects do not reflect the main effect of valence predicted by generalized asymmetry. Also, the modest negative attenuation-corrected correlation between positive and negative feelings is consistent with the bidimensional rather than the bipolar conceptualization of ad-evoked feelings.

All of the relationships studied had significant nonartifactual variance, which signifies nonhomogeneity of effect sizes. This indicates that the effects of positive and negative ad-evoked emotions are context dependent rather than generalizable. It shows that estimated effect sizes are a function of (and must be interpreted in light of) the study designs that produce them. Thus, the similar magnitudes of positive and negative feeling effects in the overall analysis do not constitute prima facie evidence of symmetry. Further analyses were necessary to assess the moderator effects of study design characteristics on the effects of positive and negative ad-evoked feelings.

Moderator Analyses

We conducted moderator analyses by using bootstrapping to regress the correlations between feelings and ad and brand attitudes against the coded study charac-

---

[7]Credibility intervals represent intervals around the corrected mean correlations based on variances that have been corrected for statistical artifacts (in this case, sampling error). Thus, they represent only "true" (i.e., nonartifactual) variance and are always smaller than the confidence intervals (Whitener 1990).

Table 2
Descriptive Statistics for Pairwise Relationships

Relationship	Cumulative N	Observed $\bar{r}$	Corrected $\bar{r}$	Sampling error/s_c^2	95% confidence interval for corrected $\bar{r}$	95% credibility interval for corrected $\bar{r}$	$\chi^2_{(n-1)}$*
Positive feelings and negative feelings (k = 16)	3788	−.229	−.262	.067	−.722 ≤ ρ ≤ .235	−.706 ≤ ρ ≤ .182	240.19$_{(15)}$
Positive feelings and A_{ad} (k = 25)	3762	.482	.551	.012	−.462 ≤ ρ ≤ 1.000	−.456 ≤ ρ ≤ 1.000	2071.16$_{(24)}$
Negative feelings and A_{ad} (k = 17)	3068	−.428	−.494	.015	−1.000 ≤ ρ ≤ .406	−1.000 ≤ ρ ≤ .340	1132.75$_{(16)}$
Positive feelings and A_b (k = 19)	3062	.330	.367	.042	−.283 ≤ ρ ≤ 1.000	−.269 ≤ ρ ≤ 1.000	449.84$_{(18)}$
Negative feelings and A_b (k = 14)	2739	−.342	−.389	.028	1.000 ≤ ρ ≤ .318	1.000 ≤ ρ ≤ .308	494.37$_{(13)}$
Positive feelings and purchase intention (k = 14)	2387	.241	.280	.082	−.204 ≤ ρ ≤ .764	−.184 ≤ ρ ≤ .744	171.43$_{(13)}$
Negative feelings and purchase intention (k = 9)	1996	−.172	−.200	.139	−.539 ≤ ρ ≤ .139	−.515 ≤ ρ ≤ .115	64.97$_{(8)}$
Positive feelings and beliefs (k = 3)	381	.154	.173	.741	−.023 ≤ ρ ≤ .369	.118 ≤ ρ ≤ .228	4.05$_{ns}$
Negative feelings and beliefs (k = 2)	369	−.329	−.390	.095	−.787 ≤ ρ ≤ .007	−.767 ≤ ρ ≤ −.013	21.04$_{(1)}$
Positive feelings and recall (k = 4)	354	.065	.083	>1.00	−.056 ≤ ρ ≤ .222	−.443 ≤ ρ ≤ .609	1.79$_{ns}$
Negative feelings and recall (k = 2)	235	−.175	−.238	.399	−.508 ≤ ρ ≤ .032	−.444 ≤ ρ ≤ −.032	5.02$_{(1)}$
Positive feelings and brand cognitions (k = 4)	562	.256	.295	.135	−.114 ≤ ρ ≤ .706	−.087 ≤ ρ ≤ .677	29.67$_{(3)}$
Negative feelings and brand cognitions (k = 3)	442	−.242	−.292	.162	−.659 ≤ ρ ≤ .075	−.625 ≤ ρ ≤ .042	18.49$_{(2)}$
Negative feelings and attitude toward advertising (k = 2)	362	−.036	−.036	>1.00	−.124 ≤ ρ ≤ .052	. . .	.73$_{ns}$

*(n – 1) refers to the degrees of freedom for this test. All values are significant at $p < .05$ unless otherwise indicated.

teristics.[8] In these analyses, each observation was weighted by its sample size relative to the cumulative bootstrap sample size. For each relationship, we drew 200 bootstrap samples with replacement from the original sample, reran the regression for each bootstrap sample, and then used the resulting parameter estimates to generate a frequency distribution for each parameter across the 200 regressions. We then examined the proportion of parameter estimates that had the same sign. If more than 95% of the parameter estimates were positive, we inferred that the parameter is positive and statistically significant at the 5% level. The median parameter estimate across the 200 regressions serves as the point estimate for each independent variable (Efron and Tibshirani 1986).

To evaluate the relative effects of positive and negative feelings, we first treated all of the individual study correlations between feelings and A_{ad} and feelings and brand attitude as absolute values (regardless of valence) and specified a dummy variable to indicate positive and negative feelings (i.e., the dummy variable was set to 1 for negative feelings and 0 otherwise). Second, we incorporated the main effect of valence and terms representing interactions between valence and each coded study characteristic into the regression models. Third, as described previously, we performed 200 bootstrapped regressions for both the A_{ad} and brand attitude models.

We conducted these analyses as a series of nested model tests. Experimental instructions and cover story were correlated substantially (i.e., most studies that did not instruct subjects to attend to target advertisements also used disguised cover stories), which caused data dependencies between these two dummy-coded study characteristics. Judge and colleagues (1985) recommend imposing linear constraints as a means of dealing with collinearity when a theoretical reason exists to believe that the explanatory variables are related. In this case, we assessed whether instructions and cover story represent parallel indicators of the same underlying latent construct by testing the linear constraint that the effect of cover story equals zero.

We regressed the individual study correlations against the main effects of valence, medium, experimental instructions, and product type and the interactions between valence and each coded study characteristics except cover story. We then regressed the residuals from this analysis against the main effect of cover story and the interaction between valence and cover story.[9] A significant main effect of valence would be consistent with generalized asymmetry, whereas significant interaction terms would indicate contingent asymmetry. The results are presented in Table 3.

Consistent with the findings of the overall analyses, the main effect of valence was not significant in either the A_{ad} or brand attitude models, which indicates that the results are not consistent with generalized asymmetry. However, consistent with contingent asymmetry, valence interacted with experimental instructions in the A_{ad} model (beta = .251, $p < .01$) and with both experimental instructions (beta = .305, $p < .01$) and cover story (beta = .091, $p < .05$) in the brand attitude model.

---

[8]These analyses were conducted only on the four relationships for which an ample number of observations (i.e., at least ten) existed.

[9]We also conducted the analysis by constraining the main effect of instructions and the valence × instructions interaction to equal zero in the first run and then testing this constraint by regressing the residuals from the first run against instructions and the valence × instructions interaction. The results were identical substantively to those obtained in the analysis reported here.

We then conducted additional analyses to assess the specific effects of the coded study characteristics on relationships involving positive and negative feelings. These analyses were conducted using bootstrapped regressions performed in the same nested fashion described previously. We report the results in Table 4. On average, the coded study characteristics accounted for between 49 and 79% of the variance in effect sizes, which suggests that these four coded study characteristics have substantial ability to explain between-study variance in the effects of ad-evoked feel-

Table 3
Results Of Bootstrapped Regressions With Interaction Terms

	Models	
Predictors	A_{ad}	A_b
Valence	−.082	−.118
Instructions	.059	−.040*
Medium	.163*	.140
Product Type	.236***	−.074**
Valence × Instructions	.251***	.305**
Valence × Medium	−.008	.059
Valence × Product Type	.059	.125
Median R^2	.43	.53
Cover Story	.017	.041*
Valence × Cover Story	.068	.091**
Median Incremental R^2	.08	.12

*indicates $p < .10$.
**indicates $p < .05$.
***indicates $p < .01$.

Table 4
Results of Bootstrapped Regressions Testing Specific Effects of Positive and Negative Feelings

	Predictors (Coded Study Characteristics)				
Dependent Variable	**Instructions[a]**	**Cover Story[b]**	**Medium[c]**	**Product Type[d]**	**Median R^2**
Positive–A_{ad}	.064	−.008	.145*	.226**	.50
Negative–A_{ad}	−.302**	−.046	−.133**	−.312**	.49
Positive–A_b	−.039*	.023	.127	−.077**	.62
Negative–A_b	−.241*	−.112**	−.150**	−.018	.79

[a]0 = instructed to attend; 1 = not instructed to attend.
[b]0 = undisguised; 1 = disguised.
[c]0 = television; 1 = print.
[d]0 = novel; 1 = familiar.
*indicates $p < .10$.
**indicates $p < .05$.

ings.[10] The moderator effects of each coded study characteristic are discussed in the following sections.

Experimental Instructions

Consistent with the contingent asymmetry perspective, experimental instructions moderated the effect of negative feelings on A_{ad} (beta = $-.302$, $p < .05$) but did not moderate the effects of positive feelings on A_{ad} (beta = .064, n.s.). Experimental instructions also moderated the negative feelings–brand attitude relationship (beta = $-.241$, $p < .10$) in the manner predicted by contingent asymmetry. Experimental instructions moderated the effects of positive feelings on brand attitude (beta = $-.039$, $p < .10$), but this effect was opposite in direction to the effect of instructions on the negative feelings–brand attitude relationship. Positive feelings had a greater effect on brand attitude when instructions focused subjects' attention on target advertisements. A plausible explanation for this unexpected effect is that subjects who are instructed specifically to attend to advertisements that obviously are intended to evoke positive feelings might exaggerate their affective responses.

Cover Story

Cover story moderated the effects of negative feelings on brand attitude (beta = $-.112$, $p < .05$) but not on A_{ad} (beta = $-.046$, n.s.). It did not moderate significantly the effects of positive feelings on either A_{ad} (beta = $-.008$, n.s.) or brand attitude (beta = .023, n.s.). The significant moderating effect of cover story on the negative feelings–brand attitude relationship and the absence of significant moderating effects on relationships involving positive feelings again are consistent with contingent asymmetry. The effect of cover story on the negative feelings–A_{ad} relationship was directionally consistent with the contingent asymmetry prediction, even though it was not statistically significant.

Medium

The results did not support the prediction of stronger feeling effects for television advertisements than for print advertisements. Medium had significant effects on the positive feelings–A_{ad} (beta = .145, $p < .10$), negative feelings–A_{ad} (beta = $-.133$, $p < .05$), and negative feelings–brand attitude (beta = $-.150$, $p < .05$) relationships. However, the direction of these effects was opposite to the prediction. For each relationship, feelings had stronger effects in studies using print advertisements than in those using television advertisements. Results for the positive feelings–brand attitude relationship, though not significant, were directionally consistent. The reason for these findings is not immediately clear. Further research is warranted to investigate the effects of feelings across media.

---

[10]We also coded sample type (student versus nonstudent) but did not include it in the bootstrapped regressions, because the presence of several samples that could not be classified unambiguously as one or the other (e.g., Burke and Edell 1989) seriously would have reduced the number of observations available for the multivariate analysis. Independent analyses revealed no significant effects of sample type, though the number of studies using nonstudent samples was extremely small (as indicated in Table 2).

Product Type

Product type (novel/familiar) moderated the effects of positive feelings on both A_{ad} (beta = .226, $p < .05$) and brand attitude (beta = −.077, $p < .01$). However, these effects were in opposite directions. Contrary to expectation, the positive feelings–A_{ad} relationship was stronger for familiar products. It is possible that familiar advertisements for existing products cued retrieval of ad-related affect from memory. If ad-related affect is a well-defined feature of familiar brand schemas, it could cause stronger feelings–A_{ad} relationships than spontaneous experience of ad-related affect for novel products.

The effect of product type on the positive feelings–brand attitude relationship was in the expected direction. This relationship was stronger for novel products than for familiar products. This is consistent with the premise that ad-evoked emotions have greater impacts on brand attitude for novel brands for which prior brand attitudes are nonexistent (Moore and Hutchinson 1983).

The relationship between negative feelings and A_{ad} was also stronger for familiar products (beta = −.312, $p < .05$). Although contrary to expectation, this result is consistent with the effect of product type on the positive feelings–A_{ad} relationship reported previously. Product type did not moderate the negative feelings–brand attitude relationship (beta = −.018, n.s.). This result is inconsistent with our prediction of a stronger relationship for new products. The fact that product type differentially moderated relationships involving ad and brand attitudes suggests the need for research to investigate when and why feelings affect A_{ad} and brand attitude differently.

Mean Correlations by Subgroup

Table 5 reports the weighted mean correlations by subgroups based on levels of the coded study characteristics. On the basis of the aggregated data, these provide some interesting insights regarding the relative strength of positive and negative feelings under specific study conditions. For example, Table 5 shows that the effects of negative (compared with positive) feelings were stronger when experimental interest in target advertisements was disguised. However, the effects of positive (compared with negative) feelings were stronger when interest in target advertisements was undisguised. The plots of subgroup means for the two levels of experimental instructions shown in Figure 1 illustrate this pattern.[11] These subgroup patterns clearly show differential effects of study characteristics on the effects of positive and negative feelings and constitute a useful basis of comparison for further research (Lehmann 1996). The subgroup analyses also show that feelings–A_{ad} relationships were stronger than feelings–brand attitude relationships. This is consistent with the premise that feelings–A_{ad} relationships are direct, whereas feelings–brand attitude relationships are indirect. The subgroup comparisons are also useful in demonstrating the utility of bootstrapping for testing moderator effects in meta-analysis.

The Utility of Bootstrapping

The utility of bootstrapping for conducting moderator analyses can be seen by comparing the regression results with those of independent t-tests. The bootstrapped

---

[11]Although the subgroup means for cover story reveal a similar pattern, they are not plotted because of the substantial overlap between cover story and instructions.

Table 5
Subgroup Comparisons of Moderator Effects

Relationship	In-structed to Attend	versus	Not In-structed to Attend	Undis-guised Cover Story	versus	Dis-guised Cover Story	TV	versus	Print	Novel	versus	Famil-iar
Positive–A$_{ad}$ .620*	.554	versus	.538	.502	versus	.665*	.535	versus	.543	.470	versus	
Negative–A$_{ad}$	-.396	(18 versus 7) versus	-.778*	-.343	(11 versus 8) versus	-.771**	-.461	(20 versus 3) versus	-.397	-.505	(12 versus 9) versus	-.642
Positive–A$_b$ .256*	.360	(12 versus 5) versus	.286	.354	(7 versus 7) versus	.270	.311	(13 versus 2) versus	.486	.388	(9 versus 5) versus	
Negative–A$_b$	-.239	(12 versus 6) versus (8 versus 5)	-.485**	-.208	(9 versus 4) versus (7 versus 4)	-.512*	-.292	(13 versus 3) versus (10 versus 2)	-.342	-.383	(11 versus 4) versus (9 versus 2)	-.403

*denotes $p < .05$.
**denotes $p < .01$.

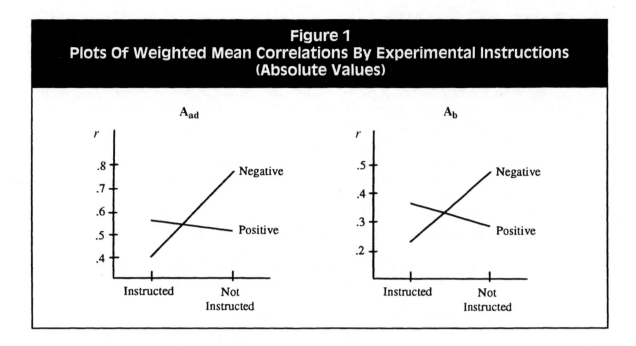

Figure 1
Plots Of Weighted Mean Correlations By Experimental Instructions
(Absolute Values)

regressions identified several significant moderator effects (instructions on positive feelings–A_{ad}, medium on both positive feelings–A_{ad} and negative feelings–brand attitude, and product type on negative feelings–A_{ad}) that independent t-tests could not detect.[12] The regressions also correctly found that the moderating effects of cover story on positive feelings–A_{ad} and negative feelings–A_{ad} that appear clearly in the subgroup analyses are redundant with the effects of instructions.

More important, the bootstrapped regressions assessed the joint effects of the study characteristics. Analyzing the moderator effects individually can lead to attributing moderator effects to the wrong variables. For example, the subgroup analysis suggests that the negative feelings–A_{ad} relationship is slightly (but not significantly) stronger for studies using television advertisements ($r = -.461$ versus $r = -.397$). After partialing the effects of the other coded study characteristics, however, the bootstrapped regression leads to the opposite conclusion: Negative feelings influence A_{ad} more strongly in studies using print advertisements. Ability to account for these partialing effects, even with the small samples typical of moderator analyses in meta-analysis, is a major advantage of the bootstrapped multivariate regression.

Discussion

In this study, we extend previous research by (1) comprehensively summarizing existing research on ad-evoked feelings, (2) providing summary evidence consistent with the contingent asymmetry theoretical perspective (but not with bipolarity or generalized asymmetry), (3) showing the context dependency of relationships involving ad-evoked feelings, and (4) presenting a useful new way of assessing moderator effects in meta-analysis. Our findings improve the interpretability of existing data

---

[12]These analyses used a small sample t-test described by Winer (1971, pp. 41–42), which previously has been used for meta-analysis by Brown (1996) and Mathieu and Zajac (1990).

and provide information useful for theory development and the design of new research.

Consistent with contingent asymmetry, study design characteristics related to amount of cognitive elaboration (i.e., experimental instructions and cover story) interacted with valence of feelings in relation to ad and brand attitudes. Also consistent with contingent asymmetry, experimental instructions and cover story moderated effects of negative feelings on advertising responses but, for the most part, did not moderate the effects of positive feelings. Effects of negative feelings on advertising responses were generally greater under conditions that did not encourage cognitive elaboration of target advertisements, whereas effects of positive feelings were generally strong regardless of study conditions.

We found several minor but notable exceptions to the pattern predicted by contingent asymmetry. First, cover story did not moderate the effects of negative feelings on A_{ad} as contingent asymmetry would have predicted. In this case, the additional variance explained by cover story after accounting for other moderator effects (average incremental $R^2 = 6\%$) was not statistically significant. Much of the variance explained by cover study was redundant with that explained by experimental instructions. However, cover story did contribute uniquely to explained variance in the brand attitude model (19% incremental R^2), which suggests the potential for each of these study characteristics to influence effect sizes independently.

A second minor discrepancy from the prediction of contingent asymmetry was the significant moderating effect of experimental instructions on the positive feelings–brand attitude relationship. This effect was in the opposite direction from the effects of instructions on relationships involving negative feelings. Positive feelings were related more strongly to brand attitude when subjects were instructed to attend to target advertisements than when they were not instructed to attend. A plausible explanation is that instructing subjects specifically to attend to target advertisements might create demand effects. Viewing positive emotional advertisements in a critical evaluation set might lead to exaggeration of positive feeling effects. Subjects easily can recognize and appreciate that good advertisements "work" on an emotional level, and this can influence their responses when they are aware during exposure that those responses are of interest to the researchers. Overall, the results are consistent with the contingent asymmetry predictions.

The evidence was not consistent with other theoretical perspectives. The attenuation-corrected correlation between positive and negative ad-evoked feelings ($r = -.262$) clearly indicated nearly orthogonal independent dimensions rather than bipolar ends of a single continuum. Also, though the effects of positive and negative feelings were virtual mirror images in the overall analyses, these mean correlations did not estimate generalizable population parameters. Subsequent analyses demonstrated contingently asymmetric effects of positive and negative feeling effects. Thus, our findings lead to the conclusion that positive and negative ad-evoked feelings are bidimensional rather than bipolar and that their effects on advertising response variables are not symmetrical.

The absence of a main effect of valence in both the overall analysis and bootstrapped regression was inconsistent with generalized asymmetry. The results made clear that the relative strength of positive and negative feeling effects was context dependent rather than generalizable (i.e., the direction of asymmetry differed across contexts). There was no evidence to suggest that, in general, negative feelings are given greater weight than positive feelings or vice versa. Thus, the conclusion that feelings are contingently rather than generally asymmetrical is warranted.

Aspects of study designs clearly bias effect sizes systematically and create potential confounds with explanatory variables. Both the magnitude and direction of the effects of study design characteristics depended on the valence of ad-evoked feelings. The effects of negative feelings on ad and brand attitudes were greater when study procedures did not direct attention to target advertisements. In contrast, the effects of positive feelings were greater when procedures did direct attention to target advertisements. A clear implication for basic and applied research is that exposure conditions influence observed relationships between feelings and ad and brand attitudes. Results of applied copy tests and basic research on the effects of ad-evoked feelings will be most accurate and valid when exposure to target advertisements occurs under realistic exposure conditions. Study procedures that focus subjects' attention on target advertisements generally will produce results that do not generalize to realistic exposure conditions.

In addition to the moderators of processing goals, we identified other methodological factors that influenced relationship strength. Novel versus familiar product and advertising medium both had significant effects. These also suggest the need for additional research to understand why ad-evoked feelings influence attitudes toward the ad more strongly for familiar than for novel products. This effect was contrary to expectation and the moderating effects of feelings on brand attitudes (which, as expected, were stronger for novel brands). It seems likely that viewing familiar advertisements (or familiar types of advertisements) for a known brand may cue retrieval of stored affect from memory (Stayman and Batra 1991). This memory-based advertisement affect already might be associated closely and specifically with attitudes toward the brand's advertising, which leads to stronger effects of feelings on A_{ad} for familiar brands. These results suggest the need for research investigating why product type (novel/familiar) differentially moderates the effects of ad-evoked feelings on ad and brand attitudes.

Our study also demonstrates the advantages of using bootstrapping to test moderator effects in meta-analyses. The lack of distributional assumptions makes it generally applicable to the types of moderator analyses typically conducted in meta-analyses. Sample sizes in these analyses are almost invariably small, and no consensus has developed regarding the best way of assessing moderator effects. The methods most generally used involve testing effects of one moderator at a time (cf. Hunter and Schmidt 1990; Rosenthal 1984). As we have shown, this often leads to erroneous conclusions regarding (1) statistical significance of moderator effects and (2) attribution of moderator effects to the correct explanatory variables. Bootstrapping enables researchers to overcome both of these problems and thus enhances the validity of moderator analyses.

Our review suggests several additional worthwhile directions for further research. For example, we found unexpectedly strong effects of ad-evoked feelings in studies that used print advertisements. Contrary to expectation, the negative feelings–A_{ad} and negative feelings–brand attitude relationships were stronger in studies using print advertisements than in studies using television advertisements. Although these results should be interpreted with caution because of the small number of studies using print advertisements, it would be worthwhile for further research to investigate moderating effects of media in more detail.

It also would be worthwhile to reevaluate models of cognitive and affective factors that mediate the effectiveness of advertisements intended to evoke negative feelings. The dual mediation model (MacKenzie, Lutz, and Belch 1986), for example, does not appear to represent accurately the intended effects of this type of advertising. Our findings indicate strong and robust negative effects of negative feelings on ad and brand attitudes (cf. Burke and Edell 1989; Edell and Burke 1987; Stayman and Aaker 1988). However, other research demonstrates that advertising designed to elicit negative emotions can have positive effects on motivation, attitude, and persuasion (e.g., Bagozzi and Moore 1994; Ray and Wilkie 1970; Sternthal and Craig 1974). It is important to understand better how fear appeals and other advertising designed to evoke negative emotions affect advertising outcomes.

Another issue for further research is the operationalization of A_{ad}. Previous research has established A_{ad} as a multidimensional construct (Madden, Allen, and Twible 1988; Olney, Holbrook, and Batra 1991; Shimp 1981). Researchers primarily have used global measures of A_{ad} that do not discriminate between cognitive and affective elements. Cognitive and affective reactions are likely to constitute separate dimensions of A_{ad}, and antecedent and moderating factors may influence these dimensions differentially (e.g., Madden, Allen, and Twible 1988).

In conclusion, our results suggest that the effects of positive and negative ad-evoked feelings are contingently asymmetrical. They demonstrate that the strength of effects of ad-evoked feelings depends systematically on the valence of emotion, study design characteristics, and cognitive evaluation set. These findings are important for interpretation of empirical findings, design of further research, and further theory development. We hope our results will stimulate and guide further research. Research designed to provide a more detailed understanding of the specific causes and effects of each type of emotion is needed.

References

Aaker, David A., Douglas M. Stayman, and Michael R. Hagerty (1986), "Warmth in Advertising: Measurement, Impact, and Sequence Effects," *Journal of Consumer Research*, 12 (March), 365–81.

Bagozzi, Richard P. (1993), "An Examination of the Psychometric Properties of Measures of Negative Affect in the PANAS-X Scales," *Journal of Personality and Social Psychology*, 65 (October), 836–51.

———— and David J. Moore (1994), "Public Service Advertisements: Emotions and Empathy Guide Prosocial Behavior," *Journal of Marketing*, 58 (January), 56–70.

Bangert-Downs, Robert L. (1986), "Review of Developments in Meta-Analytic Method," *Psychological Bulletin*, 99 (3), 388–99.

Batra, Rajeev and Michael L. Ray (1986), "Affective Responses Mediating Acceptance of Advertising," *Journal of Consumer Research*, 13 (September), 234–49.

———— and Douglas M. Stayman (1990), "The Role of Mood in Advertising Effectiveness," *Journal of Consumer Research*, 17 (September), 203–14.

———— and Debra Stephens (1994), "Attitudinal Effects of Ad-Evoked Moods and Emotions," *Psychology and Marketing*, 11 (May/June), 199–215.

Baumgartner, Hans, Mita Sujan, and James R. Bettman (1992), "Autobiographical Memories, Affect, and Consumer Information Processing," *Journal of Consumer Psychology*, 1 (1), 53–83.

Bentler, Peter (1969), "Semantic Space Is (Approximately) Bipolar," *Journal of Psychology*, 71 (January), 33–40.

Biel, Alexander L. and Carol A. Bridgwater (1990), "Attributes of Likable Television Commercials," *Journal of Advertising Research*, 30 (June/July), 38–44.

Bless, Herbert, Gerd Bohner, Norbert Schwarz, and Fritz Strack (1990), "Mood and Persuasion: A Cognitive Response Analysis," *Personality and Social Psychology Bulletin*, 16 (June), 331–45.

Bone, Paula F., Subhash Sharma, and Terence A. Shimp (1989), "A Bootstrap Procedure for Evaluating Goodness of Fit Indices of Structural Equation and Confirmatory Factor Models," *Journal of Marketing Research,* 26 (February), 105–11.

Brown, Steven P. (1996), "A Meta-Analysis and Review of Organizational Research on Job Involvement," *Psychological Bulletin*, 120 (September), 235–55.

――― and Douglas M. Stayman (1992), "Antecedents and Consequences of Attitude Toward the Ad: A Meta-Analysis," *Journal of Consumer Research*, 19 (June), 34–51.

Burke, Marian Chapman and Julie A. Edell (1989), "The Impact of Feelings on Ad-Based Affect and Cognition," *Journal of Marketing Research*, 26 (February), 69–83.

Chaiken, Shelly and Alice H. Eagly (1983), "Communication Modality as a Determinant of Persuasion: The Role of Communicator Salience," *Journal of Personality and Social Psychology*, 45 (August), 241–56.

Curren, Mary T. and Katrin R. Harich (1994), "Consumers' Mood States: The Mitigating Influence of Personal Relevance on Product Evaluations," *Psychology and Marketing*, 11 (March/April), 91–107.

Derbaix, Christian M. (1995), "The Impact of Affective Reactions on Attitudes Toward the Advertisement and the Brand: A Step Toward Ecological Validity," *Journal of Marketing Research*, 32 (November), 470–79.

Diener, Ed and Robert A. Emmons (1984), "The Independence of Positive and Negative Affect," *Journal of Personality and Social Psychology*, 47 (5), 1105–17.

Edell, Julie A. and Marian Chapman Burke (1987), "The Power of Feelings in Understanding Advertising Effects," *Journal of Consumer Research*, 14 (December), 421–33.

Efron, Bradley and R. Tibshirani (1986), "Bootstrap Methods for Standard Errors, Confidence Intervals, and Other Measures of Statistical Accuracy," *Statistical Science*, 1 (February), 54–77.

Farley, John U. and Donald R. Lehmann (1986), *Meta-Analysis in Marketing: Generalization of Response Models.* Lexington, MA: Lexington Books.

Frijda, Nico H. (1986), *The Emotions.* New York: Cambridge University Press.

Goldberg, Marvin E. and Gerald J. Gorn (1987), "Happy and Sad TV Programs: How They Affect Reactions to Commercials," *Journal of Consumer Research*, 14 (December), 387–403.

Goodstein, Ronald C., Julie A. Edell, and Marian Chapman Moore (1990), "When Are Feelings Generated? Assessing the Presence and Reliability of Feelings Based on Storyboards and Animatics," in *Emotion in Advertising: Theoretical and Practical Explorations*, S. J. Agres, J. A. Edell, and T. M. Dubitsky, eds. Westport, CT: Quorum Books, 175–93.

Gorn, Gerald J., Marvin E. Goldberg, and Kunal Basu (1993), "Mood, Awareness, and Product Evaluation," *Journal of Consumer Psychology*, 2 (3), 237–56.

Green, Donald P., Susan L. Goldman, and Peter Salovey (1993), "Measurement Error Masks Bipolarity in Affect Ratings," *Journal of Personality and Social Psychology*, 64 (6), 1029–41.

Greenwald, Anthony G. and Clark Leavitt (1984), "Audience Involvement in Advertising: Four Levels," *Journal of Consumer Research*, 11 (June), 581–92.

Holbrook, Morris B. and Rajeev Batra (1987), "Assessing the Role of Emotions as Mediators of Consumer Responses to Advertising," *Journal of Consumer Research*, 14 (December), 404–20.

Homer, Pamela M. and Rajeev Batra (1994), "Attitudinal Effects of Character-Based Versus Competence-Based Negative Political Communications," *Journal of Consumer Psychology*, 3 (2), 163–85.

――― and Sun-Gil Yoon (1992), "Message Framing and the Interrelationships Among Ad-Based Feelings, Affect, and Cognition," *Journal of Advertising*, 21 (March), 19–33.

Howard, Daniel J. and Thomas E. Barry (1994), "The Role of Thematic Congruence Between a Mood-Inducing Event and an Advertised Product in Determining the Effects of Mood on Brand Attitudes," *Journal of Consumer Psychology*, 3 (1), 1–27.

Hunter, John E. and Frank L. Schmidt (1990), *Methods of Meta-Analysis: Correcting Error and Bias in Research Findings.* Newbury Park, CA: Sage Publications.

Inman, J. Jeffrey and Leigh McAlister (1993), "A Retailer Promotion Policy Model Considering Promotion Signal Sensitivity," *Marketing Science*, 12 (4), 339–56.

Isen, Alice M. (1987), "Positive Affect, Cognitive Processes, and Social Behavior," in *Advances in Experimental Social Psychology*, Vol. 20, Leonard Berkowitz, ed. New York: Academic Press, 203–54.

——— (1993), "Positive Affect and Decision Making," in *Handbook of Emotions*, Michael Lewis and Jeannette M. Haviland, eds. New York: The Guilford Press, 261–77.

———, Thomas E. Shalker, Margaret S. Clark, and Lynn Karp (1978), "Affect, Accessibility of Material in Memory, and Behavior: A Cognitive Loop?" *Journal of Personality and Social Psychology*, 36 (1), 1–12.

Johnson, Blair T. and Alice H. Eagly (1989), "Effects of Involvement on Persuasion: A Meta-Analysis," *Psychological Bulletin*, 106 (2), 290–314.

Judge, George G., W. E. Griffiths, R. Carter Hill, Hulmut Lutkepohl, and Tsoung-Chao Lee (1985), *The Theory and Practice of Econometrics*. New York: John Wiley & Sons.

Krugman, Herbert (1965), "The Impact of Television Advertising: Learning Without Involvement," *Public Opinion Quarterly*, 29 (Fall), 349–56.

Lazarus, Richard S. (1984), "On the Primacy of Cognition," *American Psychologist*, 39 (February), 124–29.

——— (1991), *Emotion and Adaptation*. New York: Oxford University Press.

Lehmann, Donald R. (1996), "Presidential Address: Knowledge Generalization and the Conventions of Consumer Research: A Study in Inconsistency," in *Advances in Consumer Research*, Vol. 23, Kim P. Corfman and John G. Lynch Jr., eds. Provo, UT: Association for Consumer Research, 1–5.

Lutz, Richard J. (1985), "Affective and Cognitive Antecedents of Attitude Toward the Ad: A Conceptual Framework," in *Psychological Processes and Advertising Effects*, Linda F. Alwitt and Andrew A. Mitchell, eds. Hillsdale, NJ: Lawrence Erlbaum & Associates, 45–64.

MacInnis, Deborah J. and C. Whan Park (1991), "The Differential Role of Characteristics of Music on High- and Low-Involvement Consumers' Processing of Ads," *Journal of Consumer Research*, 18 (September), 161–73.

MacKenzie, Scott B., Richard J. Lutz, and George E. Belch (1986), "The Role of Attitude Toward the Ad as a Mediator of Advertising Effectiveness: A Test of Competing Explanations," *Journal of Marketing Research*, 23 (May), 130–43.

Mackie, Diane M. and Leila T. Worth (1989), "Processing Deficits and the Mediation of Positive Affect in Persuasion," *Journal of Personality and Social Psychology*, 57 (1), 27–40.

——— and ——— (1991), "Feeling Good But Not Thinking Straight: The Impact of Positive Mood on Persuasion," in *Emotion and Social Judgments*, Joseph P. Forgas, ed. New York: Pergamon, 201–209.

Madden, Thomas J., Chris T. Allen, and Jacquelyn L. Twible (1988), "Attitude Toward the Ad: An Assessment of Diverse Measurement Indices Under Different Processing Sets," *Journal of Marketing Research*, 25 (August), 242–52.

Mathieu, John E. and Dennis M. Zajac (1990), "A Review and Meta-Analysis of the Antecedents, Correlates, and Consequences of Organizational Commitment," *Psychological Bulletin*, 108 (September), 171–94.

Mitchell, Andrew A. and Jerry C. Olson (1981), "Are Product Attribute Beliefs the Only Mediator of Advertising Effects on Brand Attitudes?" *Journal of Marketing Research*, 18 (August), 318–22.

Mizerski, Richard W. (1982), "An Attribution Explanation for the Disproportionate Influence of Unfavorable Information," *Journal of Consumer Research*, 9 (December), 301–10.

Moore, Danny L. and J. Wesley Hutchinson (1983), "The Effects of Ad Affect on Advertising Effectiveness," in *Advances in Consumer Research*, Vol. 10, Richard P. Bagozzi and Alice M. Tybout, eds. Ann Arbor, MI: Association for Consumer Research, 503–508.

Olney, Thomas J., Morris B. Holbrook, and Rajeev Batra (1991), "Consumer Responses to Advertising: The Effects of Ad Content, Emotions, and Attitude Toward the Ad on Viewing Time," *Journal of Consumer Research*, 17 (March), 440–53.

Petty, Richard E. and John T. Cacioppo (1986), *Communication and Persuasion: Central and Peripheral Routes to Persuasion.* New York: Springer-Verlag.

Ray, Michael L. and William Wilkie (1970), "Fear: The Potential of an Appeal Neglected by Marketing," *Journal of Marketing,* 34 (January), 54–62.

Roseman, Ira (1991), "Appraisal Determinants of Discrete Emotions," *Cognition and Emotion,* 5 (3), 161–200.

Rosenthal, Robert (1984), *Meta-Analytic Procedures for Social Research.* Newbury Park, CA: Sage Publications.

Russell, James A. (1979), "Affective Space Is Bipolar," *Journal of Personality and Social Psychology,* 37 (February), 1161–78.

Sackett, Paul R., Michael M. Harris, and John M. Orr (1986), "On Seeking Moderator Variables in the Meta-Analysis of Correlational Data: A Monte Carlo Investigation of Statistical Power and Resistance to Type I Error," *Journal of Applied Psychology,* 71 (April), 302–10.

Schwarz, Norbert (1990), "Feelings as Information: Informational and Motivational Functions of Affective States," in *Handbook of Motivation and Cognition: Foundations of Social Behavior,* Vol. 2, E. Tory Higgins and Richard Sorrentino, eds. New York: Guilford Press, 527–61.

———, Herbert Bless, and Gerd Bohner (1991), "Mood and Persuasion: Affective States Influence the Processing of Persuasive Communications," in *Advances in Experimental Social Psychology,* Vol. 24, Mark Zanna, ed. San Diego: Academic Press, 161–99.

——— and Gerald L. Clore (1983), "Mood, Misattribution, and Judgments of Well-Being: Informative and Directive Functions of Affective States," *Journal of Personality and Social Psychology,* 45 (September), 513–23.

——— and ——— (1996), "Feelings and Phenomenal Experiences," in *Social Psychology: A Handbook of Basic Principles,* E. Tory Higgins and Arie Kruglanski, eds. New York: Guilford Press, 433–65.

Shimp, Terence A. (1981), "Attitude Toward the Ad as a Mediator of Consumer Brand Choice," *Journal of Advertising,* 10 (2), 9–15.

Smith, Craig A. and Phoebe C. Ellsworth (1985), "Patterns of Cognitive Appraisal in Emotion," *Journal of Personality and Social Psychology,* 48 (4), 813–38.

Stayman, Douglas M. and David A. Aaker (1988), "Are All the Effects of Ad-Induced Feelings Mediated by A_{ad}?" *Journal of Consumer Research,* 15 (December), 368–73.

——— and Rajeev Batra (1991), "Encoding and Retrieval of Ad Affect in Memory," *Journal of Marketing Research,* 28 (May), 232–39.

Sternthal, Brian and Samuel Craig (1974), "Fear Appeals: Revisited and Revised," *Journal of Consumer Research,* 1 (December), 22–34.

Stout, Patricia A. and John D. Leckenby (1986), "Measuring Emotional Response to Advertising," *Journal of Advertising,* 15 (4), 35–42.

——— and ——— (1988), "The Nature of Emotional Response to Advertising: A Further Examination," *Journal of Advertising,* 17 (4), 53–7.

Tellegen, Auke (1985), "Structures of Mood and Personality and Their Relevance to Assessing Anxiety, With an Emphasis on Self-Report," in *Anxiety and the Anxiety Disorders,* A. H. Tuma and J. D. Maser, eds. Hillsdale, NJ: Laurence Erlbaum Associates, 681–706.

Van Trijp, Hans C. M., Wayne D. Hoyer, and J. Jeffrey Inman (1996), "Why Switch? Product Category-Level Explanations for True Variety-Seeking Behavior," *Journal of Marketing Research,* 33 (August), 281–92.

Walker, David and Tony M. Dubitsky (1994), "Why Liking Matters," *Journal of Advertising Research,* 34 (May/June), 9–18.

Watson, David A., Le Anna Clark, and Auke Tellegen (1988), "Development and Validation of Brief Measures of Positive and Negative Affect: The PANAS scale," *Journal of Personality and Social Psychology,* 54 (6), 1063–70.

——— and Auke Tellegen (1985), "Toward a Consensual Structure of Mood," *Psychological Bulletin,* 98 (2), 219–35.

Weinberger, Marc G., Chris T. Allen, and William R. Dillon (1981), "Negative Information: Perspectives and Research Directions," in *Advances in Consumer Research*, Vol. 8, Kent B. Monroe, ed. Ann Arbor, MI: Association for Consumer Research, 398–404.

Whitener, Ellen M. (1990), "Confusion of Confidence Intervals and Credibility Intervals in Meta-Analysis," *Journal of Applied Psychology*, 75 (June), 315–21.

Winer, B. J. (1971), *Statistical Principles in Experimental Design*. New York: McGraw-Hill.

Yoon, Carolyn (1991), *Tears, Cheers, and Fears: The Role of Emotion in Advertising*. Cambridge, MA: Marketing Science Institute.

Zajonc, Robert B. (1984), "On the Primacy of Affect," *American Psychologist*, 39 (2), 117–23.

Zevon, M. A. and Auke Tellegen (1982), "The Structure of Mood Change: An Idiographic/Nomethetic Analysis," *Journal of Personality and Social Psychology*, 43 (1), 111–22.

6

An Informal, Qualitative Analysis of Shortages and Abundances in Academic Advertising Research

James H. Leigh
Texas A&M University

Research on advertising topics has significantly expanded in recent years. The emphasis on investigating particular subjects has allowed for the accumulation of research findings in sufficient numbers to enable other researchers to perform meta-analyses of these works to search for generalizable threads across different study contexts. At the same time, because there is a finite number of researchers who conduct academic advertising research, the accumulation of studies in one domain comes at the expense of research on other topics. The purposes of this article are twofold: to comment on the meta-analysis conducted by Brown, Homer, and Inman (1998) regarding the relationship between feelings evoked by advertising and subsequent advertising responses and to place the focus of that meta-analysis within the broader context of advertising topics that constitute the domain of topics available to researchers for investigation. Particular emphasis is placed on identifying those areas in which an abundance of studies have already been conducted and on those areas in which there is a shortage of substantive findings and a need for concentrated work in the future.

Meta-Analytic Research: Ad-Evoked Feelings and Advertising Response Relationships

Brown, Homer, and Inman's (1998) comprehensive and illuminating meta-analysis provides an important synthesis and extension to the advertising literature regarding the relationship between positive and negative feelings evoked by an advertisement and relevant responses. These authors examine generalizations that emerge from the more than 50 studies that have focused on these matters. Their research is particularly important in that they apply a strong theoretical framework to the data that involves a direct assessment of countervailing theoretical positions in terms of their generalizability across study contexts. In other words, the authors investigate whether positive and negative affective feelings have symmetrical or asymmetrical relationships with advertising responses and whether study design characteristics moderate the strength of the relationships uncovered.

The authors are to be commended for employing meta-analysis in a manner that the developers of the technique originally intended as a means of theory testing and application. It is only in this way that the limits and qualifications to general findings can be determined. Their article is a textbook example of how meta-analysis can and should be conducted if the available data allow for use of the technique in the intended manner.

In many advertising domains, however, the studies that have been conducted are insufficient in number to allow for such a thorough and useful investigation. Moreover, the lack of commonalities across multiple parts of study domains does not allow for extraction and examination of reliable and valid estimates of variable relationships. In subsequent sections of this article, I identify those topic areas that have generated substantial researcher interest for several years and for which a sufficient number of studies have already been conducted to allow for a similar detailed meta-analysis. Equally, if not more important, I identify those areas in serious need of further research attention so that, in time, a body of research findings can be accumulated for similar meta-analytic pursuits.

What Advertising Research Is and What It Is Not

In recent years, several studies have been published that use advertisements for the purpose of communicating to study participants the desired objects under investigation. In some of those cases, the focus might reasonably and correctly be considered one of advertising research. In others, however, it would be stretching the province of advertising to consider the research study relevant to the practice of advertising.

McGrath and Brinberg (1983) propose a partial resolution to the lengthy debate on how research should be conducted for application purposes. In their comment article on the dialogue between Calder, Phillips, and Tybout (1982, 1983) and Lynch (1982, 1983) regarding the positions that are outlined in the article by Calder, Phillips, and Tybout (1981), McGrath and Brinberg (1983) present three distinct paths of relations among the conceptual, substantive, and methodological domains associated with a discipline. Each of these paths represents a legitimate area of inquiry. Moreover, for maximal progress to be realized, continued development and refinement activities are also required in each of the separate disciplines associated with each domain.

The first path McGrath and Brinberg identify entails proposing and testing a formulated new design or possible application in an experimental or real-life setting. An example of this path might be an investigation of the possible effectiveness of ten-second commercials, if they had not been used before, or consideration of the possible benefits or shortcomings of the use of a black-and-white print advertisement in a medium that has only included four-color advertisements in the past.

A second path McGrath and Brinberg forward involves the development of testable hypotheses extracted from theoretical concepts and the evaluation of these hypotheses using appropriate research methods. This pathway encompasses the majority of experiment-based research that has been published in advertising-oriented outlets. The third McGrath–Brinberg path concerns the extraction of a set of observations from the real world followed by an explanation of them using existing theory. Examples of this path include research studies in advertising that are based on content analysis of advertisement headlines, information content, and execution-related factors.

In advertising, the first path is usually undertaken by practitioners when they test a new possible way of promoting a good or service. Nevertheless, after a promotion is implemented, it is incumbent on advertising researchers in academia to identify the practice and search for possible theory-based explanations for the outcomes experienced. One important role of academic advertising research is to examine what is being done in practice by advertisers (i.e., the third path). Qualitative examination and content-analytic investigation of actual advertising content using the third path represent the most appropriate methodologies for the assessment of advertising practice.

Alternatively, new approaches might be tested using the second McGrath–Brinberg path in experimental and applied settings. My work on umbrella advertisements (1984) and Edell and Keller's (1989) work on coordinated media campaigns appear to have been precipitated by recent use by advertisers and reports in the popular press such as *Advertising Age*.

Another area that defines the province of academic research on advertising topics is to test theory-based hypotheses regarding advertising and audience-based principles in an experimental or applied setting using the second McGrath–Brinberg path. The advertising literature contains many examples of studies that employ this focus.

The domain of advertising can be considered to be applied social science. As a result, most, if not all, theories that have been advanced in psychology, sociology, microeconomics, and cultural anthropology can be readily applied to the investigative task. Conversely, some of the methodologies appropriate for examining advertising outcomes are unique to advertising, such as Starch Readership scores, or the context or focus is different from the core discipline, and refinement or modification is warranted. Because of this uniqueness, a final province of academic advertising research is one of methodological development. Work that investigates the viability of using outcome measures drawn from other social science branches, research work that is concerned with refining and improving existing outcome measures, and examinations of relationships among measures within the province of advertising also represent legitimate advertising emphases.

Taken together, these alternative pathways encompass a wide assortment of research domains under the advertising umbrella. Nevertheless, simply because a research study uses advertisements or commercial executions as its manipulated stimuli does not necessarily place it in the domain of academic advertising research. To qualify as an advertising research study, the advertisements should be typical of advertising in practice. For example, if the study uses advertisements simply as a vehicle to test theoretical propositions regarding consumer behavior or human behavior in general, and some or all of the test advertisements are necessarily ones that would never be encountered (e.g., a claim that the product is overpriced and will not last very long), the study should be considered to be about behavior and not advertising per se. Because of the focus of this article is on advertising and the research to investigate such phenomena no further discussion or attention is given to such emphases.

Abundances and Shortages in Advertising Research

A review of academic research articles published on advertising topics reveals several subjects that have been heavily researched in recent years and are deserving of meta-analytic work to identify the commonalities and discrepancies among the research findings. Equally important is the identification of those research domains that have not received much recent attention, yet are deserving of additional work. In the remainder of this article, I provide a qualitative assessment of the state of advertising knowledge and point out those areas that have been heavily researched and those in need of more work.

By way of background, I am a co-founder and co-editor of the *Journal of Current Issues and Research in Advertising* since its inception in 1978. I am also a member of the editorial review board for the *Journal of Advertising* and have served in that capacity since it was formed in 1991. Moreover, I am an occasional ad hoc reviewer of advertising and consumer behavior manuscripts for the *Journal of Consumer Research*, and for AMA's *Journal of Marketing* and *Journal of Marketing Research*. Finally, I have been an active researcher in advertising for many years. By serving in these capacities, I have had the opportunity to both observe and participate first hand in academic advertising research. It is clear to me, at some times painfully so, that a few hot topics are investigated by several different investigators and get virtually all collective intellectual attention. Often the incremental contributions made across studies are small. At the same time, other equally, if not more important, subjects get little, if any, attention. It is hoped that by pointing out the excesses and shortages, interest can be stimulated in the neglected areas.

The Appendix lists several areas in advertising that have been the subject of investigation and highlights those areas in need of additional work. Items denoted with one asterisk are in need of additional study, those with two asterisks have not been studied much at all and are in serious need of concentrated study, and those with no asterisk have been studied extensively and are likely candidates for meta-analytic work. This list is by no means a complete accounting of all subject areas that have been used in investigations, and it might not cover unstudied subject areas that should be the focus of investigation but have not been studied to date.

Table 1 lists different measures of advertising effectiveness that have been the focus of many studies. The McGuire (1978) hierarchy-of-effects framework is used for organizational purposes. In most cases, one or more of the factors given in the Appendix have been used in a study as the predictor or manipulated factors, and one or more of the factors shown in Table 1 are incorporated as criteria for evaluation.

If a particular area has been slighted in the Appendix or Table 1, please accept my apologies and add your favorite items to the list. This compendium is intended as a guide for future research efforts. Advertising researchers are part of a relatively small special interest group of a fairly small, compact discipline compared with other, more established social sciences. For this reason, I hope that serious thought and consideration are given to my observations so that the collective efforts of

Table 1
Selected Measures of Effectiveness

Attention/awareness	Recognition, aided and unaided recall, cognitive responses
Comprehension	Unaided, aided recall of advertising facets
Interest/evaluation	A_{ad}, A_{brand}, cognitive responses
Desire/yielding	Persuasion
Intention	Likelihood of purchase
Action	Purchase

researchers can be of maximal benefit in the long run to uncovering the wide assortment of unknowns associated with the science and practice of advertising.

Stimulus, Contextual, and Individual Factors

The factors provided in the Appendix are organized into categories of advertising stimulus factors, contextual factors, and individual factors. Advertising stimulus factors are further subdivided into factors that pertain to the information characteristics of a commercial or print advertisement, factors associated with the medium of presentation, and campaign-related factors.

Without question, informational factors have been the most heavily researched dimension in advertising, though some factors have received more attention than others. Factors in need of additional study include the following: emotional versus rational appeals; information complexity or internal clutter within an advertisement; stimulus meaningfulness or clarity; format effects such as integrated or umbrella appeals; grammatical structure and other rhetorical vehicles; and the myriad of different stimuli linkages among product characteristics, branding, advertising copy, spokesperson, visual, and audio elements. Some research has been conducted on each of these informational factors, but an insufficient number of articles have appeared to merit meta-analytical work at this point in time. Moreover, the subject of linkages among advertising elements is sufficiently complex that it alone could occupy the complete attention of academic researchers for several years before a body of research findings can be assembled to warrant a general meta-analysis of linkage effects. I cannot overemphasize the importance and potential benefit of dedicated attention to disentangling linkage effects.

In contrast, several studies have analyzed affect direction, fear appeals, the use of humor, comparative versus noncomparative appeals, message sidedness, fine print captions, stimulus novelty, and imagery in advertising content. Advertising spokesperson characteristics and role portrayals in advertising have also been popular topics. It seems appropriate at this point to perform meta-analyses on these heavily studied factors and to devote attention to the understudied information-related factors.

Unquestionably, print is the most commonly used medium in studies. As a result, much is known about characteristics related to print advertisements, such as size, layout, headline usage, the presence of visuals, and the use of color. In contrast, television and radio media have been employed much less frequently. In light of the tremendous amounts of money devoted to television and, to a lesser extent, radio advertisements, the overemphasis on print is a cause for concern.

A few researchers have studied campaign-related factors, but these are the exception, not the rule. Edell and Keller's (1989) work on the coordinated effects of different media vehicles is exemplary of the direction research efforts should take. In addition to media vehicle strategy considerations, issues associated with pulsing, repetitions, and commercial duration over an entire campaign are but a few of the many issues that remain unresolved and in need of further work.

Other issues in need of study include contextual factors associated with the use of appropriate media vehicles to enhance commercial or print advertisement effectiveness, clutter-related issues, and exposure environment factors. Little is known about the circumstances surrounding exposure, which is unfortunate in light of the important effects situational factors seem to have on consumer behavior.

Much work has been done in recent years on individual involvement and self-monitoring activities, and a case can be made for redirecting study efforts to other individual factors that have been researched less heavily. In particular, the effect that prior knowledge or experience has on information processing of advertisements is still in its infancy. Furthermore, consumer interest and other predispositions play an important role in advertising, yet little is known relative to the other, more heavily researched areas. Outside the realm of advertising oriented toward children, researchers know little about those factors that affect the adult consumer's capacity to process advertisement information.

Effectiveness Measures

Table 1 shows some of the different criterion measures of effectiveness that are available for use in studies. The typical approach is to employ only one or two of the available measures of effectiveness. Some studies apply recognition measures of

---

Appendix
Selected Stimulus, Contextual, and Individual Factors

I. Advertising Stimulus Factors
  A. Information-related
    1. Nature of the appeal (emotional/rational,* affect direction/intensity, fear/guilt, humor, comparative/noncomparative, message sidedness, fine print)
    2. Amount and complexity of the information, internal clutter*
    3. Meaningfulness, clarity*
    4. Novelty
    5. Format (integrated/nonintegrated)*
    6. Imagery
    7. Grammatical structure/rhetoric*
    8. Spokesperson characteristics/role portrayals
    9. Linkages: product, brand, copy, spokesperson, visuals, audio*
  B. Transmission- or execution-related
    1. Audio (radio)*
    2. Audio/video (television)* (silence versus background music)
    3. Print
      a. Color/black and white
      b. Size
      c. Layout
      d. Headline
      e. Visuals
      f. Signature
  C. Campaign-related
    1. Nature and extent of exposure frequency (media vehicles, pulsing strategy, repetition)*
    2. Execution adjustment (10 sec/30 sec)*
II. Contextual Factors
  A. Program/medium* (pleasantness, arousal)
  B. Commercial clutter*
  C. Others present, noise, and other distractions**
III. Individual Factors
  A. Prior knowledge*
  B. Predisposition/interest level*
  C. Involvement
  D. Self-monitoring
  E. Cognitive capabilities*

---

*Indicates that factor is understudied.
**Indicates that factor is highly understudied.
No notation indicates that factor has been studied extensively.

awareness and perhaps measures of attitude toward the ad and brand, whereas others use aided recall and cognitive response measures. However, as Leigh (1991) points out, the use of multiple indicants of awareness and attitude provides important diagnostic information. A number should be used in tandem fashion to isolate the nature and generality of the relationships under investigation. In particular, I recommend employment of unaided recall measures of advertising facets and cognitive responses, followed by aided recall and recognition measures of awareness. Measures of attitude toward the ad and brand and possibly behavioral intentions should then be assessed. In this way, interstudy comparisons can be made across multiple indicants.

Conclusion

The purpose of this article is to provide an overview of the field of advertising as an academic discipline with an emphasis on the topic areas that have been heavily researched and are amenable to performing meta-analytic work. I also discuss those topic areas that have not received much research attention and are in need of research. Several topics are identified in each group; as an editor, reviewer, and researcher, I encourage fellow researchers to concentrate on topics that have not received adequate attention in the literature. It is hoped that an appreciation for the underresearched areas in advertising has been developed and that new avenues of inquiry will be stimulated. The potential benefits of such efforts are enormous.

References

Brown, Stephen P., Pamela M. Homer, and J. Jeffrey Inman (1998), "A Meta-Analysis of Relationships Between Ad-Evoked Feelings and Advertising Responses," *Journal of Marketing Research*, 35 (February), 114–26.

Calder, Bobby J., Lynn W. Phillips, and Alice M. Tybout (1981), "Designing Research for Application," *Journal of Consumer Research*, 8 (September), 197–207.

———— (1982), "The Concept of External Validity," *Journal of Consumer Research*, 9 (December), 240–44.

———— (1983), "Beyond External Validity," *Journal of Consumer Research*, 10 (June), 112–14.

Edell, Julie and Kevin Lane Keller (1989), "The Information Processing of Coordinated Media Campaigns," *Journal of Marketing Research*, 26 (May), 149–63.

Leigh, James H. (1984), "Recall and Recognition Performance for Umbrella Print Advertisements," *Journal of Advertising*, 13 (4), 5–18, 30.

———— (1991), "Information Processing Differences Among Broadcast Media: Review and Suggestions for Research," *Journal of Advertising*, 20 (June), 71–75.

Lynch, John G., Jr. (1982), "On the External Validity of Experiments in Consumer Research," *Journal of Consumer Research*, 9 (December), 225–39.

———— (1983), "The Role of External Validity in Theoretical Research," *Journal of Consumer Research*, 10 (June), 109–111.

McGrath, Joseph E. and David Brinberg (1983), "External Validity and the Research Process: A Comment on the Calder/Lynch Dialogue," *Journal of Consumer Research*, 10 (June), 115–124.

McGuire, William J. (1978), "An Information Processing Model of Advertising Effectiveness," in *Behavioral and Management Sciences in Marketing*, Harry L. Davis and Alvin J. Silk, eds. New York: Ronald Press, 156–80.

7

Advertising Modification Strategies: Appealing to Minority Consumers

Gail Ayala Taylor
Northwestern University

Miriam Stamps
University of South Florida

The emergence of segmented media has made it possible for advertisers to expand conversations with different consumers in their target audiences. However, how firms can modify their advertisements to communicate more effectively with various members of their target audiences should be addressed. The projected growth of minority consumers makes this topic particularly relevant today and in the future. In an exploratory analysis, we examine current practices regarding advertising modification strategies by studying firms that advertise the same products in both *Essence* and *Glamour* magazines. From this comparison, we determine that firms are (1) using the exact same advertisements in both media, (2) changing only the race of the model across magazines, (3) changing the layout of the advertisement, or (4) changing multiple advertising elements, such as race of the model, advertisement copy, and layout.

Changes in the ethnic makeup of the United States have fueled the idea that minority markets are crucial to the strategic focus of a firm. Whereas historically firms had the luxury of either understanding the consumption behavior of minority markets or not, the demographic changes occurring in the United States make it imperative that firms serve these consumers in an effective and efficient manner. Even the term "minority" is undergoing questioning in states such as California, where the minority population will soon be the majority. In addition to demographic changes, there is evidence that many members of ethnic groups are holding on to their cultural patterns rather than blindly and completely acculturating to the patterns of the majority culture (Valencia 1989). Ethnicity has been shown to affect attitudes toward media, media behavior, and consumption behavior (Green 1992; Hirschman 1981).

Although early studies often examined minority groups monolithically (Barban and Cundiff 1964; Kerin 1979), it became apparent that not all consumers of a specific ethnic group behave similarly. Explanations for these differences vary and some of the demographic and psychographic segmentation variables used in research on

Anglo consumers have been adopted (Stamps 1986). However, other research indicates not only that degree of acculturation has an influence on consumer behavior but that different consumers from a specified ethnic group identify differentially with the group (Larouche, Kim, and Tomiuk 1998; Williams and Qualls 1989). Stayman and Deshpandé (1989) indicate that ethnicity can also be a situational variable; that is, the level of ethnic identity possessed by a particular individual will differ depending on the situation.

Thus, as the demographic makeup of the domestic market rapidly changes and the need for the successful business to operate in a global marketplace grows, new marketing demands arise. Contemporary marketing managers must be able to grasp consumer differences among various cultural and subcultural groups. They must tackle a myriad of issues in all aspects of the marketing process. One of these issues pertains to whether or not modifications are to be made to the marketing strategy to attract consumers who are not in the mainstream. This phenomenon is perhaps most evident in the area of advertising communications.

Vast opportunities are available to the savvy, market-oriented firm; however there are issues for the firms to consider when they decide whether to modify their advertising messages. Some of these are the following:

1. Minority populations are not monolithic, and therefore a great danger exists when changes are made that overgeneralize or stereotype.
2. The marketer must consider the risk of alienating other consumers if a modification strategy that is too extreme is adopted.
3. Budgetary constraints may exist that limit the number of targeted advertising campaigns the firm can implement.

The dilemma of how much to modify advertising messages in various advertising media (i.e., television, radio, print, or others) and with many different cultural groups, both domestic and international, is apparent. Rossman (1994) states, "the truth is that to succeed with African-Americans, ads must be relevant to their lifestyle and must reflect a positive image of them as consumers." This statement is critical considering the magnitude of the African American consumer market. According to Census Bureau reports, in 1996, 12.8% of the U.S. population, or approximately 34 million people, were African American. The median income was approximately $24,500. Also, this segment of the population had a $11,899 per capita income, which leads to a total income of over $400 billion.

The African American Market

As stated previously, demographic changes occurring in the U.S. marketplace make it imperative that marketers become proficient in appealing to minority consumers. The Census Bureau estimates that minorities will make up approximately 50% of the U.S. population by the year 2050. Just as marketers have realized that international markets can make the difference in profitability and growth for their businesses, they are also slowly beginning to realize that minority markets can do the same. In fact, Snuggs (1992) has suggested that minority markets will define the consumer of the twenty-first century.

However, minority markets need to be further dissected into specific population groups. Hispanic, Asian, and African American consumers all have their specific profiles, needs, and concerns. We focus on one of these minority groups: African Americans.

Since 1980, the African American market has grown faster than both the total population and the white population. The increase was an average of 1.5% per year for African Americans between 1980 and 1994, whereas the average per year growth for whites was 0.9%. In 1996, African Americans made up 12.8% of the population, a total of 33.9 million people. This population is unevenly geographically disbursed: 55% live in the south, 17% in the northeast, 20% in the midwest, and 8% in the west (Collins 1996).

Not only is the African American population growing in terms of size, but it is also faring better educationally and economically. For example, in 1980, 51% of African Americans 25 years of age and older had at least a high school diploma, and 8% had at least a bachelor's degree. However, in 1995, these figures were 74% and 13%, respectively (Collins 1997). African American households saw an increase in median income from $20,032 to $21,027 between 1993 and 1994. This represented an increase of 5% (Collins 1996). African American incomes rose another 3.6% between 1994 and 1995 (Collins 1997).

Targeted Advertising

The concept of targeted advertising is increasingly controversial. Some of the criticisms have dealt with the targeting of so-called vulnerable populations (Sims 1997; Smith and Cooper-Martin 1997). Turow (1997) introduces the idea that target marketing was problematic because it led to the breakup of America. His thesis is that though media historically has helped to shape a unified view of America, current efforts to target specific groups lead to the lack of a shared vision. At one juncture he argues that "the U.S. is experiencing a major shift in balance between society-making media and segment-making media" (p. 3). Turow goes on to state that "Segment-making media are those that encourage small slices of society to talk to themselves, while society-making media are those that have the potential to get all those segments to talk to each other" (p. 3). However, the notion of targeted advertising is not as new as the Turow article suggests. Specialized media designed to appeal to special groups based on demographics such as race, sex, or age are not new, particularly in newspapers or magazines.

At one time, advertising featuring African American models generally was found only in African American publications. For example, Shuey, King, and Griffith (1953) find that in 1949–50, advertisements in general magazines that featured African Americans constituted only .57% of all advertisements. African American publications also carried advertisements that featured white models; however, the advertisements were seldom, if ever, integrated. Later, during the Civil Rights era, the argument was made that integrated advertisements could help change the image of Africans Americans in society (Cox 1970, p. 41). Thus, modified advertisements became a social marketing tool, not attempting to improve the bottom line of businesses, but rather showing that major corporations were willing to take on their social responsibilities. In the current milieu, the motivation has changed yet again to one that is strictly business: Companies must devise advertising strategies that will ensure their market success at a time when the market is undergoing significant demographic changes. The academic and popular discussion of whether companies should modify their advertising to reach minority consumers more effectively is an old and heated topic. In addition to the concerns about targeted advertising mentioned previously, other managerial concerns are efficiency and effectiveness. Efficiency deals with cost–benefit issues—how many people can be reached for a particular cost. One of the arguments against targeted advertising is that it may not be efficient. Rather, mainstream media and advertisements may be more cost efficient. In other words, they may reach more people at a lower cost per person. However, the other issue for an advertiser is the *effectiveness* of the advertising. Communication theory suggests that targeted advertisements may be more effective; that is, they may perform better in terms of moving the consumer toward the desired outcome. Communication theory and the communication process model (see Figure 1) suggest that targeted advertising is more successful to the degree that it enhances source credibility, constructs a message that is more salient to the targeted group, and/or selects message channels that are more likely to be used by the targeted group. In fact, targeted communication is frequently used, as companies employ advertisements and media directed toward specific demographic and psychographic groups. The results of this mindset include not only the highly segmented print media that have existed for a long time (e.g., children's magazines, teen magazines, sports magazines, women's magazines) but also the recent explosion of special-interest cable television stations.

This debate of whether targeted advertising is more effective continues today. Research (Alexis and Henderson 1994; Pitts et al. 1989; Stamps 1982) suggests that blacks have a more favorable attitude toward advertising in general than whites. Furthermore, these studies show that blacks are more favorably disposed toward advertisements that include black models than toward all-white advertisements. Pitts and colleagues also argue that advertisements that are rich in cultural and value messages are particularly effective in targeting African Americans.

Cui (1997) has suggested that the literature in international marketing can help marketers derive approaches to reaching ethnic consumers. He discusses the evolution of marketing to ethnic groups from traditional marketing to separated marketing to integrated marketing to multicultural marketing. He states "The increasing purchasing power, heightened political and cultural awareness and ethnic pride have led minority consumers to reexamine many of the products and marketing practices

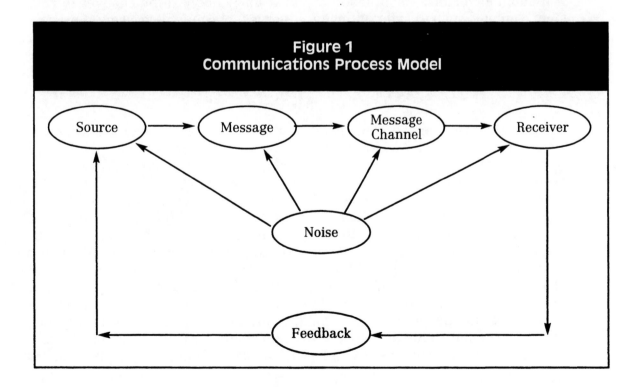

Figure 1
Communications Process Model

aimed at them, to affirm their cultural and ethnic identities and to demand more realistic and fair representation of minority groups" (p. 124). This is in keeping with Rossman's statement that advertisements must be relevant to African Americans' lifestyles and must reflect a positive image of them as consumers.

In addition to determining what marketers should do, it is also important to examine what marketers are currently doing. We add to the literature on advertising modification strategies by performing a content analysis of advertisements found in two fashion magazines targeted to women.

Content Analysis

To explore how firms are currently addressing the issue of advertising modification we conducted a content analysis. As quoted by Kassarjian (1977, p. 8), *content analysis* can be defined as "a research technique for the objective, systematic, and quantitative description of the manifest content of communication" (Berelson 1952, p.55). An alternative definition for content analysis is "a systematic technique for analyzing message content and message handling—it is a tool for observing and analyzing the overt communication behavior of selected communicators" (Budd, Thorpe and Donohew 1967, p. 2). This second definition is particularly relevant to the current study, as the purpose and intent of the study is to examine the overt communication behavior of various advertisers.

Content analysis has a long history in the literature and is a well-accepted methodology (Kassarjian 1977). It has been used in a wide variety of studies both domestically (e.g., Hong, Muderrisoglu, and Zinkhan 1987; Spiggle 1986) and internationally (e.g., Siu 1998). Furthermore, these studies have involved various media, including newspapers (Spiggle 1986), magazines (Huhmann and Brotherton 1997), and television (Alison et al. 1998).

We will investigate whether firms strategically choose to modify their advertisements in an attempt to communicate better with African American consumers. Firms that adopt an advertisement modification strategy may exhibit changes in advertisement elements such as actor ethnicity, advertising layout, advertising copy, or a combination of these changes. We examine these elements in advertising media targeted toward the general market and media targeted specifically toward the African American consumer.

Method

An exploratory analysis was conducted to determine whether firms currently use advertising targeted to African American consumers or whether firms employ a general strategy to address concerns of all consumers simultaneously. Two magazines deemed by the researchers to be roughly equivalent, *Glamour* and *Essence*, were used in the study. *Glamour* has 86.3% white female readership and 10.4% black female readership, whereas *Essence* has 90.2% black female readership and 9.0% white female readership. All the advertising for six months (July 1997 through December 1997) of both magazines was examined. There were 748 total ads in *Glamour* for this period and 469 total advertisements in *Essence*. The first step was to isolate the companies that advertised in both magazines: 75 companies fit this profile. These companies accounted for a total of 437 advertisements. Several companies had multiple products and multiple advertisements. However, only advertisements for identical products were used in the analysis. This resulted in a total of 102 advertisement comparisons. The advertisements were placed in book form, with the advertisement for one magazine on one page and the advertisement from the other magazine on the following page. Raters were then asked to look at the advertisements and determine whether they were identical and if not, to note the differences between them.[1] The five categories on the rater sheet were no change, only race of models changed, only layout (number of pages, color, use of product, size of lettering) changed, only copy changed, or a combination of changes.

We conducted a pretest of the instrument and instructions. After further refining the instrument and directions, we conducted the preliminary analysis. Both African American and white female raters were used for the pretest and the preliminary analysis, and interrater reliability was 85% in the preliminary analysis (raters matched on 87 advertisements).

Results and Discussion

Of the 87 advertisements in which there was agreement among the raters, 29 featured no change between the general audience magazine and the targeted magazine. Twelve advertisements changed only the race of the model, and 8 advertisements featured different layouts. No advertisements featured only a change in copy, whereas 40 advertisements featured a combination of changes.

Of the 29 advertisements that ran in the same exact form in both *Glamour* and *Essence*, 9 advertisements used white models, another 9 used African American models, 8 did not use models, and 3 used integrated advertisements with both African American and white models. Basically, no one race was featured more often in unmodified advertisements. It is also interesting to note that no clear patterns emerged for type of company, type of product, or the way the product was consumed—publicly or privately. Table 1 lists all advertisements that were exactly the same in both publications.

There were also 12 advertisements in which the layout and the copy were exactly the same. The only modification was a change in the race of the models. For example, the Acuvue advertisement in *Glamour* featured a man and a woman partially in an outdoor setting and partially in an indoor setting. The advertisement in *Essence* featured a man and a woman in the same split setting, the primary difference being that the couple featured in the *Essence* advertisement was African American, whereas the couple featured in the *Glamour* advertisement was white. Of these 12 advertisements, the majority of products featured were those that were consumed privately. Personal care products seemed to be the majority of products in this category. Table 2 offers a detailed description of the advertisements in which only the race of the model changed between the two magazines.

The next category features advertisements in only the layout of the advertisement changed. The advertisements could have been of different sizes or colors, with variations in the use of human models, the positioning of the product in the advertisement, or changes in some or all of the graphics. A clear pattern emerged related to the type of products using this modification strategy. Of the eight advertisements in this category, seven were for fragrances and one was for a privately consumed medication. Although fragrance advertisements appear a few times in other categories, it is interesting to note their overwhelming presence in this category. This suggests that further research should examine the wide use of this modification strat-

---

[1]Raters were instructed to ignore retailers' names that may have been listed in an advertisement.

Table 1
Same Advertisement—No Change

Company	Brand	Race of Model	Product	Consumption
ReJuveness	ReJuveness	White	Scar removal strips	Private
Chanel	Allure	Black	Fragrance	Either
The Paddington Corporation	Bailey's Irish Cream	No model used	Liqueur	Either
Bali Company	Bali	White	Bra	Private
Hoechst Marion Roussel	Allegra	White	Allergy medication	Private
Warner-Lambert Company	Lubriderm	Black	Lotion	Private
DuPont	Lycra	Black	Spandex fiber	Private
Galderma	Cetaphil	White	Moisturizing lotion	Private
Galderma	Cetaphil	White	Skin cleanser	Private
General Motors Corporation	Chevy Metro	No model used	Automobile	Public
General Motors Corporation	Geo Prizm	Black and white	Automobile	Public
Cover Girl	Marathon	Black	Lipstick	Public
Clinique Laboratories Inc.	Superbalanced makeup	No model used	Foundation	Public
Cover Girl	Ultimate Finish	Black	Liquid powder makeup	Public
Liz Claiborne	Curve	White	Fragrance	Either
Warner-Lambert Company	EPT	No model used	Pregnancy test	Private
Gynecort	Gynecort	White	Vaginal cream	Private
Tampax Corporation	Tampax	Black	Feminine protection	Private
Philip Morris	V Wear	Black	Clothing catalog	Public
Coty Inc.	Jovan White Musk	No model used	Fragrance	Either
Ortho-McNeil Pharmaceutical	Ortho Tri-Cyclen	No model used	Birth control	Private
Revlon	New Complexion compact makeup	Black	Foundation	Public
Elizabeth Arden	Red Door	White	Fragrance	Either
OfficeTeam	OfficeTeam	Black and white	Staffing service	Public
Sally Hansen	Hard as Nails, Cuticle Defense, Power Shield, No More Peeling, Gel Cuticle Remover	No model used	Nail care	Private
Dana Perfumes Corp.	Tabu	White	Fragrance	Either
Tampax Corporation	Satin Touch, Tampax, Naturals	Black	Feminine protection	Private
Revlon	Revlon lip and nail color	Black and white	Nail and lip color	Public
Revlon	Colorstay	Black and white	Lipstick	Public

Notes: Brands may appear in this and the remaining tables multiple times if more than one advertisement comparison was conducted. This may have been the case if more than one advertisement for a brand appeared in at least one of the test magazines.

egy by fragrance companies. Table 3 provides more detail regarding the brands in this category.

There were no advertisements in which only the copy was changed. The remaining 38 advertisements in the study employed a combination approach to modification, in which more than one of the modification approaches previously discussed was used. Table 4 provides further details regarding brands in this category and modifications made. The majority of advertisements featured a change in layout cou-

Table 2 Same Advertisement—Only Difference Is Model Race			
Company	**Brand**	**Product**	**Consumption**
Johnson & Johnson	Acuvue	Clear contact lenses	Private
Whitehall-Robins	Advil	Pain reliever	Private
Coty Inc.	Exclamation	Fragrance	Either
CIBA Vision	Focus	Clear contact lenses	Private
The Gillette Company	Sensor Excel and Satin Care	Razor and shaving cream	Private
Tampax Corporation	Tampax Multi-Pack	Feminine protection	Private
Ortho-McNeil Pharmaceutical	Uristat	Urinary pain relief tablets	Private
Mary Kay Inc.	Journey	Fragrance	Either
Liz Claiborne	Liz Claiborne clothing	Clothing	Public
Brown & Williamson Tobacco	Misty	Cigarettes	Public
Rite Aid	Cosmetics Guarantee	Cosmetics Guarantee	Private
Tampax Corporation	Satin Touch, Tampax Super, Naturals	Feminine protection	Private

Table 3 Same Advertisement—Only Difference Is Layout			
Company	**Brand**	**Product**	**Consumption**
Chanel	Chanel No. 5	Fragrance	Either
Clinique	Happy	Fragrance	Either
Dana Perfumes Corp.	Dreams by Tabu	Fragrance	Either
Hugo Boss	Woman	Fragrance	Either
Giorgio Beverly Hills	Red	Fragrance	Either
Giorgio Beverly Hills	Ocean Dreams	Fragrance	Either
Giorgio Beverly Hills	Ocean Dreams	Fragrance	Either
Bristol-Meyers Squibb Company	Vagistat 1	Medication	Private

Table 4				
Combination of Changes in Advertisements				
Company	**Brand**	**Change**	**Product**	**Consumption**
GM Corporation	Pontiac Sunfire	Layout, copy	Automobile	Public
BMG Music Service	BMG Music Service	Layout, copy, race	Compact discs	Either
Hoechst Marion Roussel	Allegra	Layout, copy	Allergy medication	Private
R.J. Reynolds	Camel Lights	Layout, copy, use of model	Cigarettes	Either
R.J. Reynolds	Camel Lights	Layout, copy, use of model	Cigarettes	Either
Brown & Williamson Tobacco	Capri Superslims	Layout, race	Cigarettes	Either
DuPont	Lycra	Copy, race	Spandex fiber	Either
Caribbean Coalition for Tourism	Caribbean Vacation Planner	Layout, copy, race	Vacation planner	Private
General Motors Corporation	Cavalier	Layout, race, copy	Automobile	Public
General Motors Corporation	Cavalier	Layout, race, copy	Automobile	Public
General Motors Corporation	Prizm	Layout, copy, use of model	Automobile	Public
GM Corporation	Geo Metro	Layout, copy	Automobile	Public
Clinique Laboratories Inc.	Clinique Happy	Layout, copy	Fragrance	Either
Cover Girl	Marathon	Layout, race	Lip color	Public
Pharmacia & Upjohn	Depo-Provera	Layout, race	Birth control	Private
Wesley Jessen Corporation	Durasoft FreshLook	Layout, copy, race	Colored contact lenses	Public
Ford Motor Company	ZX2	Layout, copy, use of model	Automobile	Public
Ford Motor Company	ZX2	Layout, copy, use of model	Automobile	Public

pled with either a change in copy or a change in the race of the model. Both privately and publicly consumed products fall into this category, and almost 25% of the advertisements were for automobiles.

Conclusion

With the continued growth of targeted media such as specialized cable stations and magazines, firms are faced with the decision between running the same advertisements in all media vehicles or attempting to modify the advertisements in the hopes of better communicating with different members of their target audience. This strategy could be extremely valuable if the benefits outweigh the costs associated with additional production requirements.

	Table 4 Continued			
Company	**Brand**	**Change**	**Product**	**Consumption**
Estée Lauder	Enlighten	Layout, copy, use of model	Makeup	Public
The Gillette Company	Satin Care	Layout, copy, race	Shaving cream	Private
Hallmark Corp.	Hallmark	Layout, copy, use of model	Cards	Either
Visa U.S.A. Inc.	Visa card	Layout, copy, gender of the model	Credit cards	Public
Coty Inc.	Vanilla Musk	Layout, race	Fragrance	Either
Philip Morris	Virginia Slims	Layout, race, copy	Cigarettes	Either
Philip Morris	Virginia Slims	Layout, race, copy	Cigarettes	Either
Philip Morris	Virginia Slims	Layout, race, copy	Cigarettes	Either
Tommy Hilfiger	Tommy Girl	Layout, race, copy	Fragrance	Either
Tommy Hilfiger	Tommy Girl	Layout, copy	Fragrance	Either
Cosmair Inc.	L'Oréal	Layout, race, copy	Nail color	Public
Liz Claiborne	Liz Claiborne clothing	Layout, race	Clothing	Public
Cosmair Inc.	Excellence Creme	Layout, race, copy	Hair coloring	Public
Ortho-MacNeil Pharmaceutical	Ortho-TriCyclen	Layout, copy, use of model	Birth control	Private
Paul Mitchell	Paul Mitchell	Layout, race	Hair care	Public
Chattem Inc.	Phisoderm	Layout, copy	Skin cleanser	Private
Chattem Inc.	Phisoderm	Layout, copy	Skin cleanser	Private
National Fluid Milk Processors	Milk	Race, gender, copy	Milk	Either
Ortho-McNeil Pharmaceutical	Monistat 3	Layout, race	Medication	Private
OfficeTeam	OfficeTeam	Layout, copy, race	Administrative staffing	Private
General Motors Corporation	Saturn	Copy, race	Automobile	Public

Results of this preliminary study show that many companies are modifying their advertisements to communicate effectively with different members of their target audience. The next step in understanding the effects of modification is to determine which approach to modification is most effective. To determine the benefits of modification, experimental research should be conducted to (1) determine if consumers respond more positively to modified advertisements and (2) manipulate advertisements and modification strategies to determine which form of modification is most effective in gaining the desired consumer response.

This research focuses on identifying modifications made in one type of media on the basis of racial segmentation. Further research should expand on this approach by examining modification strategies in other media, such as broadcast, and using other bases of segmentation, such as age. The more firms can learn about how to communicate effectively to all consumers in their target audience, the more likely they are to achieve the objectives set forth in their communications plans.

References

Alexis, Marcus and Geraldine R. Henderson (1994), "The Economic Base of African-American Communities: A Study of Consumption Patterns," in *The State of Black America*. New York: National Urban League Inc., 51–84.

Alison, Alexander, Louise M. Benjamin, Keisha Hoerrner, and Darrell Roe (1998), "'We'll Be Back in a Moment': A Content Analysis of Advertisements in Children's Television in the 1950s," *Journal of Advertising*, 27 (3), 1–10

Barban, Arnold M. and Edward W. Cundiff (1964), "Negro and White Response to Advertising Stimuli," *Journal of Marketing Research*, 1 (November), 53–57.

Berelson, B. (1952), *Content Analysis in Communications Research*. Glencoe, IL: The Free Press.

Budd, R.W., R.K. Thorp, and L. Donohew (1967), *Content Analysis of Communications*. New York: Macmillan.

Collins, Laverne V. (1996), "Facts from the Census Bureau for Black History Month," press release (February 5). Washington, DC: U.S. Census Bureau.

——— (1997), "Census Facts for African American History Month," press release (January 31). Washington, DC: U.S. Census Bureau.

Cox, Keith K. (1970), "Social Effects of Integrated Advertising," *Journal of Advertising Research*, 10 (2), 41–44.

Cui, Geng (1997), "Marketing Strategies in A Multi-Ethnic Environment," *Journal of Marketing Theory and Practice*, 5 (1), 122–33.

Green, Corliss L. (1992), "Ethnicity: Its Relationship to Selected Aspects of Consumer Behavior," *Southern Marketing Association Conference Proceedings*. Atlanta: Southern Marketing Association, 106–109.

Hirschman, Elizabeth C. (1981), "American Jewish Ethnicity: Its Relationship to Some Selected Aspects of Consumer Behavior," *Journal of Marketing*, 45 (Summer), 102–110.

Hong, Jae W., Aydin Muderrisoglu, and George M. Zinkhan (1987), "Cultural Differences and Advertising Expression: A Comparative Content Analysis of Japanese and U.S. Magazine Advertising," *Journal of Advertising*, 16 (1), 55–63.

Huhmann, Bruce A. and Timothy P. Brotherton (1997) "A Content Analysis of Guilt Appeals in Popular Magazine Advertisements," *Journal of Advertising*, 26 (2), 35–46.

Kassarjian, Harold H. (1977) "Content Analysis in Consumer Research," *Journal of Consumer Research*, 4 (1), 8–19.

Kerin, Roger A. (1979), "Black Model Appearance and Product Evaluations," *Journal of Communication*, 29 (Winter), 123–28.

Larouche, Michael, Chankon Kim, and Marc A. Tomiuk (1998), "Italian Ethnic Identity and Its Relative Impact on the Consumption of Convenience and Traditional Foods," *Journal of Consumer Marketing*, 15 (2 & 3), 125–52.

Pitts, Robert E., D. Joel Whalen, Robert O'Keefe, and Vernon Murray (1989) "Black and White Response to Culturally Targeted Television Commercials: A Values-Based Approach," *Psychology and Marketing*, 6 (4), 311–28.

Rossman, Marlene (1994), "Inclusive Marketing Shows Sensitivity," *Marketing News*, (October 10), 4.

Shuey, Audrey M., Nancy King, and Barbara Griffith (1953), "Stereotyping of Negroes and Whites: An Analysis of Magazine Pictures," *Public Opinion Quarterly*, 17 (Summer), 281–87.

Sims, Rodman (1997), "When Does Target Marketing Become Exploitation?" *Marketing News*, (November 24), 10.

Siu, Wai-Sum (1998) "Hotel Advertisements in China: A Content Analysis," *Journal of Professional Services Marketing*, 17 (2), 99.

Smith, N. Craig and Elizabeth Cooper-Martin (1997), "Ethics and Target Marketing: The Role of Product Harm Consumer Vulnerability," *Journal of Marketing,* 61 (July), 1–25.

Snuggs, Thelma (1992), "Minority Markets Define the Consumer of the 21st Century," *Credit*, 18 (1), 8–11.

Spiggle, Susan (1986), "Measuring Social Values: A Content Analysis of Sunday Comics and Underground Comix," *Journal of Consumer Research*, 13 (1), 100–114.

Stamps, Miriam B. (1982), "The Black Consumer Market: A Segmentation Analysis," doctoral dissertation, Syracuse University.

——— (1986), "Impact of Race, Social Class, and Demographics on Psychographic Variables," *Southern Marketing Association Conference Proceedings*. Atlanta: Southern Marketing Association, 48–52.

Stayman, Douglas and Rojit Deshpandé (1989), "Situational Ethnicity and Consumer Behavior," *Journal of Consumer Research*, 16 (3), 361–72.

Turow, Joseph (1997), *Breaking Up America: Advertisers and the New Media World.* Chicago: University of Chicago Press.

Valencia, Humberto (1989), "Hispanic Values and Subcultural Research," *Journal of the Academy of Marketing Science*, 17 (1), 23–28.

Williams, Jerome D. and William J. Qualls (1989), "Middle-Class Black Consumers and Intensity of Ethnic Identification," *Psychology and Marketing*, 6 (4), 263–86.

Advertising Appeals

8

A Theoretical Model of Incongruity Between Sexy Pictures and Advertised Products

Andrea J.S. Stanaland
National University of Singapore

Practitioners and academic researchers alike have long been fascinated by the effects sexy models in advertising have on memory and attitude. Selected studies have examined the use of nudity or sex appeals in various product contexts and generally have concluded that a match between the sex appeal and the product category is most effective. Those studies, however, have not systematically approached classification of sexy advertisements according to congruity with the brand, incongruity with the brand, or some level in between. Drawing from the literature on congruity and picture processing, I develop a model to illustrate the effects of incongruous sex appeals on processing, affect, and ultimately memory and attitudes. The moderating effects of the viewer's sex and resolution of incongruity are included in this model.

Conceptual Development

Appropriateness of Sex Appeals

Previous research on sex appeals in advertising has touched on the general notion of relevance between the model (typically female) and the product. Kanungo and Pang (1973) examine how the presence of a male or female model affects evaluations of the effectiveness of various products. Although they do not examine sexy models in particular, they find support for a "fittingness" hypothesis, which posits that consumer evaluations of products with male versus female models in the advertisement depend on the stereotype of the products as masculine or feminine. For example, an advertisement for a product perceived as masculine that depicts a male model would be perceived as more effective than an advertisement for the same product that depicts a female model.

Peterson and Kerin (1977) examine consumer evaluations of "demure," "seductive," and "nude" models in advertisements for either body oil (which the authors consider a personal feminine product) or a ratchet wrench set (an impersonal masculine product). They found a significant model × product interaction, and the evaluations of the advertisement for body oil are higher than that for the ratchet set when both show a nude model. The authors provide a description of product/model congruency in terms of the functional role of the model. High congruity, in their estimation, includes a pictured model who communicates the message, whereas low-congruity scenarios have a model with no functional role and are therefore "exploitative." Their stimuli, however, do not seem to represent either scenario, because they feature female models, with no clear communicative role, in various stages of undress standing behind a display for the product (body oil or ratchet set).

Baker and Churchill (1977) study the potential impact of "physically attractive models" on evaluations for products with or without "romantic overtones." They use coffee (no romantic overtones) and perfume (romantic overtones). Although they find higher evaluations overall for those advertisements with attractive models than for those with less attractive models, the highest evaluations were found when the attractive model was paired with perfume.

Richmond and Hartman (1982) attempt to classify sex appeals in advertising as functional, fantasy, symbolic, or inappropriate. They do not focus on sexy models in particular but assess the way eroticism, suggestiveness, double entendre, frankness, Freudian symbols, and other features represent "sexiness." Products shown in the advertisements used to represent the dimensions include bras, perfume, liquor, condoms, cigarettes, and rice. The authors find lower recall for advertisements deemed inappropriate in their use of sex appeals.

O'Connor and colleagues (1986) pretest advertisements to develop the categories of "low sexuality/appropriate," "low sexuality/inappropriate," "high sexuality/appropriate," and "high sexuality/inappropriate." Inappropriate advertisements are defined as irrelevant to demonstrating the function of the product, but no description of actual products depicted is given. Also, pretest subjects judged advertisements on overall sexuality, not only the sexiness of the model. The authors find that in general, sexiness is positively related to recall but that higher purchase intentions result when sex appeals are appropriate to the product.

More recently, Simpson, Horton, and Brown (1996) extend Peterson and Kerin's (1977) study by including male models in the experiment. As do Peterson and Kerin, they examine the effects of models in various levels of undress on consumer evaluations of either body oil or a ratchet set. Of all conditions, they find the most favorable responses for the nude and suggestive advertisements for body oil.

None of these studies uses any type of systematic procedure for choosing products that would be appropriate or inappropriate to advertise with sexy models. With the exception of O'Connor and colleagues (1986), previous studies rely on the opinions of the researchers as to the product's fit with a sex appeal. Also, manipulation checks to determine if subjects perceived the advertisements intended to be sexy as such were not performed. Another potential limitation of the studies described here is that they all examine extremes—obviously appropriate contexts for a sexy model versus obviously inappropriate contexts for a sexy model. What might consumer reactions be to advertisements that fall in the middle, with varying levels of incongruity?

Literature on Congruity

At first glance, the marketing literature on congruity seems to contradict some of the findings described previously. Closer inspection reveals that the discrepancy might be in definitions of incongruity, including varying levels of incongruity.

Mandler's (1982) schema congruity theory explains that schema congruity (structural correspondence between the entire configuration of attribute relations associated with an object or product and the configuration specified by the schema) leads to favorable responses because consumers like things that conform to their expectations. Schema-congruent objects can be rather boring, though, and Mandler expects positive responses to be mild. With regard to schema incongruity, however, Mandler posits that (1) incongruity generates more extensive processing (because people attempt to resolve and find meaning in the incongruity) and (2) resolution of incongruity is rewarding and therefore contributes to favorable response. The theory predicts that some level of incongruity can be beneficial; however, extreme incongruity that cannot be resolved (such as a sexy female model displaying a ratchet wrench set) will only lead to consumer frustration and negative evaluations, which will be enhanced by the extensive efforts to process.

Myers-Levy and Tybout (1989) examine this theory using association between a brand's attributes and the attributes expected in the particular product category to represent congruity/incongruity. They find that products that are moderately incongruent with the associated category schemas stimulate processing that leads to more favorable evaluations (compared with congruent or extremely incongruent situations). Support for Mandler's theory is also found by Myers-Levy, Louie, and Curren (1994), in a study that examines new products with congruent, moderately incongruent, or extremely incongruent brand names. Subjects prefer products associated with moderately incongruent brand names versus congruent or extremely incongruent names.

Other research in marketing has reported consistent findings. Houston, Childers, and Heckler (1987) examine the effects of interactive pictures (in which the brand name and product class are included in a pictorial format) on consumer memory for advertising information. They find that the interactive discrepant advertisements (picture discrepant with copy included in the advertisement) elicit superior recall of copy material and brand name relative to noninteractive or consistent advertisements. Heckler and Childers (1992) develop a typology of congruence as a combination of relevance and expectation. They define these dimensions as "relevancy of information in defining the theme of the message, and expectancy of information within that context" (p. 488). They find that unexpected/irrelevant objects encourage the highest total picture recall. Their study, however, deals with pictures that contain incongruence in the scenarios depicted, rather than between the picture and product. For example, an incongruent picture (relevant and unexpected) might show an elephant sitting comfortably on an airplane. The scenario is unexpected but is relevant in the light of copy describing the spaciousness and comfort of the airline's seating. In other words, the incongruence is within the picture itself but is resolved by the advertisement's copy.

Heckler and Childers's (1992) approach to defining and testing incongruence does not accommodate situations in which the picture is decorative, showing a person or scene rather than a scenario. The authors assume that incongruity arises when the scenario depicted in an advertisement clashes with prior consumer expectations. In the case of a decorative model, however, the picture itself may create the expectation and will be compared with subsequent information about the product.

Picture-Based Persuasion

Pictorial stimuli in advertising, as opposed to verbal stimuli, have been found to be more memorable (Rossiter and Percy 1983). Edell and Staelin (1983) examine framed (when pictorial information is restated in verbal form) versus unframed pictures in advertising. They find that unframed pictures cause subjects distraction from processing brand information, and picture processing dominates. The result was lower attribute recall for advertisements with unframed pictures. It is possible, however, that attribute recall was higher for framed advertisements because subjects who viewed them were exposed to the attributes twice—in pictorial and verbal forms.

Mitchell (1986) studies the possibility that pictures in advertisements could produce affect in respondents. He finds that affect-laden photographs influence both attitude toward the ad and attitude toward the brand: Positive evaluations follow positive photographs, and negative evaluations follow negative photographs. In this case, affect produced by the pictorial component of the advertisement influences subsequent attitudes toward the ad and brand. The stimuli used in this study, though, do not match pictures to product types.

Other research on pictures has found that the pictorial component of an advertisement is more easily recalled and recognized (Childers and Houston 1984) and is processed first (Houston, Childers, and Heckler 1987; Mitchell 1983). Miniard and colleagues (1991) examine picture-based persuasion with relevant versus irrelevant pictures. Their results support the contention that pictures are processed peripherally when they do not contain product-relevant information and therefore have more impact on persuasion in low-involvement situations, as per the elaboration likelihood model.

But do pictures in advertisements always act as peripheral cues? Scott (1994), in an attempt to develop a theory of visual rhetoric, proposes that because visuals are convention based, all pictures must be interpreted according to learned patterns. In her view, pictures must therefore be processed cognitively, rather than absorbed peripherally or automatically. It may be valuable, then, to identify situations in which a picture might or might not be more elaborately processed.

Proposed Model and Propositions

A model, drawn from theory and previous empirical research, can be developed to explain how incongruity in sexy advertisements might affect consumer memory and attitudes. I suggest that though pictorial content in advertisements might normally function as a heuristic, incongruity between the picture and other elements in the advertisement (product/message) will encourage elaboration, engaging the consumer in increased processing of picture and message. This processing, it turn, will affect memory and attitudes. Heckler and Childers (1992, p. 476) explain that elaborative processing develops "a network of paths that vary in number and strength for incongruent versus congruent behaviors.... Incongruent behaviors are purported to develop this more complex set of linkages because both previous congruent and incongruent behaviors ... are retrieved during the perceiver's attempts to integrate new information. In contrast, congruent items are easily comprehended and integrated with previous expectations. Thus, less retrieval of previous information is required, and fewer and weaker pathways are developed."

Memory for picture, advertisement, and brand information should increase as model/product incongruence (and thus elaboration) increases, up to a point. In cases of extreme incongruence, I expect that the distraction effect will hinder memory for brand information.

As Scott (1994) explains, interpretation of pictures may be convention based according to learned patterns. In the light of previous research on sexy advertising, I expect the sex of the viewer to moderate the impact that sexy model/product incongruence has on affect. Women's evaluations of "cheesecake" advertisements with sexy female models have been shown to be lower than men's (Jones, Stanaland, and Gelb 1998). Drawing from schema congruity theory, I expect affect to contribute to attitudes toward the ad and brand and to be moderated by whether the incongruence can be resolved by the consumer (resolution will strengthen the positive impact of positive affect on attitudes and may help convert initial negative affect into favorable attitudes).

This formulation suggests that extreme incongruity is less likely to be resolved, which allows negative affect to proceed to negative attitudes. Because the picture in the advertisement will likely be processed first, the picture will create an expectation under which the consumer will then process the product information/message. It is at this point, after affect has been induced by the picture, that the consumer attempts to resolve any discrepancy.

Figure 1 depicts the expected relationships. Four major propositions are outlined in the figure.

P_{1a}: The level of incongruity between sexy model and product differentiates consumer recall and recognition of advertisement and brand information.
P_{1b}: The relationship stated in P_{1a} is mediated by the type of processing.
P_{2a}: The level of incongruity between a sexy model and a product differentiates consumer affect, a relationship moderated by the sex of the consumer.
P_{2b}: Consumer affect will predict attitudes toward the ad and brand and is moderated by the presence or absence of resolution of prior incongruity.

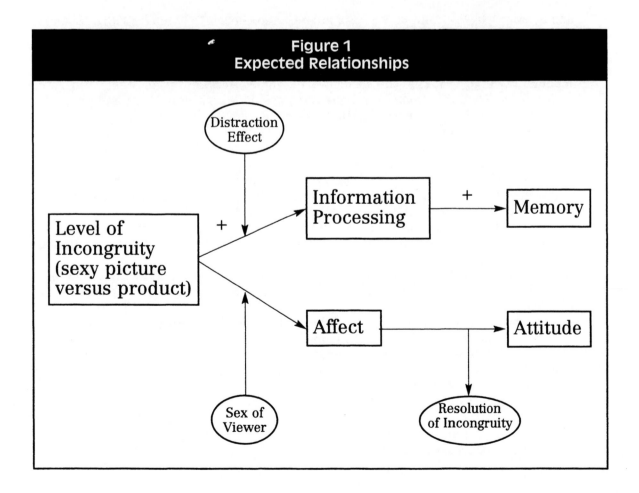

Figure 1
Expected Relationships

Conclusion

I have attempted to develop a theoretical model of incongruity between sexy pictures and advertised products. The model draws from the literature on congruity and picture processing and includes the moderating effects of the viewer's sex and resolution of incongruity. I state several propositions to suggest the expected effects of incongruous sex appeals on consumer processing, affect, memory, and attitudes. The obvious next step is to test the relationships developed here. Such an experiment should provide insight into the extent to which these various literature streams contribute to an explanation of consumer responses to sex appeals in advertising.

References

Baker, Michael J. and Gilbert A. Churchill (1977), "The Impact of Physically Attractive Models on Advertising Evaluations," *Journal of Marketing Research*, 14 (November), 538–55.

Childers, Terry L. and Michael J. Houston (1984), "Conditions for a Picture-Superiority Effect on Consumer Memory," *Journal of Consumer Research*, 11 (September), 643–54.

Edell, Julie A. and Richard Staelin (1983), "The Information Processing of Pictures in Print Advertisements," *Journal of Consumer Research*, 10 (June), 45–61.

Heckler, Susan E. and Terry L. Childers (1992), "The Role of Expectancy and Relevance in Memory for Verbal and Visual Information: What Is Incongruency?" *Journal of Consumer Research*, 18 (March), 475–92.

Houston, Michael J., Terry L. Childers, and Susan E. Heckler (1987), "Picture-Word Consistency and the Elaborative Processing of Advertisements," *Journal of Marketing Research*, 24 (November), 359–69.

Jones, Marilyn Y., Andrea J.S. Stanaland, and Betsy D. Gelb (1998), "Beefcake and Cheesecake: Insights for Advertisers," *Journal of Advertising*, 27 (2) 33–51.

Kanungo, Rabindra and Sam Pang (1973), "Effects of Human Models on Perceived Product Quality," *Journal of Applied Psychology*, 57 (2), 172–78.

Mandler, George (1982), "The Structure of Value: Accounting for Taste," in *Affect and Cognition: The 17th Annual Carnegie Symposium*, Margaret S. Clark and Susan T. Fiske, eds. Hillsdale, NJ: Lawrence Erlbaum Associates, 3–36.

Miniard, Paul W., Sunil Bhatla, Kenneth R. Lord, Peter R. Dickson, and H. Rao Unnava (1991), "Picture-Based Persuasion Processes and the Moderating Role of Involvement," *Journal of Consumer Research*, 18 (June), 92–107.

Mitchell, Andrew A. (1983), "The Effects of Visual and Emotional Advertising: An Information Processing Approach," in *Advertising and Consumer Psychology*, Larry Percy and Arch Woodside, eds. Lexington Books, MA: Lexington, 197–217.

——— (1986), "The Effect of Verbal and Visual Components of Advertisements on Brand Attitudes and Attitude Toward the Advertisement," *Journal of Consumer Research*, 13 (June), 12–24.

Myers-Levy, Joan, Therese A. Louie, and Mary T. Curren (1994), "How Does the Congruity of Brand Names Affect Evaluations of Brand Name Extensions?" *Journal of Applied Psychology*, 79 (1), 46–53.

——— and Alice M. Tybout (1989), "Schema Congruity as a Basis for Product Evaluation," *Journal of Consumer Research*, 16 (June), 39–54.

O'Connor, P.J., Aylin Baher, Bosco Gong, and Elyse Kane (1986), "Recall Levels of Sexuality in Advertising," in *AMA Educators' Proceedings*, Terrance A. Shimp et al., eds. Chicago: American Marketing Association, 2–5.

Peterson, Robert A. and Roger A. Kerin (1977), "The Female Role in Advertisements: Some Experimental Evidence," *Journal of Marketing*, 41 (October), 59–63.

Richmond, David and Timothy P. Hartman (1982), "Sex Appeal in Advertising," *Journal of Advertising Research*, 22 (5), 53–61.

Rossiter, John R. and Larry Percy (1983), "Visual Communication in Advertising," in *Information Processing Research in Advertising*, Richard Jackson Harris, ed. Hillsdale, NJ: Lawrence Erlbaum Associates, 83–125.

Scott, Linda M. (1994), "Images in Advertising: The Need for a Theory of Visual Rhetoric," *Journal of Consumer Research*, 21 (September), 252–73.

Simpson, Penny M., Steve Horton, and Gene Brown (1996), "Male Nudity in Advertisements: A Modified Replication and Extension of Gender and Product Effects," *Journal of the Academy of Marketing Science*, 24 (3), 257–62.

9

Green Advertising and its Relationship to Consumers' Environmentally Responsible Behaviors

Erika Matulich
The University of Tampa

Diana L. Haytko
Texas Christian University

Jon R. Austin
Cornell University

Environmental concerns are increasingly important in society and in the marketplace. Many practitioners believe the "green" movement has made a major impact on consumer behavior (Kaufman 1999). As consumer concern for the environment rises (Kerr 1990), corporations have responded with a flurry of green advertisements (Frankel 1992; Gillespie 1992). However, marketers do not have satisfactory measurement tools for assessing the effectiveness of such advertising or adequate means for measuring their customer's environmental attitudes, intentions, and behaviors.

Environmental themes and issues have been criticized as a passing fad because consumer purchases do not seem to reflect their attitudes and intentions as measured by environmental surveys (Phillips 1999; Troy 1993). Despite numerous studies citing that the majority of consumers include environmental concerns in their behaviors and decisions (Kleiner 1991; Teufel 1991), there is little evidence that behaviors reflect such attitudes (Schlossberg 1991; Winski 1991). However, major corporations are investing millions of dollars in developing and advertising environmental products in response to both consumer demands and regulatory requirements (Ottoman 1998; Vandermerwe and Oliff 1990).

Much of the research relevant to environmental marketing profiles the environmental consumer according to scales developed in the 1970s. Not surprisingly, current research in this area has been characterized by mixed or inconclusive results (Troy 1993). Because of the societal and legal changes that have occurred since the 1970s, surveys developed 20 years ago may no longer be valid for measuring consumers' attitudes, intentions, and behaviors.

The purpose of this research is to provide a modern, valid, reliable scale that academic researchers and business practitioners can use to assess their green advertising strategies in conjunction with the environmental attitudes of their customers. We follow Churchill's (1979) paradigm for developing better measures of marketing constructs. First, we review the literature to provide background for the development of measures of the attitude toward green advertising construct and environmental behaviors. Second, we outline the procedures to collect and analyze data. Third, we present results along with an analysis of the relationships between attitudinal dimensions and dimensions of environmental behavior. Finally, recommendations for further research are provided.

Attitude Toward Green Advertising

Before investigating how consumers respond to advertising with environmentally responsible claims, it is necessary to investigate the construct attitude toward advertising in general (A_{adG}). We use measures of A_{adG} as a basis for developing the measure for attitude toward green advertising.

Attitude Toward Advertising in General

Consumers' attitudes toward advertising in general have received increasing attention since the 1930s (Brown and Stayman 1992; Lutz 1985; Muehling 1987; Reid and Soley 1982). There are several reasons why the study of A_{adG} is important. First, there has been a proliferation of studies investigating relationships between attitude toward the advertisement (A_{ad}) and attitude toward the brand (A_{brand}) (e.g., MacKenzie, Lutz, and Belch 1986; Miniard, Bhatla, and Rose 1990; Mittal 1990). MacKenzie and Lutz (1989) assert that under certain conditions, A_{adG} will have a significant impact on A_{ad} and should be studied as an antecedent variable. Lannon (1986) indicates that A_{adG} may act as a moderating influence on the $A_{ad} \rightarrow A_{brand}$ relationship. Therefore, a reliable measure of A_{adG} is necessary to supplement and clarify measures of A_{ad} and A_{brand}.

Second, information provided by A_{adG} can benefit advertisers. The advertising industry has been criticized for being deceptive (Lantos 1987), distasteful and offensive (Durand and Lambert 1985), and insulting to the recipient's intelligence (Haller 1974; Kanter 1989). Information about the public's attitudes toward advertising in general can assist in the development of campaigns to boost the overall image and credibility of advertising. If consumers possess negative attitudes toward advertising in general, advertisers may benefit from a shift of advertising dollars to other communication vehicles, such as public relations.

The first comprehensive study of the A_{adG} construct was Bauer and Greyser's (1968) study of consumer attitudes toward advertising. An important contribution of this research was its measurement scale, which has subsequently been termed the Greyser scale (Greyser 1962; Greyser and Reece 1971). This seven-item measure has become the accepted scale for measuring the A_{adG} construct, because it allows for direct comparison among groups and an evaluation of changes in attitudes over time (Anderson, Engledow, and Becker 1978). Anderson and colleagues point out that the one constant throughout ten years of A_{adG} studies is the distinction between economic issues and social influences and the measures associated with each dimension. Their findings support the continued use of the Greyser social and economic dimensions as meaningful and stable measures of portions of the public's attitudes toward advertising.

Sandage and Leckenby (1980) take a different approach to studying A_{adG} by finding differences in attitudes toward the instrument (advertisements) and the institution (advertising). Reid and Soley (1982) take another view of the A_{adG} construct by adding generalized and personalized attitude levels to the Greyser scale. Muehling (1987) studies combined measures from previous research on A_{adG}. His measurement instrument included 20 belief items from the Greyser scale and consumer alienation scale (Durand and Lambert 1985), as well as items measuring attitudes toward institution, instruments, and advertising in general. Muehling (1987, p. 38) concluded that his measure "demonstrates a high degree of explanatory power of the variables, explaining nearly 75 percent of the variance in attitudes toward advertising in general, and suggests that each of the factors plays a unique role in shaping global attitudes toward advertising."

Haytko and Matulich (1993) combine the items and elements in the previously mentioned research to construct a modern version of A_{adG}. Their measure contains items that use the economic, social, institution, instrument, generalized, and personalized dimensions, as well as new items gleaned from consumer research and literature research since Muehling's (1987) study. Results suggest four dimensions of A_{adG}: evaluations, moral impact, quality of life, and financial impact.

On the basis of this review of attitudes toward advertising in general, Haytko and Matulich (1993) developed scale items to measure attitudes toward green advertising. Items from the A_{adG} studies were modified and adapted to reflect the green theme. In some cases, the researchers simply added the word "green" to existing item wording. In other cases, additional modifications to the original A_{adG} item were necessary.

Attitude Toward Green Advertising

To cover the domain of attitudes specific to green advertising, we undertook a comprehensive review of both academic and popular literature. Several themes emerged from this research that were unique to green advertising. For example, several authors note motivations for a firm to produce green advertising (Davis 1992; Frankel 1992; Gillespie 1992; Ottman 1992b, 1998; Zinkhan and Carlson 1995). Others research consumer responses to green advertising and products, such as loyalty (Frankel 1992), willingness to pay higher prices (Phillips 1999; Schlossberg 1992), and perceptions of product safety or harm to the environment (Davis 1994; Wheeler 1992). Finally, the positive and negative impact of green advertising on society is noted by Banerjee, Gulas, and Iyer (1995), Davis (1992), Ottman (1992b), and Schlossberg (1992). We developed twelve additional items based on these themes.

Ecological Attitudes and Knowledge

One of the most popular scales in use is the 130-item ecological attitudes and knowledge scale (EAKS) developed by Maloney and Ward (1973). These authors provide a reduced revision of 30 items with a reliability assessment (Maloney, Ward, and Braucht 1975). The scale appears to be quite situation specific, given the coverage of smog and air pollution of concern to Los Angeles residents at the time. Surprisingly, few revisions have been made to the scale since then. One exception is Synodinos (1990), who makes only minor modifications (e.g., "congressman" was changed to "congressional representative"). The author notes in his conclusion that "future studies should investigate the changes of environmental attitudes across time" (p. 168), because his results do not match those found in the previous literature.

The EAKS also presents items in true/false format rather than in scaled responses. The true/false format has statistical analysis limitations (McDaniel and Gates 1993). It is apparent that new measurement tools are necessary to investigate consumers' intentions and behaviors with respect to environmental variables. In addition, corporate practitioners require a method for assessing whether their expenditures on green advertising are having a positive impact on those consumers.

We determined potential items in addition to those found in EAKS in a further literature review. Hines, Hungerford, and Tomera (1986) point out that self-reported knowledge can affect environmental behaviors. Consequently, we added three general knowledge items: "I strive to learn as much as possible about environmental issues," "I do my best to keep up-to-date on environmental issues," and "I feel that I am very knowledgeable about environmental issues." In addition, items regarding conservation of resources (water, home utilities) were added on the basis of research conducted by Weigel (1985). Finally, we borrowed items from the more recent environmental efforts scales (Brown and Wahlers 1998), including items on supporting environmental causes and actively seeking out environmentally friendly products.

The Measures

The construction of a measurement instrument is important in data collection and analysis and the interpretation of results (Churchill 1979). This study uses a combination of several previously used measures that have not been studied simultaneously, in addition to new items thought to tap the domains of attitudes toward green advertising and environmental behaviors. All items use a five-point Likert scale, where 5 = strongly agree and 1 = strongly disagree.

The attitude toward green advertising scale contains 35 items: 23 were adapted from items used in past A_{adG} scales, and 12 items were constructed on the basis of reviews of green marketing literature. The scale was pretested and evaluated for wording and comprehension by 123 undergraduate business students. After minor changes in terminology and sentence structure, the final items appear in Table 1. Items adapted from the A_{adG} studies are noted with an asterisk.

The environmental behavior scale was largely adapted from EAKS. Wording changes were necessary for two reasons. First, items needed to be suitable for scaled responses rather than true/false responses. Second, wording was changed to modernize terms (e.g., "ozone alert" rather than "smog" or "air pollution"). Finally, other terms were generalized (e.g., "environmental contamination" replaced "air pollution"). Again, the scale was evaluated by the same 123 respondents. Several items were deleted as a result of the pretest. These included "I feel fairly indifferent to the statements: 'The world will be dead in 40 years if we don't remake the environment,' 'I'm usually not bothered by so-called noise pollution,' and 'I get depressed on smoggy days.'" After further wording changes, the final 21 items appear in Table 2.

Data Collection

The survey was mailed to a random sample of 1000 residents in Wisconsin and Texas. Responses provided 246 usable surveys. Green advertising was described to the respondents as promotions using any of the following claims: recyclable, environmentally friendly, nontoxic, biodegradable, refillable, compostable, reusable,

Table 1
Attitude Toward Green Advertising Measure

Item	Source Adapted From	Mean	Standard Deviation
Green advertising takes advantage of consumers' environmental concerns.	Davis (1992)	3.36	1.17
Green advertising leads people to be more socially responsible.	Ottman (1992a)	3.72	.84
Products and services that are advertised as green are safer to use.	Wheeler (1992)	2.90	.96
A company that uses green advertising is trustworthy.	Frankel (1992)	2.70	.99
Green advertising is valuable to society.*	Sandage and Leckenby (1980)	3.80	.91
Green advertising exploits environmental issues instead of addressing them.	Schlossberg (1992)	2.86	1.05
Green advertising is unnecessary.*	Sandage and Leckenby (1980)	1.96	.86
Green advertising promotes materialism.*	Haytko and Matulich (1993)	2.06	1.03
I think green advertising is good.*	Muehling (1987)	3.77	.88
Green advertising is deceptive.*	Sandage and Leckenby (1980)	3.01	.99
Green advertising is interesting to see.*	Haytko and Matulich (1993)	3.38	.92
Advertisements that focus on environmental concerns persuade people to buy products they do not really need.*	Greyser (1962)	2.35	.94
Green advertising is a weak form of advertising.*	Sandage and Leckenby (1980)	2.19	.91
Green advertising results in better products.*	Greyser (1962)	2.71	1.01
I have more confidence in advertised green products than in unadvertised green ones.*	Haller (1974)	2.54	.99
Green advertising is unprofessional.*	Haytko and Matulich (1993)	1.95	.82
Green advertising results in higher prices for products.*	Greyser (1962)	3.25	1.09
I don't pay much attention to green advertising.*	Haytko and Matulich (1993)	2.66	1.12
Sponsors of green advertising have sincere intentions.*	Sandage and Leckenby (1980)	3.10	.85
Green advertising is wasteful.*	Haytko and Matulich (1993)	2.03	.81
Green advertising is a good source of information about products/services.*	Haller (1974)	3.37	.97
I have an unfavorable view of green advertising.*	Muehling (1987)	2.14	.96

Item	**Source Adapted From**	**Mean**	**Standard Deviation**
Green advertising presents a true picture of the product being advertised.*	Greyser (1962)	2.63	.80
Green advertising helps to solve environmental problems.	Davis (1992)	3.10	1.07
Most green advertising insults people's intelligence.*	Greyser (1962)	2.07	.99
I would pay more for products or services that were advertised as being green.	Schlossberg (1992)	2.84	1.13
Green advertising is believable.*	Reid and Soley (1982)	3.23	.90
I believe the claims in green advertising are truthful.*	Muehling (1987)	3.15	.85
Green advertising is good at addressing environmental problems.	Davis (1992)	3.45	1.00
I tend to be more loyal to products from companies that practice green advertising.	Frankel (1992)	3.02	.98
Green advertising shows the consumer that the firm is addressing consumers' environmental concerns.	Davis (1992)	3.77	.91
Green advertising claims are insincere.*	Sandage and Leckenby (1980)	2.49	.95
Products and services that are advertised as green are less expensive to society in the long run.*	Greyser (1962)	3.36	.94
Green advertising is a good business practice.	Gillespie (1992)	3.92	.76
Companies use green advertising to protect their reputations.	Ottman (1992b)	2.71	.90

Table 1 Continued

*Items adapted from A_{adG} studies.

environmentally safe, made from recycled materials, degradable, less polluting, energy efficient, ozone friendly, good for the environment, or ecology-minded (Hemphill 1991; Newell, Goldsmith, and Banzhaf 1998). Response rates and responses between Wisconsin and Texas were not significantly different, so all responses were combined for purposes of data analysis.

Data Analysis and Results

The following procedures were performed on both the attitude toward green advertising scale and the environmental behavior scale. First, we assessed overall reliabilities (Paul 1979, 1981). Second, we performed principal components factor analysis to ascertain the dimensionality of each scale. Then we assessed reliabilities for subdimensions. Finally, we determined the relationships among attitude toward green marketing dimensions and environmental behavior dimensions.

Table 2
Environmental Behaviors Measure

Item	Mean	Standard Deviation
I often urge my friends to use products that are advertised as being green.	2.55	1.24
It frightens me to think that much of the food I eat may be dangerous because of environmental contamination.	3.18	1.34
I regularly keep track of my congressional representatives' voting records on environmental issues.	1.68	.98
I would be willing to join a group or club which is concerned solely with ecological issues.	2.58	1.20
It is the government's job to help the environment, not mine.	1.69	.86
I would be willing to stop buying products from companies guilty of harming the environment, even though it might be inconvenient.	3.59	1.23
I regularly contact community agencies to find out what I can do to help the environment.	1.64	.88
I'd be willing to write my congressional representative concerning ecological problems.	2.71	1.24
I probably would go to a house to distribute literature on the environment.	2.00	1.03
I consider myself to be an environmentalist.	2.61	1.16
I would be willing to pay an environmental tax to help decrease environmental problems.	3.26	1.16
I am a strong supporter of environmental regulation.	3.38	1.18
I often subscribe to ecological publications.	1.59	.85
I strive to learn as much as possible about environmental issues.	2.62	1.12
I've often bought products just because they were safer for the environment.	3.04	1.20
I'd be willing to ride a bicycle or use public transportation to go to work/school to reduce air pollution.	2.87	1.35
I try hard to use less heat in the winter and use less air conditioning in the summer to conserve energy.	2.84	1.23
I would be willing to donate a day's worth of pay to a foundation to help them improve the environment.	2.87	1.20
I make a special effort to buy products with environmentally friendly packaging.	3.21	1.15
I become upset when I think about the harm being done to the environment.	3.64	1.08
I have changed my choice of many products for ecological reasons.	2.73	1.05
I do my best to keep up-to-date on environmental issues.	2.77	1.11
When I think of the ways industries are destroying the environment, I get frustrated.	3.53	1.11
I make every attempt to join environmental cleanup drives.	2.01	1.05
I often attend meetings of an organization specifically concerned with bettering the environment.	1.79	.98
I rarely ever worry about the effects of the environment on me and my family.	2.25	1.05
I strive to conserve water in my home.	2.99	1.21
I feel people worry too much about environmental contaminants in food products.	2.53	1.08
I am willing to give up driving on a weekend due to an ozone/smog alert.	2.75	1.23
It makes me angry to think that the government doesn't do more to help control environmental problems.	3.41	1.04
I feel that I am very knowledgeable about environmental issues.	2.71	1.13

Attitudes Toward Green Advertising

Coefficient alpha is an important measure of reliability. Nunnally (1978, p. 245) suggests that an acceptable level of coefficient alpha in exploratory analyses is .70. A linear combination (Nunnally 1978, p. 248) gives a coefficient alpha for the entire green advertising measure of .90, which suggests that the items tap a significant amount of the common core of attitude toward green advertising.

We used exploratory factor analysis to assess the dimensionality of the attitude toward green advertising construct. Before analysis, we recoded appropriate items so that all items ran in the same direction. We performed principal components analysis with VARIMAX rotation. Initial default extraction produced ten factors with eigenvalues greater than 1.0. However, this solution was not interpretable. An eigenvalue scree plot suggested that between two and four factors could be appropriate. Careful analysis of factor solutions between two and four solutions resulted in the selection of the three-factor solution as the most interpretable and cleanest (with the fewest cross-loadings), which accounted for 39% of the variance explained. The rotated factor matrix scores are presented in Table 3, along with an indication of which other factor the item cross-loaded on with a score of greater than .3500.

The first factor seems to describe cognitive and affective responses to green advertising in general. This corresponds to a similar dimension found in Haytko and Matulich's (1993) study of advertising in general. Coefficient alpha for items within this dimension was .87. The second factor appears to be consumers' responses to the companies and their green products, which is similar to the institution dimension defined by Sandage and Leckenby (1980), where $\alpha = .76$. Finally, the third factor is some type of moral factor of the ethical impact of green advertising ($\alpha = .75$). An ethical dimension also appeared in Haytko and Matulich's (1993) study and has components of the social dimension defined by Greyser (1962).

Environmental Behaviors

Coefficient alpha for all 21 items was .94, which indicates that items tap a large part of the environmental behavior domain. A few items had low item-to-total correlations but were retained until their reliability could be assessed within dimensions.

The default factor analysis extraction produced seven factors with eigenvalues greater than 1.0. However, seven factors were not readily interpretable. An eigenvalue scree plot suggested that two to five factors could be appropriate. Careful analysis of factor solutions between two and five solutions resulted in the selection of the four-factor solution, which accounted for 55% of the variance explained, as most interpretable. The rotated factor matrix is presented in Table 4.

The first factor describes environmental activism. These items describing strong and overt forms of environmental behavior together had a coefficient alpha of .91. The second factor seems to describe current, personal, everyday environmental thoughts and behaviors. The item stating, "It is the government's job to help the environment, not mine" was deleted from further analysis because of a low item-to-total correlation, which resulted in $\alpha = .79$. The third factor depicts the respondent's emotional response to environmental problems ($\alpha = .82$), whereas the fourth factor appears to describe possible future behaviors ($\alpha = .76$).

Relationships Between Green Attitudes and Green Behaviors

To examine the relationships between green attitudes and behaviors, it was first necessary to compute overall scores for each of the dimensions found previously.

Table 3
Dimensions of Attitude Toward Green Advertising

Factor 1: Response to Green Advertising α = .87	Factor Score	Cross-Load
I have an unfavorable view of green advertising.	.5338	3
Green advertising is a good source of information about products/services.	.3889	
Green advertising helps to solve environmental problems.	.3572	
Green advertising is believable.	.4760	2
Green advertising is good at addressing environmental problems.	.4558	
Green advertising is a good business practice.	.7176	
Green advertising is a weak form of advertising.	.4320	3
I believe the claims in green advertising are truthful.	.4586	2
I don't pay much attention to green advertising.	.4334	
Green advertising is unnecessary.	.6627	3
I think green advertising is good.	.7021	3
Green advertising is valuable to society.	.6987	
Green advertising leads people to be more socially responsible.	.5290	
Green advertising is interesting to see.	.5891	

Factor 2: Response to Companies and Their Products α = .76	Factor Score	Cross-Load
Green advertising presents a true picture of the product being advertised.	.5741	
I would pay more for products or services that were green.	.4395	1
A company that uses green advertising is trustworthy.	.7041	
Products and services that are green are safer to use.	.5946	
I am more loyal to products from companies that practice green advertising.	.5204	1
Firms address environmental concerns with green advertising.	.5310	
Green advertising results in better products.	.4446	
I have more confidence in green products than nongreen ones.	.4362	
Companies use green advertising to protect their reputations.	.4781	1,3
Sponsors of green advertising have sincere intentions.	.4935	

Factor 3: Ethical Impact of Green Advertising α = .75	Factor Score	Cross-Load
Green advertising claims are insincere.	.5145	
Green products are less expensive to society in the long run.	.4258	
Green advertising is deceptive.	.4538	2
Green advertising results in higher prices for products.	.4875	
Green advertising persuades people to buy products they do not really need.	.5304	
Green advertising is wasteful.	.5046	1
Most green advertising insults people's intelligence.	.4971	1
Green advertising takes advantage of consumer's environmental concerns.	.5372	
Green advertising promotes materialism.	.4882	
Green advertising exploits environmental issues instead of addressing them.	.4858	
Green advertising is unprofessional.	.4550	1

This was accomplished by averaging scores of all items within a particular factor for each respondent (appropriate items were reverse coded before computation), which resulted in three green attitude scores and four environmental behavior scores. The mean for the response to green advertising dimension was somewhat positive at

Table 4
Dimensions of Environmental Behaviors

Factor 1: Environmental Activism α = .91	Factor Score	Cross-Load
I regularly contact community agencies to find out what I can do to help the environment.	.7877	
I probably would go to a house to distribute literature on the environment.	.7120	
I consider myself to be an environmentalist.	.4413	3, 4
I strive to learn as much as possible about environmental issues.	.6416	
I often subscribe to ecological publications.	.7443	2
I do my best to keep up-to-date on environmental issues.	.6492	2
I make every attempt to join environmental cleanup drives.	.7815	
I regularly keep track of my congressional representatives' voting records on environmental issues.	.5761	
I feel that I am very knowledgeable about environmental issues.	.5682	
I often attend meetings of an organization specifically concerned with bettering the environment.	.8522	
I would be willing to join a group or club that is concerned solely with ecological issues.	.4662	2

Factor 2: Normal, Everyday Behaviors α = .79	Factor Score	Cross-Load
I often urge my friends to use products that are advertised as being green.	.4222	3,1
I strive to conserve water in my home.	.3615	
I make a special effort to buy products with environmentally friendly packaging.	.7186	
I've often bought products just because they were safer for the environment.	.5825	
I try hard to use less heat in the winter and use less air conditioning in the summer to conserve energy.	.4961	4
I would be willing to stop buying products from companies guilty of harming the environment, even though it might be inconvenient.	.5234	
I'd be willing to write my congressional representative concerning ecological problems.	.6572	

Factor 3: Emotional Response to Environmental Problems α = .82	Factor Score	Cross-Load
I rarely ever worry about the effects of the environment on me and my family.	.6388	
It frightens me to think that much of the food I eat may be dangerous because of environmental contamination.	.6322	
It makes me angry to think that the government doesn't do more to help control environmental problems.	.6453	
I feel people worry too much about environmental contaminants in food products.	.5922	
When I think of the ways industries are destroying the environment, I get frustrated.	.6470	2
I am a strong supporter of environmental regulation.	.5543	4
I have changed my choice of many products for ecological reasons.	.4899	1,3
I become upset when I think about the harm being done to the environment.	.5661	2

Factor 4: Possible Future Behaviors α = .76	Factor Score	Cross-Load
I am willing to give up driving on a weekend due to an ozone/smog alert.	.7336	
I'd be willing to ride a bicycle or use public transportation to go to work/school to reduce air pollution.	.6372	2
I would be willing to pay an environmental tax to help decrease environmental problems.	.6807	
I would be willing to donate a day's worth of pay to a foundation to help them improve the environment.	.5561	2

3.518, whereas responses to the company were lower at 2.742. Finally, respondents had a fairly neutral reaction to the ethical impact of green advertising, with a mean of 3.291. The mean for the environmental activism dimension was 2.305, which indicates that respondents are not very proactive in overt environmental behaviors. Respondents were fairly neutral in their level of everyday environmental behaviors (mean = 3.1962) and possible future behaviors (mean = 2.944). However, respondents tended to agree that they experienced negative emotions in response to environmental problems (mean = 3.654).

The next step was to split the respondents into groups. Respondents who uniformly exhibited positive attitudes toward green advertising (for whom each dimension score was greater than three) were placed into one group, whereas those with negative attitudes (for whom dimension scores were less than three) were placed in the other group. T-tests were performed to determine significant differences (at $p <$ .01) between groups for each of the environmental behavior dimensions. Not surprisingly, respondents with positive attitudes toward green advertising were significantly more likely to exhibit environmental activism traits, perform everyday proactive environmental behaviors, and show high emotional response to the state of the environment. There was no significant difference between groups regarding their intentions to perform other environmental behaviors in the future (Table 5).

Similarly, respondents who uniformly exhibited proactive environmental behaviors (for whom each dimension score was greater than three) were placed into one group, whereas those less likely to exhibit proactive behaviors (for whom dimension scores were less than three) were placed in the other group. T-tests were performed to determine significant differences (at $p <$ .01) between groups for each of the attitude toward green advertising dimensions. Respondents exhibiting higher levels of proactive environmental behavior were significantly more likely to have higher-than-average responses to green advertising and responses to the advertising companies/advertised products. Surprisingly, there was no significant difference between more and less proactive respondents and their attitudes toward the ethical impact of green advertising (Table 6).

Conclusion

In this study, a measurement instrument designed to assess attitude toward green advertising was developed and empirically tested. On the basis of this investigation, it appears that this measure shows strong internal consistency (reliability).

Table 5
Attitudes Toward Green Advertising by Environmental Behavior Dimensions

Environmental Behavior Dimension	Overall Mean	Positive Green Attitude Mean	Negative Green Attitude Mean
Environmental activism	2.305	2.384	1.939
Everyday environmental behaviors	3.196	3.366	2.409
Emotional response to environmental problems	3.654	3.804	2.961
Possible future behaviors (n.s.)	2.944	3.078	2.318

Table 6
Environmental Behaviors by Attitudes Toward Green Advertising Dimensions

Attitudes Toward Green Advertising Dimension	Overall Mean	More Behaviors Group Mean	Less Behaviors Group Mean
Response to green advertising	3.518	3.884	3.274
Response to competition and its products	2.747	3.167	2.468
Ethical impact of green advertising (n.s.)	3.291	3.443	3.189

This measurement instrument contributes to advertising research because it establishes dimensionality to the attitude toward green advertising construct that differs from A_{adG}. The three dimensions found were a cognitive response to green advertising, a response to companies and the products being advertised as green, and an ethical impact of green advertising factor. Respondents had less favorable attitudes toward the companies and products than they had toward green advertising itself.

In addition, an updated instrument was provided for the measurement of environmental behavior. The new scale modernizes the popular EAKS by changing terminology and allowing scaled responses better suited to statistical analysis. Results showed that the measurement instrument had high reliability overall and within the four dimensions found. The four dimensions were environmental activism, normal behaviors, emotional response to environmental problems, and possible future behaviors. Overall, respondents were not strong on environmental activism but showed emotional concern about the state of the environment.

Finally, an initial exploratory analysis was undertaken to determine if any relationships existed among the attitude and behavior dimensions. In general, respondents with positive attitudes toward green advertising tended to engage in more proactive environmental behaviors, and vice versa. However, there were no significant differences in response to the ethical impact of green advertising based on environmental behaviors. This indicates that green advertising may only be effective for consumers who already practice proactive environmental behaviors and does not convert other consumers.

Further research is needed to provide a better-understanding of the conceptual foundations of attitude toward green advertising and corresponding environmental behaviors. The next step, according to Churchill (1979) and Gerbing and Anderson (1988), would be to use the purified instrument to collect additional data and perform confirmatory factor analysis using the new factors. In addition, despite the inclusion of multiple dimensions, a large portion of the variance is yet to be explained for both measures. Further research could explore possible additional variables that tap the same domain of the these constructs. In addition, further research should use a sample containing a wide range of ages, educational levels, or incomes. Mohai and Twight (1987) find that age is strongly related to environmental concern, and other authors have found additional variables related to responsible environmental behavior. Weigel (1977) found that high levels of proecology behavior were found in subjects who were liberal and more educated and had higher occupational status. Hines, Hungerford, and Tomera (1986) find that knowledge, locus of control, commitment, and sense of responsibility were related to environmental behaviors.

These purified, multidimensional scales provide a broader perspective of the attitude toward green advertising and environmental behavior constructs than previous research. This perspective is necessary for studying the influence of attitude toward green advertising in general on specific advertisements, especially in the light of advertising's changing role in society. In addition, advertising practitioners can benefit from the results by using these measures to determine how their market is responding to the green advertisements being produced. Finally, this study provides a foundation for further research.

Acknowledgment

Dr. Matulich thanks the generous contribution to research expenses made by the American Marketing Association Faculty Research Grant program.

References

Anderson, Ronald D., Jack L. Engledow, and Helmut Becker (1978), "How *Consumer Reports* Subscribers See Advertising," *Journal of Advertising Research*, 18 (December), 29–24.

Banerjee, Subhatra, Charles S. Gulas, and Easwar Iyer (1995), "Shades of Green: A Multidimensional Analysis of Environmental Advertising," *Journal of Advertising*, 23 (Summer), 21–31.

Bauer, Raymond A. and Stephen A. Greyser (1968), *Advertising in America: The Consumer View*. Boston: Harvard University.

Brown, Joseph D. and Russell G. Wahlers (1998), "The Environmentally Concerned Consumer: An Exploratory Study," *Journal of Marketing Theory and Practice*, 6 (2), 39–47.

Brown, Steven P. and Douglas M. Stayman (1992), "Antecedents and Consequences of Attitude Toward the Ad: A Meta-analysis," *Journal of Consumer Research*, 19 (June), 34–51.

Churchill, Gilbert A. (1979), "A Paradigm for Developing Better Measures of Marketing Constructs," *Journal of Marketing Research*, 16 (1), 64–73.

Davis, Joel J. (1992), "Ethics and Environmental Marketing," *Journal of Business Ethics*, 2 (11), 81–87.

——— (1994), "Consumer Response to Corporate Environmental Advertising," *Journal of Consumer Marketing*, 11 (2), 25–37.

Durand, Richard M. and Zarrel V. Lambert (1985), "Alienation and Criticisms of Advertising," *Journal of Advertising*, 14 (3), 9–15.

Frankel, Carl (1992), "Blueprint for Green Marketing," *American Demographics*, 14 (4), 34–38.

Gerbing, David W. and James C. Anderson (1988), "An Updated Paradigm for Scale Development: Incorporating Unidimensionality and Its Assessment," *Journal of Marketing Research*, 25 (May), 186–92.

Gillespie, Robert J. (1992), "Pitfalls and Opportunities for Environmental Marketers," *Journal of Business Strategy*, (July/August), 14–17.

Greyser, Stephen A. (1962), "Businessmen RE Advertising: 'Yes, but...,'" *Harvard Business Review*, 40 (3), 20–30+.

——— and Bonnie B. Reece (1971), "Businessmen Look Hard at Advertising," *Harvard Business Review*, 49 (3), 18–26, 157–65.

Haller, Thomas F. (1974), "What Students Think of Advertising," *Journal of Advertising Research*, 14 (February), 33–38.

Haytko, Diana L. and Erika Matulich (1993), "The Conceptualization and Measurement of Consumer Attitudes Toward Advertising in General," *AMA Winter Educators' Proceedings: Marketing Theory and Applications*, Vol. 4, P. Rajan Varadarajan and B. Jaworski, eds. Chicago: American Marketing Association, 411–19.

Hemphill, Thomas (1991), "Marketer's New Motto: It's Keen to Be Green," *Business and Society Review*, (Summer), 39–44.

Hines, Jody M., Harold R. Hungerford, and Audrey N. Tomera (1986), "Analysis and Synthesis of Research on Environmental Behavior: A Meta-Analysis," *Journal of Environmental Education*, (18), 1–8.

Kanter, Donald L. (1989), "Cynical Marketers at Work," *Journal of Advertising Research*, 28 (December/January), 28–34.

Kaufman, Lois (1999), "Selling Green: What Managers and Marketers Need to Know About Consumer Environmental Attitudes," *Environmental Quality Management*, 8 (Summer), 11–20.

Kerr, Kevin (1990), "AdWeek's Marketing Week Poll: Thinking Green Is No Longer Just a Hippie Dream," *AdWeek's Marketing Week*, (July 9), 18–19.

Kleiner, Art (1991),"What Does It Mean to Be Green?" *Harvard Business Review*, 69 (July/August), 38–47.

Lannon, Judie (1986), "New Techniques for Understanding Consumer Reactions to Advertising," *Journal of Advertising Research*, 26 (3), RC6–RC9.

Lantos, Geoffrey P. (1987), "Advertising: Looking Glass of Molder of the Masses?" *Journal of Public Policy & Marketing*, 6, 104–128.

Lutz, Richard J. (1985), "Affective and Cognitive Antecedents of Attitude Toward the Ad: A Conceptual Framework," in *Psychological Processes and Advertising Effects: Theory, Research, and Application*, Linda Alwitt and Andrew A. Mitchell, eds. Hillsdale, NJ: Lawrence Erlbaum Associates, 189–212.

——— (1991), "The Role of Attitude Theory in Marketing," in *Perspectives in Consumer Behavior*, Eds. Harold H. Kassarjian and Thomas S. Robertson, eds. Englewood Cliffs, NJ: Prentice Hall, 317–39.

MacKenzie, Scott B. and Richard J. Lutz (1989), "An Empirical Examination of the Structural Antecedents of Attitude Toward the Ad in an Advertising Pretesting Context," *Journal of Marketing*, 53 (April), 48–65.

———, ———, and George E. Belch (1986), "The Role of Attitude Toward the Ad as a Mediator of Advertising Effectiveness: A Test of Competing Explanations," *Journal of Marketing Research*, 23 (May), 130–43.

Maloney, Michael P. and Michael P. Ward (1973), "Ecology: Let's Hear from the People: An Objective Scale for the Measurement of Ecological Attitudes and Knowledge," *American Psychologist*, 28 (July), 583–86.

———, ———, and G. Nicholas Braucht (1975), "Psychology in Action: A Revised Scale for the Measurement of Ecological Attitudes and Knowledge," *American Psychologist*, 30 (July), 787–90.

McDaniel, Carl and Roger Gates (1993), *Contemporary Marketing Research*, 2d ed. St. Paul, MN: West Publishing.

Miniard, Paul W., Sunil Bhatla, and Randall L. Rose (1990), "On the Formation and Relationship of Ad and Brand Attitudes: An Experimental and Causal Analysis," *Journal of Marketing Research*, 27 (August), 290–309.

Mittal, Banwari (1990), "The Relative Roles of Brand Beliefs and Attitude Toward the Ad," *Journal of Marketing Research*, 27 (May), 209–20.

Mohai, Paul and Ben W. Twight (1987), "Age and Environmentalism: An Elaboration of the Buttel Model Using National Survey Evidence," *Social Science Quarterly*, 68, 798–815.

Muehling, Darrel D. (1987), "An Investigation of Factors Underlying Attitude-Toward-Advertising-In-General," *Journal of Advertising*, 16 (1), 32–40.

Newell, Stephan J, Ronald L. Goldsmith, and Edgar J. Banzhaf (1998), "The Effect of Misleading Environmental Claims on Consumer Perceptions of Advertisements," *Journal of Marketing Theory and Practice*, 6 (2), 48–60.

Nunnally, Jum C. (1978), *Psychometric Theory*, 2d ed. New York: McGraw Hill Book Company.

Ottman, Jacquelyn (1992a), "The Four E's Make Going Green Your Competitive Edge," *Marketing News*, (February 3), 7.

——— (1992b), "Industry's Response to Green Consumerism," *Journal of Business Strategy*, 13 (July/August), 3–7.

——— (1998), "Back Up Green Programs with Corporate Credibility," *Marketing News*, (October 12), 9–10.

Peter, J. Paul (1979), "Reliability: A Review of Psychometric Basics and Recent Marketing Practices," *Journal of Marketing Research*, 16 (February), 6–17.

——— (1981), "Construct Validity: A Review of Basic Issues and Marketing Practices," *Journal of Marketing Research*, 18 (May), 133–45.

Phillips, Lisa E. (1999), "Green Attitude," *American Demographics*, 21 (4), 46–47.

Reid, Leonard N. and Lawrence C. Soley (1982), "Generalized and Personalized Attitudes Toward Advertising's Social and Economic Effects," *Journal of Advertising*, 11 (3), 3–7.

Sandage, C. H. and John D. Leckenby (1980), "Student Attitudes Toward Advertising: Institution vs. Instrument," *Journal of Advertising*, 9 (2), 29–32.

Schlossberg, Howard (1991), "Americans Passionate About the Environment? Critic Says That's Nonsense," *Marketing News*, (September 16), 8.

——— (1992), "Marketers Warned to Heed Message of 'Ecologism,'" *Marketing News*, (March 30), 6.

Synodinos, Nicolaos (1990), "Environmental Attitudes and Knowledge: A Comparison of Marketing and Business Students with Other Groups," *Journal of Business Research*, 20 (2), 161–70.

Teufel, Robert (1991), "Are Marketers Turning Green?" *Direct Marketing*, 53 (February), 27–30.

Troy, Lisa Collins (1993), "Consumer Environmental Consciousness: A Conceptual Framework and Exploratory Investigation," *AMA Educators' Proceedings*, David W. Cravens and Peter R. Dickson, eds. Chicago: American Marketing Association, 106–114.

Vandermerwe, Sandra and Michael D. Oliff (1990), "Customers Drive Corporations Green," *Long Range Planning*, 23 (December), 10–16.

Weigel, Russel H. (1977), "Ideological and Demographic Correlates of Proecology Behavior, *Journal of Social Psychology*, 117 (3), 39–47.

——— (1985), "Ecological Attitudes and Actions," in *Ecological Beliefs and Behaviors: Assessment and Change*, D.B. Gray, ed. Westport CT: Greenwood, 96–103.

Wheeler, William A., III (1992), "The Revival in Reverse Manufacturing," *Journal of Business Strategy*, 13 (July/August), 8–13.

Winski, Joseph M. (1991), "Big Prizes, But No Easy Answers," *Advertising Age*, (October 28), GR3.

Zinkhan, George M. and Les Carlson (1995), "Green Advertising and the Reluctant Consumer," *Journal of Advertising*, 24 (2), 16.

10

The Soapbox Versus the Soap: The Application of Negative Political Advertising Tactics In the NonPolitical Marketplace

Paul Hensel
University of New Orleans

Karen James
Louisiana State University Shreveport

This article is a combination of efforts by both authors from work presented at various academic meetings and symposia. Parts of this article have been published or presented previously.

Negative advertising is best regarded as a specific and unique variant of comparative advertising, which attacks, degrades, or impugns a specific competitor for the purpose of promoting a negative attitude change toward the competitor targeted by the advertisement. Although empirical research specific to the use of negative advertising in the marketing of goods and services is nonexistent, this study borrows from and extends concepts developed in existing research in negative political advertising, comparative advertising, the negativity bias, and attitude toward the ad for the purpose of developing a series of testable hypotheses under the attitude framework known as the Dual Mediation Model of Attitudes.

Prior to addressing the negative political advertising research, it is first necessary to justify the assumption that empirical findings from the political arena are generalizable to the study of negative advertising in the context of goods or services. The reader very well may point to the fact that several important characteristics distinguish the political product category and the political decision process from more typical goods and services purchasing conditions. The argument can be advanced logically that these characteristics have important implications with respect to issues related to the effective use of the negative advertising technique.

In an effort to address this issue, we first provide support for generalizability by paralleling the marketing of a political candidate to the marketing of goods and services. In an attempt to analyze the impact of marketplace differences, we next examine the nature of the voter decision process and the characteristics of the political product class, placing particular emphasis on those attributes unique to or characteristic of the political marketplace that are thought to contribute to the successful use of negative advertising. We conclude this section with a discussion of how the generalizability of political research findings can be maximized by developing an experimental research design characterized by a decision process and product class consistent with that found in the political marketplace.

In the second section of this article, we present an example of empirical research designed to test the hypotheses that negative advertising techniques are applicable to the nonpolitical marketplace. This research is designed in a way that maximizes the possibility that significant findings may occur, the logic being that if negative advertising ultimately proves ineffective under conditions deemed most favorable for its successful use, a strong case may be made for the relative ineffectiveness of this technique compared with other advertising alternatives. The maximizing process relies on the discussion in the first section of the article to develop a nonpolitical market scenario that is as similar as possible to the political marketplace.

Characteristics of the Political Marketplace

Although parallels certainly exist between the marketing of a political candidate and the marketing of goods and services, certain key conceptual and fundamental differences are present as well. In the political context, the "product" component of the marketing mix consists of "a complex blend of many potential benefits which voters believe will result if the candidate is elected" (Niffenegger 1989, p. 47). The expected benefits are summarized in the party platform (Newman and Sheth 1987; Niffenegger 1989). Also influencing voters' benefit expectations are the candidate's past record, the candidate's personal characteristics, and the image of the party sponsoring the candidate (Niffenegger 1989) in much the same fashion that prior product experience/family brand experience and parent company image influence benefit expectations in the goods industry. From a product management perspective, political consultants perform the chore of packaging these benefits in different ways to attract the various political market segments and, similar to product managers, engage in research (polling), marketing, fund-raising, advertising, and public relations (Niffenegger 1989). Although the candidate can be best thought of as an intangible service provider, similar to a physician or lawyer, there remains an important difference in that a candidate must be recruited or nominated before he or she can run at the state or federal level (Newman and Sheth 1987).

Unlike goods and services, the "price" of the candidate does not entail monetary investment in the traditional sense (Newman and Sheth 1987), but rather it could be considered in terms of those costs associated with the candidate's election. This may include economic costs in the form of higher taxes, national image costs in terms of increased or decreased national pride, and hidden psychological costs relating to the uneasiness that voters may experience due to a candidate's religious preference, ethnic origin, or stand on an important issue such as abortion or national defense (Niffenegger 1989).

Newman and Sheth (1987, p. 256) in their review of political marketing, liken the distribution element to "the process by which planning and strategy by the candidate's organization is executed so as to optimize the number of voters who come to the polling booth to make an exchange of their vote for the services of the candidate of their choice." Niffenegger (1989) delineates political marketing distribution strategy as comprising two major elements: a personal appearance program, in which the candidate appears at rallies, club meetings, universities, and other public events across the country for the purpose of talking to interested voters; and a volunteer worker program in which volunteers function as intermediary channel members who work to get the voters interested, registered, and at the polling booth on election day via canvassing, sign posting, and campaign fund-raising (Newman and Sheth 1987; Niffenegger 1989).

Finally, both Newman and Sheth (1987) and Niffenegger (1989) note that the promotion element of the marketing mix (encompassing both advertising and public relations) is used by political marketers in a fashion similar to that of goods and services marketers. Niffenegger (1989) argues that most media consultants view promotion as the key marketing element in presidential elections, as it can be used to not only promote the candidates, but also mold public opinion. Newman and Sheth (1987) assert that political marketers use many of the same vehicles—television, newspapers, radio, magazines, direct mail—to promote candidates as do goods and services marketers in the commercial market.

There are several parallels between the political and goods/services marketing efforts discussed to this point; but one key difference affecting the promotional component of the marketing remains to be discussed. In the political marketplace, advertising is viewed as free speech and as such is protected under the tenets of the First Amendment. Goods and service advertising, more commonly called commercial speech, is considered somewhat less fragile and afforded a lesser amount of protection. This is evidenced by the fact that political advertising does not fall under the jurisdiction of the Federal Trade Commission (FTC) and as such *cannot* be regulated for truthfulness; prior substantiation of claims is not required. Furthermore, although Section 315 of the Communications Act of 1934 allows broadcasters the privilege to refuse product or service advertisements that they feel are deceptive or misleading, this act explicitly denies them the privilege of refusing deceptive or misleading political advertising, even in its most blatant form (Merritt 1984). Finally, the Supreme Court ruling in the 1964 *New York Times v. Sullivan* case set an important precedent when the opinion rendered made it clear that public figures faced a difficult task in attempting to recover damages for defamatory statements that hurt their reputations (Merritt 1984). Goods and services marketers are not constrained on this front, a fact that is reflected in the ever-increasing number of corporations that are going to court over comparative advertising claims (Millman 1992).

The discussion delineated here raises some interesting speculations. The reader might argue that the lack of regulatory control in the political marketplace favors the use of untruthful messages, which, due to the negativity bias, in turn may affect attitudes and outcome profoundly in a manner benefiting the negative advertisement initiator. From a research perspective, one might question, then, whether the hypotheses and empirical findings pertinent to political advertising can be generalized to a nonpolitical marketplace. To the advertising practitioner, the question becomes, Will negative advertising be an effective technique under the highly regulated goods and services marketplace?

Although the lack of regulatory control represents a significant difference between the political and nonpolitical marketplaces, the effect that this variable is likely to have on the generalizability of hypotheses, and differences in actual measures of negative advertising's effectiveness, is minimal. Research from the political arena has indicated that those advertisements that are perceived as being the least truthful typically fare poorly in terms of influencing consumers against the targeted opponent (Garramone 1984) and, in fact, may result in "backlash," or substantially less favorable attitudes toward the candidate initiating the advertisement (Garramone 1984, 1985; Hill 1989; Merritt 1984).

However, when this issue is considered from the standpoint of the marketing practitioner, the difference in regulatory control and its implication for litigation would appear to make negative advertising a less desirable strategy. Historically, a loophole in the Lanham Act prohibited only the promotion of false claims about the advertiser's brand, making no specific mention of false claims in relationship to the competition. The Trademark Law Revision Act of 1988 remedied this deficiency. The terms of this act dictate that anyone is vulnerable to a civil action who "misrepresents the nature, characteristics, qualities, or geographical origin of his or her *or another person's goods, services, or commercial activities*" (Buchanan and Goldman 1989, p. 38, emphasis added). With more and more companies now going to court over regular comparative advertising claims (Millman 1992), it seems reasonable to assume that negative advertisements will be vigorously contended in court, and the impending litigation fees may well outweigh any potential benefits that may be realized by use of a negative advertising campaign.

The following section examines issues relevant to several important differences between the marketing of political candidates and nonpolitical products that become apparent when characteristics of the political service class and the nature of the political purchase decision are considered. Particular attention is paid to those characteristics that are thought to influence the effectiveness of negative comparative advertising.

Characteristics of the Political Product Class

Politicians are classified best as service providers, not unlike insurance representatives, plumbers, or dentists, who also offer intangible benefits to the consumers choosing their services. As such, candidates may be classified as *experience goods* rather than search goods (Nelson 1970). Experience goods are those items that the consumer cannot evaluate without actually trying (or in this case, electing), in contrast to goods about which one can obtain information via inspection prior to purchase.

The political product class is unique in that it almost always introduces at least one "new" brand entry (new in the sense that typically at least one candidate has never served as incumbent in that particular position) every election year, though it is not uncommon for the choice set to be composed of two new brand entries. The argument has been advanced that voters may use their knowledge of a candidate's past political experience in other positions as a surrogate indicator of that person's ability to perform in a given office (Newman and Sheth 1987) in a manner similar to which consumers use their knowledge of past product performance to evaluate new brand extensions (Muthukrishnan and Weitz 1991). However, it must be remembered that actual on-the-job experienced quality of the candidate in that role remains unknown. This particular criterion is important as empirical research has demonstrated that negative political advertising stands the best chance of succeeding in "open" races, as incumbency may all but eliminate the role played by advertising strategy type (positive, negative) in determining race outcome (Tinkham and Weaver-Lariscy 1991).

The size of the product category also differs substantially from the majority of nonpolitical products available in the marketplace today. In politics, the brand set is for all practical purposes artificially limited to two major brands (candidates). Although third-party candidates have been present in past elections, numerous regulations and financial limitations generally ensure that only two major candidates constitute the choice set, particularly in higher-level elections.

Another characteristic germane to the specific nature of the political service class relates to the need arousal state of the voting consumer. Unlike the majority of non-political purchases, the need to make a selection is forced artificially in politics, and the time frame for the decision is limited. Although our political system does not dictate that every person must vote, many choose to do so in spite of the fact that they may not feel a particularly strong need to choose a new candidate (or reelect the present officeholder) at the particular time dictated.

The Nature of the Purchase Decision Process

Several important dimensions differentiate the "purchase" of a political candidate from the standard purchase situation (Hensel 1998). First, and perhaps most important, the purchase itself is mandated by law; a president will be chosen whether or not an individual consumer chooses to vote for a given candidate. Although this "forced purchase" characteristic is not prevalent in most consumer goods and services industries, there are some notable exceptions. For example, many states mandate the purchase of products such as auto insurance and infant car seat carriers, and most state and governmental agencies enforce mandatory participation in some type of retirement plan.

It also seems reasonable to include under the heading of forced purchases those essential product categories that, though not mandated by law, are for all practical purposes required of the consumer due to situational factors. For example, although consumers are not forced to have a telephone in their home, those who do elect to subscribe to telephone service must choose a long-distance telephone carrier, or they will have one assigned to them. Similarly, in most felony and criminal proceedings, the defendant must hire an attorney, or risk placing the case in the hands of a public defender. Other examples include the engagement of a professional plumber when the required repairs are beyond the capabilities of the do-it-yourselfer, the selection of a medical or dental care provider when the pain becomes too great to tolerate or a life is in danger, and the purchase of health or life insurance as protection against future problems.

A second notable characteristic of the political purchase decision process is that though the "brand choice" is made by a collection of individual persons, (not withstanding the foibles of the electoral college system), the "product" is consumed by the entire country (as in presidential elections) or designated geographic area (as in all other elections) en mass (Hensel 1998). This is in some ways analogous to the industrial purchase decision made by a committee, in which the risk of a poor decision can be spread among all participating in the decision. However, several distinctions should be made.

In the industrial purchase situation, the purchasing committee members are presumed to be trained specialists. The industrial process generally is reported to be more standardized and as being somewhat cognitively rational. In industrial purchases, risk is shared with a known and limited set of decision makers versus an unknown and a priori indeterminate number of decision makers in the case of political choice. In addition, the industrial purchasing committee's individual decisions generally are known to all other decision makers. This is not the case for the typical voter. Although the risk in both instances is shared by all decision makers, the blame for a poor decision can be placed on the specified persons in the industrial setting, whereas the electorate body as a whole is likely to share the blame in the political selection task.

Another factor distinguishing the political purchase decision process from that of the more typical nonpolitical purchase process is that the consequences of a bad decision are somewhat different (Hensel 1998). Whereas claims in product advertising in effect constitute an implied warranty that the product will live up to the expectations built by the advertiser, political advertising claims (e.g., "Read my lips! No new taxes!") do not. Furthermore, avenues for "returning" a political candidate who does not perform as expected are virtually nonexistent. For example, whereas a simple majority of the voters are needed to select the president, a two-thirds majority of the senate must agree that the president needs to be impeached (i.e., returned). Practically speaking, political decisions are lived with for the length of the term, whereas the large majority of goods can be returned or, in the case of services, replaced by the customer if not satisfactory.

Enhancing the Opportunity for Negative Advertising's Effectiveness

On the basis of the foregoing analysis, it would seem that the characteristics of the political product class and the nature of the political purchase decision process interact to produce a climate in which negative advertising has at least an opportunity to be successful. With an unknown experience good, no recourse is truly available for the consumer to confirm or disconfirm the advertiser's message except trial. The risk associated with making an incorrect decision is enhanced by the inability of the consumer to return or replace the candidate and by the length of time for which the candidate must be "consumed."

The impact of risk on choice behavior has direct implications for the effectiveness of negative political advertising, due to the unique product class and purchase decision characteristics found in the political arena. Prospect theory posits that when a person faces a choice, he or she will compare the expected outcome of a particular decision with a predetermined reference point, which, according to empirical studies, is typically the status quo (Currim and Sarin 1989; Fischhoff 1983; Samuelson and Zeckhauser 1988; Thaler 1980). The body of literature surrounding prospect theory indicates that the risk attitude of a person varies on the basis of this comparison. For example, a person is said to be risk-averse if he or she chooses an alternative in which the expected value of the outcome is no less than that which would be realized under any other choice scenario; therefore, the risk-averse person seeks to minimize losses. The risk-seeking person, however, would choose the alternative offering the highest possible gains, which typically also offers the most variance (positive or negative) in the potential outcome.

Interestingly enough, a phenomenon labeled "The Bowman Paradox" suggests that risk-seeking behavior is more likely to occur following periods of *poor* performance, the implication being that firms engage in risky decisions in order to catch up and compensate for previous decisions (Bowman 1980). At the personal level, Kameda and Davis's (1990) research has validated that dissatisfaction resulting from an experienced outcome being lower than a reference point typically results in a given person developing a risk-seeking attitude in subsequent decision making.

Although the negativity bias (discussed in greater detail in the "Background" subsection of the section "A Research Example") suggests that consumers will incorporate the arguments, inferences, and innuendoes portrayed in the advertisement into their information processing, the negative "framing" of the message and the inability of the consumer to experience the product prior to purchase, or to return/replace it after the decision has been made, indicates that choice behavior should be consistent with that of the risk-seeking person. In a choice between two unknown, unexperienced candidates, rather than accepting the certain "loss" (e.g., the personal faults, past conduct, policies or platform, voting record of the candidate targeted by a negative advertisement), risk-seeking voters "gamble" and attempt to maximize their gains by voting for (and possibly electing) the initiator of the negative advertisement. The likelihood of any one voter adopting a risk-seeking attitude will be influenced by prior decisions (e.g., voted Republican) and a comparison of the outcome of those decisions with a particular reference point (e.g., taxes were raised). Finally, negative advertising's impact is enhanced by the lack of trial and inability to return or replace the candidate once chosen, as this additional risk inflates the weight assigned to the negative information beyond that allocated in purchase situations involving search goods, or products that can be returned or replaced easily if the consumer is not satisfied.

The presence of "new" or unfamiliar brands is also beneficial in creating an environment favorable to the use of negative advertising. A variety of persuasion-based theories and research suggests that prior brand knowledge and experience should result in selective attention to those message arguments that are consistent with a person's preexisting beliefs and experiences, whereas counterargumentation should result against those messages that are inconsistent (e.g., Petty and Caccioppo's [1981, 1986] Elaboration Likelihood Model of Persuasion). In the absence of this knowledge base, the arguments presented in a negative advertisement may be taken at face value, due in part to the negativity bias, and are likely to be more effective. Furthermore, as comparative advertising studies typically have found that new brands benefit most from comparative advertising whereas market leaders benefit least (Gorn and Weinberg 1984; James 1994; Shimp and Dyer 1978; Sujan and Dekleva 1987), it would seem reasonable to assume that nonpolitical negative advertising stands a better chance of working in purchase situations in which choice is limited to unknown and unexperienced "brands."

In the political marketplace, the forced choice characteristic and the implied forced consumption of a single service provider (the winning candidate) by voters and nonvoters alike work hand-in-hand to favor the use of negative advertising. The fact that some voters may become disgusted by negative advertising and choose not to exercise their individual right to vote is irrelevant, as a candidate will be selected by the majority of the people taking part in the election and "consumed" en mass.

In the nonpolitical marketplace, such a scenario is highly unlikely. Only on extremely rare occasions do the decisions of a group as a whole force a person to accept a single service or good provider (e.g., cable provider for a township), and even then, the person typically has the freedom to determine whether he or she will choose to consume (e.g., subscribe to cable) this service or good. The end result of these differences is that the potential payoff of a successful negative advertising strategy is limited in the nonforced, individual consumption situation to those people who directly choose to purchase the negative advertiser's good or service, whereas the potential payoff in the political situation is much higher.

When the purchase decision is not forced or required in some manner, it stands to reason that negative advertising has a smaller chance of being effective. The feelings of dislike engendered by a negative advertisement, and the deflation in brand evaluations and purchase intentions towards both the target and the initiator may reach the point where the consumer becomes so disgusted that (in a product category of only two brands) he or she abandons the purchase decision process and in effect chooses not to choose.

The discerning reader well may wonder if such would be the likely case in a non-forced purchase decision involving a product category comprising more than two brands. First, consider by way of example the 1992 presidential election, which was unique in that for much of the race, it was characterized by three viable candidates. Following Ross Perot's formal reentry into the race, President Bush employed a negative advertising strategy against Clinton. Although Clinton's poll ratings did decrease, Bush's polls did not gain, seemingly indicating that although negative advertising may have been effective in switching preference away from the intended target, it was not effective (given a third alternative) in influencing this group to swing toward the initiator of the advertisement. This observation is consistent with the reasoning of Merritt (1984, p. 27) who states:

> Negative advertising is likely in political campaigns though not in product promotion precisely because it seeks to improve the position of the sponsor by impairing the position of the competitor. To obtain gain by discouraging attraction to a competitor requires a market which has only two "brands" of the desired item. If, for example, there were only two brands of cereal, dissuading customers from purchasing the competitor's brand would benefit the sponsor because it would leave only the sponsor's brand to purchase. But in a market that has more than two brands, moving customers away from one competitor will not guarantee they move toward the sponsor.

In summary, the size of the political product class is of critical importance to the success of negative political advertising and should be replicated in the initial exploratory study of negative goods or services advertising. The greater the number of brand alternatives available in a product category, the more reasonable it becomes to expect that the consumer will purchase a brand other than that of the negative advertisement initiator, particularly as research so consistently has shown that negative advertising reduces brand evaluations and purchase intentions for the initiating brand as well as the one being targeted.

The artificial time constraint imposed on the political decision process also favors the use of negative advertising, as research has shown that negative information becomes more important to consumers as the time allotted for the decision is reduced (Wright 1973). Furthermore, the limited time frame for media placement and advertising exposures in political marketing contributes to the novelty and distinctiveness of negative information, which naturally otherwise would decrease over the prolonged exposure period available in a nonconstrained setting. As Hamilton and Gifford (1976) and Hastie and Kumar (1979) found evidence that novelty and distinction increases the likelihood of information being remembered and recalled, one would also expect the effectiveness of negative advertising to decrease with prolonged exposure.

Implications for Testing Negative Advertising in a Nonpolitical Context

The foregoing analysis was conducted for the purpose of identifying the specific combination of political product class and purchase decision characteristics that are instrumental in creating an environment favorable to the use of negative political advertising. As this research represents the first attempt to study negative advertising in the context of nonpolitical products, developing a purchase decision process and product class similar to that found in the political marketplace is highly appropriate.

The preceding analysis suggests that an experience good, such as a service, be chosen for study from a product class in which (1) the need to make a selection is artificially forced, either due to legal mandates or practical circumstances; (2) the time frame for that decision is severely limited; (3) the alternative offerings are unknown or unexperienced brands; and (4) the number of brand alternatives are severely constrained, ideally to only two. Furthermore, the nature of the decision process should be such that the purchase decision (1) is made by a collection of individual persons for mass consumption by the target population and (2) once made, cannot be immediately returned, revoked, replaced, or changed but rather must be "lived with" and consumed for some specified time period.

From the perspective of the researcher, replication of these characteristics allows empirical findings from the political arena to be generalized to the goods and services context with a high degree of confidence and lends credibility to proposition generation and modeling efforts.

Not only is this decision beneficial to the researcher, but it ensures that the findings will be of value to the advertising practitioner as well. If the results of this study ultimately determine that negative advertising is not an effective alternative under the most optimal of all marketplace conditions, common sense suggests that it hardly seems likely that negative advertising will be generally effective under those conditions governing the majority of goods and services sold.

Although it is certainly true that this claim can only be validated through replication of results and additional research, the benefit to the advertising practitioner is that he or she will be able to make a better informed decision with respect to the general advisability of using a negative advertising strategy based on objective evidence. Not only would such a study foster a superior understanding of how advertising treatment type and argument quality influence attitude toward the ad, brand evaluations, and purchase intentions, it would also provide a direct comparison of how negative advertising fares against the direct comparative and noncomparative alternatives. The rational advertising practitioner will be able to use this information to make effective advertising decisions in a manner that maximizes allocations of financial and creative resources.

A Research Example

The primary purpose of this preliminary research is to evaluate the relative effectiveness of negative comparative advertising in relation to the direct comparative and noncomparative advertising alternatives in other than the political market. Researchers have been interested in the study of comparative advertising since the early 1970s when the FTC gave comparative advertisements its stamp of approval. The bulk of academic research typically has addressed definitional and typology issues, its effectiveness and measurement, and its relationship to the Hierarchy of Effects Model or Situational Effects Model (Ash and Wee 1983; Rogers and Williams 1989; Turgeon and Barnaby 1988). However, the scope of comparative advertising research suffers in that a specific variant of this format—negative comparative advertising—has never been studied empirically outside of the political arena (James 1994). From an academic perspective, this deficiency presents an opportunity to extend our knowledge in the area of advertising effects and effectiveness.

Negative Advertising Defined

For all its frequent use by the media, practitioners, and the public, the term "negative advertising" rarely has been defined formally (*Advertising Age* 1988;

Battaglio 1988; Colford 1988, 1992a, b, c, d, e, f; Garfield 1992; Levy 1987; Miller 1985). An examination of the academic literature reveals that most definitions are rooted in the political context. Surlin and Gordon (1977) laid the groundwork for later definitions of negative political advertising with references to political advertisements that "attack" the other candidate personally, the opponent's platform, or the party of the other candidate.

Negative advertising is similar to comparative advertising in that both forms name or otherwise identify the competitor (Merritt 1984). However, negative advertising is regarded best as a specific and unique variant of comparative advertising. Whereas comparative advertisements identify the competitor for the purpose of claiming superiority, thereby enhancing perceptions of the initiator, negative advertising specifies the competitor for the purpose of imputing inferiority (Merritt 1984). Merritt (1984, p. 27) defines negative advertising within the political context as "advertising designed to evoke negative images of the sponsor's (e.g., initiator's) opponent."

James and Hensel (1991) were the first to extend the definition of negative advertising beyond the political context. According to these authors, negative advertising attacks, degrades, or impugns a specific competitor for the purpose of promoting a negative attitude change toward the target of the advertisement. James and Hensel (1991) also note that the intent of a negative advertisement (to impute inferiority) in and of itself does not preclude the inclusion of some positive message arguments favorable to the brand initiating the advertisement. James and Hensel (1991, p. 56) formally define negative advertising as follows:

> [A]dvertising in which consumers perceive a violation of "fair play" standards and perceive derogatory references or image damaging inferences made by an initiator through the use of either non-mistakable visual stimuli or an explicit verbal reference naming the competitor in a malicious or vicious personal attack against a specific brand, service, issue, company, or candidate.

Background

Although political advertising, and negative political advertising in particular, has received a substantial amount of coverage in the popular literature (*Advertising Age* 1988; Battaglio 1988, Colford 1988, 1992a, b, c, d, e, f; Garfield 1992; Levy 1987; Miller 1985) as well from the academic community (Caywood and Laczniak 1985; Devlin 1989; Garramone 1984, 1985; Garramone and Smith 1984; Garramone et al. 1990; Hill 1989, 1991; Jamieson 1989; Kaid and Boydston 1987; Lang and Lanfear 1990; McClure and Patterson 1974; Merritt 1984; Meyer and Donohue 1973; Roddy and Garramone 1988; Surlin and Gordon 1977; Tinkham and Weaver-Lariscy 1991, 1993) the study of negative comparative advertising in relationship to the marketing of nonpolitical goods and services is virtually nonexistent. Indeed, no empirically based studies of negative or "attack" good or service advertising exist (Hensel and James 1997; James 1994; James and Hensel 1991).

Attribution theory and the phenomenon known as the negativity bias provide the strongest theoretical support for negative advertising when effectiveness is defined solely in terms of attitude change toward the candidate/ brand targeted. The negativity bias refers to research that consistently indicates that consumers tend to favor or assign disproportionate value to negative information in the decision-making process (Arndt 1967; Fiske 1980; Gatignon 1989; Kalish 1986; Kanouse 1984; Kanouse and Hanson 1972; Leonard-Barton 1985; Mahajan, Muller, and Kerin 1984;

Mizerski 1982; Reynolds and Darden 1972; Richins 1983; Weinberger 1986; Wilson and Peterson 1989; Wright 1973).

In the case of negative political advertising, the negativity bias would seem to offer a reasonable explanation for laboratory findings indicating that a negative attitude change occurred toward the targeted candidate following the use of negative advertising (Garramone 1984, 1985; Garramone and Smith 1984; Kaid and Boydston 1987) as well as for those instances in which negative political advertising historically has been credited with influencing poll ratings or election outcome in a substantial fashion (Colford 1988; Diamond and Bates 1984; Niffenegger 1989; Tinkham and Weaver-Lariscy 1991).

Restricting measures of "effectiveness" to outcome, however, provides too simplistic a picture. The political media analysts who so frequently hail negative advertising as the catalyst of poll changes or election outcome do so without the benefit of research validating that advertising is the causal agent. This fact is of critical importance, as the cautious researcher will recognize that intervening variables may moderate the relationship between advertising and outcome. Alternatively, some variable other than advertising may be the true causal agent. Measuring the impact that negative advertising has on the targeted candidate or brand, and using these measures alone, is of limited value in determining effectiveness. Although the purpose of negative advertising is to generate less favorable evaluations of the candidate or brand being targeted, negative advertising also influences perceptions of the candidate or brand that initiated the advertisement.

Negative political advertising research has demonstrated that attitude toward the initiator is highly germane to the effectiveness issue when evaluated in terms of candidate (brand) evaluation and voting (behavioral) intentions. Of the utmost importance is the fact that though negative advertisements may be successful in reducing perceptions of the *targeted* candidate to a greater or lesser degree under varying circumstances and conditions (Garramone 1985; Garramone and Smith 1985; Hill 1989; Kaid and Boydston 1987; McClure and Patterson 1974; Merritt 1984), negative political advertising invariably results in poorer evaluations of the candidate *initiating* the advertisement (Garramone 1984; 1985; Hill 1989; Kaid and Boydston 1987; McClure and Patterson 1974; Merritt 1984).

Theoretical Model

We use the negativity bias in conjunction with the Dual Mediation Model of Attitudes (MacKenzie, Lutz, and Belch 1986; Mitchell and Olson 1981) to explain and predict both attitude toward the brand (A_B) and behavioral intentions (BI) under noncomparative, direct comparative, and negative comparative ad treatments.

Under the tenets of Dual Mediation (DMH), A_{AD} influences A_B directly, and indirectly via brand cognitions (C_B). Attitude toward the brand in turn influences behavioral intentions, or in the case of politics, voting intentions. MacKenzie, Lutz, and Belch (1986) reason that the DMH is consistent with Lutz and Swasy's (1977, p. 132) cognitive structure/cognitive response model of communication effects, arguing that "consumers' affective reactions to an advertisement influence their propensity to accept the claims made in the ad on behalf of the brand: the more favorable they feel toward the advertisement, the more receptive they are to its content." The DMH is also highly compatible with Petty and Cacioppo's (1981) Elaboration Likelihood Model of Persuasion.

Empirical Research

Empirical research provides strong support for the Dual Mediation Model. MacKenzie, Lutz and Belch's (1986) work is of particular significance as they compared four alternative causal models in an effort to determine A_{AD}'s role as a causal mediator with respect to brand attitudes, brand cognitions, and behavioral intentions. Although the Affect Transfer, Reciprocal Mediation, Independent Influences, and Dual Mediation hypotheses were each consistent with the general hierarchy of effects framework, the theoretical links among A_{AD}, C_B, A_B, and BI varied. Using LIS-REL V and a variety of goodness-of-fit measures, MacKenzie, Lutz, and Belch (1986) conclude that the Dual Mediation proposition best fit the data, although the predicted path between C_B and A_B did not reach significance. Support for the Dual Mediation Hypothesis has proven robust to effects such as involvement levels, brand consideration set, variations in advertising type, advertising medium, brand familiarity, product type, argument strength, and message sidedness, and the decomposition of A_{AD} into claim and nonclaim dimensions as well as affective and cognitive components (Gardner 1985; Homer 1990; MacKenzie, Lutz, and Belch 1986; Miniard, Bhatla, and Rose 1990). Although additional studies such as that conducted by Homer (1990) have validated the significance of the C_B to A_B path, the strength of the direct effect of A_{AD} on A_B has been found to vary widely among studies (Brown and Stayman 1992).

In their effort to assess the true robustness of the Dual Mediation model, Brown and Stayman (1992) conducted a meta-analysis. Drawing data from 47 studies across the A_{AD} research stream, Brown and Stayman estimated chi-square statistics, goodness-of-fit indexes, and root mean square residuals for each of the hypotheses originally proposed and tested by MacKenzie, Lutz, and Belch (1986). The results indicated that the affect transfer, reciprocal mediation, and independent influences hypotheses fit the data very poorly when compared with the Dual Mediation Model. However, even the Dual Mediation Model's chi-square was significant at the $p < .01$ level. Despite this significance, Brown and Stayman (1992) argue convincingly that the extreme disparity in the chi-square statistics, as well as a comparison of the goodness-of-fit indexes and root mean square residuals, provided overwhelming support for the superiority of the Dual Mediation Model of Attitudes and advertising effects.

In the context of the current study, we measure A_B and BI for the brand initiating the advertising as well as for the competing brand being targeted or mentioned in the advertisement where appropriate. To eliminate the spurious impact of a priori attitudes, moderating variables thought to influence brand attitude and behavioral intentions will be covaried out using MANCOVA. The moderators addressed by this study include attitude toward advertising in general ($A_{AD/GEN}$), attitude toward comparative advertising in general ($COMP_{GEN}$), attitude toward negative advertising in general (NEG_{GEN}), and demographic variables such as race, age, and education.

Research Propositions

We use the following symbols and abbreviations in delineating the research propositions:

A_{AD} = Attitude toward the ad
$A_{B/INIT}$ = Attitude toward the brand initiating the advertisement
$A_{B/TARG}$ = Attitude toward the targeted competitor
BI_{INIT} = Behavioral intentions toward the initiator of the advertisement
BI_{TARG} = Behavioral intentions toward the competitor

Attitude-Toward-the-Ad Propositions

P_1 and P_2 are grounded in academic research in the negative political advertising literature (Hensel and James 1997; James 1994).

> P_1: The negative comparative advertising treatment will result in less favorable A_{AD} evaluations than will the direct comparative advertising treatment.
>
> P_2: The negative comparative advertising treatment will result in less favorable A_{AD} evaluations than will the noncomparative advertising treatment.

Research has demonstrated that negative advertising is perceived as unethical (Surlin and Gordon 1977) and, more important, is disliked actively (*American Demographics* 1984; Johnson and Copeland 1987). Furthermore, candidates (i.e., brands) engaging in negative advertising are perceived to be untrustworthy, dishonest, and unlikable (Stewart 1975). These perceptions of the advertiser influence an advertisement's perceived credibility, which in turn influences (P_3) A_{AD} negatively (Lutz 1985; MacKenzie and Lutz 1989), resulting in A_{AD} scores that are less favorable than that which would be expected under the direct comparative and noncomparative treatments (P_1 and P_2).

Although Hill's (1989) research provides results contrary to P_1 and P_2, the majority of the political advertising research supports these propositions. Typically, exposure to negative advertisements inspires a negative affective reaction toward either the candidate initiating the advertisement (Garramone 1984, 1985; Merritt 1985) or the candidate targeted by the advertisement (Garramone 1985; Kaid and Boydston 1987). As A_{AD} consistently has been proven to influence B_A directly and indirectly (Brown and Stayman 1992), it seems highly probable that A_{AD} would be negative as well. In the absence of additional research validating Hill's (1989) results, these propositions seem justified.

Brand Attitude Propositions

Although some propositions are contrary to the findings of the Hill (1989) study, P_3–P_5 derive from the following information and logic (Hensel and James 1997; James 1994):

> P_3: The negative comparative advertising treatment will result in less favorable $A_{B/INIT}$ than will the direct comparative advertising treatment.
>
> P_4: The negative comparative advertising treatment will result in less favorable $A_{B/INIT}$ than will the noncomparative advertising treatment.
>
> P_5: The negative comparative advertising treatment will result in less favorable $A_{B/TARG}$ than will the direct comparative advertising treatment.

These three propositions flow directly from the tenets of Dual Mediation theory. Muehling's (1987, p. 47) admonishment that "if an ad produces a negative affect, no matter how potentially informative and useful its information, unfavorable reactions to the sponsoring brand are likely to result" in particular reinforces these propositions, as descriptive studies and surveys pertinent to negative political advertising traditionally have found that consumers dislike negative advertising. Furthermore, the tenets of learning theory and findings from the A_{AD} literature suggest that the negative ad cognitions and affect inspired by a negative political advertisement are transferred toward the candidate initiating the advertisement via the classical conditioning mechanism (Shimp 1981).

The negative political advertising literature pertaining to backlash supports P_3 and P_4. In its most extreme form, backlash occurs when an advertisement inspires sympathy among voters for the candidate targeted by the advertisement, resulting in less favorable evaluations of the candidate who initiated the advertisement (backlash), and better evaluations of the targeted candidate (boomerang) than existed before it was run. Taylor, Taylor, and Greene (1989) purport that backlash is more likely to occur when negative advertisements attack a candidate on a personal rather than job related level. Garramone (1984) believes the perceived truthfulness of the advertisement to be a key determinant of whether backlash occurs; attacks perceived as being untruthful, undocumented, or in any way unjustified inspire negative affect toward the sponsor, rather than the target.

Support for each of the propositions related to brand attitude also is derived from the literature surrounding the negativity bias. The distinctiveness, novelty, and informational power of negative information (Jones and Davis 1965; Kanouse and Hanson 1972; Mizerski 1982) suggests that a person's attitude toward the targeted brand will be less favorable under the negative advertising treatment than it will be under the direct comparative treatment. Furthermore, the multitude of findings indicating that the impact of negative information persists, even after it has been refuted (Ross and Hubbard 1975; Tybout, Calder, and Sternhal 1981; Wegner, Coulton, and Wenzlaff 1983; Weinberger 1986) lends support to the contention that attitude toward the targeted brand will be less favorable under the negative advertising treatment than under the direct comparative treatment.

Behavioral Intention Propositions

Given our expectations for measures of A_{AD} and A_B, the BI propositions should come as no surprise (Hensel and James 1997; James 1994):

P_6: The negative comparative advertising treatment will result in less favorable BI_{INIT} than will the noncomparative advertising treatment.

P_7: The negative comparative advertising treatment will result in less favorable BI_{TARG} than will the direct comparative advertising treatment.

P_8: The negative comparative advertising treatment will result in less favorable BI_{TARG} than will the noncomparative advertising treatment.

These propositions are justified, as to declare otherwise would run counter to the tenets of Dual Mediation Theory. Additional support can be found in the experimental literature surrounding the negativity bias. Arndt (1967), Reynolds and Darden (1972), and Wilson and Peterson (1989) find evidence supporting the contention that negative information depressed purchase intentions. Wilson and Peterson's (1989) additional finding that negative information affects the purchase decision to a greater extent than does positive information also justifies P_7 and P_8. In summary, these propositions provide a stringent test for negative advertising's relative effectiveness, particularly in light of the following discussion.

Method

As this preliminary research represents our first attempt to study negative comparative advertising in the context of nonpolitical marketing, the experimental scenario was marked by a decision process and a product category whose characteristics mimic those found in the political marketplace as closely as possible. The logic to this approach is that if negative advertising ultimately proved to be ineffective under conditions deemed most favorable for its successful use, the results of this study would provide strong evidence of negative advertising's relative ineffectiveness for product marketing when compared to other advertising alternatives.

James (1994) discusses in detail political marketplace factors thought to be most beneficial in creating an environment favorable to the successful use of negative advertising. In brief, that analysis suggests that an experience good, such as a service, be chosen for study from a product class in which (1) the need to make a selection is artificially forced, either due to legal mandates or practical circumstances (similar to elections); (2) the time frame for that decision is severely limited (similar to elections); (3) the alternative offerings are unknown/unexperienced brands (to avoid potential confounding of study results); and (4) the number of brand alternatives are constrained severely, ideally to only two (similar to typical nonprimary elections). Furthermore, the nature of the decision process should be such that the purchase decision (1) is made by a collection of individual persons for mass consumption by the target population and (2) once made, cannot be immediately returned, revoked, replaced, or changed but rather must be "lived with" and consumed for some specified time period, as is typical with an elected official (issues of impeachment aside).

From the researcher's perspective, replication of these characteristics allows empirical findings from the political arena to be generalized to the goods and services context with a high degree of confidence and lends credibility to proposition generation and modeling efforts. It also ensures that the findings will be of value to the advertising practitioner. If the results of this study ultimately determine that negative advertising is not an effective alternative under the most optimal of all marketplace conditions, common sense suggests that it hardly seems likely that negative advertising generally will be effective under those conditions governing the majority of goods and services sold (Hensel and James 1997; James 1994).

Experimental Scenario

The product class ultimately chosen for study was long-distance telephone service, and the experimental scenario asked students to imagine a situation in which only one long distance carrier would be made available to students living in residence halls for an entire academic year. The choice was limited to two fictitious brands, and subjects were informed that the carrier would be selected on the basis of a vote, with the brand preferred by the majority of students being awarded the contract (Hensel and James 1997; James 1994).

Sample

A convenience sample of 95 undergraduate business students at a major university in the southern United States served as the sample in this exploratory study. Subjects were assigned randomly to treatment conditions. Of the 94 usable responses received, 9 students who classified themselves as foreigners were eliminated to avoid confounding the study results, yielding a final sample of 85 subjects. Testing was undertaken in a classroom setting; most subjects finished the experiment in less than 25 minutes (Hensel and James 1997; James 1994).

Although the use of a student sample limits the generalizability of the experiment's results, it was appropriate for this study. As the primary purpose was to test whether negative advertising works outside of the political arena under conditions that enhance the probability of its successful use, limiting the number of brands to two and satisfying the forced purchase and joint consumption criteria were more realistically feasible given the unique characteristics afforded by the use of a student sample. Also, using a student sample helped to control those demographic variables that seem to make a difference in how people respond to different types of advertising. Controlling for these variables is desirable, as this study is interested in examining the relative differences between advertising treatments. Furthermore, the biases that did exist with respect to the age and education of subjects typically worked to negative advertising's advantage. This enhanced the probability for negative advertising's success and makes findings deeming negative advertising the relatively lesser effective technique all the more significant. Finally, students were an appropriate sample because long-distance telephone service represents a legitimate service choice, and one that is used by the large majority of the students living in the residence halls (Hensel and James 1997; James 1994).

Experimental Stimuli

The experimental stimuli were composed of twofold, six-panel (three each side) direct mail brochures. Each experimental stimulus featured the same base paper stock, the same font family, and the same basic layout and design. This allowed for control over nonverbal forms of communication that otherwise might have confounded interpretation of the experiment's results.

Stimuli Development

For each ad treatment cell, half of the experimental stimuli named Telecol as the initiator of the advertisement, and the other half identified Techtel as the advertisement's initiator. In the direct comparative and negative comparative treatments, the company not named as the initiator was identified as the targeted brand. This controlled for any potentially confounding effects that might result from unintended associations or preferences stemming from the use of a particular brand name, despite a previously conducted brand name pretest (Hensel and James 1997; James 1994).

Advertising Treatment Manipulations

The front cover panel, mailer panel, and the two panels constituing the business reply card were identical across each treatment condition. With respect to the brochure cover, only the name of the brand allegedly initiating the advertisement was altered. The advertising treatment manipulation was confined to the first two inner panels of the brochure. Every attempt was made to use consistent wording throughout the treatments. However, the nature of the manipulation required that some variations in text exist (Hensel and James 1997; James 1994).

The noncomparative advertising treatment discussed only the attributes and benefits associated with the service provided by the long-distance company initiating the direct mail brochure. No implicit or explicit references to competitors were made in the text of the advertisement. The intent of this treatment type, as with the direct comparative treatment, was to increase attitudes and preference for the advertisement initiator (Hensel and James 1997; James 1994).

The direct differentiative comparative advertising treatment compared the attributes and benefits of the service provider initiating the advertisement with that of the service provider who allegedly was competing for the university contract as well. This competitor was identified by name (Hensel and James 1997; James 1994).

The negative comparative advertising treatment focused primarily on the competitor being targeted by the advertisement's initiator. The content of these brochures aggressively impugned, degraded, and attacked the attributes and weaknesses of the targeted competitor's service, with little mention being made of the attributes and benefits to be received by selecting the initiator as the service provider. Instead, attention was focused on the attributes and benefits that would *not* be realized if the competitor's brand was selected. The intent of this manipulation was to decrease attitudes and preferences toward the competitor being targeted (Hensel and James 1997; James 1994).

Covariant and Dependent Measures

The proposed covariants and dependent measures were composed of seven-point semantic differential measures corresponding to scales consistent or compatible with prior Dual Mediation and comparative advertising research. With the exception of NEG_{GEN}, each of these scales had been used successfully in prior research, and content validity had been demonstrated.

$A_{AD/GEN}$, $COMP_{GEN}$, and NEG_{GEN} were each composed of five items: honest/dishonest, attractive/unattractive, interesting/dull, offensive/ inoffensive, and ethical/unethical. These items were used by Grossbart, Muehling, and Kangun (1986) when comparative and noncomparative print ads were the stimuli in their study. These measures were found to be significant covariates to the A_{AD}, A_B, and BI measures, demonstrating acceptable levels of reliability (coefficient alpha for $A_{AD/GEN}$ = .75; $COMP_{GEN}$ = .85) (Hensel and James 1997; James 1994).

The dependent measures of interest were adapted from the research of MacKenzie and Lutz (1989), MacKenzie, Lutz, and Belch (1986), and Mitchell and Olson (1981). Mitchell and Olson's (1981) work is cited frequently as the first study to provide evidence in support of the Dual Mediation Model, and their operationalization of A_{AD} is perhaps the most commonly used for measuring a global A_{AD} (Brownlow and Bruner 1994); MacKenzie, Lutz and Belch's (1986) and MacKenzie and Lutz's (1989) operationalizations for A_{AD}, A_B, and BI were developed specifically within the context of the Dual Mediation Model. The operationalizations used in the context of this research reflect global construct evaluations as opposed to dimensional (claim/nonclaim, affective/cognitive) orientations. Global evaluations are appropriatehere, as we are interested in overall measures of the dependent variables, rather than individual determinants (Hensel and James 1997; James 1994).

Six items were chosen to represent the A_{AD} construct (pleasant/unpleasant, favorable/unfavorable, good/bad, interesting/dull, like/dislike, and irritating/nonirritating). The first three items exhibited a reliability of .86 when used by MacKenzie and Lutz (1989); the last three were used in the research of Mitchell and Olson (1981) where they exhibited a reliability of .87. One item was modified slightly from that used in prior research: "Not-interesting" was replaced by "dull," as this word was judged to be a superior semantic opposite to "interesting" and also was more consistent with the semantic pairings used in the attitude toward advertising in general scale and variants (Hensel and James 1997; James 1994).

Six items (favorable/unfavorable, good/bad, pleasant/unpleasant, interesting/ dull, like very much/dislike very much, and high quality/poor quality) were chosen to represent the $A_{B/INIT}$ and $A_{B/INIT}$ constructs. The first three items exhibited a reliability of .86 when used by MacKenzie and Lutz (1989); the last three were used in Mitchell and Olson's (1981) research, in which a .88 coefficient alpha was observed.

Finally, four items (likely/unlikely, possible/impossible, probable/ improbable, existent/nonexistent) were selected to represent the behavioral intention measures,

Table 1
Scale Reliabilities for Dependent Measures & Covariates

Variable	Number of Cases	Number of Items	Alpha
$A_{ADGLOBAL}$	82	5	.9204
$A_{B/INIT}$	85	5	.9715
$A_{B/TARG}$	85	5	.9540
BI_{INIT}	85	4	.9670
BI_{TARG}	85	4	.9311
$A_{AD/GEN}$	85	5	.6113
$COMP_{GEN}$	84	5	.6163
NEG_{GEN}	84	5	.7802

BI_{INIT} and BI_{TARG}. These items resulted in high levels of reliability (.88 and .90) when used previously by MacKenzie, Lutz, and Belch (1986).

Data Analysis and Results

All analyses were conducted using SPSS. F-tests and planned group comparisons via MANCOVA tested the propositions. MANCOVA is appropriate here, as we are interested in relative group differences and not in determining the amount of variance explained by each measure. A significance level of .05 was used in all analyses (Hensel and James 1997; James 1994).

Results

The reliability of the global A_{AD} measure was high (see Table 1). The reliabilities of the $A_{AD/GEN}$ (a= .61), and $COMP_{GEN}$ (a = .62) scales were of some concern, as reliabilities achieved in this exploratory study were less than what had been reported in prior research (Grossbart, Muehling, and Kangun 1986).

The full MANCOVA model specified the independent variables of advertisement type (noncomparative, direct comparative, and negative comparative) against the dependent variables of A_{AD}, $A_{B/TARG}$, $A_{B/INIT}$ and BI_{TARG}, BI_{INIT}. $A_{AD/GEN}$, $COMP_{GEN}$, and NEG_{GEN} were specified as covariates along with race, sex, and class (Hensel and James 1997; James 1994).

In the initial run of the full model, we also specified brand name (Telecol and Techtel) as an independent variable in order to verify that the brand names selected for the hypothetical brands featured in this study did not confound the results through either a main or interaction effect. The brand name main effect test and the brand by ad interaction tests did not result in any significant findings at the .05 level on any of the dependent variables; therefore, we dropped this variable out of the model and reran the MANCOVA analysis (Hensel and James 1997; James 1994).

We found a main effect significant at the .05 level for each of the dependent variables when analyzed according to treatment type (A_{AD}: $p <= .05$; $A_{B/INIT}$: $p <= .05$; $A_{B/TARG}$: $p <= .05$; BI_{INIT}: $p <= .05$; BI_{TARG}: $p <= .05$). Examination of the dependent measure mean scores indicated that the evaluations of the negative advertisement treatment were in the direction expected. Analysis of the significance of covariates found that race was significant with respect to $A_{B/INIT}$ measure ($p <= .05$), but all other covariates failed to exhibit a significant relationship with at least one of the dependent variables (Hensel and James 1997; James 1994).

Validity of Measures

Convergent validity was demonstrated for the dependent measures and covariates via correlations between the mean of each semantic differential global measure and the corresponding log base 10 value of the magnitude scaling judgment. As the logarithmic form of the magnitude scaling score is similar to the linear relationship of an interval scale (Lodge 1991, p. 17), we took significant correlations as evidence of convergent validity. Using the one-tailed t-test, every covariate and dependent measure was significantly correlated to its corresponding magnitude scaling measure at the .01 or better level, indicating that convergent validity was present, though only NEG_{GEN}, A_{AD}, $A_{B/INIT}$ and BI_{INIT} were correlated at the .50 or greater level (Hensel and James 1997; James 1994).

Discriminant validity is evidenced by demonstrating that a measure does not correlate highly with a measure from which it should differ (Peter 1981). The ten-item abbreviated version of the Marlowe-Crowne Social Desirability Scale was selected for this purpose. This scale version exhibited a reliability of .70 among university males, .66 among university females, and .61 among college females in the original developmental study (Strahan and Gerbasi 1972) and .67 among college students in general in the study conducted by Fraboni and Cooper (1989).

As none of the dependent measures reasonably should be expected to correlate with this scale, a lack of statistically significant correlation was accepted as evidence of discriminant validity. As only one variable ($A_{B/INIT}$) significantly correlated with the social desirability bias measure ($p < .05$), discriminant validity was deemed to be present for each variable except $A_{B/INIT}$. The significant correlation (.1885) between $A_{B/INIT}$ and SDBIAS is somewhat puzzling. Although it is possible that respondents felt obligated to evaluate the brand initiating the advertisement in a socially desirable manner, it is more probable that this finding was simply an artifact of the sample size correlating by chance alone (Hensel and James 1997; James 1994).

Nomological validity refers to whether a construct behaves as expected with respect to other constructs to which it is related theoretically. In terms of the dependent measures, nomological validity was assessed in the research itself. As the premise behind Dual Mediation theory suggests that a relationship exists between A_{AD}, A_B, and BI, a significant model was accepted as evidence of nomological validity (Hensel and James 1997; James 1994).

Discussion

To assess fully the potential managerial implications of this research, it is necessary to reconsider first the constraints under which this experiment was conducted. We made every effort to develop an experimental scenario biased toward the successful use of negative advertising. This required limiting the purchase decision to two unknown, unexperienced brands, designing a socialized purchasing system, and requiring forced choice and consumption of the service for a time period of one year.

Although the purpose of negative advertising is to influence brand evaluations and behavioral intentions toward a competitor unfavorably, such an action makes little sense if the initiator does not hope to profit from this reaction in some fashion. In a two-brand marketplace, in which choice and consumption are forced, the fact that negative advertising did not have a relatively more positive impact on brand evaluations and behavioral intentions toward the *initiator* under this most favorable of all scenarios provides strong evidence that negative advertising is not as effective as the direct comparative or noncomparative advertising alternatives.

Furthermore, it is highly probable that in a marketplace composed of more than two brands, behavioral intentions toward the initiator may decrease substantially when consumers are given an option to purchase a brand other than the initiator's or the target's. This would be consistent with the negative impact on brand evaluations toward the initiator observed in this study, the tenets of Dual Mediation theory, and results published in the political advertising literature.

The relaxation of the forced-choice, forced-consumption, socialized buying scenario in effect should decrease the level of risk perceived by consumers as being associated with making an incorrect decision. This very well could deflate the impact that negative advertising has on brand attitudes and behavioral intentions toward the targeted brand. Similarly, the availability of product trial, and prior experience with brands also may contribute to a lessening of negative advertising's ability to fulfill its primary purpose (i.e., damaging brand evaluations and behavioral intentions of the targeted competitor).

The major implication of this study is that the use of negative advertising may be best limited to situations in which the initiator is unconcerned about potential negative attitude changes toward its own brand, and where the sole purpose of the advertisement is to damage the reputation, image, or evaluation of, or behavioral intentions toward, a specific competitor. Practical circumstances falling within this realm of possibility are very limited but may include campaigns that attack goods or services in particularly vulnerable positions, such as new product test marketing and/or launches, goods returning to the market after major problems (e.g., the Tylenol relaunch), and possibly those goods that are associated with high levels of risk and cost, and/or infrequent purchase or decision, such as with proxy fights.

An additional implication of this study is that negative advertising would seem to be a short-term tactic at best; the use of this technique damages evaluations and intentions toward the initiator's brand, as well as those of the targeted competitor. Although we did not address specifically the effect that repetitive exposure to negative advertising may have on brand attitudes, learning theory and the A_{AD} literature suggest that the negative feelings and evaluations inspired by negative advertising toward the initiator may become more deeply ingrained over time, perhaps to the point where they influence behavioral intentions. Although this specific link was not supported by this research, the data from the political arena indicate that this relationship very well may exist.

We find that negative advertising does result in less favorable evaluations toward the initiator. Thus, one further managerial implication is that negative advertising probably is used most effectively in a campaign complemented by noncomparative and/or regular comparative advertising. The use of these more traditional forms of advertising may help to repair the damage done by negative advertising to the initiator's brand by positioning the initiator more positively in the consumers' minds and providing consumers with reasons to purchase the initiator, as opposed to reasons not to purchase a competitor.

Limitations and Recommendations for Further Research

There are several limitations in this research study, most of which resulted from the need to maximize internal validity at the expense of generalizability, as well as from the need to establish an experimental scenario marked by a decision process and a product category that mimicked the political marketplace as closely as possible. This trade-off was recognized and accepted as a necessary prerequisite for addressing the primary research question, which sought to evaluate the relative effectiveness of negative advertising under conditions most favorable to its successful use, and in the absence of confounding or moderating factors. Thus the generalization of these results is limited by the nature of the sample, the product class being studied, and the advertising execution employed.

The replication of findings from the political marketplace in the context of long-distance telephone services advertising is exciting, as it suggests that many of the findings from the negative political advertising literature may be generalizable to the marketing of goods and services. Yet before the results from the political arena can be accepted with confidence as appropriate for goods and services, the current study must be replicated with a larger sample.

It also would be interesting to undertake additional research using a product or service class from a more traditional marketplace unencumbered by a socialized buying system, forced product choice and consumption, and competition that is limited to two unknown brands. Natural extensions of the present research should manipulate the number of brands in the marketplace, the service or good category being studied, the brand familiarity and market position of the respective brands, consumer predisposition and loyalty toward the various brands, and key characteristics of the choice process (e.g., time frame for decision, opportunity for trial and return). Investigation of these constraints and the impact of their removal on negative advertising's effectiveness represents a primary stream of potential research.

Other key variables that could be manipulated include the medium used to create and display advertising executions, the involvement level of the consumer, and the intensity of the negative advertising effort. Manipulations of intensity would allow for greater understanding of how boomerang and backlash effects have an impact on brand attitudes and behavioral intentions. Consumer's processing of negative comparative advertising also could be studied more extensively with respect to other theoretical models, such as the Elaboration Likelihood Model of Persuasion and Attribution Theory. The long-term effects of negative advertising and its relationship to memory presents an interesting area of research as well. Finally, issues related to affect and emotion also should be explored in further research.

References

Advertising Age (1988), "Where to Start the Cleanup," 59 (November 14), 16.

American Demographics (1984), "Nix, Nein, Nay, No, Uh-Uh," 14 (November), 14.

Arndt, Johan (1967), "Role of Product-Related Conservations in the Diffusion of a New Product," *Journal of Marketing Research*, 4 (August), 291–95.

Ash, Stephen B. and Chow-Hou Wee, (1983), "Comparative Advertising: A Review with Implications for Future Research," in *Advances in Consumer Research*, Vol. 10, Richard D. Bagozzi and Alice B. Tybout, eds. Ann Arbor, MI: Association for Consumer Research, 370–76.

Battaglio, Stephen (1988), "Frankenberry: The Man Who Locked Mike Dukakis in a Revolving Door," *Adweek,* 29 (October 31), 50.

Bowman, E. H. (1980), "A Risk-Return Paradox for Strategic Management," *Sloan Management Review*, 23, 17–31.

Brown, Steven P. and Douglas M. Stayman (1992), "Antecedents and Consequences of Attitude-Toward-the-Ad: A Meta-Analysis," *Journal of Consumer Research*, 19 (June), 34–51.

Brownlow, Thomas L. and Gordon C. Bruner, II (1994), "Measure Development Out of Control: A Critical Review of A_{AD} Scales," working paper, College of Business Administration, Southern Illinois University at Carbondale.

Buchanan, Bruce and Doron Goldman (1989), "Us vs. Them: The Minefield of Comparative Ads," *Harvard Business Review*, (May–June), 38–50.

Caywood, Clarke and Russell N. Laczniak (1985), "Unethical Political Advertising," in *Marketing Communications: Theory and Research*, M.J. Houston and R. Lutz, eds. Chicago: American Marketing Association, 37–41.

Colford, Steven W. (1988), "Campaign Flak Flies: Pol's Ads Have Negative Charge," *Advertising Age,* 59 (October 31), 4.

——— (1992a), "Buchanan Takes Off the Gloves in N.H.," *Advertising Age,* 63 (January 27), 3.

——— (1992b), "Bush Adman: 'My Most Frustrating Time,'" *Advertising Age,* 63 (November 9), 1, 42.

——— (1992c), "Bush Boosters Plan Anti-Democratic Blitz," *Advertising Age,* 63 (March 16), 3, 49.

——— (1992d), "Campaign Ads Get Down and Dirty," *Advertising Age,* 63 (March 2), 32.

——— (1992e), "Clinton Adman Says Bush Ads Backfired," *Advertising Age,* 63 (November 9), 1, 42.

——— (1992f), "Tsongas Relents on Negative Ads," *Advertising Age,* 63 (March 9), 51.

Currim, I. S. and R. K. Sarin (1989), "Prospect Versus Utility," *Management Science,* 35 (1), 22–41.

Devlin, L. Patrick (1989), "Contrasts in Presidential Campaign Commercials of 1988," *American Behavioral Scientist,* 32 (March/April), 389–414.

Diamond, Edwin and Stephen Bates (1984), *The Spot: The Rise of Political Advertising on Television.* Cambridge, MA: MIT Press.

Fischhoff, B. (1983), "Predicting Frames," *Journal of Experimental Psychology,* 9 (1), 103–16.

Fiske, Susan T. (1980), "Attention and Weight in Person Perceptions: The Impact of Negative and Extreme Behavior," *Journal of Personality and Social Psychology,* 38 (6), 889–906.

Fraboni, Maryann and Douglas Cooper (1989), "Further Validation of Three Short Forms of the Marlowe-Crowne Scale of Social Desirability," *Psychological Reports,* 65, 595–600.

Gardner, Meryl Paula (1985), "Does Attitude-Toward-the-Ad Affect Brand Attitude Under a Brand Evaluation Set?" *Journal of Marketing Research,* 22 (May), 192–98.

Garfield, Bob (1992), "Mudslinging Sinks Buchanan," *Advertising Age,* 63 (March 3), 32.

Garramone, Gina M. (1984), "Voter Responses to Negative Political Ads," *Journalism Quarterly,* 61 (Summer), 250–59.

——— (1985), "Effects of Negative Political Advertising: The Roles of Sponsor and Rebuttal," *Journal of Broadcasting & Electronic Media,* 29 (Spring), 147–59.

——— and Sandra Smith (1984), "Reactions to Political Advertising: Clarifying Sponsor Effects," *Journalism Quarterly,* 61 (Winter), 771–75.

———, Charles K. Atkin, Bruce E. Pinkleton, and Richard T. Cole (1990), "Effects of Negative Political Advertising on the Political Process," *Journal of Broadcasting & Electronic Media,* 34 (Summer), 299–311.

Gatignon, Hubert and Thomas S. Robertson (1989), "Technology Diffusion: An Empirical Test of Competitive Effects," *Journal of Marketing,* 53 (January), 35–49.

Gorn, Gerald J. and Charles B. Weinberg (1983), "Comparative Advertising: Some Positive Results," in *Advances in Consumer Research,* Vol. 10, Richard P. Bagozzi and Alice Tybout, eds. Ann Arbor, MI: Association for Consumer Research, 377–80.

Grossbart, Sanford, Darrel D. Muehling, and Norman Kangun (1986), "Verbal and Visual References to Competition in Comparative Advertising," *Journal of Advertising,* 15 (1), 10–23.

Hamilton, David L. and Robert K. Gifford (1976), "Illusory Correlation in Interpersonal Perceptions: A Cognitive Basis of Stereotype Judgments," *Journal of Experimental Social Psychology,* 12 (4), 392–407.

Hastie, Reid and Purohit Anand Kumar (1979), "Person Memory: Personality Traits as Organizing Principles in Memory for Behaviors," *Journal of Personality and Social Psychology,* 37 (1), 25–58.

Hensel, Paul J. (1998), "Soap Box Versus the Soap," presentation at the Advertising Special Interest Group meeting of the American Marketing Association's Winter Conference, Austin, TX (February). From Hensel, Paul J., Karen E. James, and Gordon C. Bruner II (1989), "To Sling Mud or Blow Your Own Horn: An Analysis of Negative Advertising," working paper, College of Business and Administration, Southern Illinois University at Carbondale.

―――― and Karen F. James (1997), "A Constrained Exploration of the Communication Effectiveness of Negative Advertising in the Nonpolitical Market Place," in Proceedings of the Special International Group Conference of the American Marketing Association, Dublin, Ireland (June), (CD-ROM).

Hill, Ronald Paul (1989), "An Exploration of Voter Responses to Political Advertisements," *Journal of Advertising,* 18 (December), 14–22.

―――― (1991), "Political Advertising in the 1990s: Expected Strategies, Voter Responses, and Public Policy Implications," in *Advances in Consumer Research*, Vol. 18, Rebecca H. Holman and Michael R. Solomon, eds. Ann Arbor, MI: Association for Consumer Research, 212–18.

Homer, Pamela M. (1990), "The Mediating Role of Attitude-Toward-the-Ad: Some Additional Evidence," *Journal of Marketing Research*, 27 (February), 78–86.

James, Karen E. (1994), *The Relative Effect of Negative Comparative, Direct Comparative and Noncomparative Advertising Under Varying Conditions of Argument Quality on Attitude-Toward-the-Ad, Brand Attitudes, and Behavioral Intentions.* Ann Arbor, MI: UMI Dissertation Services.

―――― and Paul J. Hensel (1991), "Negative Advertising: The Malicious Strain of Comparative Advertising," *Journal of Advertising,* (June), 53–69.

Jamieson, Kathleen H. (1989), "Context and the Creation of Meaning in the Advertising of the 1988 Presidential Campaign," *American Behavioral Scientist*, 32 (March/April), 415–24.

Johnson, K. S. and G. Copeland (1987), "Setting the Parameters of Good Taste: Negative Political Advertising and the 1986 Elections," paper presented at the International Communication Association Convention, Montreal.

Jones, Edward E. and Keith E. Davis (1965), "From Acts to Dispositions: The Attribution Process in Person Perception," in *Advances in Experimental Social Psychology*, Vol. 2, Leonard Berkowitz, ed. New York: Academic Press, 218–66.

Kaid, Lynda Lee and John Boydston (1987), "An Experimental Study of the Effectiveness of Negative Political Advertisements," *Communication Quarterly,* 35 (Spring), 193–201.

Kalish, Shlomo and Gary L. Lilien (1986), "A Market Entry Timing Model of New Technologies," *Management Science*, 32 (February), 194–205.

Kameda, T. and J. H. Davis (1990), "The Function of Reference Point in Individual and Group Decision Making," *Organizational Behavior and Human Decision Processes*, 46, 55–76.

Kanouse, David E. (1984), "Explaining Negativity Biases in Evaluation and Choice Behavior: Theory and Research," in *Advances in Consumer Research*, Vol. 11, Thomas C. Kinnear, ed. Provo, UT: Association for Consumer Research, 703–708.

―――― and L. Reid Hanson Jr. (1972), "Negativity in Evaluations," in *Attribution: Perceiving the Causes of Behavior*, Edward E. Jones, et al. eds. Morristown, NJ: General Learning Press., 47–62.

Lang, Annie and Patrick Lanfear (1990), "The Information Processing of Televised Political Advertising: Using Theory to Maximize Recall," in *Advances in Consumer Research*, Vol. 17, Marvin Goldberg, Gerry Gorn, and Rick Pollay, eds. Provo, UT: Association for Consumer Research, 149–58.

Leonard-Barton, Dorothy (1985), "Experts as Negative Opinion Leaders in the Diffusion of a Technological Innovation," *Journal of Consumer Research*, 1 (March), 914–26.

Levy, Robert (1987), "Big Resurgence in Comparative Ads," *Dun's Business Month*, 129 (February), 56–58.

Lodge, Milton (1991), *Magnitude Scaling. Quantitiative Measurement of Opinions.* Newbury Park, CA: Sage Publications.

Lutz, Richard J. (1985), "Affective and Cognitive Antecedents of Attitude-Toward-the-Ad: A Conceptual Framework," in *Psychological Processes and Advertising Effects: Theory, Research and Application*, L. F. Alwitt and A. A. Mitchell, eds. Hillsdale, NJ: Lawrence Erlbaum Associates, 45–63.

—— and John L. Swasy (1977), "Integrating Cognitive Structure and Cognitive Response Approaches to Measuring Communication Effects, in *Advances in Consumer Research*, Vol. 4, W. D. Perreault Jr., ed. Atlanta: Association for Consumer Research, 363–71.

MacKenzie, Scott B. and Richard J. Lutz (1989), "An Empirical Examination of Structural Antecedents of Attitude-Toward-the-Ad in an Advertising Pretesting Context," *Journal of Marketing*, 53 (April), 48–65.

——, ——, and George C. Belch (1986), "The Role of Attitude-Toward-the-Ad as a Mediator of Advertising Effectiveness: A Test of Competing Explanations," *Journal of Marketing Research*, 23 (May), 130–43.

Mahajan, Vijay, Eitan Muller, and Roger A. Kerin (1984), "Introduction Strategy for New Products with Positive and Negative Word-of-Mouth," *Management Science*, 30 (December), 1389–404.

McClure, Robert D. and Thomas E. Patterson (1974), "Television News and Political Advertising: The Impact of Exposure on Voter Beliefs," *Communications Research*, 1 (January), 3–31.

Merritt, Sharyne (1984), "Negative Political Advertising: Some Empirical Findings," *Journal of Advertising*, 13 (September), 27–38.

Meyer, Timothy P. and Thomas R. Donohue (1973), "Perceptions and Misperceptions of Political Advertising," *Journal of Business Communication*, 10 (Winter), 29–40.

Miller, Gregory (1985), "The Fine Art of the Proxy Nastygram," *Institutional Investor*, 19 (October), 172–73.

Millman, Nancy (1992), "Attack Advertising Goes Beyond Politics: Marketers Hop on the Negative Bandwagon," *Chicago Tribune*, 7 (August 30), 3.

Miniard, Paul W., Sunil Bhatla, and Randall L. Rose (1990), "On the Formation and Relationship of Ad and Brand Attitudes: An Experimental and Causal Analysis," *Journal of Marketing Research*, 27 (August), 290–303.

Mitchell, Andrew A. and Jerry C. Olson (1981), "Are Product Attribute Beliefs the Only Mediator of Advertising Effects on Brand Attitude?" *Journal of Marketing Research*, 18 (August) 318–32.

Mizerski, Richard W. (1982), "An Attribution Explanation of Disproportionate Influence of Unfavorable Information," *Journal of Consumer Research*, 9 (December), 301–8.

Muehling, Darrel D. (1987), "Comparative Advertising: The Influence of Attitude-Toward-the-Ad on Brand Evaluation," *Journal of Advertising*, 16 (December), 43–49.

Muthukrishnan, A. V. and Barton A. Weitz (1991), "Role of Product Knowledge in Evaluation of Brand Extension," in *Advances in Consumer Research*, Vol. 18, Rebecca H. Holman and Michael R. Solomon, eds. Ann Arbor, MI: Association for Consumer Research, 407–13.

Nelson, Philip (1970), "Information and Consumer Behavior," *Journal of Political Economy*, 78 (March), 311–39.

Newman, Bruce I. and Jagdish N. Sheth (1987), "A Review of Political Marketing," in *Research in Marketing*, Vol. 9, Jagdish N. Sheth, ed. Greenwich, CT: JAI Press, Inc., 237–66.

Niffenegger, Phillip B. (1989), "Strategies for Success from the Political Marketers," *Journal of Consumer Marketing*, 6 (Winter), 45–51.

Peter, J. Paul (1981), "Construct Validity: A Review of Basic Issues and Marketing Practices," *Journal of Marketing Research*, 18 (May), 133–45.

Petty, Richard E. and John T. Cacioppo (1981), *Attitudes and Persuasion: Classic and Contemporary Approaches*. Dubuque, IA: William C. Brown Company.

—— and —— (1986), "The Elaboration Likelihood Model of Persuasion," in *Advances in Experimental Social Psychology*, Vol. 19, L. Berkowitz, ed. New York: Academic Press, 123–205.

Reynolds, Fred D. and William R. Darden (1972), "Why the Midi Failed," *Journal of Advertising Research*, 12 (August), 39–46.

Richins, Marsha L. (1983), "Negative Word-of-Mouth by Dissatisfied Consumers: A Pilot Study," *Journal of Marketing*, 47 (Winter), 68–78.

Roddy, Brian L. and Gina M. Garramone (1988), "Appeals and Strategies of Negative Political Advertising," *Journal of Broadcasting & Electronic Media*, 32 (Fall), 415–27.

Rogers, John C. and Terrell G. Williams (1989), "Comparative Advertising Effectiveness: Practioners' Perceptions Versus Academic Research Findings," *Journal of Advertising Research*, 29 (October/November), 22–37.

Ross, L., M. R. Lepper, and M. Hubbard (1975), "Perserverence in Self Perception and Social Perception: Biased Attributional Processing in the Debriefing Paradigm," *Journal of Personality and Social Psychology*, 32, 880–92.

Samuelson, W. and R. Zechhauser (1988), "Status Quo Bias in Decision Making," *Journal of Risk and Uncertainty*, 1, 7–59.

Shimp, Terence A. (1981), "Attitude Toward the Brand as a Mediator of Consumer Brand Choice," *Journal of Advertising*, 10 (June), 9–15.

―――― and David C. Dyer (1978), "The Effects of Comparative Advertising Mediated by Market Position of Sponsoring Brand," *Journal of Advertising*, 8 (June), 13–19.

Stewart, C. J. (1975), "Voter Perception of Mudslinging in Political Communication," *Central States Speech Journal*, 26, 279–86.

Strahan, Robert and Kathleen Carrese Gerbasi (1972), "Short, Homogeneous Versions of the Marlow-Crowne Social Desirability Scale," *Journal of Clinical Psychology*, 28, 191–93.

Sujan, Mita and Christine Dekleva (1987), "Product Categorization and Inference Making: Some Implications for Comparative Advertising," *Journal of Consumer Research*, 14 (September), 372–78.

Surlin, Stuart H. and Thomas F. Gordon (1977), "How Values Affect Attitudes Toward Direct Reference Political Advertising," *Journalism Quarterly,* 54 (Spring), 89–98.

Taylor, Ronald D., Jan C. Taylor, and Steven Greene (1989), "Negative Political Advertising: An Evaluation from Theory and Practice," *Journal of Midwest Marketing,* 4 (Spring), 20–25.

Thaler, R. (1980), "Mental Accounting and Consumer Choice," *Marketing Science*, 4 (Summer), 199–214.

Tinkham, Spencer F. and Ruth Ann Weaver-Lariscy (1991), "Advertising Message Strategy in U.S. Congressional Campaigns: Its Impact on Election Outcome," *Current Issues and Research in Advertising*, 13 (1 and 2), 207–26.

―――― and ―――― (1993), "A Diagnostic Approach to Assessing the Impact of Negative Political Television Commercials," *Journal of Broadcasting and Electronic Media* (Fall), 377–99.

Turgeon, Normand and David J. Barnaby (1988), "Comparative Advertising: Two Decades of Practice and Research," *Current Issues in Advertising Research*, 11 (1 and 2), 41–65.

Tybout, Alice M., Bobby J. Calder, and Brian Sternthal (1981), "Using Information Processing Theory to Design Marketing Strategies," *Journal of Marketing Research*, 18 (February), 73–79.

Wegner, Daniel M., G. Coulton, and R. Wenzlaff (1983), "Processing Denials: The Impact of Briefing in the Debriefing Paradigm," work in progress.

Weinberger, Marc C. (1986), "Products as Targets of Negative Information: Some Recent Findings," *European Journal of Marketing*, 20 (3–4), 110–28.

Wilson, William R. and Robert A. Peterson (1989), "Some Limits on the Potency of Word-of-Mouth Information," in *Advances in Consumer Research*, Vol. 16, Thomas K. Srull, ed. Provo: Association for Consumer Research, 23–29.

Wright, Peter L. (1973), "The Cognitive Processes Mediating Acceptance of Advertising," *Journal of Marketing Research*, 10 (February), 53–62.

IV

Creativity

Creativity

George M. Zinkhan
University of Georgia

Introduction

Creativity is a key aspect of many human endeavors. Thus, it is not surprising that creativity is such a key component of successful advertising and marketing strategies. In the past, advertising researchers have found creativity to be a difficult topic to write about and to investigate. For example, it is not possible to outline the "seven steps" for creative advertising or the seven steps for creative and successful Web sites. By nature, a creative solution breaks the mold and gets a message across in a new or innovative way.

The ad copywriter's job is not unlike the task faced by a poet or artist. Both work within the confines of a medium and a tradition. The poet uses sound and rhythm to express feelings, thoughts, and experiences. In the same way, within a confined space, the advertiser strives to send forth messages that reflect dimensions of universal truth that may resonate deeply within the target audience. Within the past 15 years, advertising researchers have been increasingly interested in topics such as consumer experiences, feelings, images fantasies, metaphors, emotions, and satisfaction. Poetry provides a way to explore these important advertising topics and concepts. A few examples are presented in the next section.

Five Poems

The following five poems deal with themes in the commercial world. Issues illuminated include brand spokespersons, image advertising, consumer behavior, retail shopping, temptation, commercial content, and excitement in the marketplace.

"Scenes from a TV"

buxom boisterous girls
frolic as the beer flows
and the men huddle
scheming their next play
life is gay, when you drink
what they drink

waspish thin waifs
in sexy repose
lounge and passively smoke
what you should smoke
if you want to look lifeless,
like them

winsome wives whine
about rings around collars
while their husbands are out
laundering money and hustling
high-powered clients who will dump them
in the end

towheaded children toddle and play
in their crispy clean clothes
that mommy shopped for at the mall
consuming on credit and killing time
waiting for daddy to come home
and save her

Anne L. Balazs, Mississippi University for Women

"Window on the World"

All of the excitement in my life
    comes in quick Technicolor bursts —
much like the 30-second commercials
    that slide across my large-screen TV.

George M. Zinkhan, University of Georgia

"watching   (and watching) TV"

With large promise, the green soul
    of advertising offers up high-flown ideas
    and blown up images.

Bits and pieces of Wagner fill in the blank spaces
    as, en masse, we learn how
    to calm our fevers and soothe our tired limbs.

Time after time, that which seems so close —
    clinging to the tips of our eager fingers —
    seems to slip away, just out of our sifting grasp.

In the end,
    our lives become little more
    than naked desire herself.

George M. Zinkhan, University of Georgia

"Enough"

witnessing this marriage
of cunning and fur
and arrogance
    tempts me to accept
the challenge of her grin.
    I would object
had I but bag and rope and well
    and she one life, not nine.

John F. Sherry Jr., Northwestern University

"gargoyles"

we shopped for gargoyles
    early one chicago spring
and picked our way
    across a broken field
of sidewalk soldiers,
    homeless hawkers
passing streetwise
    who might as well
have fallen
    from those dark facades
so far above our heads
    as yet to rest unnoticed
save for pigeon fells
    commencing on the spouts
and ending here
    before our step

he rested
    half the weight
of his young life
    against the float pane
palms on glass and
    brow on backhand
talking to the plaster
    phalanx more than me,
this is it, this
    is the place
there's gargoyles here,
    and over here,
his eager fingers
    searching for the hinge
that might admit him
    to this
retail reliquary
    now

John F. Sherry Jr. Northwestern University

V

Strategic Issues in Advertising

11

Research Issues in Targeting Neglected Segments

Subodh Bhat
San Francisco State University

Targeting specific groups of people is a well-accepted marketing practice. Marketers have targeted groups on the basis of demographic factors such as age, sex, race, and ethnic identity. Other types of groups that have been the subject of marketing efforts have been very diverse: fans of a sports team, graduates of a university, and members of a social association are a few examples. Although targeting is extensively practiced, literature on the strategic issues involved in targeting is hard to find. Therefore, this article focuses on a few important issues related to the rewards and risks of targeting. Starting with a survey of the advantages and criticisms of targeting, I go on to discuss several issues that arise when marketers target specific groups. The first issue concerns the assumptions that underlie targeting. I critically analyze these assumptions and discuss the resulting caveats for target marketers. This article also examines other reasons marketers may engage in targeting and the possible effects of targeting on the marketer, the target group, and other groups.

Motivations for Targeting

Targeting is an effective business practice because it recognizes the spending potential of the groups that are targeted. Often, it results in the development of a product and an advertising, promotions, and distribution mix tailored to the needs of a specific group. The target group benefits from the satisfaction of its specific needs and preferences, and the marketer reaps the resulting rewards of patronage. Targeting minorities or other special groups also makes sense in an increasingly diverse and expressive American society, especially because it focuses on the group's desire for recognition or legitimacy. Targeting strategies make it easy to build enduring relationships with members of a group, an important objective for most marketers. It may also serve as a way to differentiate a brand within a specific group. For example, Subaru of America Inc. has long targeted lesbians through advertisements in gay media and by supporting gay organizations, which has resulted in strong loyalty to the Subaru brand among lesbians. One dealer estimated that one-third of the Subaru vehicles he sells are purchased by lesbians (Alsop 1999). In addition, society benefits from the targeting of "desirable" products and images (e.g., that of a role model) to certain disadvantaged groups (e.g., by showing an African American woman as a corporate boss).

Yet, targeting has often been criticized in situations in which marketers of products such as alcohol, cigarettes, and sneakers have appealed to specific minorities, youths, or children (see Brown 1992; Johnson 1992; Pollay 1993; Scott, Denniston, and Magruder 1992). Academics have devoted considerable attention to the public policy issues in targeting, especially when the target groups are perceived as vulnerable (for a review, see Ringold 1995).

Methods of Targeting

Targeting can take many forms. The most obvious example is a product that has been tailored to meet the needs of a specific group. For example, long distance companies have been adept at targeting ethnic communities with special programs for calls to their countries of origin. Another method that is practiced widely is targeting a group with advertisements or other promotional materials that focus on their differences from other groups. Common approaches include depicting members of the target group in advertisements or placing advertisements in media patronized by target group members. For example, Fleet Boston Corporation, a banking company, appealed to lesbians with advertisements in gay newspapers that showed a woman touching her female partner's hand and pregnant body (Alsop 1999). Direct marketing and personal selling are other activities that lend themselves well to the targeting of specific groups. Several insurers, such as MONY Life Insurance and New York Life Insurance, have been successful in their targeting of ethnic Indians, such as Gujaratis, by employing people with close ethnic and linguistic ties to those communities (Louis 1999). A final method of targeting is distributing products through stores patronized by members of the target group.

Marketers have long targeted groups such as African Americans and others on the basis of sex and age. Increasingly, however, interest has focused on emerging ethnic minorities such as Hispanics and Asian Americans. This makes sense given the increasing size and growing wealth of these groups. For example, a recent study by the Strategy Research Group estimated the size of the Hispanic population in the United States to be at 34 million in the year 2000 (approximately 12% of the total U.S. population) with buying power of $325 billion (Cantu 1999). Similarly, Asian Americans, who are the fastest growing immigrants, are expected to increase to 8% of the population by 2020 (Bureau of the Census 1996) and given their affluence, education, and occupational status are an attractive target group (Taylor and Stern 1997). Marketers have also aimed specific marketing mixes at groups that share common nondemographic interests or preferences that result in affiliation to the group by individual members. Students at a university, members of a profession, and supporters of a cause, to cite just a few examples, have all been targets of various marketing efforts. More recently, marketers have begun to pay more attention to nontraditional groups, whose composition is unrelated to conventional demographic factors or to commonality of interests or preferences; examples include gays and lesbians and the disabled. Most of these groups have existed for a long time, but in the new climate of openness and assertiveness, they are striving for public recognition and legitimacy. With their increasing political and economic clout, these previously neglected groups are beginning to attract the attention of marketers. Therefore, although this article discusses general strategic issues in targeting, particular attention is given to the special issues involving these neglected groups, given the regency of marketers' efforts in targeting them and the lack of academic research about them. A discussion of the assumptions behind targeting follows.

The Assumption of Within-Group Homogeneity

Underlying the strategy of targeting specific groups is the assumption of considerable homogeneity within the target group. In other words, marketers assume that members of a target group are similar in their preferences and behaviors simply because of their membership in that group. This assumption lies at the foundation of developing marketing mixes directed at all members of a target group. However, such an approach, though cost-effective, might be problematic when the assumed homogeneity is lacking or is slight in nature. For example, not all homosexuals have the same preferences for a product or react similarly to a marketing tactic. Similarly, Asian Americans and Hispanic Americans vary widely in their consumption habits and preferences. The following paragraphs examine issues related to the assumption of group homogeneity.

One key factor that marketers should examine before making a targeting decision is whether the assumed homogeneity within a target group translates into homogeneity in responding to a product offering or other marketing action. For example, it makes sense for delivery companies to target Haitian Americans with a plan that has special rates to their country of origin. However, it is not as meaningful to offer special international rates to fans of the Baltimore Orioles because their homogeneity in terms of being Orioles fans probably does not lead to homogeneity in their preferences for international delivery.

Another factor to consider is that often within-group homogeneity with respect to a certain characteristic is not a dichotomous issue of presence or absence of that characteristic but rather a range of possibilities. It is this degree of within-group homogeneity that should be of real interest to marketers. For example, all graduates of a university are unlikely to have the same degree of school spirit and therefore may react differently to a credit card that emphasizes affiliation with that university. There is usually a distribution of such consumption-related preferences and behaviors, and savvy target marketers must try to understand the nature of this distribution. Such information will provide marketers even more opportunity to segment and target a particular group. Even when there is considerable homogeneity within a target group with respect to a product or marketing mix, a marketer has to evaluate whether the target group is large enough to justify a separate targeting effort.

Marketers should also not assume that group homogeneity with respect to one characteristic means homogeneity with respect to other probably unrelated characteristics. In other words, the nuances of differences within groups should be clearly understood. One example of this is the concept of an Indian American market. Although the members of this group might share the trait of being born in or otherwise affiliated with India, they come from different religions, classes, regions, ethnic backgrounds, and castes and speak different languages. Anecdotal evidence exists of Indian Americans being irked by telemarketers, who were soliciting long-distance telephone service, speaking in an unfamiliar Indian language.

The Assumption of Intergroup Heterogeneity

Another important assumption in targeting is the degree of heterogeneity between the target group and other groups of interest to the marketer. Targeting is worthwhile only if meaningful differences exist in the responses of the target group and the other groups with respect to specific products or marketing tactics. If that is not the case, marketers may be better off with a broader product marketing strategy because of cost considerations. Continuing a previous example, it may not make sense for delivery companies to target Haitian Americans with a specific plan for domestic delivery because consumption-related differences between Haitian American consumers and others are unlikely to exist, and such a strategy may simply increase overall marketing costs. Similarly, using an advertisement that depicts a disabled person or sponsors an event targeted to academics may make sense only if the pattern of preferences for the appeal among the disabled and academics on the one hand, and other groups on the other hand, is sufficiently different. Thus, the question that marketers should ask themselves is whether the target group's preferences and behaviors with respect to the targeted product or marketing tactic are sufficiently distinct from those of other groups the marketer is targeting. If not, the cost of separate targeting efforts might not be justified.

It is also possible that neglected groups are being slowly acculturated into mainstream groups. The exchange of behavioral patterns between dominant and neglected populations is quite common. Marketers should closely watch how the dominant culture might be affecting preferences and behaviors among neglected groups. For example, acculturation trends suggest that diet drinks will become popular in the Hispanic community (Dick Thomas, cited in Cantu 1999). If the neglected groups are assimilating mainstream consumption patterns, separate targeting efforts might not be worth the extra time and money.

Acculturation flows both ways, and it is possible for the tastes and preferences of a minority to go mainstream. For example, the widespread acceptance of salsa, the sauce and the music, is a testimony to the way minority groups have influenced the mainstream. Given the rapid increase in the Hispanic population, Hispanic values such as family, togetherness, and trustworthiness are predicted to dominate mainstream values such as independence, individualism, and convenience in the near future (Dick Thomas, cited in Cantu 1999). Marketers might study the preferences and behaviors of long-neglected groups to find out which of their preferences and behaviors might become popular.

A Target Group's Special Traditions

An important issue in targeting any group is to understand that group's special and sacrosanct traditions. This is especially the case with previously neglected groups because marketers might be unfamiliar with their customs and traditions. Marketers have to be careful about the kind of products they target. For example, when targeting Muslims, the fastest growing religion in the United States, financial companies should remember that offering interest on savings may be anathema to devout Muslims. Similarly, advertising and direct selling pitches should not offend the sensibilities of target groups.

Sensitivity to Targeting

Individual members of a targeted group may not always like being targeted as members of that group. They may feel little affiliation with the target group or believe that the marketer is trying to gain an advantage by exploiting their membership in that group. This is particularly likely with members of neglected groups because they have little history of being targeted by marketers. Not much is known about how members of neglected groups react to the targeting tactic. Marketers should therefore be sure to research these groups' sensitivity to being the objects of targeting.

Effect of Targeting on Other Groups

One possibly unintended consequence of targeting a small group is the effect it has on other groups that become aware of the targeting. Sometimes, the effect may be negative. At the least, groups may not be able to relate to the targeted group. For example, an advertisement that depicts an actor with many piercings might not evoke the desired response in groups that cannot empathize with those that favor piercings. More gravely, groups that oppose or dislike targeted groups may feel offended enough to engage in complaining or even boycotting. For example, Christian groups called for a boycott of Walt Disney products when it became known that Disney had created gay-themed attractions to attract a homosexual audience. For this reason, marketers need to monitor how their targeting of specific groups affects other groups of customers or stakeholders. The issues raised in the preceding paragraphs require that marketers examine the financial pros and cons of a specific targeting decision. However, financial consequences are not the only criteria for deciding whether to target a specific group. Marketers may have other strategic considerations for wishing to target specific groups, and these are examined subsequently.

Marketer's Desire for Inclusiveness

Marketers might want to target previously neglected groups to convey to the broader audience a sense of the marketers' inclusiveness. They may believe that doing so is simply the right thing and part of their responsibility as good corporate citizens. Perception of a marketer's inclusiveness might result in a positive image for the marketer or the brand in some circles, and more generally, might lead to brand awareness among a larger set of potential customers. For example, in contrast to the young, heterosexual couples typically found in advertisements, IKEA, the Swedish furniture chain, used diverse actors such as a middle-aged couple, a male homosexual couple, a family with an adopted son, and a divorced woman in a series of advertisements that it characterized as inclusive. IKEA received an enormous amount of publicity for its efforts, probably raising its brand awareness and burnishing its image among socially conscious customers.

Marketer's Desire to be Perceived as Being on the Cutting Edge

Another objective for targeting neglected groups might be to enhance consumers' perceptions of the marketer being on the cutting edge. Targeting groups that have been neglected by other marketers is likely to position the target marketer as one that bravely ventures into new areas. The use of advertisements depicting AIDS patients and gays by apparel vendors such as Calvin Klein and Benetton is an attempt to position their products as being on the cutting edge in fashion.

Conclusions

This article focuses on strategic issues in the targeting of groups, particularly traditionally neglected groups. Targeting offers several advantages that result from a better understanding of target market needs. Designing a product and marketing mix specifically for a target market that is appreciative has the potential to increase sales and profits. Also, targeting can differentiate a brand from competing brands in the marketplace while helping build enduring relationships with the target group. Targeting makes increasing sense in a world in which groups previously neglected by marketers are becoming more aware and assertive about their identity.

At the same time, there are several caveats for marketers who want to target these "new" groups. Assumptions about the homogeneity within the target group and the heterogeneity between the targeted and other groups must be seriously examined to ensure that targeting remains effective. Marketers also need to consider whether members of the target group want to be targeted as a group. In addition, marketers would be best served if they examined the repercussions of targeting on other groups that may be hostile or indifferent to those targeted. Apart from the financial consequences of these caveats, some marketers might still wish to target these neglected groups because it is simply the right thing to do or to achieve an image of being on the cutting edge.

References

Alsop, Ronald (1999), "In Marketing to Gays, Lesbians are Often Left Out," *The Wall Street Journal*, (October 11), B1.

Brown, J.W., Jr. (1992), "Marketing Exploitation," *Business and Society Review*, 83 (4), 17.

Bureau of the Census (1996), *National Population Estimates*. Washington, DC: U.S. Department of Commerce.

Cantu, Hector D. (1999), "Hispanics Influence, Affluence Will Grow," *San Francisco Examiner*, (October 31), B3.

Johnson E.M. (1992), "Harmful Targeting," *Business and Society Review*, 83 (4), 16–17.

Louis, Meera (1999), "Help Wanted: Gujarati Speakers to Sell Insurance," *The Wall Street Journal*, (October 12), B1.

Pollay, Rick W. (1993), "Targeting the Young is an Old Story: A History of Cigarette Advertising to the Young," in *Contemporary Marketing History: Proceedings of the Sixth Conference on Historical Research in Marketing and Marketing Thought*, J. B. Schmidt, S.C. Hollander, T. Nevett, and Jagdish N. Sheth, eds. Atlanta, GA: 263–82.

Ringold, Debra Jones (1995), "Social Criticisms of Target Marketing," *American Behavioral Scientist*, 38 (4), 578–92.

Scott, B.M., R.W. Denniston, and K.M. Magruder (1992), "Alcohol Advertising in the African-American Community," *Journal of Drug Issues*, 22 (2), 455–69.

Taylor, Charles R. and Barbara B. Stern (1997), "Asian-Americans: Television Advertising and the 'Model Minority' Stereotype," *Journal of Advertising*, 26 (2), 47–61.

12

The Fusion of Design and Marketing: Implications for Merchandising, Consuming, and Ownership

Angela H. Patton
University of Houston

Marketing and design are progeny of business and art. Their traits are genetic. Business glorifies the practical; art pays homage to impulse. Business prefers clarity and precision; art flourishes in ambiguity. Business is prone to making rules; art revels in breaking rules. These polarized (albeit stereotyped) attributes give rise to the adage "opposites attract." Despite differences in their heritage, marketing and design have an affinity for each other that is consummated in material culture.

As subsets of art and business, design and marketing are not part of the inner circle. They are kindred spirits living on the outskirts of the disciplines that spawned them. With a utility-based disposition, design, an applied art form, is at the low end of the art world's food chain. Marketing seems frivolous, its stature is diminished, when it stands between its serious-minded siblings, management and finance. As misfits, design and marketing are well-suited companions that share a vanity. They both want to be noticed. Design has the face, but marketing has the moves. When marketing and design join forces the line between them blurs like rubbed chalk.

In the early days of their courtship, marketing and design watched hand-in-hand as consumer culture was cultivated (Ewen 1988). It has been said that couples that live together start to resemble each other. It isn't that basic features change but that people who share intimate lives often adopt similar gestures, expressions, movements, and mannerisms that animate their physical form and give rise to a similarity that transforms their physical characteristics. Such is the case of design and marketing's long-lived relationship. Their individuality is tangled in a hybrid of art and commerce, and it is not always easy to know where one ends and the other begins.

Design and marketing have aged well together; they are comfortable and prosperous. Their union has spawned subsidiaries, such as advertising and merchandising, that are distinct fields with their own idiosyncrasies, interests, and points of view. In the age of genetic engineering, hyphenates (e.g., designer–marketer) are old technology. Partnering has given way to fusion.

When design, marketing, advertising, and merchandising are bound together, they create an alloy that encapsulates a full range of thinking. From the depths of intuition, ideas emerge that are based on aesthetic sensibility and creative awareness. Ideas pilot rational and strategic thinking. Planning offers a bird's-eye perspective that gives form and direction to conceptual thinking and sets the stage for devising persuasive tactics. The fusion of these fields seamlessly melds looks, brains, charm, and a charismatic personality. It is an aggregate that is programmed to stimulate and satiate in the same stroke.

In this chapter, I focus on the fusion of design and marketing in the context of two case studies. The first example comes from the world of art—the controversial exhibition, SENSATION, representing British contemporary art from the Saatchi collection. The second case study comes from the world of business—the ubiquitous Martha Stewart Living Omnimedia (MSLO) that has built an empire on tasteful living. After presenting the two case studies, I examine design and marketing in relation to merchandising, consumption, and ownership. My discussion encompasses the natural progression from retailer (merchandising) to user (consuming and owning).

At a glance, these two case studies do not suggest commonality. SENSATION takes viewers to a visual precipice and hurls them over the edge, whereas MSLO models composure and domesticated discretion. Beyond their images, however, SENSATION and MSLO share similar characteristics; they are both composite entities of aesthetic awareness and marketing savvy that transcend conventional forms of advertising and merchandising. SENSATION is loud and shrill, whereas MSLO speaks in measured responses, and yet they are both prototypes of fabricated realities that are targeted to a consumer market.

SENSATION

At the heart of the controversy surrounding the exhibition SENSATION is the collector Charles Saatchi of the high profile advertising agency Saatchi and Saatchi. Critics suggest that Saatchi (because of his binge buying and selling practices) does not simply collect art; he controls Britain's contemporary art market. According to their accounts, rather than sipping and savoring art, Saatchi guzzles and devours it. Saatchi counters by saying that art is his passion and he has a big appetite. In either case, his inhaling and exhaling of art creates enough breath to sway the market.

SENSATION's first public viewing was in 1997 at the Royal Academy of Arts. The exhibition struck a nerve and attracted crowds eager for a jolt. The media decreed SENSATION scandalous and dubbed the Academy "the Royal Academy of Porn." All of this prompted an art critic to observe that, "SENSATION went exactly as planned" (Solomon 1999, p. 46). When SENSATION traveled to its only North American venue, the Brooklyn Museum of Art, it offended and enraged the mayor of New York City. In a knee-jerk response, Mayor Giuliani withheld approximately half a million dollars in city funding, threatened to evict the museum from city property, and considered filing a personal lawsuit.

There is more to this exhibition than a grouping of provocative and, in some cases, repulsive artifacts. The art is rivaled by an equally visible phenomenon—advertising. As Mark Twain (1889, p. 202) noted more than 100 years ago, "Many a small thing has been made large by the right kind of advertising."

It is common practice to inform the public when viewer discretion is advised. The Brooklyn Museum of Art's Web site (www.brooklynart.org) introduces SENSATION with a health warning: "The contents of this exhibition may cause shock, vomiting, confusion, panic, euphoria, and anxiety. If you suffer from high blood pressure, a nervous disorder, or palpitations, you should consult your doctor before viewing this exhibition." This portentous yellow and black sign appears to be taped to the page, suggesting the work of a health official rather than a museum director. The patronizing tone and graphic presentation provide the right tingle to entice thrill seekers.[1]

The sincerity of the health warning seems additionally dubious in the light of the toll-free number through which tickets to the exhibition can be purchased, 1-87-SHARKBITE, a caustic reference to Damien Hirst's haunting "pickled shark" piece, which is one of the objects on display. For added hyperbole, British rock and roll icon David Bowie narrates the audio tour and features SENSATION on his own Web site.

Merchandising opportunities include SENSATION T-shirts that simply state the First Amendment or duplicate the health warning. There are pins, along with posters and postcards, that say, "Danger Art" or "Censorship." Viewer advisories, theme-oriented toll-free ticket numbers, audio tours, and T-shirts are not uncommon features of exhibitions. The shape of these features, however, suggests that SENSATION is more synthetic than organic.

Saatchi's advertising background doesn't go unnoticed: "Saatchi brings an adman's eye to the practice of connoisseurship; he favors art that makes an instant impact, art that surprises you and lodges in your brain, art with kicked-up visual appeal" (Solomon 1999, p. 49). It was also reported that reproductions of these works are slated to be used as images in a Saatchi restaurant chain called Sensation (Lynch 1999).

Some argue that SENSATION should be taken at face value—an exhibition showing on-the-edge and over-the-edge art that "provokes, challenges, and rewards the viewer," according to Arnold L. Lehman, the Brooklyn Museum of Art's director. Controversy is not new to art. Others contend that what is on exhibit is not art but advertising—capitalizing on controversy is not new to marketing. And others believe that the real artist is Saatchi himself and SENSATION is a carefully orchestrated large-scale performance piece. The existence of all these assertions as viable choices gives credibility to a fourth option—all of the above.

On the one hand, SENSATION is a traveling exhibition of contemporary British art from the Charles Saatchi collection. In the words of New York artic critic Peter Schjeldahl, it is "an exhibition ... of works by an assortment of sometimes strenuously naughty young British artists, [that] was fun to start with, not to mention good" (Schjeldahl 1999, p. 104). On the other hand, SENSATION displays a "deliberately provocative bid for attention" (Johnson 1999, p. 5D). Regardless of the quality of the art, the artists have received celebrity status simply by association. In writing about current strategies in marketing, Douglas Rushkoff (1999, p. 19) observes that "Advertisers have dispensed with the idea of promoting a product's attributes in favor of marketing a product's image."

SENSATION, like Art Happenings of the 1960s, depends on audience participation. It is not insignificant that this exhibition attracts hoards of people yearning to be unnerved. Without viewer frenzy, SENSATION fizzles. It is the response that fuels the high voltage of the exhibition and Saatchi, as performance artist, who flips the

---

[1]Subsequently, the Brooklyn Museum of Art's director, Arnold Lehman, posted a letter on the museum's Web site to address questions of professional ethics that the SENSATION exhibition raised. Lehman concedes that the health warning on the Web site "lent itself to interpretations of commercialism" but states that the real intention was to capture "broad audience appeal."

switch. As one proponent of pop culture over high culture writes, "Your opinion of what's quality is not more valid than mine. Popularity *is* quality. And so marketers *are* today's real artists" (Barry 1999, p. 187).

SENSATION is in your face, mocking and probing viewers' darker sensibilities. The exhibition delves beneath surfaces, peeling back the facade of acceptability and exposing the raw side of human nature. SENSATION levels its sights at viewer comfort and pulls the trigger. SENSATION asks the question "Is it live or is it Memorex?" Is it art or is it advertising? In an interview with Charles Saatchi, art critic Deborah Solomon comments that "Ours is the era in which advertising became more artful, and art became more like advertising" (Solomon 1999, p. 49).

SENSATION's projection of a multiple personality highlights its aggregate quality. The fusion of design and marketing results in a diverse, more dimensional enterprise that has wider appeal and greater market value.

MSLO

A less sensational example of fusion is MSLO, which has successfully built a financial empire around Martha Stewart's persona as an artful homemaker. SENSATION's bid for discomfort is positioned 180 degrees from the color-coordinated comfort of MSLO. Unlike SENSATION, MSLO treads closer to the safety of surfaces where appearances are lodged and offers a view of the world that is neatly folded and tucked away. MSLO, through an infusion of aesthetic awareness and handcrafted sensibility, promotes household rituals as leisure activities rather than domestic chores. This slant on homemaking marks a revival of the preindustrial household.

Since the 1920s, homemaking has been shaped by the promotion of labor-saving devices: "No longer the repository of craft and self-sustaining values, the home of the 1920s saw the massive influx of industrial goods and values which made most of those crafts superfluous" (Ewen 1976, p. 161). To cultivate the domestic market, the use of mass-produced goods and mechanized appliances was advertised as a way for homemakers to enjoy leisure time outside of the home. The Electrical Development Association forwarded this idea in its 1928 publicity slogan: "No longer tied down by housework. Spring-clean with Electricity" (Forty 1986, p. 207). In contrast, MSLO promotes a domestic philosophy that advocates style first and ease as an irrelevant factor. Regardless of these different points of view, what the pre- and postindustrial households have in common is the influence of advertising.

Through palpable imagery, MSLO constructs domestic fantasies tailored toward escapism. An uneventful snack is visually transformed into an elegant hors d'oeuvre when herbed creamed cheese is delicately piped into sensual lines on celery stalks. The visual presentation has fed the imagination.

MSLO capitalizes on sentimental association (e.g., holidays, family gatherings, weddings) and staple experiences (e.g., fried chicken 101) that reflect more provincial values. *Living*, one of MSLO's publications, is a vicarious feast that offers respite and repose to frenzied lives.

Stewart's gracious demeanor and unassuming appearance disguises her steel-eyed business agenda and reputedly high-strung character. This disjunction between appearance and reality provides spin to the adage, "Live as I say, not as I do." The effort to fashion and maintain Stewart's lifestyle is the antithesis of frugality, simplicity, and ease. To actualize Martha's world requires the combined effort of a multimillion dollar conglomeration to create and maintain.

In the era of branding, Stewart reigns as queen. On October 19, 1999, MSLO was publicly traded for the first time. Stewart (in character) stood outside the New York Stock Exchange with a tray of brioche. On the first day of trading, the stock doubled, giving the company a market value of $2.52 billion. MSLO has carefully woven design, marketing, advertising, and merchandising into a single (albeit synthetic) fiber. "Design is her [Stewart's] medium, but marketing is her art" (Patton and Zinkhan 1998, p. 27).

Merchandising

Although SENSATION and MSLO make opposite impressions, they represent a new strategy of consuming that is the synergetic outcome of fusion: "the whole is greater than the sum of the parts." Like the tensile strength of the alloy chrome nickel steel that is intensified by ten times its weakest component and six times its strongest one (Baldwin 1996, p. 68), SENSATION and MSLO are strengthened by their use of fusion. Combining intuitive processing, instinct, use of visual tools, strategic thinking, and persuasion results in a highly integrated, coordinated, and packaged enterprise that has roots in an earlier advertising phenomenon—the ensemble.

The idea of merchandising ensembles originated more than 75 years ago. According to Roland Marchand, author of *Advertising the American Dream*, "The popularization of the idea of the ensemble expanded the definition of consumer 'necessities' ... and represented a notable success in the transfer of elite tastes and ideas to the consumer masses" (1985, p. 132). The ensemble is a larger concept than packaging merchandise and represents the precursor to theme-based marketing and contemporary branding practices.

The core value of MSLO is style. Its mantra is stylish living. As a lifestyle, consultant Martha Stewart offers ensemble advice. The company fashions staged vignettes that are assemblages of purchasable products that enable consumers to select, try on, and hang the lifestyle of Martha Stewart in their closets. Assuming an identity requires significantly more commitment than just casual browsing. Identity builds context. Context creates its own market and fuels proliferation. MSLO merchandises products and services that promote the masquerade. Martha's world is a visual aberration that consumers can own through her 27 books, seasonal products, and services (e.g., a syndicated advice column).

SENSATION is more than a controversial visual experience. Organizers adopted a merchandising strategy that aligns SENSATION with debatable and emotionally charged issues (e.g., freedom of speech). This approach to merchandising "organizes individuals into masses" (Slater 1997, p. 73). SENSATION is a highly integrated, packaged concept that appears to have been created in a single stroke. The ensemble aspect of SENSATION is SENSATION itself.

Ensemble merchandising introduces the concept of the authority figure. According to Marchand (1985, p. 138), "authority must come from above." Both SENSATION and MSLO, in building context, establish credibility and an authoritative position. SENSATION's prestige comes from its institutional setting—the art museum. MSLO influence comes from Stewart's ubiquitous media presence that proliferates her image as a lifestyle advisor. "What would Martha do?" (WWMD) is a popular cultural construct.

SENSATION and MSLO both use visual tools and aesthetics to access the emotions. SENSATION is harsh and unadorned and, like salt in a fresh wound, stings and numbs at the same time. Settings in *Living* are delicately lit and use a short depth of field to achieve a slightly out of focus image that has a daydream quality. A carefully composed collection of jarred capers is elevated to the stature of still life. SENSATION and MSLO dilate the senses and make consumers vulnerable to merchandising.

SENSATION and MSLO use multimedia strategies for reaching consumers. Up close, viewers of SENSATION are confronted by the rawness of a rotting cow's head swarming with maggots. At a safer distance, virtual viewing can be equally hazardous. The exhibition does not have to be viewed in person to elicit response. In the same way, thumbing through *Living* or *Martha by Mail* or logging on to www.martha.com, readers can vicariously slip into Martha's world. In the Whitney Museum's exhibition catalog, *High Styles: Twentieth-Century American Design*, associate curator Lisa Phillips (1985, p. ix) writes, "Simulated and secondhand images have transformed our sense of the real, competing successfully with direct experience. As a result, it is no longer the function of an object but the received image of it that is the fundamental stimulus of consumption."

SENSATION and MSLO are synthetic enterprises that have commerce-based objectives; they have something to sell. Fusion offers a strengthened position by viewing design, marketing, advertising, and merchandising as a single entity. SEN-SATION and MSLO rely on fusion to fabricate realities that create a plausible context. In both cases, context is synonymous with culture. To understand this phenomenon, it is necessary to isolate design and marketing and consider their relationships in the context of consumption.

Consuming

Design and marketing are entwined in the complexity of a consumer-based ecosystem that is preoccupied with materiality and the value of materialism. Some argue that consumer culture is an oxymoron and view culture in terms of higher ideals. In this respect, culture is reserved for the refinement of taste through aesthetic and intellectual awareness. Others contend that culture is a more general term that merely describes social thinking regardless of the point of view (Slater 1997). Culture is also defined as cultivation or tillage, which suggests that it is an outcome of hands-on work. In biology, culture is understood as growth in a defined and controlled medium. For the purposes of my discussion, I adopt a hybrid point of view and consider culture the outcome of directed effort in a defined medium.

The act of consuming is a fundamental characteristic of the biosphere. People breathe, eat, drink, and, in the process, consume the elements needed to survive—"the stuff of the gene, the thousands of individual carbon, hydrogen, oxygen, and other atoms that comprise it are in constant exchange with the world outside" (Dossey 1982, p. 73). Consuming transpires at levels beyond the reach of human awareness. Cells engulf nutrients, and black holes devour galaxies.

From the vantage point of biology, consumption is part of a highly integrated system that distributes energy. Rather than an end, consuming is part of a chain of events aimed at synthesizing the world. The instinct to consume is present at every point of transformation. Consuming is pervasive and unending: "the incessant flow of matter from living organisms forms endless chains of connections (Dossey 1982, p. 76).

Within organisms, catalysts in the form of enzymes facilitate consumption. These macromolecules accelerate the process of metabolism by lowering the amount of activation energy needed to start the process of transformation. In the context of the marketplace, design and marketing (advertising and merchandising fall under the rubric of marketing) form a coenzyme that provides the catalytic boost. Collectively, they generate the heat that stimulates consumption and facilitates the flow of energy.

The Second Law of Thermodynamics states that in exchanges of energy, some energy is lost. Each link in the chain passes on less energy than the preceding link, which results finally in an entropic state. First-order consumers (plants) absorb solar energy and feed second-order consumers (herbivores), who in turn feed third-order consumers (carnivores) and so on. This principle of hierarchical ordering can be applied to design and marketing.

Consumption itself reveals a loss of energy at each exchange (e.g., plants receive 100% of solar energy, herbivores through plants receive 10%, and carnivores receive 1%). In terms of design and marketing, the process of consuming is filtered through perception en route to fuel the body, mind, and soul.

The quality of first-order experiences defines the range and scope of the sustainable energy. Experiences must be packed with enough energy to reach subtler levels of gratification. Consider the vigor of an original piece of art compared with a mass-produced reproduction. In this case, the reproduction has less vitality because it is removed from the intention (psychic energy) that shaped the original work, which reduces its life span as an experience.

The energy that feeds immediate pleasure cannot sustain itself and burns out at the surface, leaving the emotions and psyche hungry. In some respects, low energy experiences are viewed as optimal. If the first order of consumption is met (i.e., the purchase is made), it is to the advantage of those that control the distribution chain (e.g., merchandisers) that consumers are left hungry and rooting around for more. "Design and advertising, as co-conspirators, can inspire discontent as a means to fuel consumption" (Patton and Zinkhan 1998, p. 30).

Consumer culture places an emphasis on acquisition. "The sole purpose of marketing is to get more people to buy your product, more often, for more money" (Zyman 1999, p. 11). By this definition, marketing is focused on the first order of consumption. Purchasing serves to arrest consuming. It is the culmination of a process. Purchasing transforms consumption into ownership.

Ownership

People acquire things to add comfort to their lives, both physically and psychologically. Ownership alters the relationship people have to their surroundings. Ownership gives shape to identity and a framework to human value systems. It publicly declares who a person is. Branding, for example, is a marketing strategy based on ownership.

Ownership is the double-edged sword of capitalism. Through ownership people gain comfort and status but at the same time assume a physical and financial burden. Consuming, in the context of distributing energy as sustenance, requires a catalyst that has a life span beyond acquisition. What enables marketing to go beyond first-order consuming is its coenzyme, design.

Thoreau (1854, p. 60) once noted that ownership is in the eye of the beholder: "The owner does not know it for many years when a poet has put his farm in rhyme, the most admirable kind of invisible fence, has fairly impounded it, milked it, skimmed it, and got all the cream and left the farmer only the skimmed milk." By setting thoughts and feelings to verse, the poet owns the beauty of the farm without the physical burden of being a landowner. Recording the experience creates a means to revisit it, even from the distance of space and time.

Artfulness is a sustaining quality. In addition to tempting the senses and ego with style and fashion, design's aesthetic viewpoint assists marketing as it facilitates the flow of energy beyond the first order of acquiring. Design provides the means to fuel deeper levels of consuming as people ingest outside experiences. As philosopher Albert Borgmann (1995, pp. 13–19) suggests, "Think of design as the excellence of material objects.... [D]esigners are charged with making the material culture conducive to engagement.... Artisanship is required for the shaping of engaging environments."

Conclusion

The fusion of design and marketing transcends the individual attributes of each field and provides a new tool for commerce. These fields (in combination) regulate the process of consumption. Their fusion results in a new medium that can stimulate and satiate at the same time, which gives greater control.

Design proliferates, shapes, and directs the contour of the material world. It adds weight and dimension through products, lifestyles, and environments. Objects are physical manifestations of ideas that can be exchanged, have value, and give rise to the need for managing exchange. Marketing focuses on this exchange. It serves to intimate, allude, connote, and in the process, persuade consumers through advertising and merchandising.

SENSATION and MSLO exemplify the use of fusion to construct high-energy enterprises. High energy is necessary to sustain the vitality of a consumable experience. Experiences that reach deeper into the process of consuming are transformed into sustenance for the human body. The success of SENSATION and MSLO is that they have a fractal character. That is, SENSATION and MSLO are fabricated realities that perpetuate this process of reality fabrication. These realities create context that gives rise to cultures favorable to the practice of merchandising. Through the fusion of design and marketing, a viable, high-energy consumer culture is cultivated. In previous studies of consumer culture, culture is treated as if it were created almost spontaneously. It is true that consumers themselves have a role to play in the creation of a consumer culture. Nonetheless, as described here, the fields of design and marketing also have important roles to play.

References

Arnheim, Rudolf (1971), *Entropy and Art: An Essay on Disorder and Order*. Berkeley, CA: University of California Press.

Baldwin, J. (1996), *Bucky Works: Buckminster Fuller's Ideals for Today*. New York: John Wiley & Sons.

Barry, Maxx (1999), *Syrup*. New York: Viking Press.

Borgmann, Albert (1995), "The Depth of Design," in *Discovering Design: Explorations in Design Studies*. Chicago: University of Chicago Press, 13–22.

Csikszentmihalyi, Mihaly and Eugene Rochberg-Halton (1981) *The Meaning of Thing: Domestic Symbols and the Self*. Cambridge: Cambridge University Press.

Dossey, Larry (1982), *Space, Time and Medicine*. Boston: Shambhala.

Ewen, Stuart (1976), *Captains of Consciousness: Advertising and the Social Roots of the Consumer Culture*. New York: McGraw-Hill.

——— (1988), *All Consuming Images: The Politics of Style in Contemporary Culture*. New York: HarperCollins Publishers.

Forty, Adrian (1986), *Objects of Desire: Design and Society Since 1750*. London: Thames and Hudson.

Johnson, Patricia (1999), "Sensation Flurry Obscures the Art," *Houston Chronicle*, (October 13), 1D, 5D.

Lynch, Don (1999), "Draw the Line at Elephant Dung on the Virgin Mary," *Houston Chronicle,* (September 29), 29A.

Marchand, Roland (1985), *Advertising the American Dream.* Berkeley, CA: University of California Press.

Patton, Angela H. and George M. Zinkhan (1998), "Cultural History as a Thematic Study: Analyzing Advertisements to Interpret American Home Design," *Journal of Interior Design*, 24 (2), 25–32.

Phillips, Lisa (1985), Introduction to *High Styles: Twentieth-Century American Design.* New York: Summit Books, ix–xi.

Rushkoff, Douglas (1999), *Coercion: Why We Listen to What They Say.* New York: Riverhead Books.

Schjeldahl, Peter (1999), "Those Nasty Brits: How Sensational Is Sensation?" *The New Yorker*, (October 11), 104–105.

Solomon, Deborah (1999), "The Collector," *The New York Times Magazine,* (September 26), 44–49.

Slater, Don (1997), *Consumer Culture and Modernity.* Cambridge: Polity Press.

Thoreau, Henry David (1854), *Walden*, 29th ed. New York: The New American Library.

Twain, Mark (1889), *A Connecticut Yankee in King Arthur's Court.* New York: C.L. Webster & Company.

Zyman, Sergio (1999), *The End of Marketing As We Know It.* New York: HarperBusiness.

13

Environmentalist–Business Collaborations: Social Responsibility, Green Alliances, and Beyond

Edwin R. Stafford
Utah State University

Cathy L. Hartman
Utah State University

Marketers are engaging in cooperative relationships with environmental, non-government organizations (NGOs) to form *green alliances*. In practice, many green alliances have encountered skepticism from consumers and criticism from other stakeholders because of perceptions that the cohesive environmentalist-marketer ties were inappropriate, given their relationship structure or activities. This article advances a green alliance credibility framework to describe how consumers and other stakeholders make sense of and respond to green alliances. Specifically, it proposes that the ability of a partnering environmental NGO's *organizational credibility* to enhance the marketer's credibility and image is contingent on the partnership's *relationship credibility*. The framework specifies the dimensions and criteria that consumers and other stakeholders use to evaluate organizational and relationship credibility. Implications for sustainable marketing communications management and research are offered.

Introduction

In the spring of 1989, Loblaws, Canada's largest food retailer, launched a new private-label product line called, "GREEN," which was designed to be "environmentally friendly" and to fill growing consumer demand for green products (Kohl 1990). The products obtained significant market share, in part, because of a novel and exclusive cooperative relationship with Pollution Probe, an environmental NGO, that certified the product line (Stafford and Hartman 1996; Westley and Vredenburg 1991). Pollution Probe intended that its certification would educate consumers, shift market demand toward environmentally preferable products, and ultimately influence industry to become more environmentally sensitive.

The innovative partnership, however, proved controversial. The agreement, which had been negotiated in secrecy for competitive reasons, provided Pollution Probe a 1% royalty on sales to cover the NGO's research and certification expenditures. When this arrangement was announced publicly, many Pollution Probe scientists and staff who were not briefed beforehand resigned in protest over what they perceived as an inappropriate relationship. Greenpeace, another environmental group, was suspicious of the certification and analyzed Loblaws's GREEN fertilizer, finding traces of toxins. Greenpeace publicly criticized Pollution Probe's ambiguous certification criteria and accused the partnership as simply exploitation to sell products and raise funds for the NGO (Manolson 1989). Other activists staged demonstrations in Loblaws's parking lots by handing out satirical leaflets that denounced Loblaws's GREEN products as "Pure GREED" (Stafford and Hartman 1996). The negative publicity ultimately forced Pollution Probe to dissolve the relationship, and the NGO became a weaker, less credible environmental force (Murphy and Bendell 1997).

The widely publicized Pollution Probe–Loblaws endorsement partnership illustrates the inherent paradox of environmental NGO–marketer relationships. Long and Arnold (1995, p. 33) summarize the paradox as follows:

> [Environmental groups] face a unique challenge when they enter into partnerships. They risk losing ground in other areas when they gain ground through the partnership. Many environmental organizations were built on the principle of fighting the offenses of corporations and the intrusions of government. They receive financial support from thousands of individuals who value their "watchdog" role. When nonprofits tap into the potential of partnerships, they must work hard to educate their membership and avoid compromising either their independence or their ability to maintain the public's trust.

Striking the right balance between environmental progress and credibility is crucial for environmental NGO–marketer relationships. As an unanticipated "public" or stakeholder reacting to the partnership, Greenpeace shattered the social credibility of the Pollution Probe–Loblaws relationship by calling its intent into question. Stakeholders, defined as "any group or individual who can affect or is affected by" (Freeman 1984, p. 46) an organization's objectives or actions, warrant careful consideration for environmental NGO–marketer partnerships because of how they respond to green marketing activities and their ability to engage and influence other social entities, such as the media and consumers (Polonsky 1996). Environmental stakeholders may include consumers, channel members, employees, shareholders and the financial community, environmental NGOs, academia, government agencies and policymakers, and the general public. Thus, environmental NGO–marketer cooperation faces a network of stakeholder influences (Rowley 1997). Table 1 summarizes traditional environmental stakeholders, their primary interests, potential environmental messages, and useful marketing communications vehicles to reach these stakeholders. Stakeholder management suggests that organizations need to adapt their strategies and marketing communications to meet or address stakeholder interests (Freeman 1984; Polonsky 1996). Procuring stakeholder support may be instrumental in achieving green marketing performance goals (Clarkson 1995; Donaldson and Preston 1995).

Following the Pollution Probe–Loblaws relationship, the 1990s have witnessed a proliferation of *green alliances*, defined as collaborative partnerships between environmental NGOs and businesses that pursue mutually beneficial ecological goals (Stafford and Hartman 1996), with such NGOs as the Environmental Defense Fund

Table 1
Environmental Stakeholders and Their Information Needs

Stakeholders	Primary Interests	Environmental Messages	Promotional Vehicles
Customers	Product quality; prices; product safety and liability	Selling environmentally sound products; willingness to contribute to consumer safety; environmental problems	Advertising; press information; product labeling; hotlines; direct mail; Web sites
Channel Members	Product quality; prices; product demand; product safety and liability; litigation risk; ISO-certification	Disclosure of environmental problems; desire to meet channel member demands	Environmental report; press information; newsletter; product labeling; Web site
Competitors	Product positioning; environmental benchmarking	Product, price, and environmental performance comparisons	Environmental report; advertising; press information; Web site
Shareholders/ Financial Community	Financial results; reporting of all liabilities; limitation of future liabilities; litigation risk	Risk management; cost savings through improved environmental management	Environmental report; annual report; newsletter; press information; Web site
Employees/Unions	Job security; salaries; pride; industrial safety; education	Transparency of decision making; environmental policies, objectives, and results	Environmental report; social report; annual report; notice board; internal newsletter; negotiations; Web site
Community	Health hazards; noise; odors; discharges to land, water, and air; knowledge of business activities	Pollution reduction; responsible waste management; attention to neighbors' concerns	Environmental report; site visit; newsletter; information department; press information; ad-hoc troubleshooting groups; public meetings; Web site
Government Agencies and Regulators	Compliance with environmental regulations and policies; ISO-certification	Environmentally responsible activities; overview of costs and benefits of environmental actions	Environmental report; negotiations; press information; Web site

Table 1
continued

Stakeholders	Primary Interests	Environmental Messages	Promotional Vehicles
Environmental NGOs	Site/neighbor information; impacts on ecosystems; compliance with environmental regulations and policies; fit with environmental agenda	Improvement of environmental performance; interest/involvement in environmental NGO cooperation to improve matters	Environmental report; site visit; annual report; negotiations; newsletter; press information; Web site
Academia/Scientific Community	Monitor corporate/industry trends; comparative studies	Current and future environmental policies; regulatory compliance record; details of environmental management systems; environmental performance results	Environmental report; annual report; site visit; newsletter; press information; Web site
Media	Information dissemination	Disclosure of environmental objectives and environmental progress	Environmental report; press information; newsletter; site visit; Web site

Adapted from Azzone et al. (1997); Kolk (1998)

(EDF), Ducks Unlimited, the National Wildlife Federation, the Natural Resources Defense Council (NRDC), World-Wide Fund for Nature (WWF), and even Greenpeace on the forefront of the movement (see Crane 1998; Hartman and Stafford 1998; Lober 1997; Murphy and Bendell 1997). Promotions and media attention thrust green alliances into the public spotlight, and the perceived credibility of such partnerships among stakeholders is fundamental to *legitimacy*, defined as the organization's appearance of meeting the expectations of external constituents (Oliver 1990). Oliver (1990, p. 246) asserts that, "Attempts to enhance legitimacy through relationship formation will be directed especially toward organizations whose level of legitimacy is perceived by the focal organization to be considerably higher than its own." In green alliances, marketers seek well-known and reputable environmental NGO partners to legitimize and enhance the credibility of their own environmental and social images, operations, and products.

Although *source credibility*, the overall trustworthiness of the source (Petty and Capioccio 1981), has been extensively researched, most studies have focused on the "individual" as source (Hammond 1987) with few concentrating on the "organization" as source or *organizational credibility* (Haley 1996). Previous research confirms that nonprofit environmental organizational sources are perceived to be more credible than commercial sources (Cooper 1994). For example, Ozanne and Vlosky (1998) found that consumers perceived environmental NGOs as the most trustworthy to provide a sustainably harvested wood products certification, whereas the wood products industry was perceived as the least trustworthy. Such evidence supports marketers' motives to ally with environmental NGOs (Milne, Iyer, and Gooding-Williams 1996). However, given environmental NGOs' adversarial "watchdog" role, *relationship credibility* becomes a significant issue (Stafford and Hartman 1996). That is, do stakeholders believe a cooperative relationship is in the best interest of the environment and society? Under what conditions are such relationships appropriate? What are the implications for marketing communications?

Little research has examined how stakeholders make sense of green alliances, and this analysis explores this issue by advancing a framework that specifies the dimensions and criteria that stakeholders use to evaluate the credibility of and formulate responses to environmental NGO–marketer relationships. It is proposed that the environmental NGO's ability to enhance a marketer's environmental image is contingent on the perceived relationship credibility between the NGO and the marketer. This article first presents a brief overview of the environmental NGO–marketer cooperation movement, describing the basic forms of cooperation and the significance of relationship credibility. The framework is then developed using source credibility and stakeholder research, supplemented by specific case examples to illustrate implications. Recommendations for structuring credible relationships and sustainable marketing communications are discussed, and future research directions are proposed.

Environmental NGO–Marketer Cooperative Relations

Over the past decade, the culture of the environmental movement has been transforming from one of protest to one of practical solutions. Environmental NGOs have become increasingly interested in working "within the system" (Milne, Iyer, and Gooding-Williams 1996, p. 203), favoring market, social, and public policy reforms to encourage environmentally sensitive corporate practices over "command-and-control" regulatory mechanisms that typically pit business interests against environmental concerns (Krupp 1994; Lober 1997). For environmental initiatives to be adopted widely, environmental NGOs are recognizing that the needs of businesses, employees, customers, and other stakeholders must be considered simultaneously.

Likewise, marketers are increasingly facing social, legal, and global market pressures to operate more sustainably (Zinkhan and Carlson 1995). Many are realizing that cooperative environmental NGOs can be allies for facilitating the development of appropriate and credible environmental initiatives (Lober 1997). The increasing use of interorganizational relationships to facilitate more credible green products and communications implies a recognition that individual marketers on their own cannot provide the most effective solutions to environmental problems (Crane 1998). A recent study conducted by Roper Starch Worldwide (1998, p. 25) for The Nature Conservancy found that 69% of Americans polled believe that having corporations work with environmental groups is the "most effective way for corporations to improve the environment." Similarly, the study found that 72% of those polled believe having environmental NGOs work with corporations is the "most effective way for environmental groups to improve the environment" (p. 25). As partners, an environmental NGO can provide marketers (1) technical and legal expertise, (2) an enhanced social image, and (3) commercial venture opportunities (Dutton 1996; Milne, Iyer, and Gooding-Williams 1996). The Pollution Probe–Loblaws partnership, for example, attempted to achieve both profit and environmental progress by capitalizing on the growing demand for green products through certification.

Gray (1989, p. 5) defines *collaboration* as a "process through which partners who see different aspects of a problem can constructively explore their differences and search for solutions that go beyond their own limited vision of what is possible." Thus, environmentalist-marketer collaboration encourages finding the "common ground" between ecological and commercial interests through environmental entrepreneurial activities, referred to as *enviropreneurship*—innovations and technological approaches that address environmental problems and accommodate societal needs to meet economic objectives (Menon and Menon 1997). Indeed, both Loblaws and Pollution Probe considered their certification alliance a "win-win-win" for the environment, society, and economics. In addition to green products, enviropreneurial strategies can lead to operational efficiencies through resource reductions and competitive advantages through new technologies (see Menon and Menon 1997; Porter and van der Linde 1995). Although not all environmental initiatives achieve competitive gains (see Esty and Porter 1998), a confluence of ecological, social, and market objectives is possible from green alliances because they create collaborative forums for environmental stakeholders to define problems, discuss needs, establish common ground, and implement mutually agreeable environmental programs to address the needs of involved parties (Gray 1989). Table 2 summarizes several recent successful green alliances and their enviropreneurial objectives.

Types of Green Alliances

In practice, six forms of environmental NGO–marketer cooperation have been identified by Hartman and Stafford (1997; Stafford and Hartman 1998), ranging from simple to complex. The simplest form is *licensing*, whereby a marketer licenses an environmental NGO's name and offers products under the NGO's "brand" (e.g., Bushnell licenses the National Audubon Society's name for its binoculars). If an environmental "brand" possesses high recognition and perceived value, licensing offers a way for marketers to access new markets; customers affiliated with environmental

Table 2
Examples of Environmental NGO–Marketer Cooperation and Their Enviropreneurial Initiatives

Name	Key Participants	Location	Principal Time Frame	Enviropreneurial Initiatives
Bronx Community Paper Company	Natural Resources Defense Council (Advisor), MoDo Paper Company, S.D. Warren Company, The Banana Kelly Bronx Community Improvement Association	New York City	1994–Present	For-profit joint venture for recycling and pulp deinking of New York City office waste
Greenfreeze Campaign	Greenpeace, Foron Household Appliances	Germany	1992–93	Marketing of an ozone-safe refrigerator motivating industrywide adoption of eco-technology
McDonald's Sweden Environmental Program	The Natural Step, McDonald's Sweden	Sweden	1995–96	Employee/management training and consultation in environmentally sensitive packaging, waste management, energy conservation, and alternative construction materials
The Nature Conservancy Georgia Pacific Roanoke River Project	The Nature Conservancy, Georgia Pacific	North Carolina, United States	1994–Present	Biodiversity protection and timber production using ecosystem management principles
Paper Task Force	Environmental Defense Fund, Duke University, Johnson & Johnson, McDonald's, Prudential Insurance, Time Inc.	United States	1993–95	Environmentally sensitive paper buying/use recommendations to facilitate operational efficiencies and technological advances
Partnership for Regulatory Innovation and Sustainable Manufacturing (PRISM)	Environmental Defense Fund, General Motors, Environmental Protection Agency, Dayton Power & Light, various community groups	Primarily United States	1996–99	Promote innovative environmental management and regulatory systems in vehicle manufacturing
Ricelands Habitat Partnership (RHP)	The Nature Conservancy, Ducks Unlimited, California Waterfowl Association, California Rice Industry Association, Sacramento Valley Rice Farmers	Sacramento Valley of California, United States	1990–Present	Postharvest winter field flooding program to create temporary waterfowl habitat and facilitate rice stubble decomposition
Waste Reduction Task Force	Environmental Defense Fund, McDonald's	Primarily United States	1990–91	42-step waste reduction program for McDonald's to facilitate operational efficiencies

groups compose attractive markets because of their affluence and high education levels (Harris 1992). However, licensing does not appear to fulfill an effective "communications" role about the interorganizational relationship to consumers; under an environmental NGO's brand name, the manufacturer may neither be associated with the product nor receive public recognition (Mendleson and Polonsky 1995). Therefore, licensing provides limited environmental image credibility for either organization, and relationship credibility is weak.

Another simpler form in which the environmental NGO–marketer relationship is more explicit is *corporate sponsorships* in which marketers donate resources to the environmental NGO through involvement in relevant causes (e.g., Eastman Kodak's funding of the World Wildlife Fund's environmental literacy program). For the marketer, the goals of environmental sponsorships are to enhance the marketer's image or increase brand awareness by promoting the marketer's association with the environmental NGO or cause (Cornwell and Maignan 1998). A moderately complex form of cooperation involves *product endorsements* or *certifications*, whereby an environmental NGO approves a product as "environmentally preferable" (e.g., Rainforest Alliance certifies "SmartWood" harvested from "sustainably managed" forests). As with the Pollution Probe–Loblaws certification partnership, the environmental NGO must be perceived as expert and trustworthy for making a valid endorsement (Hovland, Janis, and Kelly 1953), and the intent of the relationship must be perceived to be in the public's and environment's interests.

A more complex form of environmentalist-marketer cooperation includes *task forces* in which environmental NGOs and marketers collaborate to analyze corporate practices to propose economically feasible environmental solutions (e.g., EDF-McDonald's Waste Reduction Task Force). Although the key strategic objective of task forces centers on improving the environmental performance of operations and processes, publicity and promotions play a significant role for "selling" the legitimacy of the task force and its outcomes to stakeholders. A special form of task forces is the public policy task force in which environmental NGOs collaborate with marketers and public policymakers to study and propose market-based environmental government policies. (For example, Partnership for Regulatory Innovation and Sustainable Manufacturing [PRISM], initiated by EDF, promotes environmental management and regulatory systems in vehicle manufacturing.) The central purpose of these alliances is to curtail economically burdensome "command-and-control" environmental regulations and to promote policies that provide firms compliance flexibility (e.g., through tradable pollution permits) or enviropreneurial innovation incentives (e.g., green tax credits) (see Porter and van der Linde 1995; Stavins and Whitehead 1997). Because marketers' efforts to influence environmental public policies may be viewed with suspicion, communications surrounding public policy task forces play a critical role in shaping stakeholders' beliefs about the intent of proposals.

The most complex form of cooperation is *green systems alliances* in which environmental NGOs and marketers collaborate to implement economically feasible environmental solutions (e.g., Bronx Community Paper Company, a joint venture employing ecologically responsible processes, uniting NRDC, MoDo Paper Company, S.D. Warren Company, and the Kelly Community Improvement Association). Compared with task forces (which tend to be shorter-term and issue-specific), green systems alliances entail more strategically comprehensive relationships that involve greater resource investment among partners and multiple enviropreneurial value chain activities (Hartman and Stafford 1998). Similar to task forces, however, public scrutiny and media attention are critical for legitimizing green alliance initiatives and outcomes.

In green alliances, appropriate environmental partners provide marketers social influence and bridges to other social entities to support enviropreneurial initiatives (Brown 1991; Westley and Vredenburg 1991). Through their credibility, environmental groups can leverage marketer relationships with other diverse social stakeholders, such as consumers, government agencies, other environmental NGOs, and the media, which may traditionally be skeptical, critical, or ambivalent toward marketers but nevertheless possess resources critical to support marketers' environmental programs (Mendleson and Polonsky 1995). For example, consumers may be willing to buy a marketer's green products if they believe the environmental NGO has endorsed the product or contributed to the product's development. Likewise, government agencies may be more flexible regarding environmental policies for firms or industries that are working with environmental NGOs (Cardskadden and Lober 1998; Hemphill 1996).

The ability of an environmental NGO to build social support for a marketer's products or initiative hinges on the environmental NGO's reputation and image within society (Lober 1997; Westley and Vredenburg 1991). Paradoxically, as illustrated by the Pollution Probe–Loblaws partnership case, perceptions of the collaborative relationship itself can imperil the environmental NGO's public credibility. As cooperative partners, environmental NGOs are like elephants walking a tight rope. Perceptions that the environmental NGO is "selling out" to corporate interests can seriously harm the green alliance's credibility, potentially jeopardizing the environmental NGO itself, enviropreneurial initiatives, and environmental gains. Our framework, presented next, attempts to discern how stakeholders make sense of environmental NGO–marketer relationships by specifying the determinants that contribute to perceived credibility.

Organizational and Relationship Credibility: Framework Overview

Our framework of stakeholders' understandings of environmental NGO–marketer cooperative relations extends Haley's (1996) model of consumer assessment of organizational credibility by drawing from green alliance cases. It is anchored in stakeholder perceptions of four key elements, including the (1) marketer, (2) environmental NGO, (3) environmental issue, and (4) stakeholder's self-perception. The framework illustrates how stakeholders link these perceived elements to assess the overall credibility of a green alliance. Specifically, green alliance research suggests that when the marketer's organization credibility is deficient with respect to its environmental objectives, an environmental NGO partner's organizational credibility can help close this gap (Fuller 1999; Milne, Iyer, and Gooding-Williams 1996; Murphy and Bendell 1997). We propose, however, that this credibility enhancement through the partnership is contingent on the environmental NGO–marketer's *relationship credibility* that we define as the trustworthiness and legitimacy of the cooperative activities between the partners. The green alliance's overall credibility will determine a stakeholder's evaluation of the partnership's appropriateness and response (i.e., supportive or critical). Figure 1 illustrates the framework and summarizes the proposed determinants that stakeholders use to evaluate linkages between the perceived elements.

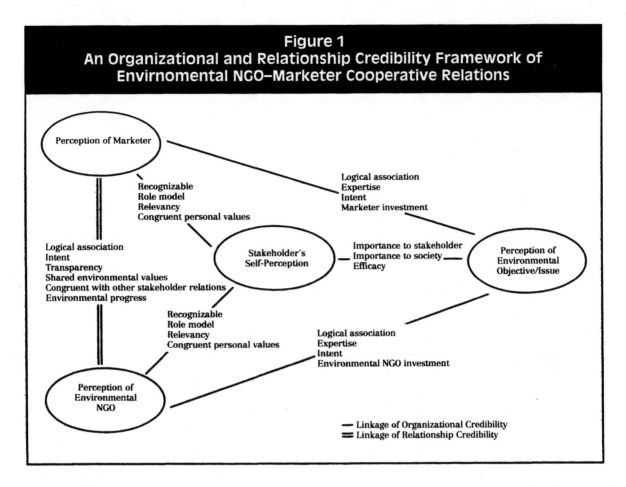

Figure 1
An Organizational and Relationship Credibility Framework of
Envirnomental NGO–Marketer Cooperative Relations

Following Haley (1996), organizational credibility of green alliance partners is made up of three elements and is represented by two triads in Figure 1. Marketer organizational credibility is composed of (1) a stakeholder's self-perception, (2) perception of the environmental objective/issue, and (3) perception of the marketer. Environmental NGO organizational credibility is composed of (1) a stakeholder's self-perception, (2) perception of environmental objective/issue, and (3) perception of the environmental NGO. Relationship credibility encompasses the linkage between the stakeholder's perception of (1) the marketer and (2) the environmental NGO.

Organizational Credibility of Environmental NGOs and Marketers

When evaluating an environmental NGO's or marketer's organizational credibility, stakeholders compare their self-perceptions to their perceptions of each organization. Environmental NGO or marketer credibility is enhanced if stakeholders perceive the organization to be (1) recognizable, (2) a role model, (3) relevant to their interests, and (4) sharing common values with them (Haley 1996). In terms of recognizability, stakeholders will consider whether the organizations and their products or missions are well-known (Vanden Bergh, Soley, and Reid 1981). With regard to being a role model, stakeholders will consider organizational histories and actions, products or achievements, and community service (Dutton 1996; Winters 1986). Some marketers, such as Ben & Jerry's Homemade Ice Cream, The Body Shop, and

Patagonia, have positioned themselves as environmentally and socially responsible by advocating industry "best ecological practices" and adhering to standards such as ISO 14000 (Chouinard and Brown 1997; Curren 1994; Shrivastava 1995). Likewise, effective environmental NGOs maintain strong public images as environmental role models. EDF has built a reputation as a skilled corporate collaborator, facilitating substantive environmental progress with high-profile corporations (Fastiggi 1999). Stakeholders also consider the relevancy of the organization, that is, the extent that the environmental NGO or marketer has some pertinence to or can affect them (Donaldson and Preston 1995; Freeman 1984). Last, stakeholders contemplate to what extent the environmental NGO or marketer shares values with them. Environmental NGOs that advocate militant behavior or marketers that sell objectionable products may be offensive to some stakeholders. In summary, the linkage between the stakeholder's self-perception and that of the organization is an important component of organizational credibility.

In addition, stakeholders will consider the linkage between their perceptions of each organization and the environmental issue (Haley 1996). Stakeholders will perceive an environmental NGO or marketer as more credible if the organization appears to have (1) a logical association, (2) relevant expertise, (3) appropriate intent, and (4) investment and commitment to the environmental issue. With regard to logical association, the organization must be perceived as having some identifiable relevance to the environmental issue. Many environmental NGOs identify with specific environmental causes (e.g., Ducks Unlimited with waterfowl habitat conservation; Hartman and Stafford 1998), and stakeholders will consider how marketers "connect" with their environmental causes or objectives (e.g., Patagonia with organically grown cotton; Chouinard and Brown 1997). In terms of expertise (Hovland, Janis, and Kelly 1953), marketers are likely to be perceived as not having the necessary expertise with their environmental objectives (e.g., McDonald's and waste reduction), and the partnering environmental NGO's expertise is expected to compensate for the marketer's deficiency (e.g., EDF partnered with McDonald's to address the restaurant's excessive waste output in the Waste Reduction Task Force; Stafford and Hartman 1996) (Milne, Iyer, and Gooding-Williams 1996; Vincett 1991). For intent, stakeholders will assess the genuineness of the organization's commitment and devotion to its environmental mission. If marketers stand to make significant economic gains by promoting an environmental image, stakeholders may question motives. Last, stakeholders will consider the significance of the organization's investment in the environmental issue. For both environmental NGOs and marketers, programs, resources, and funding devoted to environmental causes demonstrate investment (Fastiggi 1999). On balance, the linkage between the organization and the environmental issue in question is another critical component of organizational credibility.

Finally, stakeholders assess the relationship between their self-perceptions and their perceptions of the environmental issue in terms of its (1) importance to the stakeholder, (2) importance to society, and (3) efficacy (Haley 1996). Stakeholders will consider whether the environmental issue is important to their personal lives and well-being. For example, coffee retailer Starbucks faces the "double-cup" problem—having to use two, stacked disposable cups for each serving to ensure customers' comfort (*EDF Letter* 1996). To reduce waste, Starbucks encourages customers to bring in their own cups. Although potentially inconvenient, consumers may support this idea if waste reduction is of importance to them and they can appreciate its importance to society in terms of environmental sustainability. With regard to efficacy, stakeholders will consider if any actions can address the organization's environmental issue effectively. Research suggests that consumers respond favorably to environmental causes if they believe their personal actions will make a difference (Ellen, Winer, and Cobb-Walgren 1991). Another issue facing coffee retailers is the need to grow some coffee varieties in full sunlight, which is a leading cause for tropical forest clear-cutting (Tasker 1998). As a means of "protecting" rain forests, some marketers and environmental NGOs are advocating that consumers drink "shade-grown" coffee that is planted beneath canopies of trees, making it "rain forest friendly." Stakeholders will evaluate whether saving the rain forest is possible and if "my action can help" (Haley 1996, p. 30); that is, if their loyalty to shade-grown coffee can meaningfully lessen rain forest destruction. In summary, organizational credibility involves how stakeholders link perceptions about themselves, the organization (marketer or environmental NGO), and environmental issue. Relationship credibility between an environmental NGO and a marketer is another important contingency.

Relationship Credibility of Environmental NGO–Marketer Cooperation

Our significant departure from Haley's (1996) framework is the concept of *relationship credibility*, defined as the overall trustworthiness and legitimacy of the cooperative activities between the environmental NGO and the marketer. In other words, does the stakeholder believe the relationship is in the best interest of the environment and society? Previous conceptual and case research on green alliances (Stafford and Hartman 1996; Westley and Vredenburg 1991) suggests that relationship credibility is contingent on the (1) logical association between partners, (2) intent of the relationship, (3) transparency of the relationship, (4) shared environmental values between the partners, (5) whether the green alliance is congruent with other stakeholder relationships engaged by the partners, and (6) extent of environmental progress.

To determine relationship credibility, stakeholders will consider whether the green alliance partners have a logical association (Vincett 1991). The relationship between the environmental NGO and the marketer must appear relevant in that the marketer's environmental deficiency or objective is being addressed by an appropriate environmental NGO partner. For example, the Rainforest Alliance certifies "SmartWood" because it is harvested from "sustainably managed" forests (Ozanne and Vlosky 1998) and shade-grown coffee because it is grown under rain forest canopy (Tasker 1998). These certifications assess the effect of forest activities against stakeholder-endorsed standards, assuring the public of independent and professional judgment. Green alliance marketing communications need to educate stakeholders of the partners' logical association.

Stakeholders will also evaluate the intent of the relationship (Westley and Vredenburg 1991). Green alliance activities should advance the common good, and promotions and press information need to inform consumers and other stakeholders about the social responsibility of the relationship. Greenpeace's criticism of the Pollution Probe–Loblaws's certification partnership centered largely on how the partnership's structure—secretive negotiations, exclusive certification, ambiguous certification criteria, and sales royalty—potentially compromised the partnership's genuineness for enhancing consumer demand for green products and transforming industry (Manolson 1989).

One of the risks of corporate sponsorships of environmental NGOs is that marketers may engage in them for reasons other than the attainment of environmental progress. As such, critical stakeholders may question the intent of corporate sponsorships, regarding them only as superficial image-building (Hartman and Stafford 1997). One illustration involved Coca-Cola's sponsorship of the National Parks and Conservation Association, in which the marketer planted a tree in the California Redwood National Park for each proof-of-purchase emblem from Minute Maid products and 75-cent donation mailed in by consumers. The sponsorship was criticized because of Minute Maid's nonbiodegradable aseptic packaging. Mockingly, another environmental NGO publicly disparaged Minute Maid with its "Wastemaker Award," and the corporate sponsorship's environmental intent lost credibility (Mendleson and Polonsky 1995). Demonstrating the green alliance's genuine and socially acceptable intent is critical for relationship credibility.

Related to intent is the need for transparency where the environmental NGO–marketer agreement parameters and partnership activities are open to stakeholder scrutiny and feedback (Dutton 1996; Murphy and Bendell 1997). Failure to involve organizations, policymakers, media, and other stakeholders reduces the partnership's impact, regardless of the environmental progress made by the participants (Gray 1989; Long and Arnold 1995). Transparency has been particularly critical for the Marine Stewardship Council (MSC), established in February 1997 from a partnership between the WWF and Unilever to institute industrywide certifications and market incentives for sustainably harvested fish products (Fowler and Heap 1998). As one of the world's largest fish marketers, Unilever controls approximately 25% market share of the frozen fish industry in Europe and the United States, and declining global fish stocks is threatening Unilever's business. Ideally, sustainable fish harvesting standards that are adhered to by a variety of disparate stakeholders, including competitors, customers, suppliers, and fishing fleets across nations, are critical. WWF and Unilever provided seed money to establish MSC, and its principles and criteria were developed from consultation with a broad range of stakeholders. Fowler and Heap (1998) report that "National Working Groups" established in various European countries provide communication between fisheries' representatives and the MSC Advisory Board, with dialogue processes also being instituted in Latin America. Although Unilever's competitors tolerated the company's involvement in the early stages of the partnership, in June 1998, Unilever officially ended its financial and managerial support to demonstrate the partners' intent to make MSC an independent, standard-setting, and accreditation body. Ultimately, informing stakeholders of Unilever's severed ties was critical for creating stakeholder confidence in MSC's authority (see Fowler and Heap 1998). The transparency of environmental NGO–marketer relationships is fundamental for building stakeholder support and establishing relationship credibility.

The shared environmental values between the environmental NGO and the marketer need to be communicated clearly and convincingly. The marketer must be perceived as part of the environmental problem's solution (Dutton 1996). In the Ricelands Habitat Partnership (RHP), Sacramento Valley rice farmers posted signs on their properties declaring, "Wildlife Habitat Managed by Landowner," to inform the community of their participation in a postharvest, winter field flooding program that eliminated their need to burn rice straw and provided habitat for migratory waterfowl (Hartman and Stafford 1998). Before the partnership's formation in 1990, rice farmers were criticized for postharvest field burning of rice straw that polluted the air and destroyed bird habitat. When new clean air legislation restricted field burning, the Nature Conservancy, Ducks Unlimited, and the California Waterfowl Association came forward to partner with the California Rice Industry Association and persuade the U.S. Bureau of Reclamation to provide farmers water to initiate field flooding as an alternative disposal method. The flooded fields simultaneously created temporary waterfowl nesting places and feeding grounds where the birds aided microbial decomposition of the straw by trampling it and adding their droppings. The rotting straw that otherwise would have been burned returned nutrients to the soil. The posted signs communicated the farmers' shared concerns for waterfowl, enhancing their social image as a protector of the valley's wildlife (Hartman and Stafford 1998).

Stakeholders will also compare the green alliance to associations the partners have with other social and community entities. The green alliance should be perceived as congruent with other stakeholder relationships maintained by the environmental NGO and the marketer, reinforcing stakeholders' existing organizational beliefs and expectations (Javalgi et al. 1994). The Waste Reduction Task Force between McDonald's and EDF in 1990 was a first for both organizations. Despite the negative publicity surrounding McDonald's environmental record, the marketer maintained a strong positive social image from its long history of proactive community outreach involving the Ronald McDonald House (lodging for families visiting critically ill children in hospitals) and affiliated children's charities (Livesey 1991). Just before the green alliance, McDonald's had increased its environmental education projects with other environmental NGOs aimed primarily at elementary school children. McDonald's participation in the Waste Reduction Task Force appeared to be the next logical step in its stakeholder/community relationships. In contrast, before its partnership activities, EDF's motto had been "Sue the Bastards," and the environmental NGO had a reputation as an aggressive environmental litigator (Stafford and Hartman 1996). The task force with McDonald's appeared to be an about-face, and some critics saw this as EDF's "sell out" to business interests (see Dowie 1995). Despite initial skepticism, the task force's eventual success at reducing McDonald's waste stream transformed EDF's image to a results-oriented corporate collaborator. Since the McDonald's project, EDF has successfully partnered with several *Fortune* 500 companies, implementing a variety of practical, market-based solutions for improving environmental performance (Fastiggi 1999). Environmental NGOs that work with businesses do not see themselves as "selling out" to business interests but rather "buying in" to corporate consciousness (Dowie 1995).

Last, consumers and stakeholders will assess whether environmental progress results from the environmental NGO–marketer relationship (Long and Arnold 1995; Vincett 1991). In the RHP, winter field flooding created the most cost-effective method for compliance with mandated air quality laws, and the public witnessed an immediate improvement in air quality and bird populations. Legislators and regulatory agencies were pleased with the proactive environmental program, and farmers earned a more favorable relationship with public policymakers on environment and farming issues (Hartman and Stafford 1998).

The most publicized outcome of the EDF–McDonald's Waste Reduction Task Force was the discontinued use of the polystyrene clamshell packaging (Murphy and Bendell 1997). After a year of collaboration, however, the task force had launched 41 additional waste reduction initiatives (many of them cost-saving), ranging from reduced napkin sizes to reusable shipping pallets to composting of restaurant waste (see Environmental Defense Fund and McDonald's Corporation 1991). By 1995, the number of waste reduction initiatives expanded to more than 100 (Murphy and Bendell 1997), and McDonald's "McRecycle USA" program reached the milestone of $1 billion in purchases of products made from recycled materials, five years ahead of schedule (Stafford and Hartman 1996). A "ripple effect" also resulted in which Burger King and other fast-food restaurants adopted similar waste reduction programs (Stafford and Hartman 1996). Publicizing tangible results can dispel potential stakeholder cynicism of green alliances.

Our framework proposes that green alliance credibility is founded on the organizational and relationship credibilities of the green alliance partners, which are derived from stakeholders' perceptions of the linkages among four key elements, including the (1) marketer, (2) environmental NGO, (3) environmental issue, and (4) stakeholder's self-perception. The framework suggests several implications for stakeholder communications.

Implications for Marketing Communications

Marketing communications (advertising, sales promotion, personal selling, and publicity) play a significant role in enviropreneurial marketing and the strategic positioning of environmental NGO–marketer collaboration. Although marketing communications often are criticized as a source of puffery and misinformation (e.g., "green washing"), the legitimate purpose of marketing communications is to provide complete and appropriate information about products and market alternatives to foster the customer's ability to make informed choices (Fuller 1999). In enviropreneurial marketing, sustainable marketing communications has been proposed as marketing's responsibility to establish a "continuous, multilevel, and consistent exchange between the organization and its customer-publics" (Harrison 1994, p. 8) to reinforce an organization's environmental orientation and encourage useful input and output and stakeholder feedback.

Motivated by the need for environmental *sustainability*, the appropriate and efficient use of resources so that demand does not outrun or damage the environment's long-term life-supporting ability (Franck and Brownstone 1992), marketing must turn away from traditional one-way, preprogrammed messages to designated targets and encourage interactive information exchanges with customers and stakeholders to nurture environmental transparency and credibility (Harrison 1994). Sustainable marketing communications establish stakeholder relationships for responding to dynamic forces and channels involved in environmental performance and reputation. In short, sustainable marketing communications must strive to (1) educate diverse stakeholders about environmental issues, (2) build communications relationships, and (3) establish and maintain environmental credibility (Fuller 1999).

For green alliances, sustainable marketing communications must educate other stakeholders about enviropreneurial initiatives and deliver genuine messages that the green alliance is meeting stakeholder interests, as summarized in Table 1. The determinants proposed in our framework represent practical communication aims for green alliance promotion managers. For example, using the promotion vehicles noted in Table 1, the objective of establishing relationship "transparency" may be realized through open, detailed, and frequent communications with stakeholders for feedback. Perceptions of "environmental progress" may be reinforced by publicizing tangible environmental outcomes and publishing environmental audits and reports.

Given the general suspicion of and the commercial connotations associated specifically with advertising, some environmental NGOs, such as EDF, restrict the use of their names in their marketing partners' mass promotions and point-of-sale messages, preferring to allow marketers to discuss their cooperative activities and outcomes only in annual environmental reports or similar fact-based, nonadvertising forms of communications (Fastiggi 1999). Conspicuous inclusion of the environmental partner's name in mass advertising could foster stakeholder perceptions that the NGO is "selling out" to the marketer's commercial interests, and Ottman (1995) recommends that advertising should play a "low-key" role in green marketing. In contrast, owing to its greater perceived believability, publicity in the form of press releases and environmental reports originating from the environmental NGO may be particularly convincing.

An effective sustainable marketing communications program, however, cannot compensate for poorly structured green alliance agreements and relationships. Green alliance partners must consider the determinants of organizational and relationship credibility when crafting and executing their cooperative initiatives to deflect negative publicity and stakeholder disapproval. The past experiences of some green alliances have generated important lessons for organization and relationship credibility and implications for marketing communications.

Green Alliance Partners Should Maintain an "Arm's-Length" Relationship

One key criticism of the Pollution Probe–Loblaws alliance involved the sales royalty. The environmental NGO appeared to be working for rather than with the food retailer as a true partner, which called into question the relationship's intent. Therefore, it is important for green alliance partners to work collaboratively but maintain independence. The American Oceans Campaign (AOC) has worked with oil companies on oil recycling while standing as one of the oil industry's most obstinate public critics (Hartman and Stafford 1997). Protests in the media of the oil industry maintains the NGO's organizational credibility as a crusader for the environment, and AOC views public protest as a "stick" to motivate businesses to cooperate with it.

Likewise, EDF has exercised great caution in developing arm's-length relationships with its corporate partners. EDF and its project with the Pew Charitable Trusts, called the Alliance of Environmental Innovation (AEI), use a carefully crafted "memorandum of agreement" (Fastiggi 1999) that declares that partners can exit their relationships at any time and must assume responsibility for their expenses. No money is ever to change hands. Furthermore, the partners agree to disagree with each other; if necessary, each partner can pen separate position statements on issues of disagreement in the partnership's final environmental reports, which are ultimately made public to facilitate transparency. Stipulations of EDF's agreements with business are presented to the media to communicate intent. Sustainable marketing communications stemming from green alliances need to emphasize the independence partners maintain within the relationship.

Green Alliance Programs and Objectives Should Be Clear and Defensible

Another controversy surrounding the Pollution Probe–Loblaws partnership was its ambiguous product certification criteria. Pollution Probe had also endorsed a GREEN "dioxin-free" disposable diaper made of pulp and plastic. Activists believed that because the diaper was intended for one-time use and could not be disassembled or biodegraded, the dioxin-free benefit was comparatively inconsequential to justify certification (Murphy and Bendell 1997; Stafford and Hartman 1996). Well-defined and respected evaluation mechanisms must be used to determine which products and processes meet acceptable environmental practices. Moreover, evidence of the environmental testing, if applicable, needs to be made public (Gallon 1991). Environmental standards and criteria must be incorporated into the green alliance's marketing communications to demonstrate intent and facilitate transparency.

The EDF–McDonald's partnership also encountered controversy over its abandonment of polystyrene clamshell sandwich packaging for quilted paper-polyethylene wraps. The quilted wraps could not be made of recycled content, owing to FDA restrictions regarding recycled materials' contact with food, nor was the wrapping biodegradable (Stafford and Hartman 1996). The polystyrene industry criticized the green alliance's alternative, suggesting that polystyrene was "better" for the environment. EDF and McDonald's countered those charges with the fact that the new wrapping used fewer resources and discharged less pollution at the point of manufacture. The EDF–McDonald's partnership was able to weather the controversy by grounding its actions in the defensible environmental objective of "resource reduction." McDonald's ultimately adopted an all-paper, biodegradable wrapping. Media attention and promotions surrounding these moves reinforced the partnership's intent to reduce McDonald's waste stream and communicated meaningful environmental progress.

It should be noted, however, that collaborative processes in green alliances that attempt to integrate competing demands of the environmental NGO, the marketer, and other stakeholders (e.g., consumer preferences or government requirements) are likely to result in compromised rather than ideal environmental solutions (Gray 1989). Environmental science is still an emerging discipline, and environmentalists, scientists, and policymakers continue to debate rather than come to consensus regarding appropriate ecological measures (Fuller 1999). As such, stakeholder criticism of green alliance outcomes is inevitable. Sustainable marketing communications, however, need to draw the connection between the marketer's socially acceptable environmental objectives (e.g., McDonald's need to reduce waste) and the environmental NGO's expertise (e.g., EDF's resource life cycle know-how) to signal the partners' coherent association with each other, invite stakeholder feedback, and communicate environmental progress.

Green Alliances Should Not Be Exclusive and Outcomes Must Be Shared With Broader Society

Another aspect of the Pollution Probe endorsement of Loblaws's GREEN products was that the eco-certification was not immediately available to other grocery retailers. Although this may have promoted product differentiation for Loblaws, it impeded relationship credibility. Murphy and Bendell (1997) point out that a general concern with green alliances centers on whether an environmental NGO should provide environmental services to a marketer, particularly when the marketer may achieve significant competitive advantages through the alliance (e.g., environmental risk reductions, eco-efficiencies, new technologies, product differentiation). Is it appropriate for a nonprofit environmental group, which may rely on grassroots donations from the general public (and consumers), to collaborate and support just one marketer that may, in turn, demand price premiums from consumers for "green" products resulting from that collaboration? Such consumer and stakeholder perceptions can call into question the relationship's intent and whether partners genuinely have shared environmental and social values.

In its green alliance agreements, EDF and AEI demand that task force outcomes be shared with others through the media and the final environmental report so that the work with one company can be amplified (Alston and Prince Roberts 1999). EDF has used its environmental reports (e.g., Environmental Defense Fund 1995; Environmental Defense Fund and McDonald's Corporation 1991) as mechanisms to communicate methodologies, results, and recommendations for public scrutiny. These environmental reports have facilitated knowledge transfer to other firms and expanded market demand for the green processes that result from green alliances. The EDF–McDonald's widely publicized move to abandon polystyrene clamshell packaging ultimately motivated other fast-food concerns to follow suit (Stafford and Hartman 1996). This validated the green alliance's environmental progress benefiting broader society.

To support relationship credibility, sustainable marketing communications should underscore the marketer's willingness to share environmental outcomes and practices that result from a green alliance, authenticating the marketer's intent and exemplifying the marketer's investment toward furthering environmental causes. Moreover, promotions should accentuate how disseminating green alliance results to other firms supports the shared environmental values of the environmental NGO and marketer. Given that enviropreneurial outcomes, technologies, and recommendations must be shared to preserve the green alliance's credibility, marketers should view their partnerships as avenues for "early-mover" advantages in which enviropreneurial technologies and processes can be enjoyed and expanded before the competition can adopt green alliance recommendations and reconfigure environmental processes (Hartman and Stafford 1997).

Environmental NGO "Champions" Should Facilitate Stakeholder Communication and Mutual Understandings

Lober (1997) observes that environmental NGOs typically take the role of "collaborative entrepreneur" or green alliance "champion" to inspire collaboration and foster support among stakeholders. Champions steward the vision, the goals, and the agenda that serve as the foundation of the partnership (Long and Arnold 1995). Effective champions build strategic bridges and networks among external stakeholders whose support may be necessary for the social acceptance of the green alliance (Polonsky 1996; Westley and Vredenburg 1991). In the RHP, for example, conservationists targeted prominent farmers in the community to engage in the winter field flooding program who, in turn, encouraged others to follow their lead (Hartman and Stafford 1998). The various environmental NGOs involved in the RHP also championed the partnership's objectives among state and federal government agencies and legislators, who, in turn, granted farmers flexibility in acquiring necessary water and resources to implement the program.

Likewise, in a green alliance between Greenpeace Germany and Foron Household Appliances for the marketing of an ozone-safe, hydrocarbon refrigerator in 1992, Greenpeace championed Foron's product among the scientific community, the media, and consumers through a grassroots effort (Beste 1994; Kalke 1994). The partnership represented the first time that Greenpeace endorsed a commercial product. Despite a disinformation campaign instigated by Foron's threatened competitors, Greenpeace was able to communicate to critical stakeholders the partnership's intent and the environmental benefits that could be gained with the hydrocarbon technology. The scientific community and media declared their support for the product, and consumer demand eventually encouraged other German appliance manufacturers to launch comparable products. By 1994, virtually the entire German refrigeration industry had converted to the hydrocarbon technology (Walsh 1995). Environmental NGOs need to champion the cause of the green alliance to establish relationship credibility and build stakeholder support.

Research Implications

Our framework brings together a complex set of perceptual elements and organizes them into two interdependent constructs—organizational and relationship credibility—providing insights into factors marketers must consider to build and strengthen the communications effects from green alliances. Refinement of our framework necessitates a systematic program of study that includes two important avenues of research to understand more fully the process of establishing credibility as well as sustaining its effects. We recommend beginning with studies using qualitative research paradigms, particularly grounded theory (Strauss and Corbin 1990) and case analysis (Yin 1994), followed by quantitative studies to develop measurements of our proposed constructs.

The first avenue of research involves a thorough assessment of how stakeholders assess green alliance credibility. Although the core perceptual elements and criteria in our framework have been identified from case analysis, along with stakeholder and source credibility research, information is needed to understand more precisely how the assessment process takes place. That is, how do stakeholders evaluate credibility determinants, compare credibility between green alliance partners, and collectively determine relationship credibility? Certain credibility dimensions may be more pertinent to some stakeholder groups than others, and this will affect how promotion managers should position green alliances and implement sustainable communications for specific stakeholders effectively. Research needs to uncover these potential differences among stakeholder groups. This avenue of research has a methodological component as well. Measurement of the different credibility criteria is needed (Haley 1996). Once measurements are derived, a more systematic understanding of the determinants of credibility, along with the interactions between stakeholders and germane organizational and relationship credibility criteria, is possible.

The second avenue of study focuses on the design and implementation of sustainable marketing communications. The design of communications must take into account that message recipients—consumers and other stakeholders—consider not only their individual values and perceptions, but also those related to their "ecological self," defined as the environmental end goals a person perceives as important and connected to his or her well-being. How stakeholders compare their values with cooperative relations between environmental NGOs and marketers warrants further examination. Marketing researchers and theorists are just beginning discourse on sustainable marketing communications (Fuller 1999; McDonagh 1998). In general, the discussion suggests that sustainable communications need to inform and educate consumers and stakeholders about environmental issues and redirect purchases toward ecologically sensitive products. Our framework adds a more comprehensive strategic focus, suggesting that sustainable communication strategy needs to provide convincing information about potential benefits that result from cooperative strategic efforts, including green alliances. This is a challenge given the lack of scientific data and consensus to unequivocally support environmental purchasing, consumption, and disposal choices (Fuller 1999). Thus, stakeholder perceptions of organizational and relationship credibility of green alliances must be built through ongoing, two-way communications with a diverse set of interest groups. Establishing appropriate promotional vehicles that efficiently and credibly facilitate information exchanges with stakeholders warrants exploration.

Research also needs to focus on how communications can effectively provide clear, concise, and credible messages to a wide variety of stakeholders who may subsequently engage in word-of-mouth communications with and influence one another (Polonsky 1996). How promotion managers interact with coalitions and networks of stakeholder groups needs further consideration (Rowley 1997). Managerially, the challenge is to send out persuasive messages that educate and sensitize stakeholders to the intent and achievements of green alliances while being receptive and willing to act on stakeholder feedback.

Conclusion

Green alliances are likely to continue to a play a prominent role for advancing environmental sustainability (Murphy and Bendell 1997). Given environmental NGOs' traditional "watchdog" role in society, however, the social acceptability of green alliances is likely to be a concern among consumers and other stakeholders, and promotion managers need to position green alliances as credibly meeting stakeholder expectations and facilitating environmental progress. Our framework is designed to illustrate the dimensions and determinants of organizational and relationship credibility to understand how stakeholders make sense of and respond to environmental NGO–marketer cooperation. The next step is to consider how green alliances build sustainable communication exchanges and long-term relationships with stakeholders. Green alliances are a new phenomena that will warrant further study if they are to succeed and contribute to global marketing and ecological sustainability in the twenty-first century.

References

Alston, Ken and Jackie Prince Roberts (1999), "Partners in New product Development: SC Johnson and the Alliance for Environmental Innovation," *Corporate Environmental Strategy*, 6 (2), 111–28.

Azzone, Giovanni, Michael Brophy, Giuliano Noci, Richard Welford, and William Young (1997), "A Stakeholders' View of Environmental Reporting," *Long Range Planning*, 30 (5), 699–709.

Beste, Dieter (1994), "The Greenfreeze Campaign," *Akzente*, (December), 26–29.

Brown, L. David (1991), "Bridging Organizations and Sustainable Development," *Human Relations*, 44 (8), 807–31.

Cardskadden, H. and D.J. Lober (1998), "Environmental Stakeholder Management as Business Strategy: The Case of the Corporate Wildlife Habitat Enhancement Programme," *Journal of Environmental Management*, 52 (2), 183–202.

Chouinard, Yvon and Michael Brown (1997), "Going Organic: Converting Patagonia's Cotton Product Line," *Journal of Industrial Ecology*, 1 (1), 117–30.

Clarkson, Max B.E. (1995), "A Stakeholder Framework for Analyzing and Evaluating Corporate Social Performance," *Academy of Management Review*, 20 (1), 92–117.

Cooper, Steve (1994), "Our Environment," *Better Homes and Gardens*, (March), 20.

Cornwell, T. Bettina and Isabelle Maignan (1998), "An International Review of Sponsorship Research," *Journal of Advertising*, 27 (Spring), 1–21.

Crane, Andrew (1998), "Exploring Green Alliances," *Journal of Marketing Management*, 14 (August), 559–79.

Curren, Mitch (1994), "Ben & Jerry's Scoop on Environmentalism," *Forum for Applied Research and Public Policy*, (Summer), 33–37.

Donaldson, Thomas and Lee E. Preston (1995), "The Stakeholder Theory of the Corporation: Concepts, Evidence, and Implications," *Academy of Management Review*, 20 (1), 65–91.

Dowie, Mark (1995), *Losing Ground: American Environmentalism at the Close of the Twentieth Century*. Cambridge, MA: MIT Press.

Dutton, Gail (1996), "Green Partnerships," *Management Review*, 85 (January), 24–28.

Ellen, P.S., J.L. Winer, and C. Cobb-Walgren (1991), "The Role of Perceived Consumer Effectiveness in Motivating Environmentally Conscious Behaviors," *Journal of Public Policy & Marketing*, 10 (Fall), 102–107.

EDF Letter (1996), "Alliance Projects Aim to Make Business Greener," (November), 1, 3.

Environmental Defense Fund (1995), *Paper Task Force Recommendations for Purchasing and Using Environmentally Preferable Paper*. New York: Environmental Defense Fund.

——— and McDonald's Corporation (1991), *Waste Reduction Task Force Final Report*. New York: Environmental Defense Fund and McDonald's Corporation.

Esty, Daniel C. and Michael E. Porter (1998), "Industrial Ecology and Competitiveness: Strategic Implications for the Firm," *Journal of Industrial Ecology*, 2 (1), 35–43.

Fastiggi, Elizabeth (1999), *Catalyzing Environmental Results: Lessons in Advocacy Organization-Business Partnerships*. Boston, MA: Alliance for Environmental Innovation.

Fowler, Penny and Simon Heap (1998), "Learning from the Marine Stewardship Council: A Business-NGO Partnership for Sustainable Marine Fisheries," *Greener Management International*, 24 (Winter), 77–90.

Franck, Irene and David Brownstone (1992), *The Green Encyclopedia*. New York: Prentice-Hall.

Freeman, R.E. (1984), *Strategic Management: A Stakeholder Approach*. Boston, MA: Pitman Publishing Company.

Fuller, Donald A. (1999), *Sustainable Marketing: Managerial-Ecological Issues*. Thousand Oaks, CA: Sage Publications.

Gallon, G. (1991), "The Green Product Endorsement Controversy: Lessons from the Pollution Probe/Loblaws Experience," *Alternatives*, 18 (3), 17–25.

Gray, Barbara (1989), *Collaborating: Finding Common Ground for Multiparty Problems*. San Francisco, CA: Jossey-Bass Publishers.

Haley, Eric (1996), "Exploring the Construct of Organization as Source: Consumers' Understandings of Organizational Sponsorship of Advocacy Advertising," *Journal of Advertising*, 25 (Summer), 19–35.

Hammond, Sharon (1987), "Health Advertising: The Credibility of Organizational Sources," in *Communication Yearbook*, Vol. 10, M.L. McLaughlin, ed. Newbury Park, CA: Sage Publications, 613–28.

Harris, James T. (1992), "Working with Environmental Groups," *Public Relations Journal*, 48 (May), 24–35.

Harrison, E. Bruce (1994), "The E-Factor: Going Green, Sustainably," *Green Business Letter*, (September), 8.

Hartman, Cathy L. and Edwin R. Stafford (1997), "Green Alliances: Building New Business with Environmental Groups," *Long Range Planning*, 30 (2), 184–96.

——— and ——— (1998), "Crafting Enviropreneurial Value Chain Strategy Through Green Alliances," *Business Horizons*, 41 (March–April), 62–72.

Hemphill, Thomas A. (1996), "The New Era of Business Regulation," *Business Horizons*, 39 (July–August), 26–30.

Hovland, Carl, Irving Janis, and Harold Kelly (1953), *Communication and Persuasion*. New Haven, CT: Yale University Press.

Javalgi, Rajshekhar G., Mark B. Traylor, Andrew C. Gross, and Edward Lampman (1994), "Awareness of Sponsorship and Corporate Image: An Empirical Investigation," *Journal of Advertising*, 23 (4), 47–58.

Kalke, Marion (1994), "The Foron-Story," *Akzente*, (December), 20–25.

Kohl, Helen (1990), "Are They Nature's Choice?" *Financial Post Moneywise*, (April), 16–29.

Kolk, Ans (1998), "From Voluntary to Obligatory? Trends in Corporate Environmental Reporting," paper presented at the 7th International Conference of the Greening of Industry Network, Rome, Italy (November 15–18).

Krupp, Fred (1994), "EDF and the Third Wave Environmentalism," *Pulp & Paper*, 68 (July), 132.

Livesey, Sharon (1991), "McDonald's and the Environment," *Harvard Business School Case N9-391-108.* Boston, MA: Harvard Business School.

Lober, Douglas J. (1997), "Explaining the Formation of Business-Environmentalist Collaborations: Collaborative Windows and the Paper Task Force," *Policy Sciences*, 30 (February), 1–24.

Long, Frederick J. and Matthew B. Arnold (1995), *The Power of Environmental Partnerships.* Fort Worth, TX: The Dryden Press.

Manolson, Michael (1989), "Big Business is Cashing in on Environmental Worries While Industry Keeps Polluting," *Globe and Mail*, (July 10), A7.

McDonagh, Pierre (1998), "Towards a Theory of Sustainable Communications in Risk Society: Relating Issues of Sustainability to Marketing Communications," *Journal of Marketing Management*, 14 (August), 591–622.

Mendleson, Nicola and Michael Jay Polonsky (1995), "Using Strategic Alliances to Develop Credible Green Marketing," *Journal of Consumer Marketing*, 12 (2), 4–18.

Menon, Ajay and Anil Menon (1997), "Enviropreneurial Marketing Strategy: The Emergence of Corporate Environmentalism as Market Strategy," *Journal of Marketing*, 61 (January), 51–67.

Milne, George R., Easwar S. Iyer, and Sara Gooding-Williams (1996), "Environmental Organization Alliance Relationships Within and Across Nonprofit, Business, and Government Sectors," *Journal of Public Policy & Marketing*, 15 (Fall), 203–215.

Murphy, David F. and Jem Bendell (1997), *In the Company of Partners: Business, Environmental Groups, and Sustainable Development Post-Rio.* Bristol, England: The Policy Press.

Oliver, Christine (1990), "Determinants of Interorganizational Relationships: Integration and Future Directions," *Academy of Management Review*, 15 (2), 241–65.

Ottman, Jacquelyn A. (1995), "Mandate for the 90s: Green Corporate Image," *Marketing News*, (September 11), 8.

Ozanne, Lucie K. and Richard P. Vlosky (1998), "Willingness to Pay for Environmentally Certified Wood Products: A Consumer Perspective," *Forest Products Journal*, 47 (6), 39–48.

Petty, Richard E. and John T. Capioccio (1981), *Attitudes and Persuasion: Classic and Contemporary Approaches.* Dubuque, Iowa: Wm. C. Brown Company Publishers.

Polonsky, Michael Jay (1996), "Stakeholder Management and Stakeholder Matrix: Potential Strategic Marketing Tools," *Journal of Market Focused Management*, 1 (3), 209–29.

Porter, Michael E. and Claas van der Linde (1995), "Green and Competitive: Breaking the Stalemate," *Harvard Business Review*, 73 (September–October) 120–34.

Roper Starch Worldwide/The Nature Conservancy Report (1998), "The Power of Two: Conservation and Corporate Environmental Responsibility," Washington, DC: Roper Starch Worldwide Inc.

Rowley, Timothy J. (1997), "Moving Beyond Dyadic Ties: A Network Theory of Stakeholder Influences," *Academy of Management Review*, 22 (4), 887–910.

Shrivastava, Paul (1995), "Environmental Technologies and Competitive Advantage," *Strategic Management Journal*, 16 (Summer), 183–200.

Stafford, Edwin R. and Cathy L. Hartman (1996), "Green Alliances: Strategic Relations Between Businesses and Environmental Groups," *Business Horizons*, 39 (March–April), 50–59.

—— and —— (1998), "Toward an Understanding of the Antecedents of Environmentalist-Business Cooperative Relations," in *American Marketing Association's*

Summer Educators' Conference Proceedings, Ronald C. Goodstein and Scott B. MacKenzie, eds. Chicago, IL: American Marketing Association, 56–63.

Stavins, Robert and Bradley Whitehead (1997), "Market-Based Environmental Policies," in *Thinking Ecologically: The Next Generation of Environmental Policy*, Marian R. Chertow and Daniel C. Esty, eds. New Haven, CT: Yale University Press, 105–117.

Strauss, Anselm and Juliet Corbin (1998), *Basics of Qualitative Research: Techniques and Procedures for Developing Grounded Theory*. Thousand Oaks, CA: Sage Publications.

Tasker, Georgia (1998), "Eco-Friendly Coffee Farms for the Birds," *Salt Lake Tribune*, (April 1), C2.

Vanden Bergh, Bruce, Lawrence Soley, and Leonard Reid (1981), "Factor Study of Dimensions of Advertiser Credibility," *Journalism Quarterly*, 58 (4), 629–31.

Vincett, John (1991), "Forging an Effective Working Relationship with Environmental Groups," in *The Canadian Green Marketing Handbook*, Michael J. Meagher and Ian Rhind, eds. Don Mills, Ontario: Southam Business Communications, 269–76.

Walsh, Mary Williams (1995), "Case Study: Company Puts Faith in Freon-Free Fridge," *Los Angeles Times*, (January 10), 4.

Westley, Frances and Harrie Vredenburg (1991), "Strategic Bridging: The Collaboration Between Environmentalists and Business in the Marketing of Green Products," *Journal of Applied Behavioral Science*, 27 (March), 65–90.

Winters, Lewis (1986), "The Effect of Brand Image on Company Image: Implications for Corporate Advertising," *Journal of Advertising Research*, 26 (April–May), 54–59.

Yin, Robert K. (1994), *Case Study Research: Design and Methods*. Thousand Oaks, CA: Sage Publications.

Zinkhan, George M. and Les Carlson (1995), "Green Advertising and the Reluctant Consumer," *Journal of Advertising*, 24 (2), 1–6.

14

Marketing Activities and Organizational Success: An Application to the Health Care Industry

Misty K. Ritchie
Bank of America

T he treatment of substance abuse in the United States is a relatively recent development. Private treatment of substance abuse is an even newer manifestation within the industry. With many facilities competing for private and public resources, treatment centers are searching for new ways of creating a competitive advantage. Because substance abuse treatment provides an intangible and poorly understood service, treatment centers rely heavily on image. A distinct, positive image generates legitimacy with constituents. Centers must not only establish legitimacy with customers to differentiate themselves from competitors, but also manage their identities in such a way that legitimizes the business of substance abuse treatment. The author examines firmographic characteristics, competitive factors, strategic positioning, and imaging strategies as they affect the development of legitimacy. The author addresses how the interaction of these variables contributes to organizational performance.

Organizational Image, Performance, and Legitimacy

Organizational legitimacy generates credibility and confidence among an organization's constituents. Credibility and confidence attract customers, which translates into high levels of organizational performance. Legitimacy presupposes that an organization, its abilities, and its goals are valid (Hoekstra 1995). It infers that organizational actors are capable of providing a good or service, that they provide goods or services of satisfying quality, and that the organization is a reliable and trustworthy agency (Baum and Oliver 1992; Hinings and Greenwood 1988; Silverman and Grover 1995). Organizational performance and legitimacy are tightly linked, especially in young industries. Indeed, in such cases, organizational performance is a strong correlate of organizational legitimacy as well as the legitimacy of the industry (Baum and Oliver 1992).

Image is a way for individuals to categorize and compartmentalize complex packages of information. The image becomes the symbol of what an organization means to social audiences, condensing the evaluations and connotations of an organization into a meaningful and manageable form (Baum and Oliver 1992; LeBlanc and Nguyen 1996). Countless authors believe that organizational legitimacy and a positive image are invaluable organizational assets. A positive reputation helps an organization weather the entrance of new competitors in the market and retain market share from existing competitors. A positive image can directly affect organization performance.

Because "image is basically the product being sold," it is especially important for service providers (Zahradnik 1986). Similar to other service organizations, substance abuse treatment centers have various ranges of services and capabilities, and each center must do its best to emphasize its assets to constituents. "Creating, communicating, enhancing and maintaining a corporate image is a task that is critical to a company's success" (Brendsel 1993, p. 9).

Health care organizations are becoming increasingly aware of the value of a positive organizational image. Administrators are discovering the importance of using imaging strategies to disseminate information about their firms in ways that shape their external identities. Through planning or by default, every organization has an identity or image. Similarly, all organizations have the ability to develop or alter their capabilities and their image to some degree. Through advertisements, relationship marketing, and other programs, potential clients (both individual and organizational) are informed about an organization's professional reputation, special capacities, and particular programs or services. Imaging strategies can be used to differentiate health care organizations more effectively and efficiently from their competitors by strategically presenting a recognizable image to constituents. Imaging strategies include any positioning tactic, approach to image-building, or competitive strategy that enables an organization to differentiate itself positively from competitors and gain credibility in the eyes of its stakeholders.

Substance abuse treatment facilities are one type of health care organization whose success is particularly tied to the benefits of a positive image and organizational legitimacy. Every substance abuse treatment center has a mission to assist clients with their addiction problems and, thus, to improve their quality of life. However, treatment centers have to face the business realities of meeting expenses and attracting customers. To survive and thrive, centers must communicate to customers what they are; they need to define themselves to their constituents (Zahradnik 1986). In doing this, administrators must take into account the organizational environment, the resources and capabilities of the firm, and the expectations of the potential market. As stated by Aaker (1995, p. 4), "The scope of a business is defined by the products it offers and chooses not to offer, by the markets it seeks to serve and not serve, [and] by the competitors it chooses to compete with and to avoid." The decisions that are made regarding positioning and strategy lay the groundwork for the creation of a corporate image.

Treatment centers must generate legitimacy in a way that distinguishes them from competing centers. Just as important, however, is the need for such centers to legitimate the business of substance abuse treatment, especially considering the barriers and misconceptions that prevent the use of substance abuse treatment programs. The stigma associated with substance abuse can inhibit individuals from seeking treatment (Abel and Kruger 1995; Moore 1992). Personal weakness, immorality, criminal behavior, and psychiatric problems are often linked with substance abuse. Attempting to avoid such associations, substance abusers might resist seeking formal treatment. Although drug treatment professionals have attempted to inform the public that alcoholism and drug addiction are "diseases like any other," much confusion still exists regarding the nature of substance abuse.

Substance abuse and substance abuse treatment are often misunderstood by the general public. A study by Moore (1992) shows that the public often holds competing views of substance abuse and people who abuse drugs. She finds that in many cases people simultaneously believe not only that substance abuse is a disease, but also that it is a moral flaw. That is, though they tend to acknowledge that there is some physical component to addiction, people also believe that users of illegal drugs are criminals. Public opinion oscillates between sympathy and blame when it comes to alcohol and drug abuse.

Because so many recovering substance abusers have used Alcoholics Anonymous or have "self-recovered" (Humphreys, Moos, and Finney 1995; Mulford 1994), the need for a formal treatment program might seem unnecessary to some or fraudulent to others. Moreover, many people, citing high relapse rates as evidence, believe that it is rare for an addict to be treated for addiction successfully.

Another barrier to the legitimization of substance abuse treatment is the public's perception of the best-known centers. The treatment facilities that receive the most publicity often provide treatment for wealthy, celebrity clients. Because of the upscale nature of these centers, the public sometimes associates substance abuse treatment with a spa- or resort-like "vacation" and not as serious medical treatment.

Adding to the misconceptions regarding treatment centers is that treatment of substance abuse is poorly understood. The average person has little information about how a substance abuser is transformed into a "healthy" patient. There is no standardized protocol for treating substance abuse. Detoxification, aversion therapy, group counseling, vocational training, prescription drugs, and art therapy are just a few of the many options offered to clients who want to enter formal treatment programs. Various programs have different philosophies and treatment regimens. The variety of options often proves overwhelming to consumers.

As discussed previously, there is a great deal of room for misunderstanding what substance abuse treatment really is and to what degree it can be effective. Treatment centers must not only battle other centers for market share, but also establish images that legitimate substance abuse treatment in the mind of the public. Because most substance abusers do not seek treatment at all (Weisner and Schmidt 1995), legitimating substance abuse as a treatable disease could be the best way to increase the overall market share and enhance organizational performance.

Literature on organizations most often discusses the concepts of legitimacy and image in the framework of institutional theory. However, interest in these topics typically is concentrated at the industry level, which involves explaining and predicting how new industries establish themselves and how they become "taken for granted" through institutional processes such as isomorphism, regulatory efforts, or networking activities (Baum and Oliver 1992; Deephouse 1996; DiMaggio and Powell 1983; Hannan et al. 1995; Podolny, Stuart, and Hannan 1996; Scott 1993). Other studies provide discussions of the possible mechanisms for achieving legitimacy but offer no empirical evidence (Meyer and Scott 1992; Oliver 1991). Few analyses have examined how organizations establish and maintain images and legitimacy within an industry. This analysis proposes to use quantitative data to examine how competition factors, positioning strategies, and imaging strategies (such as marketing activities) interact to affect image and organizational performance and, thus, legitimacy.

Literature Review

Competition, legitimacy, and success are intimately related to one another, but until now, no one has attempted to draw an explicit connection among these topics or pull them together under one organizational theory. As several authors note, image and legitimacy are essential for organizational success (Baum and Oliver 1992; Brendsel 1993; Hinings and Greenwood 1988; LeBlanc and Nguyen 1996; Meyer and Scott 1992). Organizations are embedded within "a wider social system which is the source of 'meaning,' legitimacy, or higher-level support which makes the implementation of the organization's goals possible" (Parsons 1960, pp. 63–64). Institutional theory presents a fitting overarching framework for understanding how the concepts of legitimacy and image manifest themselves in the field of substance abuse treatment. In the past, institutional theory has been criticized for being too passive and difficult to test empirically. This analysis provides an excellent opportunity to explore the usefulness of institutional theory to explain such dynamic concepts as competition and imaging strategies and to test institutional theory with quantitative data. In addition, it allows for the integration of institutional theory with population ecology theory and contingency theory.

Researchers such as Scott (1995) and Hinings and Greenwood (1988) have noted the connections between ecological theories and institutional theory and between contingency theory and institutional theory. Hinings and Greenwood (1988, p. 55) contend that "the notions of contingency theory with their rational, technological, adaptive thrust derive from the institutional legitimations of business." Scott notes a "convergence between ecological and institutional approaches to organizations" (1995, p. 108) in his discussion of the relationships between organizational growth and death rates as they are affected by the "processes of institutional environments" (1995, p. 109). Scott (1993, p. 271) suggests that pursuing organizational theory from a variety of "perspectives ... provides only a partial account of the complex phenomena we observe." As such, he (1993, p. 272) proposes that organizational theory would benefit from attempts to combine various strains of organizational theory "in a layered or nested fashion," allowing for a more comprehensive and integrated perspective. This analysis proposes to do just that by combining population ecology theory, contingency theory, and institutional theory to provide an understanding of the ways in which competition, niche width, and strategy interact to affect organizational image and performance. A positive organizational image should lead to the development of legitimacy among constituents.

Institutional Theory

Institutional theory suggests that "many structures, programs, and practices in organizations attain legitimacy through the social construction of reality" (Wright and McMahan 1992, p. 313). Institutional theory has provided much insight into the ways organizations are affected by processes such as isomorphism, professionalization, and external regulation. Although institutional theory has enjoyed considerable support among organizational researchers, "the major criticisms of institutional theory have been its assumptions of organizational passivity and its failure to address strategic behavior and the exercise of influence" (Oliver 1991, p. 173; see also Coveleski and Dirsmith 1988; DiMaggio 1988; Perrow 1985; Powell 1985).

Institutional theory has gone through many transformations and periods of revitalization (see Scott 1995), but currently one of the more exciting and promising topics addressed within this field is in what Scott refers to as the "cognitive pillar" of new institutional theory. This area of research examines the manner in which the meanings and symbols pervading organizations are constructed, maintained, and transmitted. According to Scott (1995, p. 40), "Symbols—words, signs, and gestures—have their effect by shaping the meanings we attribute to objects and activities. Meanings arise in interaction and are maintained." Developed by various organizational actors, these representations come to be reified and institutionalized within and across populations. Although early theories of institutionalism were criticized for being passive or reactionist, able only to respond to external changes, the new institutionalism recognizes the proactive role organizations can take in constructing their realities. That is, "Organizations are creatures of their institutional environments, but most modern organizations are constituted as active players, not passive pawns" (Scott 1995, p. 132). Strategy combines with environmental conditions to produce many kinds of organizations and many avenues to creating successful organizations.

In his 1993 article, Scott suggests that present efforts in organizational theory and research should focus on combining the views of institutionalism with other organizational theories. The topic of legitimacy is one that holds the potential for integrating institutional theory with two other widely held theories: population ecology theory and contingency theory. Legitimacy is an elusive concept whose definition has been taken for granted. It has often gone undefined in the literature, or it has been discussed indirectly, focusing more on structures or processes hypothesized to affect the legitimacy of organizations or institutions. According to institutional theory, organizational performance is highly interrelated with legitimacy and, accordingly, with organizational image. This analysis presents the opportunity to examine legitimacy in a fairly direct manner through the measurement of organizational performance measures. Performance indicators relate the degree to which organizations are accepted by individual and organizational buyers. High levels of organization performance demonstrate that an organization has created a positive organizational image and has been judged to be legitimate. The ability to develop organizational legitimacy depends on competition factors, market positioning (niche width), and imaging strategies, which draw from population ecology, contingency theory, and institutional theory. This provides an ideal opportunity to explore Scott's suggestion of the layering or nesting of organizational theories.

Although population ecology and contingency theories have different views regarding organizations' abilities to proactively use strategy to gain a competitive advantage, the basic tenets of the theories are not incompatible. Population ecology operates within an evolutionary selection framework, which suggests that successful organizations are those whose structures and processes coincidentally thrive in the environmental conditions of the time. Contingency theory lends more credence to the idea of organizations being able to "adjust their strategies and structures to match the contingencies of the flow of work and of the external environment" (Hannan and Freeman 1989, p. 30, see also Lawrence and Lorsch 1986). However, both contingency theory and population ecology theory embrace the idea that there is not one best way to organize; that is, varying environmental conditions and varying strategies are all able to produce successful organizations. Institutional theory then provides an overarching theoretical framework in which population ecology and contingency arguments are couched. All these theories essentially examine the ways in which organizational image and performance are developed through imaging strategies. A combination of these theoretical perspectives is used in this analysis to create a comprehensive view of how competition, niche width, and imaging strategies enhance organizational legitimacy through contributions to organization performance (see Figure 1).

Population Ecology Theory

Competition

Population ecology models for organizational populations are based on theories in the field of bioecology. In the early 1900s, ecologists Alfred Lotka and Vito Volterra "independently proposed models of populations dynamics that incorporate effects of competition between populations" (Hannan and Freeman 1989, p. 99). These models predicted that as competition increases, organizational performance/viability is affected nonmonotonically. When a population is at low levels and resources are in abundance, the population can sustain a high growth rate. The number of competitors will increase until the population hits its carrying capacity at which point the growth rate is zero, and resources become scarce. The number of competitors and the intensity of the competition negatively affect the ability of the members in that population to obtain the requisite amount of resources for survival. Death rates rise, and survival becomes more difficult for all members of that population.

These bioecology models were adopted by researchers of populations of organizations. Using the assumptions and equations drawn from natural ecology, Hannan

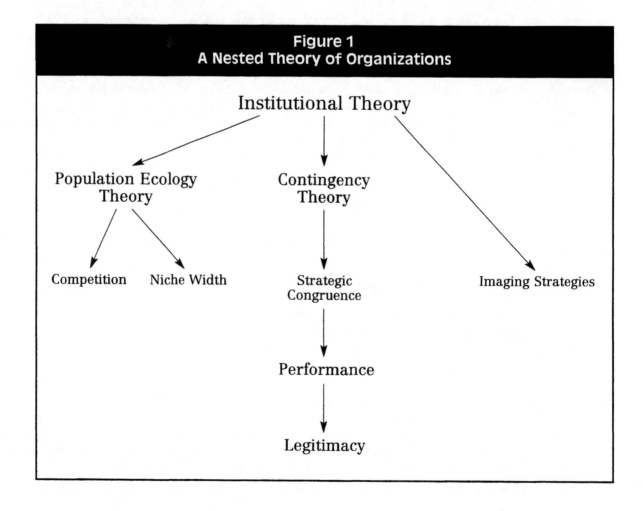

Figure 1
A Nested Theory of Organizations

Institutional Theory

Population Ecology Theory

Contingency Theory

Competition   Niche Width

Strategic Congruence

Imaging Strategies

Performance

Legitimacy

and Freeman (1977, 1983, 1989) and other organizational researchers, such as Baum and Oliver (1992); Carroll (1985); Podolny, Stuart, and Hannan (1996), have employed elements of organizational ecology to examine the topics of competition and relative positioning in the market in populations of organizations.

Results from these research projects suggest that some analogies can be drawn from biology to organizational ecology. Most of these analyses have focused on how competition affects founding rates and death rates within a population. Others have focused on the ways in which density affects how industries establish legitimacy in an organizational environment. For new industries, competitors might add legitimacy to the industry, which increases performance, lowers entry barriers, and encourages new foundings (Freeman and Hannan 1983; Oliver 1991). Initial growth leads to more growth as new organizations learn from their predecessors and attempt to mimic their successes (or avoid their failures). But as more and more organizations hop on the bandwagon, the industrial population becomes flooded. As the industry matures, swelling competition for scarce resources increases rates of organizational death and discourages new foundings (Carroll 1985; Freeman, Carroll, and Hannan 1983; Hannan and Freeman 1989). Although many organization ecology analyses focus on competition as it relates to organizational birth and death, organizational death is not the only result of competition. A more common and less extreme result is simply a decline in organizational performance.

Niche Width

Although competition is an essential element in the examination of legitimacy, another concept developed by bioecologists and adopted by organizational researchers is niche width. In bioecology terms, niche width refers to the range of environments in which a species can survive. Organizational theorists have used niche width in a similar manner that refers to the range of customers to which an organization hopes to appeal. Niche width can be described as the number and/or types of products or services offered by an organization and the way it positions itself in the marketplace. Organizations usually take one of two orientations toward the market: a generalist perspective or a specialist perspective. They take a broad view of the industry, attempting to provide a variety of services to a variety of clients. They tend to aim for a small to moderate share *of a large market*. Specialists focus on one or a few special areas, developing competencies in these areas. They attempt to attract a moderate to large share *of a smaller market*. Whether a generalist or a specialist tactic is used, an organization creates a niche in its environment.

A niche is a pocket of resources within which an organization operates: "The imagery of the niche expresses the role of a population ... in a community, a population's 'way of earning a living'" (Hannan and Freeman 1989, p. 50). Organizations' abilities to define their target markets are limited by their strengths and capabilities (or their ability to develop them) and by the opportunities presented in their environments. Selecting abilities to emphasize and segments in which to compete can combine to create a niche. Niche strategies are not exclusive to specialists; generalists use niche strategies when they develop multiple capabilities and target broad audiences.

Hannan and Freeman (1989, p. 317) note that "we are not comparing generally successful organizations with generally unsuccessful ones when we compare specialists with generalists" (see also Hannan and Freeman 1983). Adopting a strategy of specialism or generalism is not a formula for success in and of itself. Each has its own advantages and disadvantages, and each strategy interacts with the competitive environment.

Authors such as Hannan and Freeman (1983, 1989) and Aldrich and Marsden (1980) elaborate on the differences between generalists and specialists, noting that in unstable industries or during periods of industry instability (beginning stages or industry transformations), a generalist approach is usually more successful. The basic theory is that instability causes firms to "hedge their bets" by providing a variety of goods and/or services. Concentrating too much on one line of products or services could prove detrimental to survival if the industry undergoes a shift incompatible with current products and/or services. However, in stable industries or in periods of industrial stability, specialists tend to thrive. Aldrich and Marsden (1980, p. 382) note that "when environments are ... changing in predictable ways, specialism is always an optimal strategy, as specialist forms can concentrate on that portion of the environment in which they do best." Whereas generalists provide scope (a wide niche width), specialists offer depth (a narrow niche width).

Contingency Theory

Strategic Congruence

Strategic congruence is created when organizational resources are developed and communicated to constituents as core competencies of that organization. Several authors suggest that a sustained competitive advantage can be achieved through the emphasis of an organization's core competencies (Aaker 1995; Prahalad and Hamel 1990; Silverman and Grover 1995). Thus, strategic congruence is important to consider when developing any legitimacy-seeking strategy (Priem 1994). By leveraging an organization's strengths, a consistent image can be portrayed to constituents, and organizational actors can focus more effectively on its particular assets. By then emphasizing these assets through legitimacy-seeking activities, an organization can maximize the advantages of its resources by creating a strategic congruence between resources and imaging strategies or between targeting strategies and the competitive environment.

The idea of strategic congruence has its roots in contingency theory. Early contingency theorists emphasized the match between technology and organization structure (Lawrence and Lorsch 1986; Woodward 1965). They "did not incorporate the concept of strategic choice and resultant competitive capabilities" (Roth and Jackson 1995, p. 1722). Neocontingency theorists place more emphasis on strategic choice and suggest that "when there is a fit between the available resources and the firm's competitive strategies, performance should be enhanced" (Chandler and Hanks 1994). The current proposal applies Chandler and Hanks's model of strategy/resource congruence to legitimacy-seeking activities as they affect organizational legitimacy and performance. The Chandler and Hanks model suggests that the degree of fit between resources and strategy results in a more efficacious use of assets, which will result in a competitive advantage for an organization. By employing this method of analysis in examining substance abuse treatment center performance, it is predicted that agreement between the characteristics of an organization identified as assets or advantages and those characteristics of an organization that are emphasized in marketing activities will result in increased performance and likelihood of survival. Organizations that pursue a positioning strategy compatible with the local organizational environment should also enjoy the benefits of strategic congruence. Such congruence should create a competitive advantage by allowing for the best use of available resources.

Both population ecology and contingency theories illustrate that there is not a single best way to organize and manage organizations. Encompassing this perspective is the larger idea the all organizational activities must meet the central challenge of legitimizing organizations to their constituents. The nested theory of organizations presented here will allow for the examination of legitimacy through an institutional framework. Nested within this framework are the closely connected population ecology and contingency theories.

The Links Among Competition, Niche Width, Imaging Strategies, and Performance

Institutional theory provides a way to view an organization's actions in conjunction with and in response to the characteristics of the surrounding environment as imaging strategies. "Organizations must be responsive to external demands in order to survive" (Oliver 1991, p. 145; see also Meyer and Rowan 1977; Pfeffer and Salancik 1978, p. 146). Because organizational decision makers have strong preferences for certainty and stability in organizational life, they seek to employ strategies that will improve their organization's situation relative to the competition, thus, securing the future (DiMaggio 1988; DiMaggio and Powell 1983; Pfeffer and Salancik 1978; Zucker 1977).

According to Porter (1980), marketing activities are one component of an organization that can be strategically managed to create a competitive advantage. The creation of a positive image through the use of imaging strategies increases exposure of an organization and encourages use of an organization's goods or services. Well-developed imaging strategies allow for the development of a more effective and memorable organizational identity with constituents.

Although marketing and market orientations are discussed at length in this article, my analysis is not concerned with how marketing activities per se contribute to organizational performance. Instead, I describe how competition, relative positioning in the market, and marketing efforts interact to create an organizational image, enhance organizational performance, and develop organizational legitimacy.

Because substance abuse treatment is a unique mix of social movement, health care technology, and industry, special challenges are encountered when trying to construct an identity valuable to constituents. As it has grown as a sector of the health care industry and as the treatment center industry has matured, organizations that compose this segment have necessarily adopted many of the structures and processes of other business organizations—image-building being one of them. According to Gilligan and Lowe (1995, p. 14),

> The need for tighter, more professional and forward-looking management [in health care] is now greater than ever before. The managerial tools and techniques that previously were seen to be the prerogative of manufacturers ... might now possibly contribute to the better and more effective management of the health care sector. Prominent amongst these is the whole area of marketing.

Although marketing activities are taken for granted in goods industries, service industries have traditionally shied away from marketing. This has been due in large part to difficulties in developing imaging strategies for services and because management seemed unconvinced of its necessity (Gilligan and Lowe 1995). But as health care marketing increases in prevalence and importance, assessing the contribution of imaging activities to organizational performance and determining which strategies are more effective are imperative. This examination of image and performance as they affect organizational legitimacy also provides the occasion to empirically test institutional theory. Despite growing image-building efforts, only a small portion of substance abusers is actively seeking treatment (Sorbell et al. 1993). In addition to wooing existing customers, imaging strategies must focus on legitimating substance abuse as a treatable disease and substance abuse treatment as an effective cure. By informing the public about substance abuse and publicizing the benefits of formal treatment, centers can validate their worth to constituents. Legitimating the business of substance abuse treatment would encourage more people with substance abuse problems to seek treatment, thereby expanding the overall market and helping more individuals enter formal substance abuse programs.

Christensen (1995, p. 652) contends that "marketing is probably one of the most important and influential institutions of contemporary society." He (1995, p. 651) describes marketing as

> saturated with images and signs carefully devised and organized to assert, consolidate, and maintain particular identities. As the image-creating institution par excellence, marketing plays a crucial, albeit paradoxical, role in this planned articulation of identity led by contemporary organizations. Through marketing techniques of positioning and image creation, organizations of today constantly attempt to influence and shape impressions of their corporate body among their various constituencies (see also Baudrillard 1988; Berg 1989; Cheney 1992; Ewen 1988; Perniola 1980).

It is this essential tie between marketing and corporate identity that makes marketing such a valuable tool in terms of organizational performance.

Performance

Before delving into more detailed discussions about competition, relative positioning in the market, and imaging strategies, it is necessary to elaborate more on organizational performance. Performance is a difficult term to conceptualize and operationalize. It can be defined in many ways, depending on the context of the discussion. Sociologically, organizational viability has been the most prevalent measure of performance, but such a measure does not offer much depth. In business research and literature, performance is often characterized by stock prices or return on investment. For manufacturing firms, the goal might be producing defect-free products. More and more often, customer satisfaction is included as an important measure of organizational performance. However, many treatment centers are publicly funded or are not-for-profit organizations and, thus, do not view profit in the same way as for-profit centers. Evaluating the quality of services and patient care is very difficult, which makes objective judgments about the "product" difficult. Furthermore, treatment centers rarely collect detailed information about organizational or individual customers' satisfaction with their services, precluding systematic analysis of patients' evaluations of their treatment experiences. A better understanding of organizations might be lurking in the wide variability of organizational performance measures. Service industries, specifically behavioral health care, present challenges to the typical ways of measuring performance. Substance abuse treatment centers are good examples of loosely coupled organizations—organizations whose performance is more easily and more often judged by its processes than its outcomes (Meyer and

Rowan 1977). Loosely coupled organizations have "unclear and little understood methods or technologies, inconsistent and fluid participation by actors and ambiguous or uncertain goals" (Ingersoll 1993, p. 84). These factors cause outcomes to be difficult to measure.

Organizational performance is moderated by four factors: the amount of competition in the market area, niche width, relative positioning in the market, and the types of imaging strategies pursued by treatment centers. These components greatly affect the ability of a particular treatment center to create a compelling and valuable identity/image to constituents.

Although creating a meaningful image may seem a complex and daunting task, it has never been more important than it is at present. "In the recent drive by corporations to become more competitive and more market oriented, utilizing market intelligence and marketing-research-generated information has gained center-stage status" (Menon and Varadarajan 1992, p. 53). Using imaging tactics to create a corporate identity seems to be a natural fit. But using imaging strategies to create a valuable corporate identity that results in a competitive advantage is easier said than done. Strategy selection must be "compatible with the internal organization" and must "provide stakeholders with a positive sense of identity" (Aaker 1995, pp. 33, 34). According to Siegel (1993, p. 26), "To cut through the noise of the marketplace, a corporation must speak with a clear, coherent and distinctive voice." Information must be "packaged in a memorable and believable way" (Aaker 1995, p. 198). For an image to yield the desired results, it "needs to be supported with substance, consistency, and credibility" (Brendsel 1993, p. 9). As discussed briefly in a previous section, two things are clear from the organization and marketing literature: (1) organizations must construct an image in such a way that differentiates the firm from its competition, and (2) the image presented through imaging efforts must be supported by reality.

The Ties that Bind

High rates of competition within a market area make it difficult for organizations to create a unique and memorable organizational image. The number of competitors is an obvious factor to consider because organizations can assume that some types of resources will by sought by all competitors. More competitors means that it is difficult for organizations to differentiate themselves to individual and organizational buyers, to establish the legitimacy of a particular organization, and to obtain increasingly scarce resources from funding agencies. Moreover, not all competitors will compete with the same intensity as other organizations; some will present major competition, and others will offer moderate or minor competition to competing organizations. Competitors that are more similar are likely to require many of the same organizational resources and thereby present more intense competition. The number of major competitors in an organization's market area will negatively affect its ability to create a valuable image and perform successfully as an organization. The number of competitors and intensity of competition can, in turn, affect the type of positioning strategy that is successful within a market area. The overall amount of competition faced within a center's market area depends not only on the number of competitors or the intensity of the competition, but also on the availability of customers and external funding opportunities. Thus, overall competition within the market area is the most comprehensive measure of competitive forces.

The treatment industry has undergone an initial wave of consolidation, indicating its relative maturity. At an industrywide level, the number of competitors and the intensity of the competition created a difficult environment in the 1980s, causing organizational uncertainty, performance detriments, and increasing organizational death. Since then, the industry has enjoyed a period of relative stability. But treatment centers do not primarily compete on an industrywide level; they compete locally. Although industry patterns reflect local competition patterns, they do not determine them. Geography, market size, government restrictions, and type of treatment organizations will cause the amount of competition within a particular market area to vary from locale to locale.

Whether a center faces a great deal of competition or few competitive challenges, developing a niche in the environment is a way for an organization to create a distinctive voice. Niche strategies enable an organization to present a unique image to constituents by emphasizing the range of services, special capabilities, and types of programs offered. Organizations with a wide niche width might pursue a generalist strategy, attempting to appeal to a wide variety of clients with a wide variety of services. Carroll (1985, p. 1266) notes that "Organizational generalists can operate in almost every environment because of the average outcomes across a wide range of conditions." However, in some conditions, specialists can have an advantage over generalists. Specialists inhabit a smaller niche width, concentrating their efforts on a small segment of the market and offering a smaller range of services. Muddlers are those organizations that follow no distinct strategy; they can have qualities of both generalists and specialists. Relative positioning in the market is determined by the number of programs and levels of care offered, the number of specialty services provided, and the type of niche emphasized in marketing efforts.

Generalists and specialists should have a definite advantage over muddlers because muddlers have no definable "plan of action." Developing a niche in the market makes both generalists and specialists identifiable to constituents. They have an identity that they can communicate to customers in the hope of developing legitimacy, either by promoting themselves as a "full-service" center or as a center specializing in certain types of clients or treatment modalities.

As mentioned previously, environmental stability affects the effectiveness of generalist or specialist strategies. Generalist strategies should be superior when the environment is less stable, when competition is intense, and/or when the general environment is unsettled because of regulatory forces or the newness of an industry. Specialists tend to thrive in more stable conditions, which allow for concentrated efforts and more specialized planning. Although both of these adaptive strategies have the potential for success, that success is dependent on environmental forces (Freeman, Carroll, and Hannan 1983).

Currently within the treatment center industry, specialists should be expected to have an advantage. The industry has matured, and though the environment is still somewhat uncertain, it is experiencing a degree of relative stability. However, because organizational buyers of treatment services compose such a large proportion of treatment center clients' payments, a generalist strategy might be superior. Organizational buyers could be more likely to seek out a more convenient "one-stop shop" for clients instead of maintaining contracts with several "specialty" programs. Contracting with centers that have a broad range of services enables organizational buyers to serve many different types of clients without having to be especially familiar with clients' cases and without having to individually match patients with particular types of specialty centers. Still, it is likely that specialists will be more successful in general, because the substance abuse treatment center industry is stabilizing.

Whereas competition and niche width affect how well an organization can create a distinctive voice and encourage patronage from constituents, imaging strategies affect what type of identity is portrayed and whether that image is buttressed by the actual strengths and capabilities of that organization. According to Zeithaml, Berry, and Parasuraman (1998, p. 44), "Discrepancies between service delivery and external communications—in the form of exaggerated promises and/or the absence of information about service delivery aspects—can affect consumer perceptions of service quality" (see also Duncan 1995). Organizations need to "be concerned with both *delivering* and *communicating* quality elements which consumers use to assess ... quality" (Silverman and Grover 1995, p. 263, italics in original).

Imaging strategies help substance abuse treatment centers improve performance by providing an organization with opportunities to present information to constituents that differentiates them from competitors by emphasizing unique organizational assets and abilities. Whether through advertising campaigns directed toward individuals and families, advertisements in industry publications, or direct contacts with managed care or health maintenance organization (HMO) contract managers, marketing efforts afford organizations a mechanism for communicating a unique, positive image to stakeholders. Increasing degrees of fit between these resources and imaging strategies is suggested to be positively related to treatment center performance. On the basis of the findings of Chandler and Hanks (1994), strategic congruence between these two concepts will result in a more efficient use of resources and, thus, in greater competitive advantage and long-term viability. Strategic congruence of marketing efforts ensures that these communication mechanisms will efficiently and effectively portray an accurate identity of the treatment center. Those centers that have congruence between assets and marketing efforts should have a distinct competitive advantage over centers that do not.

By examining demographic characteristics of an organization (sometimes referred to in the business literature as "firmographic" information), competition factors, and the role of imaging strategies in frameworks of population ecology and contingency theory, this study should reveal factors driving organizational success and survival in the substance abuse treatment industry and in similar organizations.

Competition, relative positioning in the market, and strategic congruence of marketing activities all contribute to the creation of organizational identity, which can combine with competition factors to affect overall organizational performance. Superior imaging efforts can lead not only to an increase in market share by outperforming competitors, but also to an increase in the size of the market altogether. One additional variable should also be examined to make the picture complete. The locus of a center's marketing activities speaks to the level of dedication an organization has for developing legitimacy with customers. This variable is not couched in population ecology or contingency theory but relates to institutional theory directly. The intensity of imaging activities indicates to what degree an organization perceives legitimacy-seeking efforts as a priority.

Background on Substance Abuse Treatment

A Brief History of the Industry

This examination is not a guide on how to conduct marketing in the context of substance abuse centers, nor is it meant to contain a comprehensive review of the historical development of substance abuse treatment. Rather, this article attempts to draw out the most crucial factors affecting competition, niche width, and imaging strategies and, thus, organizational performance and legitimacy in the substance abuse treatment industry. However, to present a more complete landscape of the industry and aid in developing the context of the hypotheses, a brief history of substance abuse treatment is presented.

Private alcohol and drug treatment centers in the United States increased their numbers by 83.5% between 1982 and 1990, which is nearly four times higher than the rate of their public sector counterparts (Weisner and Schmidt 1995). Data provided by Weisner and Schmidt indicate that the private sector served 72.6% of those treated for alcohol problems in 1990. These figures highlight the significance of private substance abuse treatment facilities. Early on, the relative lack of regulations governing the setup and administration of substance abuse treatment centers resulted in low entry barriers to the treatment industry. When new industries emerge, they do so with little guidance or interference from outside agencies. As industries mature, they become increasingly regulated through external and internal agencies that monitor and control certain operating standards (Bartlett and Intagliata 1982). Low entry barriers combined with a large potential client base resulted in an attractive environment for entrepreneurs, and the number of treatment centers expanded rapidly.

The target market for treatment centers grew enormously between 1973 and 1990 because of such factors as legislation, medicalization of drug and alcohol abuse, changes in employer practices, and the mainstreaming of the problems of substance abuse (Blackwell, Conrad, and Weed 1992; Roman 1981; Scanlon 1986). Because of the enlarged client base and the opportunities for growth, a flood of entrepreneurs penetrated the market in the early 1980s. Twelve-step programs proliferated, and within a few short years, the market was saturated. The competitive environment was further aggravated by the expanding number of government regulations imposed on treatment centers and by the increased demands made by HMOs and managed care entities in the late 1980s and early 1990s (Chambliss 1996).

As centers fought for customers and legitimacy with third-party payors and credentialing agencies, the field became characterized by an increase in professionalization and institutionalization. Because of the increased financial and logistical costs of staying in business, entry barriers rose. As it matured, the industry experienced a "shake-out" in the late 1980s because of increased competition and industry and government regulations. The failure rates of substance abuse treatment centers increased (Roman and Blum 1993).

Accreditation by such agencies as the Joint Commission on the Accreditation of Healthcare Organizations (JCAHO) came to be a sign of organizational legitimacy. The JCAHO is a "private, non-profit organization ... that evaluates, accredits, consults, and sets standards" for a variety of health care organizations, including substance abuse treatment units (National Network of Libraries of Medicine 1998). Currently, treatment centers are monitored by state and local agencies as well as the JCAHO (Bartlett and Intagliata 1982). Agency guidelines result in increased costs due to higher salaries required by a more educated and professionalized clinical staff and the logistical costs of meeting the criteria for accreditation reviews and providing accountability to parent organizations and third-party payors. Managed care, employee assistance programs, and HMOs now demand certain accreditation standards and documentation of care regimens to obtain referral contracts (Freeman 1995).

Although the industry remains competitive and continues to change, these forces are becoming more predictable. Centers are better understanding how to meet the expectations of organizational buyers, referral agents, and accreditation agencies. They are also learning how to recruit and treat their clients better. New organizational entries are relatively rare, but so are failures. Initial figures from the National Substance Abuse Treatment Center Study (NSATCS) data indicate a markedly lower failure rate (10%) compared with an earlier study (Roman and Blum 1988) that found a failure rate approaching 25%. Factors such as organizational learning and the shake-out of the 1980s might have contributed to the relative stabilization. But with the industry close to its carrying capacity, competition remains an important factor. Competition and struggles for identity place the imaging function in a central role.

How Is the Treatment Field Different from Other Service Industries?

The treatment industry has a great deal in common with most service industries. Similar to other service industries, the product of substance abuse facilities is difficult to define and measure. What should the outcome look like? Does success take the form of a satisfied client, a client with improved functioning, or a client treated at minimum cost? There are no recognized industry standards or standard indicators of performance. The JCAHO has attempted to construct meaningful criteria, but has done little to create useful indicators of performance because of the difficulty in measuring the qualities of a successfully treated client.

It is difficult for both organizational and individual customers to distinguish among competitors in the treatment industry. Even accreditation standards focus almost entirely on measuring organizational processes instead of outcomes because of the difficulty of defining performance in terms of outcome. Many treatment modalities are offered, but little information is available about their quality. Individual customers are often relatively uninformed and unaided when trying to make a choice among centers. Individuals may have little knowledge about treatment in general and have little basis for making a rational decision. Unlike other services, the decision to be admitted to substance abuse treatment is often unscheduled. Clients often enter treatment after deep personal conflict and reflection, following a confrontation with family, or as the result of legal or employment problems. Their situations often demand immediate attention, and thus, the client does not have the requisite time to make a fully informed decision (for that matter their physical and/or mental state might inhibit such a process). Finally, as mentioned previously, third-party payors might limit a client's choice. Therefore, it is important for treatment centers to create easily recognizable and differentiating identities to both individual clients and third-party payors. In addition, unlike many other industries, formalized substance abuse treatment is at once augmented by and competitive with several self-help groups, which are free of cost to their clients. Although organizations such as Alcoholics Anonymous are often used in conjunction with treatment, many potential clients may opt to forgo formal treatment and just use the available self-help groups. Treatment centers must also struggle to differentiate themselves from these types of programs. The degree of competitiveness and uncertainty in the private sector suggests that treatment center administrators will have to seek out new strategies to address the changing environment. Imaging activities and strategies could play an important role in increasing certainty and stability.

Because substance abuse treatment is an intangible and somewhat mysterious service, treatment centers have a greater need for a market-focused management than most industries do (Clarke and Estes 1992). Social stigma associated with addiction, conflicting public opinion about substance abuse, and the public's lack of information about substance abuse treatment create significant obstacles for organizational performance. In turn, this creates barriers to the legitimacy of individual treatment centers, as well as for the legitimacy of the industry as a whole.

Hypotheses

Eleven variables are included in the models to be analyzed (see Table 2). The control variables include size of the treatment center, age of the treatment center, organizational type of the center, and profit status. Competition is measured by the overall perceived degree of competition in a center's market area. The effects of relative positioning in the market are assessed with relationship to the treatment industry in general. Strategic congruence between competition and local competition pressures is also examined. Competition and relative positioning in the market are used to demonstrate the usefulness of a population ecology strategy and contingency theory in addressing organizational performance. Measures of imaging strategies are also used to further the contingency model of organizational performance. Strategic congruence of marketing tactics is measured by assessing the congruence between resources and marketing tactics, the congruence between referral agents targeted by marketing, and the percentage of referrals obtained from those agents. Another imaging variable, the locus of marketing activities is also examined. All these variables are couched within the larger theoretical framework of institutionalism, integrating the ways in which organizations create a positive image and affect performance, which, in turn, develops legitimacy. Each control variable is discussed briefly, though more complete arguments are presented for variables contained in the hypotheses tested subsequently.

Independent Variables

On the basis of the arguments presented previously, the following hypotheses are proposed:

H_1: Substance abuse treatment centers facing high rates of perceived overall competition will exhibit lower levers of organizational performance.

H_2: Substance abuse treatment centers with a specialist niche width will perform better than those with a generalist orientation.

H_3: Substance abuse treatment centers with fewer levels of care will perform better than those with more levels of care.

H_4: Substance abuse treatment centers with fewer specialty programs will perform better than those with more specialty programs.

H_5: Strategic congruence between niche width and the local environment will result in a higher level of performance.

H_6: Strategic congruence between resources and legitimacy-seeking efforts will be positively related to center performance.

The locus of control for legitimacy-seeking activities is also likely to be an important control factor. Many centers handle their own marketing activities; those that are associated with a parent hospital often leave the marketing tasks to the larger hospital. Still others contract services with a separate marketing company.

Centers whose locus of marketing activities is in-house will have a better understanding of legitimacy-seeking issues as they relate specifically to substance abuse treatment. As was discussed previously, substance abuse treatment is a unique industry with unique challenges. An in-house marketing staff is likely to have a more complete understanding of what is required to effectively market to their constituents, such as which contacts to make, what type of contracts to pursue, what kind of evidence of performance to offer to managed care organizations, and what categories of referral agents are producing the highest rate of referrals. They are more likely to understand the substance abusing population and what motivates individuals to enter a formal treatment program. An in-house marketing staff is more likely to have access to relevant data about patient populations and to have the insight for meaningful analysis, which can be used to successfully create or maintain legitimacy among constituents.

> H_7: Centers whose locus of marketing is contained in-house will exhibit higher levels of success than will centers that manage legitimacy-seeking activities out-of-house.

Control Variables

Size, as measured by the number of counselors employed, is postulated to have a positive effect on treatment center performance. Larger organizations are better able to accommodate change and adjust to unexpected trends (Aldrich and Marsden 1980). Weiner and Mahoney (1981) note that size is related to profits and stock prices, which indicated greater financial resources. Greater financial resources imply that more money is available to be budgeted for marketing activities. Both arguments present organization size as being positively related to treatment center performance.

Organizational ecology literature indicates that the age of a center is also predictive of performance, with newer and older centers having an advantage over "middle-aged" centers (Hannan and Freeman 1989; Roman and Blum 1992). According to Roman and Blum (1992, p. 16), "The logic for treatment centers operating in a turbulent environment is that older centers have had a longer time to establish a niche for survival, and younger centers are more likely to be based on a complete survey of current environmental conditions prior to their founding."

Several of the respondents whose centers were part of a larger corporate structure or a hospital indicated that if the treatment center were undergoing financial difficulty during which no revenues were coming in, the larger structure would provide funds to keep them open temporarily. In addition, centers that were part of a larger organization often reported that they received the indirect benefits of being associated with the larger entity through name recognition and the general marketing of the larger organization. Similar to organizational size, organizational structure will affect the amount of resources available, the amount of organizational slack that is allowable, and the amount of time a center can stay open if it falls on hard times (Roman and Blum 1992). Centers that are part of a hospital or larger corporate structure will have a higher level of performance than other types of centers.

The profit status of a treatment center (for-profit or not-for-profit) is also postulated to be a factor in determining a center's success. Not-for-profit centers are less concerned with competition because they are not entirely reliant on revenues to keep the center open. In addition, they may get their clients through different channels than for-profit centers. For example, not-for-profit centers tend to accept more charity cases or Medicaid patients, whereas for-profit centers are more likely to lure patients with insurance or who are self-paying. For this reason, profit status could also play a role in the intensity of imaging tactics, causing not-for-profit centers to be less compelled to use advanced marketing strategies. In addition, Scott and Meyer (1983) argue that, because of their reduced need to focus on costs and other traditional performance measures, not-for-profit organizations are judged more by processes than outcomes. In other words, constituents might be more attentive to compliance with regulations or ability to document credentialing of counselors than to measures of profitability, organizational growth, or market share in a not-for-profit organization. Because for-profit and not-for-profit centers have different motivations in terms of profit performance, performance measures should include financial and nonfinancial indicators of organizational well-being. Ideally, the two groups would be analyzed separately; however, sample size limits that possibility in this case. However, by entering the profit status variable as a step in the regression analysis, the differences between for-profit and not-for-profit firms can be examined satisfactorily. It is expected that for-profit centers will outperform not-for-profit centers.

These variables were included not only because of their presumed direct effects on treatment center performance, but because of their effects on legitimacy as well. The variables included in the model are not an exhaustive list of those related to performance, but rather are those most likely to be directly associated with organizational legitimacy.

Data and Measures

This study is a result of a grant funded by the National Institutes of Health to investigate determinants of organizational survival in the field of private substance abuse treatment. The sample analyzed for this study consists of 450 private substance abuse treatment centers across the United States. Stratified random sampling was done by area codes. Within the selected area codes, the population of private substance abuse treatment centers was defined, and a random sample of the identified centers was drawn. To be included in the sample population, a center must receive no more than half of its operating funds from public agencies (this includes for-profit or not-for-profit agencies), the center must treat adult clients (though not necessarily exclusively), and it must provide substance abuse treatment (detoxification-only units and halfway houses were not included in the sample). Face-to-face interviews were conducted with the administrative director, the clinical director (or equivalent), and the individual in charge of the marketing activities at each center. In many cases, one person performed two or more functions and was interviewed in all relevant capacities (for example, at many centers the marketing activities were performed by the head administrator). The response rate for the sample of treatment centers in the NSATCS is 89%.

This analysis examines competitive pressures, niche width, and imaging strategies as they affect the performance of private substance abuse treatment centers. There are two reasons this analysis focuses only on private treatment centers. First, private treatment centers (for-profit and not-for-profit) face different pressures than their public counterparts do. There is no guaranteed revenue, and there is no guaranteed clientele. More attention must be paid to generating revenue and meeting expenses. Competition, relative positioning in the market, and marketing are more salient issues for private centers compared with public facilities because public organizations, by their definition, receive the majority of their funds from government agencies. Private centers must direct more time and effort toward the solicitation of individual customers or organizational buyers, such as managed care organizations or insurance companies. Second, private substance abuse treatment centers are more like other business organizations. Therefore, the results of this study may generalize to other private businesses. This analysis examines what effect competition has on organizational performance, which positioning strategies lead to higher levels of performance, and the ways imaging strategies interact to affect organizational performance.

Performance

Within the health care industry, performance can be measured in terms of patient outcomes, financial data, or compliance with governmental or industry regulations. For the purposes of this analysis, success is defined in terms of organizational stability and growth in a number of areas. Performance is measured in terms of whether centers are operating at a loss (in the red) or at a profit (in the black), the change in the number of staff employed by a facility over the previous year, the likelihood of closure within the next year, the percentage of patient capacity maintained over the previous year, and administrators' perceptions of the center's financial trajectory. These five measures, in different ways, capture some element of organizational success. By using several different types of indicators, a more accurate and comprehensive understanding of performance is created.

The net profit margin is determined by subtracting total annual expenditures from total annual revenues and then dividing that number by the amount of revenues. This variable is recoded into a dichotomous variable because the sample is composed of for-profit and not-for-profit organizations. Not-for-profit organizations that operate at a high level of performance might show profits at or close to the break-even point because of their tax status. If a treatment center operates at a profit or at the point of breaking even, it is coded 1. If the center operates as a loss, it is coded 0. This variable is labeled REDBLACK.

Staff growth (ECHNGYN) is determined in a similar fashion by subtracting the number of employees currently employed by the center from the number of employees working at the center a year ago. Substance abuse treatment centers that have maintained or increased the number of employees over the previous year are coded 1. Centers that experienced a decline in staff are coded 0.

In the clinical portion of the treatment center interview, the medical director is asked for an estimate of the average daily census of patients over the previous year. The medical director is then asked the capacity of the current facility. The average daily census is divided by the patient capacity to yield the percentage of use of the facility's capacity. Use percentages greater than or equal to 60% (the mean operating capacity) are coded 1 and use percentages less than 60% are coded 0. This dichotomous variable is labeled PERCAPCT.

The perceived likelihood of closure (CLOSEHL) is also an important indicator of organizational performance. Administrators are asked to rate on a scale from 1 to 10 (where 1 indicated no threat of closure in the coming year, and 10 indicated certain closure of the treatment center) how likely it was that their center would close within the next year. Centers with a score that was greater than the average score are coded 0, and those centers with a lower-than-average score are coded 1. Lower-than-average scores indicate a higher-than-average level of organizational performance.

The last dimension of performance is the administrators' assessment of the trajectory of the center's future. Administrators indicate whether financial data demonstrate a growth trend, a declining trend, or a stability trend or whether the treatment center is experiencing a period of fluctuation. Growth or stability is coded 1, and decline is coded 0. Fluctuating trends are coded 0 as well, because they reflect instability in a firm's financial situation, which indicates a more negative outlook than either a growth or stability trend. This should not inhibit the analysis because only

26 treatment centers (5.7% of all centers interviewed) indicated a fluctuating financial trend. This variable is labeled TREND10.

Because two of the independent variables were best suited to logistic regression analysis (REDBLACK and TREND10), all the dependent variables were transformed into dichotomous variables to enhance the ability to compare outcomes among analyses. Each of the five measures of performance is regressed on the various control factors, competition variables, and marketing variable to determine which organizational factors contribute significantly to the various measures of organizational performance.

The Independent Variables

Data were collected regarding the overall amount of competition faced within a self-defined market area. To encompass both the number of competitors and the intensity of competition, respondents were asked to evaluate how much competition they face in their market area overall on a scale of 1 to 10 (OTENCOMP).

Organizations are characterized as generalists or specialists on the basis of three factors: (1) how many, if any, special tracks or programs they have available as components of treatment (e.g., special programming for women); (2) whether marketing explicitly indicates that an organization is a one-stop shop (generalists) or that an organization focuses mainly on a certain demographic group, such as court referrals (specialists); and (3) the number of levels of care provided (detoxification, partial hospitalization, and so on). Treatment centers that have six or more levels of care and no specialty programming and/or those indicating a generalist perspective in their marketing efforts are labeled generalists in that functional area. Those programs that have fewer than four levels of care and one or two specialty programs and/or those indicating a specialist perspective in their marketing activities are considered specialists in that functional area. Any other values are coded "muddling," because they do not support any specific positioning strategy (see the Appendix for detailed coding requirements). Generalists and muddlers are coded 0, and specialists are coded 1. Specialists are assigned the higher value because they are predicted to perform at a higher level than generalists or muddlers. This variable is labeled RNCHWDTH.

In addition to a composite measure of niche width, two indicators of niche width are examined individually: the number of levels of care offered at a center and the number of specialty programs provided. The number of levels of care (OVNLOCS) at each center is left as a continuous variable.

The number of programs or treatment tracks provided for special populations, SPECTRAK, is also left as a continuous variable. Special programming for women or differential tracking for impaired professionals are examples of specialized programs. This type of focused programming is indicative of a specialist strategy. Thus, substance abuse treatment centers that have a small number of specialty programs would be considered specialists and are predicted to outperform programs that provide a large number of specialty programs. Even though specialty programs indicate a specialist strategy, a large number of specialty programs indicates a generalist strategy, because the objective is to provide care for a wide range of consumers.

The composite measure of niche width is also used to create an interaction term using degree of competition in the local environment and niche width. This interaction term indicates whether having any congruent strategy is superior to muddling. Testing these related hypotheses will determine whether niche width strategies contribute to organizational performance and how they interact with local and industrywide market environments. Organizations that face a high degree of competition and pursue a generalist strategy are coded 1 because they exhibit strategic congruence. Organizations facing lower rates of competition that pursue a specialist strategy are also coded 1. All other combinations are coded 0 because they do not demonstrate strategic congruence.

Strategy/resource congruence (MATCH_1) is measured by assessing the fit between what administrators and marketing personnel identify to be advantages of the center and what marketing personnel identify as qualities of the center that are emphasized in marketing efforts. The responses for these open-ended questions are categorically coded (e.g., experienced staff, low operating costs, full continuum of care, specialized care programs, family programs, medical expertise available, reputation of hospital, high performance rate). The items identified by the administrator as assets or advantages are matched to comparable responses given by the marketer as qualities that are emphasized in the centers legitimacy-seeking efforts. The degree of congruence is quantified using the number of matches between categories (those identified as assets and emphasized in marketing efforts).

The locus of a center's marketing activities (LOCUSMKT) is determined as follows: treatment centers that employ an in-house marketer or indicate that the center is responsible for marketing activities are coded 1. Centers that have their marketing activities handled out-of-house, either through external marketing firms or by the hospital or corporate parent, are coded 0. An internal locus of marketing is assigned a value of 1 because it is predicted that in-house marketers will be more in tune with organizational resources and goals and have more time and expertise to devote to marketing activities.

Organization size (CATSIZE) is determined by the number of counselors currently on staff as determined from the interviews with the program administrators. This item remains a continuous variable. Number of counselors is used rather than number of beds in a facility, because many of the treatment centers included in the sample have only out-patient services.

Organization age is determined from the data given by the administrative director about the founding date of the center as a separate identifiable entity. The age of the center is defined as 1997 minus the founding date of the center. Because it is hypothesized that middle-aged centers will not perform as well as other centers, it is necessary to divide the centers into three categories: young, middle-aged, and older. A frequency list of centers was run to determine the variable categories. The categories fell rather naturally into the following groupings: 0 to 5 years old, 5 to 16 years old and 16 or more years old.

The organizational structure of a center (HOSPCORP) is coded 1 for hospital-based centers or those that are part of a larger corporate structure such as a chain of treatment centers or part of a larger health conglomerate. Free-standing centers are coded 0. The former are coded 1 because it is expected that chemical dependency units associated with a larger structure will perform better than free-standing centers. This leaves free-standing centers in the excluded category.

The profit status of each center (FORPROFI) is identified as being for-profit or not-for-profit by the administrative directors. For-profit centers are coded 1 because they are more likely to be motivated by cost concerns and thus more likely to implement competitive strategies that will result in a higher degree of performance. Not-for-profit centers are coded 0 because they are less concerned with competitive strategies because of their reduced reliance on profits as a financial base.

Table 1 Summary of Variable Definitions		
Abbreviated Name	**Variable Name**	**Description**
DEPENDENT VARIABLES		
REDBLACK	Profit margin	1 = (Revenues − Expenses) ≥ 0 0 = (Revenues − Expenses) < 0
CLOSEHL	Likelihood of closure	1 = Likelihood ≥ 2 0 = Likelihood < 2
PERCAPCT	Operating capacity	1 = (Census/capacity) ≥ 60% 0 = (Census/capacity) < 60%
ECHNGYN	Change in # of employees	1 = (Current # of employees − # of employees one year ago) ≥ 0 0 = (Current # of employees − # of employees one year ago) < 0
TREND10	Performance trajectory	1 = Growth or stability trend 0 = Decline or fluctuating trend
CONTROL VARIABLES		
MDAGEYN	Middle-aged center	1 = Middle-aged center (3–16 years) 0 = Older (>16) or younger center (< 3)
CATSIZE	Size (# of counselors)	1 = Less than 5 2 = 5 to 10 3 = More than 10
HOSPCORP	Type of organization	1 = Hospital or corporation 0 = Free-standing center
FORPROFI	Tax status	1 = For-profit 0 = Not-for-profit
INDEPENDENT VARIABLES		
OTENCOMP	Overall amount of competition	Scaled from 1 to 10
OVNLOCS	Number of levels of care offered	Minimum = 1 Maximum = 7
SPECTRAK	Number of specialty programs/ tracks offered	Minimum = 0 Maximum = 7
RNCHWDTH	Niche width	1 = Specialist 0 = Generalist, muddler
MATCH_1	Congruence between assets and marketing	Minimum = 0 Maximum = 6
LOCUSMKT	Locus of marketing activities/ responsibilities	1 = Internal locus 0 = External locus
STCONYN	Congruence between niche width and competitive environment	1 = Strategic congruence 0 = No strategic congruence

Results

The results presented here summarize the findings of five 2-step logistic regressions. The dependent variable is first regressed on the control variables. Then, measures of competition, niche width, and imaging strategies are added to the equation. Each logistic regression has as its dependent variable one element of organizational performance: profit, employment trend, operating capacity, performance trajectory, and likelihood of closure. Ideally, these items could have been scaled to provide a general measure of organization performance, but though each variable captures one element of performance, these elements were too disparate to create a reliable scale. Therefore, each measure is analyzed individually.

Overall, most variables were in the predicted direction (see Table 2). Eight of the 11 variables were significant in at least one equation, and 4 were significant in multiple equations. Although not presented in formal hypotheses, the control variables are discussed briefly. MDAGEYN, which showed both agreement and disagreement with the expected results, was statistically significant in only one equation (ECHNGYN). In that equation, it was predicted that younger and older centers were less likely to have stability or growth in terms of staff than middle-aged centers. Perhaps these results indicate that middle-aged centers possess some degree of equilibrium not seen in older or younger centers. It appears that, relative to many other industries, substance abuse treatment is still relatively young— the majority of centers have been open less than 16 years. As such, there might not be adequate variation in age to flesh out its effects on performance. Another explanation might be that many of the centers that experienced performance problems were weeded out during the shake-out of the late 1980s, creating greater parity among centers of all ages. Because few centers could claim genuine longevity, it was not an effective indicator of organizational performance or a means of enhancing organizational legitimacy for many centers.

Size, however, did emerge as a consistent indicator of performance. Always in the expected direction and significant in predicting the likelihood of closure, larger centers were more likely to exhibit measures of positive organizational performance than smaller centers. More counselors might mean more versatility and flexibility or the ability to offer more one-on-one therapy. Size can be used as a distinguishing characteristic, both with gatekeepers such as referral agents or managed care and with customers. By promoting a wide array of counselors and by offering individualized service, size can be used as a way of improving organizational success and gaining legitimacy with consumers.

Organizational type (HOSPCORP) was expected to favor hospital-based treatment centers or organizations that were part of a corporate chain. This prediction was based on the possibility that parent organizations might have the motivation and means to support struggling facilities through difficult times. Independent centers were expected to have lower levels of performance because they have no such source of support. This did not prove to be the case. In the two equations in which organizational type was found to be significant (PERCAPCT and TREND10), centers that were part of a chain or hospital were less likely to perform at high levels than their free-standing counterparts. The possibility that independent centers would have more freedom to adapt to changing situations and be able to use that to their advantage was overlooked when predictions were made.

Profit status (FORPROFI) was significant at the .05 level only in the equation analyzing current operating capacity (PERCAPCT). The resulting parameter indicated that not-for-profit centers had a higher level of performance.

Table 2
Summary of Regression Results

	REDBLACK (1)	REDBLACK (2)	CLOSEHL (1)	CLOSEHL (2)	PERCAPCT (1)	PERCAPCT (2)	ECHNGYN (1)	ECHNGYN (2)	TREND10 (1)	TREND10 (2)
Control Variables										
MDAGEYN	-.0798 (.3231) .9233	-.1014 (.3370) .9036	.2197 (.2259) 1.2456	.2561 (.2326) 1.2918	.0035 (.2437) 1.0035	.0230 (.2488) 1.0232	-.5771 (.2592) .5615*	-.6310 (.2647) .5321*	-.1178 (.2283) .8889	-.1925 (.2411) .8249
CATSIZE	.1445 (.1996) 1.1554	.0926 (.2151) 1.0970	.3903 (.1390) 1.4774**	.3359 (.1487) 1.3991*	.1310 (.1491) 1.1400	.2817 (.1612) 1.3253	.0654 (.1619) 1.0676	.1938 (.1750) 1.2139	-.0201 (.1390) .9801	.0902 (.1536) 1.0944
HOSPCORP	.3248 (.3755) 1.3838	.4206 (.4072) 1.5229	.0906 (.2772) 1.0948	.1486 (.2914) 1.1602	-.8476 (.2928) .4284**	-.8506 (.3062) .4271**	-.1741 (.3235) .8403	-.2115 (.3358) .8094	-.6559 (.2802) .5190*	-.6726 (.2980) .5104*
FORPROFI	.7607 (.3576) 2.1399*	.7096 (.3765) 2.033	.2517 (.2290) 1.2862	.2090 (.2375) 1.2325	-.9285 (.2709) .3952**	-.8747 (.2782) .4170**	.0568 (.2719) 1.0584	.0778 (.2751) 1.0809	-.1231 (.2300) .8841	-.0500 (.2411) .9512
Independent Variables										
OTENCOMP	—	-.0880 (.0647) .9158	—	-.1437 (.0469) .8662**	—	-.0042 (.0493) .9958	—	-.0576 (.0544) .9441	—	-.1371 (.0497) .8719**
OVNLOCS	—	.3035 (.1315) 1.3547*	—	.0438 (.0872) 1.0448	—	-.2185 (.0937) .8038*	—	-.1029 (.1085) .9022	—	-.3184 (.0934) .7273**
SPECTRAK	—	-.1709 (.1058) .8977	—	.0969 (.0855) 1.1017	—	-.0160 (.0906) .9841	—	-.1227 (.0953) .8845	—	.0817 (.0876) 1.0851

Table 2
continued

Independent Variables	REDBLACK (1)	REDBLACK (2)	CLOSEHL (1)	CLOSEHL (2)	PERCAPCT (1)	PERCAPCT (2)	ECHNGYN (1)	ECHNGYN (2)	TREND10 (1)	TREND10 (2)
RNCHWDTH	—	.0252 (.4545) **2.7876***	—	.6135 (.3035) **1.8468***	—	-.0101 (.3101) **.9899**	—	.0271 (.3533) **1.0275**	—	-.8281 (.3129) **.4369****
MATCH_1	—	.1930 (.1754) **.8245**	—	.2048 (.1431) **1.2273**	—	.0469 (.1447) **1.0481**	—	-.2011 (.1458) **.8178**	—	.1774 (.1421) **1.1941**
LOCUSMKT	—	.4140 (.2338) **1.5128**	—	.2226 (.1603) **1.2494**	—	-.1445 (.1760) **.8655**	—	-.1701 (.1824) **.8436**	—	.1098 (.1641) **1.1161**
STCONYN	—	-.4724 (.3681) **.6235**	—	-.1806 (.2606) **.8348**	—	.4516 (.2770) **1.5709**	—	-.3590 (.2981) **.6984**	—	.6869 (.2729) **1.9875***
CONSTANT	.7189 (.5643)	-.2611 (.8966)	-.3210 (.4095)	-.1569 (.6264)	-.2830 (.4433)	.3813 (.6742)	1.3189** (.4804)	2.6263** (.7668)	.7955 (.4183)	2.6624** (.6804)
-2 Log Likelihood	285.964	272.656	528.124	420.771	459.929	447.352	395.826	386.670	492.523	464.039
Percent Correct	80.94%	80.27%	65.71%	67.86%	72.99%	71.78%	74.58%	74.86%	55.12%	63.13%
Number of Cases Analyzed	299	299	420	420	411	411	354	354	361	361

*$p < .05$.
**$p < .01$.
Notes: Numbers in parentheses are the standard errors. Numbers in bold are the odds ratios.

The overall rate of competition was consistently predictive of performance. Centers experiencing higher rates of competition were more likely to close than the average center and less likely to be perceived as experiencing a positive or stable trajectory. Increased competition makes valued resources more scarce (e.g., employees, funding, patients), which makes differentiation from other centers more difficult.

The OVNLOCS variable was significant in three of the five equations. In explaining likelihood of closure and performance trajectory, the number of levels of care offered by a center decreased the likelihood of favorable performance. This indicates that, as hypothesized, specialists generally outperform generalists in the current stabilizing environment. Only in the equation examining financial success did the number of levels of care offered significantly favor organizations that followed a generalist strategy.

The niche width variable (RNCHWDTH) had similar results. It was significant in three equations; in two equations (REDBLACK and CLOSEHL) the parameters had the predicted sign, but in the analysis of performance trajectory, its parameter had a sign in contradiction to the hypothesis. Specialists were correctly predicted to outperform generalists in the former; however, in the latter, generalists were favored. But as previously mentioned, in the equation evaluating performance trajectory, strategic congruence (STCONYN) was also significant, which indicates that congruence between the environment and the overall strategy are also important to performance. This variable also conveys that having a strategy, as opposed to merely muddling, is important to organizational performance. Strategic planning and image projection are important to creating legitimacy among consumers.

Although the number of specialty tracks and programs contributed to the determination of niche width, it did not surface as a significant variable in any of the equations tested here.

Table 3
Summary of Significant Variables

INDEPENDENT VARIABLE	Dependent Variable				
	REDBLACK	CLOSEHL	PERCAPCT	ECHNGYN	TREND10
OTENCOMP		*			*
OVNLOCS	*		*		*
SPECTRAK					
RNCHWDTH	*	*			*
MATCH_1					
LOCUSMKT					
STCONYN					*
MDAGEYN				*	
CATSIZE		*			
HOSPCORP			*		*
FORPROFI			*		

*Variable was significant at the .05 level or lower.

MATCH_1, the degree to which an organization's assets were featured in marketing strategies, was not significant in any of the equations. This might reflect the overall lack of strategic marketing exhibited by substance abuse treatment centers. Health care marketing and especially the marketing of substance abuse treatment is still in a fledgling stage. Very little advertising is used. Few programs have a marketing plan that is integrated well with the other aspects of operations. Most centers had a modest marketing budget. Some centers claimed to do no marketing at all. This is likely to change as marketing of these types of services becomes more acceptable and as centers gain more insight as to how their centers can be effectively marketed to their customers. Having an internal locus of marketing activities was not significantly indicative of higher levels of performance in any of the equations.

Discussion

How has this examination of treatment centers enhanced the understanding of competition, niche width, and imaging strategies as they relate to performance? Competition has been proven to diminish organizational performance. Competition inhibits the procurement of valuable resources. Increased competition makes it more difficult to carve out a distinguishing identity in the market. And as evidenced in the analysis of performance trajectory, it interacts with positioning strategy to further impact organizational performance. Increased competition makes it more difficult to gain legitimacy among constituents and significantly affects the likelihood of closure and performance trajectory—the only two variables that tap into the prospects for future success. Perhaps more than any other measure, the degree of competition determines long-range performance. These findings add support to the growing literature that links rates of competition to performance (Baum and Oliver 1992; Hannan and Freeman 1983, 1989).

Levels of care offered and relative positioning in the market (niche width) parameters both suggest that, in general, specialists outperform generalists. Focusing resources on certain demographic groups or treatment modalities do appear to enhance the opportunities for success. Specialists might find it easier to create and communicate a clear and meaningful image of their capabilities to constituents. Such centers can capitalize on their ability to position themselves as experts in a certain area with individual and organizational customers. Treatment facilities that focus on narrower niche widths enjoy some advantages over their generalist counterparts, which supports concepts discussed by Aldrich and Marsden (1980).

Although the congruence between assets and marketing emphasis did not contribute significantly in predicting organizational performance, strategic congruence between the competitive environment and relative positioning in the market did emerge as significant in explaining performance trajectory. Whereas the other four dependent variables assess current performance (operating capacity), recent performance (profit margin, changes in staff), or short-term projections (likelihood of closure), only performance trajectory addresses long-term performance projections. This suggests that strategic congruence might have its largest effect on long-term performance. By pursuing a positioning strategy that is compatible with the surrounding competitive environment, an organization can capitalize on the advantages either positioning strategy has to offer.

Competition, niche width, and strategic congruence were all significant in explaining one or more measures of organizational performance. Each concept helped further develop the understanding of how image-building and performance contribute to organizational legitimacy. The results of this analysis support a nested theory of organizations. The ecological concepts of competition and niche width have combined with the contingency theory notion of strategic congruence under the broader banner of institutional theory to elicit a more complete tale of organizational image and performance as they relate to the legitimacy of private substance abuse treatment centers. Ecological and strategic factors work individually and in tandem to affect perceptions of an organization as a legitimate entity. In this way, ecology and contingency theories are nested in institutionalism because they both affect the "social construction of reality" (Wright and McMahan 1992, p. 313).

This analysis met with several challenges. The first was identifying measures of performance for a relatively new service industry. The second was constructing a model consisting of variables centered around how legitimacy is achieved with constituents. The third challenge was to synthesize this information in support of a nested theory of organizations.

As has been noted previously, performance is not easily defined in substance abuse treatment. Historically philanthropic and often not-for-profit, organizational performance in substance abuse treatment centers cannot be characterized in something as succinct as shareholder value or profit margin, nor is it captured in the "success" rates of an organization's clients. Most organizations do not sufficiently track clients, and those that do report success rates of approximately 40%. Instead, this study identified five measures that captured various aspects of organizational performance in the treatment center industry: performance trajectory, current operating capacity, change in the number of employees, profit, and threat of closure. These variables represent long- and short-term goals, objective and subjective criteria, and financial and operational indicators, which together offer up a comprehensive understanding of organizational success. Each represents a distinct element of organization performance. Hopefully, this will contribute to the notion that performance is a more multidimensional and complex concept than is usually acknowledged in studies of organizations.

Another elusive topic, legitimacy, presented separate challenges in operationalization. Difficult to measure directly, organizational legitimacy is most readily observed as organizational performance. Performance is enhanced or inhibited through competition, relative positioning in the market, and imaging tactics. Legitimacy indicates that customers have faith in an organization and in the product or service being sold. An organization must perform well to have legitimacy with constituents. Gaining legitimacy with constituents means that some type of rapport has been established. It indicates that an organization has sufficiently distinguished itself from competitors. Only those competitors that can develop an identity or image that is recognizable and convincing will compete successfully for scarce resources. Treatment organizations, like organizations in any other industry, must be able to capitalize on any and all tools and strategies at their disposal. As stated by Seymann (1998, p. 20), "In an era when differentiation of products and services is becoming increasingly difficult and the market value of companies is determined more by intangible than tangible assets, it is important to have a plan ... a blueprint for who you are and who you are not, what you do and what you do not do." This "plan" can consist of various tactics, but all must take into account an organization's assets, the environment, and how the two interact. This analysis demonstrates how both external (environment) and internal (positioning) strategies work individually and in tandem (strategic congruence) to affect performance and, thus, achieve legitimacy with various audiences.

This analysis does indeed evidence ecological forces, institutional influences, and elements of contingency theory. Competition is shown to be a significant predictor of performance, supporting ecological theory directly and contingency theory indirectly through its interaction with niche width. The idea of strategic congruence between these two factors adds a new dimension to the concept of competition. That is, "managements have ... become aware that competition is a broad term. Enterprises compete not only with pricing and variety and quality of merchandise, but in the manner in which they operate their business (Lewis 1994, p. 19). Whereas many studies have shown competition to negatively affect organizational success (Baum and Oliver 1992; Freeman and Hannan 1983; Hannan, Carroll, and Freeman 1989), competition in this analysis also provides a context for the implementation of positioning strategies. These factors work together to create an image that is meaningful and distinctive, an image that legitimizes an organization in the minds of constituents. In an industry with an intangible, mystified, difficult to evaluate "product" that is usually purchased by either a remote insurance agency or an individual in a fairly emergent situation, image is everything. Image will drive performance. And as suggested by a nested theory of organizations, competition, niche width, and strategic congruence operate in conjunction to determine an organization's image and, thus, how well it builds legitimacy.

The advantage of using a nested theory to examine organizational performance is that it is more sophisticated than just using one particular theory. It is more complex and can therefore provide a more comprehensive understanding of success, even allowing for the explanation of apparent contradictory findings. For example, a nested theory can acknowledge that specialists will perform better overall because of the relative stability in the industry, but it can also account for the fact that generalists perform well if the local environment is more competitive. Thus, all types of strategies can be valuable and successful given the right environment. Conversely, all types of environments can be fertile given the right strategy. Treatment centers can use various combinations of factors, depending on their environment, to improve legitimacy and enhance performance.

Conclusions

The type and accessibility of care offered to private treatment center clients affects a large number of citizens. Any increase or decrease in the number of private centers is bound to have an impact on these consumers, not to mention on the public centers as well. Convenience, in terms of either location and distance or having a center that works with a particular insurance company, may have an impact on a client's decision to enter or continue with treatment. Fluctuations in the number of private centers can increase or decrease the demand for publicly funded treatment. If a variety of private centers perform well and continue to provide service within a community and if constituents see treatment providers as legitimate, the chances of substance abusing individuals finding help are enhanced. It is important to ask how competition, relative positioning in the market, and imaging strategies contribute to the performance of private centers. Understanding how these factors affect performance might help the private sector adapt and flourish in a dynamic environment and survive the dramatic changes brought about by managed care and other environmental factors. Centers will be able to create more efficient and effective imaging strategies that can help them outperform competing centers. In turn, the ability to create better communication strategies can help the industry increase the size of the overall market. As more centers learn how to flourish in a variety of environments, legitimacy of the individual treatment centers improves; but more important, the legitimacy of the industry is enhanced as well. Increased organizational legitimacy might help illustrate the value of substance abuse treatment to more organizational buyers and individual clients.

As discussed previously, substance abuse treatment as an industry is relatively new and faces a variety of obstacles. Organizational performance is equivalent to organizational legitimacy, especially in young industries. Lack of awareness or understanding of the industry creates a series of obstacles to success. Social stigma associated with substance abuse treatment, lack of understanding about substance abuse, and questions about the effectiveness of treatment act as barriers to the public's acceptance of substance abuse treatment as a valuable service. Individuals suffering from addictions may fail to seek treatment for these same reasons. As centers better learn to manage their individual identities and the public's perceptions of substance abuse treatment, they can improve their own performance and open up the possibilities of treatment for more individuals. By establishing their own legitimacy, organizations further the crusade to address substance abuse as a "disease like any other."

With such a large number of substance abusers not currently involved in a formal treatment program, the possible organizational and sociological effects of expanding the market are significant. A vast majority of individuals with substance abuse problems never find their way into treatment. Sorbell and colleagues (1993) find that anywhere from 75% to 93% of all alcoholics never enter formal treatment. Weisner and Schmidt (1995, pp. 708–709) note that "some segments of the substance-abusing population are more likely to seek help from nonspecialty services than from settings designed specifically for their needs." Mental health or welfare agencies are often contacted before substance abuse centers.

As individual organizations increase their ability to perform well in a variety of environments, they become more legitimate in the eyes of their constituents. The legitimacy generated by individual organizations carries over to the industry as a whole. Legitimacy as an industry will help individual centers grow and thrive. Increasing organizational and industrial legitimacy could convince more substance abusers of the effectiveness of treatment.

More strategic efforts to manage organizational image and legitimacy may result in reaching more affected individuals and get them the help they need. Better communicating the assets of substance abuse treatment centers and improved market positioning of organizations could result in increasing not only their proportion of the existing market share, but also the size of the overall market by reaching the large share of individuals who have not considered formal treatment.

Acknowledgments

The author thanks all the people who have contributed their time and valuable input to the creation of this document. She thanks the chairman of her committee, Paul Roman, for his guidance throughout her graduate school career and for giving her the opportunity to work on the Substance Abuse Treatment Center project. She also thanks the National Institutes of Health, whose grant funded the National Substance Abuse Treatment Center Study. She acknowledges the traineeship that lent financial support to her academic efforts for four years, NIH Grant #T32-AA-07473 from the National Institute on Alcohol Abuse and Alcoholism.

Appendix

Description of Coding Rules for Niche Width

OVNLOCS + SPECTRAK + MKTORENT = NICHE WIDTH

If all three categories had the same orientation, then that type is the niche width. (e.g., specialist, specialist, specialist = specialist niche width)

If two of the three had the same orientation, then that type is the niche width. (e.g., muddler, generalist, muddler = muddler)

If each category had a different orientation, then it is categorized as a muddler. (e.g., muddler, specialist, generalist)

References

Aaker, David A. (1995), *Strategic Market Management*. New York: John Wiley & Sons Inc.

Abel, E. L. and M. L. Kruger (1995), "*Hon v. Strohs Brewery Company*: What Do We Mean by 'Moderate' and 'Heavy' Drinking?" *Alcoholism: Clinical and Experimental Research*, 19 (4), 1024–31.

Aldrich, Howard E. and Peter V. Marsden (1980), "Technology and Organizational Structure: A Reexamination of the Findings of the Aston Group," in *A Sociological Reader in Complex Organizations*, Amitai Etzioni and Edward Lehman, eds. New York: Holt, Rhinehart and Winston, 233–50.

Bartlett, Donald P. and James Intagliata (1982), "Integration of Quality Assurance and Program Evaluation Activities in Alcoholism Treatment Programs: Part I," *Quality Review Bulletin: The Journal of Quality Assurance*, (Special Ed.), 7–12.

Baudrillard, Jean (1988), *The Ecstasy of Communication*. New York: Semiotext(e).

Berg, Peter Olaf (1989), "Postmodern Management? From Facts to Fiction in Theory and Practice," *Scandinavian Journal of Management*, 5 (3), 201–217.

Blackwell, Terry L., A. Denise Conrad, and Roger O. Weed (1992), *Job Analysis and the ADA: A Step by Step Guide*. Athens, GA: Southern Press.

Brendsel, Leland C. (1993), "Shaping Corporate Image," in *Corporate Image: Communicating Visions and Values*, Report Number 1038. New York: The Conference Board Inc.

Carroll, Glenn (1985), "Concentration and Specialization: Dynamics of Niche Width in Populations of Organizations," *American Journal of Sociology*, 90 (6), 1262–83.

Chambliss, Catherine (1996), "How Managed Care Is Dividing the Helping Professions," *Perspectives: A Mental Health Magazine*, (accessed September 15), [available at http://www.cmhc.com/perspectives/articles/art09964.htm].

Chandler, Gaylen N. and Steven Hanks (1994), "Market Attractiveness, Resource-Based Capabilities, Venture Strategies and Venture Performance," *Journal of Business Venturing*, 9, 331–49.

Cheney, George (1992), "The Corporate Person Represents Itself," in *Rhetorical and Critical Approaches to Public Relations*, E. L. Tooth and L. L. Heath, eds. Hilldale, NJ: Erlbaum Associates, 165–83.

Christensen, Lars Thoger (1995), "Buffering Organizational Identity in the Marketing Culture," *Organization Studies*, 16 (4), 651–72.

Clark, Lee and Carroll L. Estes (1992), "Sociological and Economic Theories of Markets and Nonprofits: Evidence from Home Health Organizations," *American Journal of Sociology*, 97 (4), 945–69.

Coveleski, M.A. and M.W. Dirsmith (1988), "An Institutional Perspective on the Rise, Social Transformation and Fall of a University Budget Category," *Administrative Science Quarterly*, 33 (3), 562–87.

Deephouse, David L. (1996), "Does Isomorphism Legitimate?" *Academy of Management Journal*, 39 (4), 1024–39.

DiMaggio, Paul J. (1988), "Interest and Agency in Institutional Theory," in *Institutional Patterns and Organizations: Culture and Environment*, Lynne G. Zucker, ed. Cambridge, MA: Ballinger, 3–21.

———— and Walter W. Powell (1983), "The Iron Cage Revisited: Institutional Isomorphism and Collective Rationality in Organizational Fields," *American Sociological Review*, 48 (4), 147–60.

Duncan, Tom (1995), "A Macro Model of Integrated Marketing Communication," paper presented at the Integrated Marketing Conference, Norfolk, VA (March).

Ewen, Stuart (1988), *All Consuming Images: The Politics of Style in Contemporary Culture*. New York: Basic Books.

Freeman, John, Glenn Carroll, and Michael T. Hannan (1983), "The Liability of Newness: Age Dependence in Organizational Death Rates," *American Sociological Review*, 48, 692–710.

Freeman, Michael A. (1995), "The Policy Challenges of Managed Behavioral Health Care," *Policy in Perspective*, (September), Washington, DC: Policy Resource Center.

Gilligan, Colin and Robin Lowe (1995), *Marketing and Health care Organizations*. New York: Radcliffe Medical Press.

Hannan, Michael T., Elizabeth A. Dundon, Glenn R. Carroll, and John Charles Torres (1995), "Organizational Evolution in a Multinational Context: Entries of Automobile Manufacturers in Belgium, Britain, France, Germany, and Italy," *American Sociological Review*, 60 (August), 509–528.

———— and John Freeman (1977), "The Population Ecology of Organizations," *American Journal of Sociology*, 82 (5), 929–64.

———— and ———— (1983), "Niche Width and the Dynamics of Organizational Populations," *American Journal of Sociology*, 88 (6), 1116–45.

———— and ———— (1989), *Organizational Ecology*. Cambridge, MA: Harvard University Press.

Hinings, Bob and Royston Greenwood (1988), "The Normative Prescription of Organizations," in *Institutional Patterns and Organizations: Culture and Environment*, Lynne G. Zucker, ed. New York: Harper Business.

Hoekstra, V. J. (1995), "The Supreme Court and Opinion Change—An Experimental Study of the Court's Abilities to Change Opinion," *American Politics Quarterly*, 23 (11), 109–129.

Humphreys, Keith, Rudolf J. Moos, and John W. Finney (1995), "Two Pathways Out of Drinking Problems Without Professional Treatment," *Addictive Behaviors*, 20 (4), 421–27.

Ingersoll, Richard (1993), "Loosely Coupled Organizations Revisited," *Research in the Sociology of Organizations*, 11, 81–112.

Lawrence, Paul R. and Jay W. Lorsch (1986) [1967], *Organization and Environment: Managing Differentiation and Integration*. Boston: Harvard Business School Press.

LeBlanc, Gaston and Nha Nguyen (1996), "Cues Used by Customers Evaluating Corporate Image in Service Firms: An Empirical Study in Financial Institutions," *International Review of Service Industry Management*, 7 (2), 44–56.

Lewis, Edward M. (1994), *An Introduction to Credit Scoring*. San Rafael, CA: The Athena Press.

Menon, Anil and P. Rajan Varadarajan (1992), "A Model of Marketing Knowledge Use Within Firms," *Journal of Marketing*, 56 (October), 53–71.

Meyer, John W. and Brian Rowan (1977), "Institutional Organizations: Formal Structure as Myth and Ceremony," *American Journal of Sociology*, 83, 340–63.

———— and ———— (1992), *Organizational Environment: Ritual and Rationality*. Newbury Park, CA: Sage Publications.

Moore, J. S. (1992), "Conceptions of Alcoholism," *International Journal of the Addictions*, 27 (8), 935–45.

Mulford, H. (1994) "What if Alcoholism Had Not Been Invented? The Dynamics of American Alcohol Mythology," *Addiction*, 89, 321–39.

National Network of Libraries of Medicine (1998), "DIRLINE Record for JCAHO," (accessed March), [available at http://www.nnlm.nlm.nih.gov/nnlm/jcaho.html].

Oliver, Christine (1991), "Strategic Responses to Organization Processes," *Academy of Management Review*, 16 (1), 145–79.

Parsons, Talcott (1960) [1956], "Some Ingredients of a General Theory of Formal Organization," in *Structure and Process in Modern Societies*. Glencoe, IL: The Free Press.

Perniola, Mario (1980), *The Society of Pretense*. Bologna: Cappelli.

Perrow, Charles (1985), "Review Essay: Overboard with Myth and Symbols," *American Journal of Sociology*, 91 (1), 151–56.

Pfeffer, Jeffrey and Gerald Salancik (1978), *The External Control of Organizations*. New York: Harper and Row.

Podolny, Joel M., Toby E. Stuart, and Michael T. Hannan (1996), "Networks, Knowledge, and Niches: Competition in the Worldwide Semiconductor Industry, 1984–1991," *American Journal of Sociology*, 102 (3), 659–89.

Porter, Michael E. (1980), *Competitive Strategy: Techniques for Analyzing Industries and Competitors*. New York: The Free Press.

Powell, W. W. (1985), "The Institutionalization of Rational Organizations," *Contemporary Sociology*, 14, 564–66.

Prahalad, C.K. and Gary Hamel (1990), "The Core Competence of the Corporation," *Harvard Business Review*, (May/June), 79–91.

Priem, Richard L. (1994), "Executive Judgement, Organizational Congruence and Firm Performance," *Organizational Science*, 5 (3), 421–37.

Roman, Paul M. (1981), "From Employee Alcoholism to Employee Assistance," *Journal of Studies on Alcohol*, 42 (3), 244–72.

——— and Terry C. Blum (1988), "Formal Intervention in Employee Health: Comparisons of the Nature and Structure of Employee Assistance Programs and Health Promotion Programs," *Social Science and Medicine*, 26 (5), 503–514.

——— and ——— (1992), *Proposal for the Study of Substance Abuse Treatment Facilities*. Grant Proposal National Institutes of Health.

——— and ——— (1993), "Dealing with Alcohol Problems in the Workplace," in *Recent Developments in Alcoholism*, Vol. 11, Marc Gallenter, ed. New York: Plenum Press.

Roth, Aleda V. and William E. Jackson III (1995) "Strategic Determinants of Service Quality and Performance: Evidence from the Banking Industry," *Management Science*, 41 (11), 1720–33.

Scanlon, Walter F. (1986), *Alcoholism and Drug Abuse in the Workplace: Employee Assistance Programs*. New York: Praeger.

Scott, W. Richard (1993), "The Organization of Medical Care Services: Toward an Integrated Theoretical Model," *Medical Care Review*, 50 (3), 271–304.

——— (1995), *Institutions and Organizations*. Thousand Oaks, CA: Sage Publications.

Siegel, Alan (1993), "Corporate Image: One Unique Voice," in *Corporate Image: Communicating Visions and Values*, Report No. 1038. New York: The Conference Board Inc.

Silverman, Steven N. and Rajiv Grover (1995), "Forming Perceptions of Overall Product Quality in Consumer Goods: A Process of Quality Element Integration," *Research in Marketing*, 12, 251–87.

Seymann, Marilyn (1998), "Branding Means Providing Something to Be Loyal To," *American Banker*, 163 (90), 20–21.

Sorbell, Linda C., Mark B. Sorbell, Tony Toneatto, and Gloria I. Leo (1993), "What Triggers the Resolution of Alcohol Problems Without Treatment?" *Alcoholism: Clinical and Experimental Research*, 17 (2), 217–24.

Weiner, N. and T.A. Mahoney (1981), "A Model of Corporate Performance as a Function of Environmental, Organizational and Leadership Influences," *Academy of Management Journal*, 24, 453–70.

Weisner, C. and L. A. Schmidt (1995), "Expanding the Frame of Health-Services Research in the Drug Abuse Field," *Health Services Research*, 30 (5), 707–26.

Woodward, Joan (1965), *Industrial Organization: Theory and Practice*. New York: Oxford University Press.

Wright, Patrick M. and Gary C. McMahan (1992), "Theoretical Perspectives for Strategic Human Resource Management," *Journal of Management*, 18 (2), 295–320.

Zahradnik, Rich (1986), "More Than Pretty Pictures," *Business-to-Business Guide*, B34–B41.

Zeithaml, Valerie A., Leonard L. Berry, and A. Parasuraman (1988), "Communication and Control Processes in the Delivery of Service Quality," *Journal of Marketing*, 52 (April), 35–48.

Zucker, Lynne G. (1977), "The Role of Institutionalization in Cultural Persistence," *American Sociological Review*, 42, 726–43.

15

Carving a Path to Dominance While Avoiding the Graveyard: Consumers' Brand Knowledge and Genericism

Gillian Oakenfull
Miami University

The quest for brand equity motivates marketers to build high brand awareness to place their brands first in consumers' minds. For many dominant brands, such as Kleenex and FedEx, the effort to build brand familiarity has proved so successful that consumers use the brand name to refer to the entire product category. However, extreme familiarity with a brand name could lead to the death of a brand if consumers unknowingly employ the brand name as the product category label (Zinkhan and Martin 1982). This condition, labeled "genericide" in trademark litigation, can be avoided by astute research and marketing communications.

Many brands have been used generically, that is, as the product category label; however, not all these brands have considered it a negative situation. In fact, FedEx built on consumers' use of the brand in this way by adapting its communications strategy to reinforce this usage. The success of generic brands in the marketplace and the need for corrective advertising has greatly differed among brands.

Thus, although high brand awareness is vital to build and maintain brand equity, marketers must be aware of certain situations in which customers' familiarity with the brand name can lead to genericide. To identify the potential for genericide, marketers must understand how their brands are represented in consumers' memories (Zinkhan and Martin 1987). In this study, I examine the issue of genericide within the framework of Keller's (1992) conceptualization of customer-based brand equity, which is grounded in the representation of brand knowledge as a network of associations in consumers' memories. From this viewpoint, marketers can begin to understand how consumers' differential representation of generic brands in memory may result in either category dominance or genericide. With this knowledge, marketers can detect the potential for genericism and undertake the marketing actions that are necessary to prevent customer confusion and build brand equity.

Thus, in this study I address the following issues: (1) How is genericide defined? (2) How are generic brands represented in consumer memory? (3) Why do brands become generic? (4) How does generic usage affect brand equity? and (4) How can marketers detect whether their brands are in danger of genericide?

What Is Genericide?

In the strictest sense, the term genericide was coined by trademark experts to refer to the death of a brand name resulting from a court ruling that consumers perceive the brand name as inextricably linked to the product category. Bayer's aspirin brand of acetylsalicylic acid was the first brand to lose exclusive rights to the use of a brand name. From that point, all acetylsalicylic acid tablets were known as aspirin.

In recent years, courts have weighed the efforts of marketers to educate consumers on the correct use of the brand name and to restrict misuse by competitors in the consideration of whether a brand will be deemed generic. As a result, though the expenditures on educational advertising and legal vigilance might inhibit the financial performance of the company, few firms have had to face the loss of their brand names and their equity because of court rulings of genericide.

However, although the threat of legally losing the exclusive ownership of a brand name has declined, the confusion that can result when consumers use a brand name as the product category label might well lead to an unfavorable situation in the marketplace. In this article, I refer to brand names that are used by consumers as the product category label as "generic" brands, the type of usage as "genericism," and brands that suffer a loss of performance through this confusion as victims of genericide. Thus, by my definition, genericide is not the legal loss of ownership to the brand, but the loss of brand ownership in consumers' minds.

Not all brands become generic, and generic usage does not affect all brands adversely. However, both the potential rewards of category dominance and the threat of genericide should provide marketers with a strong incentive to determine why consumers use product and brand labels interchangeably. To understand this phenomenon, it is helpful to examine how brands and product categories are represented in consumers' memories.

Representation of Generic Brands in Consumer Memory

Drawing from cognitive psychology, I conceptualize a consumer's knowledge of a brand using elements of memory structure and an associative network model (Anderson 1983). Semantic memory consists of a set of nodes and links. Nodes are stored information that are connected by links of varying strengths. The extent of retrieval in memory is determined by a spreading activation process from one node to another (Collins and Loftus 1975). A node can activate other nodes when external information is retrieved. Activation spreads from one node to another until a threshold level is reached and the information is retrieved. The extent to which this spreading activation occurs is determined by the strength of the association between nodes, which in turn determines what information is retrieved. Thus, brand information is represented in a consumer's memory not in isolation but in several contexts to which it is linked (Collins and Loftus 1975), such as product category, consumers' self-concepts (Karande, Zinkhan, and Lum 1997), or their notion of the good life (Zinkhan and Prenshaw 1994). As illustrated in Figure 1, a reference to the product category can prompt thoughts of the brand, and reference to the brand can prompt thoughts of the product category.

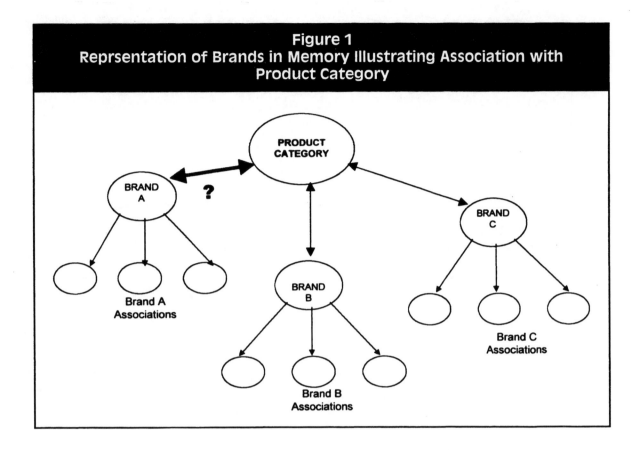

Figure 1
Reprsentation of Brands in Memory Illustrating Association with Product Category

Figure 2 depicts a memory network for a product category that contains a victim of genericide. In this case, a node for the brand (Brand A) does not exist in consumers' memories, and all the product category associations, including other brands and their respective associations, are linked to the node labeled with the brand name. Thus, exposure to the generic brand name causes consumers to think about the product category and other brands of the product. For example, when consumers hear the name Xerox, they bring to mind associations with Mita, Canon, and Konica brands of photocopiers.

However, this is not the case for all generic brands. For example, consumers might refer to all facial tissues as Kleenex, but they can still label the product correctly if presented with it. In this situation, the product category and the brand are each represented by a node in memory. Although consumers use the brand name to refer to the product category, the representations are distinct in memory, which allows consumers to link brand-specific associations to the Kleenex node.

Because most brands are separated from the product category in consumers' minds, genericism is the exception. However, given the possible negative consequences, it is important that managers are able to detect the potential for genericism early in a brand's life. This is facilitated by a clear understanding of the causes of genericism, which are discussed in the following section.

Why Do Brands Become Generic?

Throughout history, various brands have fallen to genericide. A review of previous research on brand dominance and brand structure can provide managers with

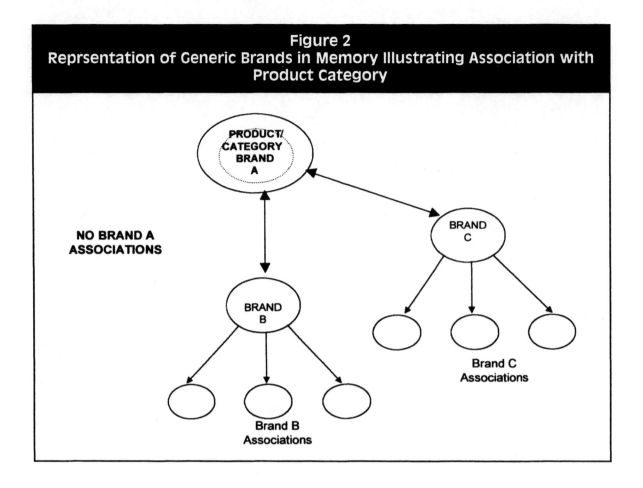

Figure 2
Reprsentation of Generic Brands in Memory Illustrating Association with Product Category

some understanding of why certain brands become inseparably linked to their product categories.

The brand was a pioneer. Pioneer brands, or brands that are first to enter the market, often have a strong influence on how consumers' preference structures are formed (Carpenter and Nakamoto 1987). As such, consumers have no prior knowledge of which product attributes are the most important or what their ideal combination of attributes might be. Thus, the pioneer brand becomes the prototype for the category. This might give the brand a competitive advantage if the firm supports it well with marketing actions and can often lead to a situation in which the prototypical brand becomes the product category label (e.g., Kleenex, Rollerblade, Xerox). A brand that is first to enter a category might exist as the sole member of the category for a long time. If so, consumers have little need to use the brand to distinguish between different offerings of the product. Thus, all associations that consumers might link to the brand node are synonymous with those of the product category, and the nodes become redundant.

The category lacks a label. A category label might not have been developed when the product was introduced to the market as a pioneer. For example, customers had no choice but to associate anything that they encoded about moving electric staircases to the node in their memory that was labeled "escalator."

The brand name is simpler to remember and easier to pronounce than the category label. The theory of bounded rationality (Simon 1969) suggests that consumers are not perfectly rational information processors and develop decision rules or heuristics to manage information in memory. According to this theory, information must be processible for consumers to encode, store, and retrieve it. In the case of aspirin, consumers simply could not pronounce or remember the term acetylsalicylic acid and used the brand name Aspirin as a heuristic. Therefore, the aspirin node replaced the category node in memory, and all associations with the product category were attached to the brand node.

The brand name is descriptive. Similarly, if the brand name is descriptive of the product, it might cause confusion by being strongly related to the category label. In this case, product information is wrongly linked to the brand name until consumers can no longer distinguish between the two.

I have discussed how a brand can become generic and the impact of these circumstances on consumers' representations of generic brands in memory. However, genericism appears to have a differential impact on brands. Some generic brands, such as Kleenex, have enjoyed high brand equity and long-standing success in the marketplace, whereas others, such as Xerox, have struggled to establish a market position and have poured thousands of dollars each year into advertising to correct the confusion. Brand equity results from consumers' association with a brand (Aaker 1991, 1996; Keller 1993). Therefore, the nature of the equity attached to the brand could be severely affected by the brand's representation as compared with the product category in consumers' memories.

Decomposing the Equity of Generic Brands

To understand how generic usage of a brand name can affect brand performance in the marketplace, it is necessary first to consider what brand equity is and how it is formed. Aaker (1991, p. 15) defines *brand equity* as "a set of brand assets and liabilities linked to a brand, its name and symbols, that add to or subtract from the value provided by a product or service to a firm or to that firm's customers." These assets include name awareness, brand associations, perceived quality, brand loyalty, and proprietary assets (Dobni and Zinkhan 1990).

Keller's (1993) conceptualization of customer-based brand equity focuses on the effect of customers' brand knowledge on their response to marketing actions. Specifically, he defines *customer-based brand equity* as "the differential effect of brand knowledge on consumers' response to the marketing of a brand" (p. 8).

Customer-based brand equity occurs when a familiar brand has favorable, strong and unique associations in consumers' minds (Keller 1993). Generic usage of a brand name occurs at the customer level; therefore, it is appropriate to consider the impact of genericism on customer-based brand equity. For a brand to have customer-based brand equity, a node for brand knowledge is formed in memory to which a variety of associations is linked. The extent of brand knowledge is explained by the consumer's awareness of the brand and the favorability, strength, and uniqueness of the brand associations in memory.

The Impact of Brand Awareness on Brand Equity

It appears that consumers are highly aware of generic brands, given their usage as product category labels. However, by examining the antecedents of brand awareness, marketers can begin to discriminate between successful and less successful generic brands.

Brand awareness is determined by the strength of the brand node in memory, that is the probability that a brand will come to a consumer's mind and the ease with which it does so. As I have discussed, generic brands might not have a brand node and nodal network that is distinct from the product category. Consequently, the ease with which a generic brand node comes to mind may vary as will the association network with which it is linked. A study of brand awareness might be the first step in differentiating among brand equity of generic brands. Researchers have shown that brand awareness is an important dimension of consumer decision making for the following reasons:

1. High brand awareness increases the likelihood that a brand will be a member of a consideration set (Nedungadi 1990).
2. Brand awareness may solely determine the result of consumers' decisions about the consideration set (Jacoby et al. 1977).
   a. Consumers may buy only familiar brands.
   b. In low-involvement decisions, consumers may choose solely on the basis of brand awareness without forming attitudes such as those suggested by the elaboration likelihood model (Petty and Cacioppo 1984).
3. Brand awareness affects the formation and strength of brand associations in memory.

Brand awareness has two dimensions—brand recognition and brand recall. Brand recognition is the extent to which a consumer can confirm prior exposure to a brand when the brand name is presented as a cue. Brand recall is measured as the consumer's ability to retrieve the brand name from memory when the product category is given as a cue.

The relative importance of recognition and recall as determinants of brand awareness depends on the situation that surrounds consumers' decision making. Consumers making a decision at the store might be exposed to the brand on the store shelf, which necessitates brand recognition only. Decisions made outside the store increase the salience of brand recall (Bettman 1979). A consideration of brand awareness and its components, brand recognition and brand recall, provides a method for delineating between generic brands.

Consumer Awareness of a Generic Brand

Awareness refers to the strength of a brand's presence in the consumer's mind and is composed of recognition and recall of the brand. As David Aaker (1996, p.10, emphasis in original) states in his book *Building Strong Brands*, "recognition reflects familiarity gained from past exposure. Recognition does not necessarily involve remembering *where* the brand was encountered before, *why* it differs from other brands, or even *what* the brand's product class is. It is simply remembering that there was a past exposure to the brand." Previous studies have shown that recognition alone can result in more positive feeling toward a brand. In one study, participants in a taste test were asked to choose between an unnamed superior peanut butter and an inferior peanut butter labeled with a brand name known to the participants but not previously purchased or used by them. Seventy-three percent of the participants chose the peanut butter with the brand name as the best-tasting, though it was inferior (Hoyer and Brown 1990). Economists explain this phenomenon as more than an instinctive response. When consumers recognize a brand, they feel that the company is putting its resources into supporting the brand. Believing that companies will not spend money to support a bad brand, they take the brand recognition as a signal that the brand is good (Aaker 1996).

Recognition of Generic Brands

There is little doubt that consumers will recognize generic brands when presented with them. Given that a brand name has entered common language, it is doubtful that a consumer could not confirm prior exposure to a brand name. Thus, brand recognition is expected to be high for all generic brands.

> P_1: Consumer recognition of all generic brands is as high or higher than recognition of nongeneric brands.

Influence of Consumers' Product Category Knowledge on Recognition of Generic Brands

As previously mentioned, though consumers might recognize the brand name, the important issue in detecting genericide is what the brand node actually represents in consumer memory. This may vary from consumer to consumer, often depending on their prior trial of the brand or their level of involvement in the product category. For example, avid roller hockey players might refer to their skates as rollerblades but know that the product category label is in-line skates. These consumers would be aware of other brands of the product. In this case, the brand is strongly associated with the product category but does not replace it. However, recreational skaters might be unaware that the Rollerblade brand even exists and refer to their skates as First Sport rollerblades. The latter situation can have serious ramifications for Rollerblade in the marketplace.

Thus, simple recognition does not identify the meaning that consumers attribute to the brand name. Some consumers may see the name Rollerblade and, while thinking of the product, in-line skates, confirm recognition of the word. A visual stimulus, such as a picture of the product that does not present the name of either the product or the brand, would determine the type of node that consumers hold in memory. As mentioned previously, despite generic usage of the brand name, it is expected that consumers who are knowledgeable about the product category will distinguish between the generic brand and the product category more readily than less experienced consumers.

> P_{2a}: For generic brands, consumers with a greater knowledge of the product category are more likely than less knowledgeable consumers to label the product with the product category label when prompted with a visual cue of the product.
>
> P_{2b}: For generic brands, consumers with little knowledge of the product category are more likely than more knowledgeable consumers to label the product with the generic brand name when prompted with a visual cue of the product.

Recall of Generic Brands

Although consumer recognition of generic brands is expected to be high, their recall of these brands can vary greatly. That is, consumers will recognize a generic brand if presented with it, but they might not always be presented with the cue to recall the node from memory. Often, inclusion in the consideration set, and therefore the shopping list, requires brand recall. If the brand is closely connected to the product category, the brand node will not be activated by the usual cues. Thus, a consumer looking at a shelf of in-line skates will undoubtedly recognize a pair of Rollerblade in-line skates; however, recall of the brand name is required for any brand decisions that are made outside of the store environment.

Generic brands can be delineated in terms of consumers' recognition and recall of the brand. Aaker (1996) refers to brands that are high in recognition and low in recall as "graveyard" brands. These brands will only be considered during in-store purchase decisions. Outside the store environment, graveyard brands will experience low consumer recognition, which leads to low customer-based brand equity. As such, generic brands that dominate the market can be expected to have higher recall than generic brands that have less market success.

P_3: Dominant generic brands experience significantly higher recall than generic brands that are less successful in the marketplace.

Impact of Brand Image on Generic Brands

The third component of customer brand knowledge is brand image. Whereas brand awareness measures the extent of consumers' familiarity with a brand, *brand image* is defined as perceptions about a brand as reflected by the brand associations held in memory (Aaker 1991). The favorability, strength, and uniqueness of these associations determine the brand's image (Keller 1993).

For a brand image to be created, a brand node must be established in memory. The nature of the brand node will affect how easily different kinds of information can be attached to the brand in memory (Keller 1993). In the most severe case of genericide, a brand node does not exist in consumers' memories. Instead, a node for the brand name is actually the product category node. Thus, the brand cannot establish an associative network to represent the brand's image.

What Lies Between the Graveyard and Dominance?

To this point, I have developed a classification system, based on the components of customer-based brand equity, to distinguish among generic brands. Graveyard brands will have high recognition, low recall, and low brand image, and therefore low customer-based brand equity, whereas dominant brands will have high recall, high recognition, and high image. However, identification of another category of generic brands that falls within these two extremes is possible upon closer consideration of brand image and the activities necessary to build and maintain it. These are brands that have high recognition and high recall among knowledgeable consumers but lack a distinctive image.

The Importance of Image-Building Marketing Communications to Generic Brands

When a brand is introduced to the market, communications with consumers must stress both the product name and the brand name to avoid genericide. However, consumers might still adopt the brand name as the category label if the brand remains the sole entrant in the market for a long period, no product category label exists, or the brand name is relatively more descriptive or difficult to remember or pronounce than the product name. Given that the brand enters into common usage, the most important factor to keep the brand name at the top of consumers' shopping lists is image-building marketing communications. To illustrate the impact of image-building activities on customer-based brand equity, consider the long-term marketing activities that followed the introduction of two generic brands: Kleenex facial tissues and Rollerblade in-line skates.

Kleenex was the first brand of facial tissue introduced to the marketplace. Although originally introduced as a disposable wipe for the removal of cold cream, the brand owners were quick to capitalize on its alternative usage by consumers. Its manufacturer, Kimberly-Clark, used extensive advertising to build and maintain a strong image throughout the life of the brand. Therefore, despite the entry of challenger brands such as Scott tissues, consumers held strong, favorable, and unique associations of Kleenex that have allowed the brand to dominate the facial tissue market since its inception.

Conversely, Rollerblade, the company that began a new recreational craze in the late 1980s, has struggled with declining market share since competitors such as Bauer and K2 entered the market. During the years in which Rollerblade enjoyed sole access to the market, the brand was supported by promotional programs designed to promote the activity of in-line skating. Team Rollerblade toured the country, and the craze took off. But when other brands, such as Bauer, entered the market, they positioned their skates as meeting the needs of distinct segments and developed a strong image, leaving Rollerblade scrambling for legal action and a belated advertising campaign. The advertising they developed still promoted the thrill of "rollerblading"; however it failed to cultivate a distinct position for the brand. Rollerblade has quickly lost share to later entrants into the market. Most alarmingly, when consumers are not faced with the Rollerblade brand during the decision process, the value of the Rollerblade brand may be diminished or nonexistent.

Thus, image-building marketing communications efforts such as image-oriented advertising can provide generic brands with a distinct image that enables consumers to recognize the existence of a brand despite the use of the brand name as a category label. However, when the product node is replaced by the brand node, communications efforts to distinguish the product will be of dubious value as consumers no longer have a node on which to build associations.

> P_4: Among generic brands with high recognition and recall, consumers hold fewer brand-specific associations for competitive generic brands than for dominant generic brands.

A Classification of Generic Brands

I have maintained that a generic brand's customer-based equity is contingent on the customer's awareness of the brand as a separate entity from the product category and the image of the brand. Although consumers' knowledge of the product category can influence the likelihood of genericide, the additional consideration of brand image enables a clearer distinction between generic brands based on their differential representation in consumer memory.

Dominant Generic Brands

A dominant generic brand has high awareness in terms of both recognition and recall. It might be strongly related to the product category, but consumers can distinguish between the two nodes enough to associate brand information with the brand node. In addition, the brand must receive strong marketing support to capitalize on consumers' brand knowledge. Therefore, a dominant brand will have high customer-based brand equity. However, the ability to leverage a dominant brand through brand extensions can be inhibited by the strength of associations with the product category. For example, consumers like Campbell's soup, but they did not like the idea of Campbell's spaghetti sauce. Campbell's was left to introduce Prego as a new brand for the spaghetti sauce category. Thus, the company could not take advantage of the usual cost savings by extending a well-liked and established brand into a new product category.

Competitive Brands

A competitive brand will have declining share in its market as new entrants seek differentiated positions and capitalize on the former market leader's lack of brand image. A competitive brand usually experiences high awareness. However, its image may be diminished by poor positioning activities, and brand confusion early in its history may inhibit the formation of brand associations.

Competitive brands are in danger of being challenged in court by "me too" brands that are positioned close to the generic brand and seek to take its name away (Carpenter and Nakamoto 1990).

Graveyard Brands

Graveyard brands have high recognition but low recall. Their only hope for being purchased is in-store purchase decisions. Graveyard brands have low customer-based brand equity when the appropriate brand cue is not given.

Determining a Brand's Potential for Genericism and Genericide

Generic brands and the likelihood of genericide can be identified using measurements of brand awareness and brand image that have commonly been used in marketing research.

Using Brand Recognition to Identify Generic Brands

Test 1

Consumers are given a visual representation of the product so that they are not primed, and then they are asked to identify the product in the picture. For a generic brand, most consumers will identify the product by referring to the brand name. Those consumers who referred to the product with a brand name are instructed to reassess the product and suggest another label. For graveyard brands, most of these consumers will be unable to suggest another label for the product. For products with dominant generic brands, most of these consumers will correctly supply the product category label.

Test 2

Consumers are shown the brand name and asked whether they are familiar with it. In this test, recognition should be high for all generic brands.

Using Brand Recall to Identify Brands with Potential for Genericide

Before exposure to the brand name, consumers are asked to recall all brands of the product shown in the picture. During this exercise, generic brands that are in danger of genericide will be mentioned infrequently, if at all, because the brand is considered the product label. Most consumers will mention dominant generic brands before other brands in the category.

Using Brand Associations to Identify Dominant Generic Brands

Consumers are asked to list the associations they hold for several brands in the category. They list far more favorable, brand-specific associations for dominant brands than for other brands in the category. Compared with other brands in the category, consumers will list far more favorable, brand-specific associations for dominant brands than less successful generic brands. However, they will be unable to list any brand-specific associations for graveyard generic brands.

Conclusion

Brand equity issues have been cited as some of the most important strategic challenges of the next decade (Aaker 1991). Companies seek to place their names at the top of every shopping list by building consumers' familiarity with the brand. However, it is vital for marketers to be aware of the potential for genericide in specific situations. When consumers begin to confuse the brand name with the product category label, companies could be employing their marketing dollars to build the equity of a brand that does not even exist as a distinct entity in consumers' minds.

Drawing on Keller's (1993) conceptualization of customer-based brand equity, I consider the extent to which consumers are aware of generic brands and hold favorable brand-specific associations. By measuring recall, recognition, and the associations that form brand image, marketers can determine (1) the likelihood that their brands may become generic; (2) whether genericism will lead to category dominance, consumer confusion resulting in a loss of performance, or the graveyard; and (3) the importance of marketing communications, especially early in a brand's life, to establish brand-specific associations in consumers' minds.

References

Aaker, David A. (1991), *Managing Brand Equity*. New York: The Free Press.

———— (1996), *Building Strong Brands*. New York: Free Press.

Alba, Joseph W. and J.W. Hutchinson (1987), "Dimension of Customer Expertise," *Journal of Consumer Research*, 13, (4), 411–54.

Anderson, John R. (1983), "A Spreading Activation Theory Of Memory," *Journal of Verbal Learning and Verbal Behavior*, 22 (June), 261–95.

Bettman, James (1979), "Memory Factors in Consumer Choice: A Review," *Journal of Marketing*, 43 (Spring), 37–53.

Carpenter, Gregory and Kent Nakamoto (1987), "Competitive Strategies for Late Entry into a Market with a Dominant Brand," *Management Science*, 36 (10), 1268–78.

Collins, A.M. and E.F. Loftus (1975), "A Spreading Activation Theory of Semantic Processing," *Psychological Review*, 82 (6), 407–28.

Dobni, Dawn and George M. Zinkhan (1990), "In Search of Brand Image: A Foundation Analysis" in *Advances in Consumer Research*, Vol. 17, M. Goldberg, G. Gorn, and R.W. Polly, eds. Provo, UT: Association for Consumer Research, 110–119.

Hoyer, Wayne D. and Stephen P. Brown (1990), "Effects of Brand Awareness on Choice for a Common, Repeat Purchase Product," *Journal of Consumer Research*, 17 (2), 141–48.

Jacoby, Jacob, George Syzbillo, Jacqueline Busato-Schach (1977), "Information Acquisition Behavior in Brand Choice Situations," *Journal of Consumer Research*, 3 (4), 209–16.

Karande, Kiran, George Zinkhan, and Alyssa Baird Lum (1997), "Brand Personality and Self Concept: A Replication and Extension," *Enhancing Knowledge Development in Marketing*, Vol. 8, William M. Pride and G. Tomas Hult, eds. Chicago: American Marketing Association, 165–71.

Keller, Kevin Lane (1993), "Conceptualizing, Measuring, and Managing Customer-Based Brand Equity," *Journal of Marketing*, 56 (January), 1–22.

Nedungadi, Prakash (1990), "Recall and Customer Consideration Sets: Influencing Choice Without Altering Brand Evaluations," *Journal of Consumer Research*, 17 (3), 263–76.

Petty, R.E. and J.T. Cacioppo (1984), "The Effects of Involvement on Response to Argument Quality and Quantity: Central and Peripheral Routes to Persuasion," *Journal of Personality and Social Psychology*, 46 (1), 69–81.

Simon, Herbert A. (1969), *The Sciences of the Artificial*. Cambridge, MA: MIT Press.

Zinkhan, George M. and Claude R. Martin (1982), "The Attitudinal Implications of a New Brand's Name," in *Advances in Consumer Research*, Vol. 9, Andrew Mitchell, ed. Provo, UT: Association for Consumer Research, 467–71.

———— and ———— (1987), "New Brand Names and Inferential Beliefs: Some Insights on Naming New Products," *Journal of Business Research*, 15 (2), 157–72.

———— and Penelope J. Prenshaw (1994), "Good Life Images and Brand Name Associations: Evidence from Asia, America, and Europe," in *Advances in Consumer Research*, Vol. 21, C. Allen and D. Roedder John, eds. Provo, UT: Association for Consumer Research, 496–500.

VI

Ethical Issues in Advertising

16

Potential Ethical Issues Associated with Qualitative Research Conducted Face to Face and in Cyberspace

Denise DeLorme
University of Central Florida

Qualitative methods have played important and varied roles in the marketing industry for many years. For example, focus groups have been widely used for creative advertising concept testing, consumer interviews involving projective techniques have been applied to uncover hidden purchasing motives, and observational methods have been employed to gain insight into consumers' shopping behaviors. These techniques have been used successfully as self-contained means of data collection or in combination with more traditional quantitative methods such as experiments and surveys.

Qualitative research is defined here as methods adopted by researchers aligned with the interpretive social science perspective (e.g., depth interviews, focus groups, observations, ethnography). *Quantitative research* is defined as methods implemented by those associated with the positivist philosophy (e.g., surveys, quasi experiments, experiments). However, it is recognized that the labels "qualitative" and "quantitative" are considered endpoints along a continuum and do not necessarily represent mutually exclusive categories (DeLorme et al. 1996).

Across disciplines, qualitative methods have grown in popularity as indicated by the prevalence of scholarly books, journals, and empirical articles. Within these sources, topics such as project design, sampling strategies, and data collection processes usually receive substantial attention. Unfortunately, one significant area that often seems overlooked is ethics. For example, Smith (1995, p. 478) notes that, "although the focus group methodology has become an increasingly popular research measure in the past fifteen years, very little has been written about the ethical issues."

Ethics is concerned with values and principles and is often referred to as philosophical thinking about morality. Ethics is certainly not a neglected topic in marketing research (e.g., Castleberry, French, and Carlin 1993; Holbrook 1994; Hunt, Chonko, and Wilcox 1984; Jacoby 1994; Kimmel 1999; Zinkhan, Bisesi, and Saxton 1989). Yet, few academic articles have directly addressed unique ethical issues associated with qualitative studies (e.g., Goode 1996; May 1980; Taylor 1987).

Although ethical concerns can arise between a variety of different stakeholders (DeLorme et al. 1996), this article focuses on ethical dilemmas specifically between researchers and those they study—the participants. Indeed, all researchers should consider the ethical consequences of their actions to "ensure the rights, privacy, and welfare of the people and communities that form the focus of their studies" (Berg 1998, p. 31). However, the application of ethical prescription is often based on the assumption that qualitative and quantitative research are the same (Cassell 1982). Because this is not the case, the purpose of this article is to identify and address some potential ethical concerns uniquely associated with qualitative research conducted face to face and in cyberspace. Some alternatives to assist researchers in resolving these ethical conflicts are then offered.

Philosophical Differences

Whether face to face or in cyberspace, potential harm to participants can be difficult to predict in qualitative research. Yet, researchers still have a responsibility to those individuals and communities they study. As qualitative methods continue to become more firmly established in the marketing discipline, it is important to give serious reflection and careful consideration to distinct points of difference that increase the complexity of ethical issues and have significant implications for researchers, informants, industry, and society as a whole (Castleberry, French, and Carlin 1993).

Qualitative research recognizes and values social interaction as part of the research process. The researcher is considered the data collection instrument and is centrally involved in informants' private social lives, including underlying emotions associated with their personal experiences (Berg 1998). During the research process, there is an attempt to maintain a balance of power (Cassell 1982). Unlike quantitative investigators who place human interpersonal interaction outside the research paradigm and attempt to be objective, detached, and distant from the data sources who are referred to as "subjects" or "respondents," qualitative researchers often label the people they study "participants" or "informants," and they are made as much an active part of the project as possible (Cassell 1982; Denzin 1989; Wax 1982).

Because qualitative research is a highly personal and interpersonal human activity, there is greater reliance on the integrity of the researcher (Richardson 1996a, b). Not only are there more opportunities for harm to occur, but it also may be more damaging or more severe than in quantitative research. The strength of the potential emotional bond between the researcher and informants places a strong responsibility on qualitative researchers to hold high ethical standards (DeLorme et al. 1996).

Qualitative studies also tend to encompass natural settings in a holistic manner. That is, the researchers aim to understand things as a whole and do not attempt to control the contexts of the investigation, which are considered potentially valuable sources of data. Cassell (1982, p. 9) notes, "Rather than interfering with what is studied, the physical, structural, social, and cultural contexts of research are significant data in their own right. Interaction is not controlled but rather it ebbs and flows freely, and a wide range of interpersonal features serve as sources of data."

However, these close ties between qualitative research and everyday social life can make ethical dilemmas more ambiguous and difficult to resolve than those associated with other methods (Eisner 1991; Punch 1986). This point is articulated by Cassell (1982, p. 23), who states:

The ethical dilemmas of fieldwork may be closer to problems of daily life than those of other methods. In fieldwork as in daily life, the line between politeness, on the one hand, and hypocrisy, on the other, may be a narrow one.

Furthermore, because qualitative research tends to be an emergent and evolving process, general ethical concerns such as invasion of privacy and deception may be inadequately anticipated (Punch 1986; Reece and Siegal 1986; Wax 1988). The practice of informed consent ensures that informants are aware of the purpose, benefits, and risks of the study and have decided to participate as an exercise of free choice (Berg 1998). This may work well for quantitative research in which designs are carefully controlled and planned in advance and provide greater ability to predict possible ethical issues (Cassell 1982).

However, in qualitative fieldwork relations are emergent, negotiable, and long term, so researchers do not always know what events will unfold (Wax 1988). As van Maanen (1988, p. 277) notes, "choices are made day in and day out in the field when deciding what data to go after, how to get them, who to talk to, how and where to record and store data, and so forth." In these cases, it can be difficult to determine in advance what to get consent about, who to get consent from, and how much consent is needed (Eisner 1991). In fieldwork, ethical problems that arise often require an immediate resolution with no opportunity for reflection and consideration (Wax 1988). Thus, the researcher may be unprepared to handle an unforeseen ethical crisis that nevertheless requires instant response.

Potential Ethical Issues Associated with Face-to-Face Qualitative Research Practices

There are several qualitative research practices involving participants that may be suspect in terms of ethics—defined here as a set of normative guidelines directed at resolving conflicts of interest so as to enhance societal well-being (French and Granrose 1995). Specifically, I discuss six qualitative research practices that are ethically questionable: gaining access through deception, asking excessive probing questions, promoting overdisclosure, observing or recording participants without permission, abandoning participants, and inadequately disguising participants' identities in publications.

Gaining Access Through Deception

The first potential ethical issue stems from the practice of researchers deliberately misrepresenting their identities, qualifications, or research purposes to gain and maintain access to participants' private worlds (Bulmer 1982a, b). Examples range from spying on consumers to deliberately misinforming them to purposefully omitting certain information. Researchers must decide whether to enter the field as an overt (i.e., announced) or covert (i.e., secret) investigator (Berg 1998). They must also address perplexing questions such as the following: (1) Is there a difference between omission of information and misinformation in terms of deception? and (2) Regarding informed consent, how much information do participants need to know?

Asking Excessive Probing Questions

A second potential ethical concern involves the practice of relentlessly asking probing questions, especially regarding sensitive topics. For example, during in-depth interviews asking repetitive probing questions regarding health issues or personal finances may be emotionally stressful or upsetting to participants and cause anxiety or discomfort. Thus, researchers might consider at what point does asking probing questions during interview situations become excessive and intrusive?

Promoting Overdisclosure

A third potential dilemma is associated with researchers creating and using relationships with participants as sources of data and professional power. Qualitative researchers often hang around in particular settings and build rapport with participants through close social interaction over time (Bulmer 1982a). Although this process is essential for successful qualitative field research, several ethical concerns may develop (Bulmer 1982a). For example, in attempting to develop rapport with participants, some researchers may express more friendship than is actually felt to further their own project goals.

In addition, if trust and friendship are established, participants may overdisclose and unveil secrets they might later regret (Eisner 1991; Smith 1995). Overdisclosure can pose even greater risks in focus group situations in which the synergistic effect of group interaction can stimulate participants to spontaneously reveal personal experiences and insights to one another as well as the researcher. This reduced confidentiality can cause concerns regarding the lack of control over what others will say when they leave the group. This concern is heightened even further if sensitive or potentially embarrassing topics are discussed.

Observing or Recording Participants Without Permission

Qualitative methods tend to be more intrusive as researchers often observe and record informants' actual words and behaviors through the use of one-way mirrors, audio recorders, cameras, or video recorders. Thus, a fourth potential ethical problem arises from investigators using observation or recording equipment during the research process without participants' knowledge and permission.

Hidden video cameras or audio recording devices have been a source of serious concern regarding consumers' privacy (Patton 1990). The recent trend of videotaping focus groups and providing clients with videotapes to support written reports raises questions as to how the tapes should be appropriately viewed and stored (Greenbaum 1996; Harris 1995; Parks 1997). For example, if participants disclose on video that they have HIV or AIDS, there may be confidentiality issues associated with the usage, storage, and availability of the tapes.

Abandoning Participants

In quantitative studies, data collection typically requires only brief contact with subjects (e.g., to administer a standardized questionnaire). However, because qualitative approaches usually involve more prolonged and persistent data collection, there are more opportunities for deception to occur. Also, investigator disengagement from the research site can be ethically problematic. When the study ends and the researcher leaves, ethical consequences arise as participants may feel exploited, betrayed, or emotionally abandoned and must cope with lost friendship and support (Bulmer 1982a, b; Punch 1986). What are the researcher's responsibilities to participants after the project has been completed?

Inadequately Disguising Participant Identities in Publications

Potential harms associated with qualitative research may occur not only during the process of the study but also at a later date when the findings are published or disseminated. Unlike quantitative studies that report means and variances generally and abstractly, well-written qualitative work involves reproducing the actual experiences, thoughts, and actions of those studied through thick descriptive accounts that are detailed, concrete, and personal. However, the researcher has no control over how the research is used when reported or other consequences of publication (Bulmer 1982a). The risks involve not necessarily what researchers may do with the findings but what sponsors, legal sources, and governmental agencies may do with them (Cassell 1982).

Thus, a sixth potential ethical problem relates to inadequately disguising actual names, occupations, and geographic locations in the published or disseminated results of qualitative studies (Punch 1986). For example, participants may be embarrassed or ashamed if they are identified in a negative context (Eisner 1991). When writing up qualitative reports, researchers should consider how much detail is sufficient to meet research standards yet still protect participants and their lives.

Qualitative Research in Cyberspace

The Internet has become a potentially powerful and intriguing qualitative data collection tool (e.g., Eisenberg 1996; Roller 1996). It allows messages of any length to be easily and instantly modified and communicated at all hours, all year long (Raman 1996). The topics that can be explored online are almost limitless. A variety of cyberenvironments, including chat rooms, electronic bulletin boards, e-mail, listservers, live chats (e.g., Internet Relay chat), MUDs (multi-user dungeons), and Usenet, offer special options for qualitative researchers considering using the Internet (Morris and Ogan 1996). As stated by Lindloff and Shatzer (1998, p. 171),

> The Internet encompasses an array of settings in which symbolic culture is performed and in which participants mean to express something coherent. The global, yet perceptibly intimate, nature of these settings and the social affiliations they spawn has attracted interest from interpretive analysts.

Marketing researchers in both academia and industry have begun conducting ethnographic studies of electronic communities (e.g., Giese and Kauffman 1998; Granitz and Ward 1996; Lindloff and Shatzer 1998; Workman 1992), online depth interviews (e.g., McMellon 1997), and focus groups (e.g., BKG America; CLT Research Associates; Greenfield Online Research; M/A/R/C group; Myers 1987; NPD Group; Research Connections, Inc.) in cyberspace.

For example, focus groups in cyberspace, sometimes called chat sessions, are conducted entirely online, from the recruitment and screening conducted by e-mail to the computer-mediated moderation of the discussion (Solomon 1996). These types of groups typically last one hour and involve six participants who remain on a panel for about a month (Peebles 1996). Kodak, for example, does its own online focus groups in addition to using outside research companies (Maddox 1997), and Viacom's Nickelodeon Network established its own private panel of children 8 to 12 years of age on the CompuServe network for focus groups designed to keep the network current on what kids think (Miller 1994).

Opportunities with Qualitative Research in Cyberspace

Qualitative data collection through the Internet will not likely replace face-to-face qualitative research, nor is it appropriate for every situation (Clapper and Massey 1996; Crowley 1996). However, it does offer several opportunities. As Solomon (1996, p. 19) notes, "The online environment has become a particularly suitable environment in which to conduct qualitative research, and a growing number of research firms are now doing so."

Many researchers have expressed praise for the Internet's real-time communication that enables them to conduct qualitative studies faster and less expensively than conventional means (Lynch 1996; Miller 1994; Murphy 1997; Peebles 1996; Roller 1996). There is a general belief that recruiting can be easier, data can be collected with less effort on the researcher's part, and there is faster turnaround as results are practically instantaneous (McQuarrie 1995). Furthermore, certain online focus groups enable participants to click on a hyperlink during the session to obtain additional information about the topic or to clarify issues (Parks 1997). Thus, qualitative research in cyberspace can offer solutions to budget and time constraints—a particularly important benefit for those in the advertising industry who are faced with tighter deadlines and budgets than ever before (Roller 1996).

Another plus is that qualitative online research can enable researchers to study and interact with a variety of people in different markets without the hassles of travel logistics (Murphy 1997). Because the Internet is a global network, it provides the opportunity for information exchange with participants who are geographically scattered throughout the world. Furthermore, by removing time and place constraints, some online research techniques can provide accessibility to groups that would otherwise be difficult to contact or too busy to participate (e.g., working mothers, physicians, attorneys, other professionals) (Murphy 1997; Peebles 1996).

On the Internet, face-to-face biases regarding social cues such as sex, age, ethnic background, and occupation can be reduced or eliminated. Unfortunately, these cues are often potentially valuable information to qualitative researchers. At the same time, however, the perceived faceless anonymity offered by qualitative research in virtual contexts can provide greater freedom for informants to vent, be candid, or discuss sensitive topics. For example, it is believed that issues such as health care or personal finance can be researched more candidly online than in person (Peebles 1996).

In addition, research in cyberspace can enable shy people to share their opinions more comfortably. Informants' perceived anonymity in this environment may reduce inhibitions and communication apprehension (Boehlefeld 1996; Clapper and Massey 1996). The removal of place constraints enables respondents to stay at home while participating; this may enhance physical comfort and stimulate thinking as "respondents are more comfortable in their own homes than they are in a room full of strangers with still more strangers hiding behind a mirror" (Peebles 1996, p. 5).

Challenges with Qualitative Research in Cyberspace

There are also several challenges with online qualitative research. Qualitative research in cyberspace is limited to consumers who have access to the Internet. Thus, the first challenge is the possible nonrepresentativeness of samples. Although the Internet is growing tremendously, many consumers are not yet on the Net. Currently, it is somewhat restricted to professionals with higher levels of education and income who are comfortable with technology. For example, computer novices, slow typists, and poor spellers might be reluctant to participate in qualitative online studies. A second challenge is that because everyone is invisible, knowing who is actually in the sample can be problematic. Finally, a third challenge is that researchers must have the skills and ability to cope with the technical difficulties that sometimes arise (e.g., downed network servers).

Because the Internet "has changed the significance of time, space, and physical location as interaction variables" (Waskul and Douglass 1996, p. 130), a major limitation of online qualitative research is the absence of visual and auditory communication and feedback. This can make gaining and maintaining participant trust and rapport much more difficult and time-consuming. Indeed, some of the human details and richness of face-to-face social interaction such as emotion and nonverbal communication (so important as qualitative data) are lost in cyberspace. For example, some online focus groups may experience reduced group dynamics and synergy due to the absence of face-to-face interaction and also boredom from the slower pace and more impersonal nature. A related concern is that some participants may not pay full attention or may even leave their computer terminals while the session is still in progress.

Another challenge involves ethical issues associated with qualitative research in cyberspace. Some argue that online qualitative research poses increased concerns over the ethics of research and researchers (Berg 1998; Eisenberg 1996; Harris 1995; Jones 1994; McQuarrie 1995). Computer technology has made it possible to perform unethical behaviors at increasingly faster rates and from distant locations (Waskul and Douglass 1996). In their enthusiasm to use the Internet, some investigators have taken shortcuts, strayed from sound practices, or implemented unacceptable data collection techniques. As Boehlefeld (1996, p. 141) notes, "when a new phenomenon crops up, like the Internet, questions arise that seem so important or exciting that researchers might, in their enthusiasm, focus more on those questions than on the fact that there are people on the 'other side' of their data."

As the Internet continues to explode, many researchers feel the need for guidance on collecting data in this new frontier. One online researcher stated, "online focus groups or depth interviews even more than survey research will require careful attention to the challenges of virtual environments" (Harris 1997, p. 14); "we urgently need an accepted ethics of online research and online marketing behavior. Without this, unscrupulous marketing tactics and resultant consumer fear will make performing online research impractical" (Harris 1997, p. 7).

Because the Internet blurs the traditional boundaries between interpersonal and mass communication—between what is "public" and what is "private"—ethical concepts are more difficult to determine (Jones 1994; McQuarrie 1995; Parks 1997; Waskul and Douglass 1996). The problems that loom large relate to the privacy and confidentiality guaranteed by interviewers (Sheehan and Hoy 1997). Although discussion and debate of ethical online research has started to appear in the literature (e.g., Bloom, Milne, and Adler 1994; Boehlefeld 1996; Foxman and Kilcoyne 1993; King 1996; Morris and Pharr 1992), there has been little focus specifically on the unique characteristics of qualitative methods. It is unclear to what extent ethical principals make sense in this new context, how ethical principles should be revised (if at all), and what specifically is the responsibility of qualitative researchers. Thus, in the next section, I address potential ethical issues associated with qualitative research practices in cyberspace.

Potential Ethical Issues in Cyberspace Qualitative Research Practices

In terms of specific practices of qualitative research on the Internet, four major concerns have been identified, including gaining access to participant information without permission, combining participant information without permission, ignoring participant perceptions of anonymity or privacy, and fabricating identities.

Gaining Access to Participant Information Without Permission

The first concern involves observing, copying, recording, or quoting informants' words and behaviors without their knowledge or permission (McQuarrie 1995; Newhagen and Rafaeli 1996). In cyberspace, security of information is a major concern as users can never really be sure who has access (Jones 1994; McQuarrie 1995). McQuarrie (1995, p. 6) states, "Theoretically, a message posted on an Internet group is accessible by anyone who has access to the Internet." In some cyberenvironments, anyone can "lurk" (i.e., be noninvolved) and peruse the group discussion without being identified (Boehlefeld 1996; Granitz and Ward 1996; Huff and Rosenberg 1989). For example, it can be difficult, if not impossible, for online focus group moderators to protect the chat room members' comments from prying computer hackers. Due in part to the simultaneous and multiple forms of online interactions, the concept of informed consent has been considered the most logistically problematic ethical issue associated with online research (Schrum 1995; Waskul and Douglass 1996). Should qualitative researchers obtain informed consent for qualitative online studies, and if so, how should they go about achieving it?

Combining Participant Information Without Permission

There is no doubt that the Internet changes the manner in which investigators collect and use information. Research on the Internet leaves tracks to an extent unmatched by that in any other context. The data are easily accessible to anyone anywhere in the world. For example, "participant demography and behaviors of consumption, choice, attention, reaction, learning, and so forth are widely captured and logged" (Newhagen and Rafaeli 1996, p. 4). Therefore, another potential problem involves data mining through the use of specialized software and the ability to track and link data sources in a way that reveals more personal information about participants than what they might voluntarily consent. To what extent should researchers use the Internet's capabilities to combine data about consumers without their knowledge?

Ignoring Participant Perceptions of Anonymity or Privacy

In virtual contexts, the researcher–informant relationship, a crucial element of qualitative research, is altered to some degree. For example, the personalities and interactions of a focus group moderator and participants may be different online than in face-to-face social interaction (Roller 1996). Participant perceptions of anonymity or privacy in various cyberenvironments can complicate online interactions and has risks that are ill-understood (Hoffman, Novak, and Peralta 1999; Nissenbaum 1999). Although cyberspace may motivate some informants to guard their words more carefully because they are afraid others are lurking, other informants may assume anonymity or privacy and blatantly reveal their true selves. Will focus group participants in a consumer behavior study be more or less forthcoming in a computer chat room when disclosing motivations behind their market purchases? How should participants' perception of anonymity or privacy on the Internet during a qualitative online investigation be handled ethically?

Fabricating Identities

Another ethical issue is associated with the capability of researchers and participants to alter or fabricate their identities, personalities, or roles during online interactions (Kolko 1999; Roller 1996). Indeed, verification of identity can be difficult in cyberspace. On the Internet, "the anonymity of interaction also allows users the option of presenting a self that is virtually unlimited in form and content" (Waskul and Douglass 1996, p. 133). For example, if a female researcher is conducting an online focus group and recruits all male participants (assumes that they are all male), should the researcher pretend to be a male with the expectation that participants will respond more openly? How does deception face to face compare with deception in cyberspace?

Summary

Many of the ethical issues that are described in this chapter remain unresolved. There are no easy answers. Some possibilities include a reliance on personal conscience (e.g., applying moral principles), industry standards (e.g., ethics codes of professional associations), or government (e.g., laws). Or perhaps researchers' "aim should be a multidisciplinary set of ethical standards and/or principles" (Waskul and Douglass 1996, p. 138). A multidisciplinary, multicontext qualitative research ethics code could be developed and implemented to provide solutions to ethical conflicts throughout the qualitative research process and could also be tailored or modified (e.g., adding an addendum) to apply to cyberspace as well. This code could serve to protect research participants from harm; heighten investigator awareness of potential issues; provide a consistent set of expectations regarding research-related actions and activities; encourage ethical behavior; enable investigators to more thoroughly anticipate ethical consequences, recognize an ethical issue when it arises, and make informed ethical decisions; guard researchers from potential legal problems; and increase public support for research, which in turn will increase consumer response rates and consequently help the social science institution as a whole (Castleberry, French, and Carlin 1993).

However, it is recognized that developing codes of ethics for qualitative research can be a complex endeavor. For example, Eisner (1991, p. 219) notes, "one way of resolving such problems is to try to appeal to some principle that guides ethical conduct.... But there can be more than one defensible principle, and at times such principles may conflict." Keeping the codes current and relevant can add to the difficulty, especially given the rapid rate of environmental change.

Regardless, it seems critical at this stage that researchers reflect about unique possible ethical dilemmas beforehand to make sensitive and informed decisions throughout the qualitative research process (Cassell 1982; Richardson 1996a, b). As Waskul and Douglass (1996, p. 138) state, "researchers must be committed to ethical behavior, and take the lead in the development of ethical guidelines, lest others decide to do it for us." Punch (1986, p. 82) believes that "common sense, academic convention, and peer control through discussion are more likely to promote understanding of the issues and compliance with them." It is hoped that this article raises a greater consciousness of the ethical issues researchers need to take into account with qualitative methods and that they consider the potential value of a multidisciplinary, multicontext (i.e., face to face and in cyberspace) qualitative research code of ethical conduct. Ongoing open discussion and debate about these issues are encouraged to continue, as marketing research is constantly adapting to environmental change and advancing in the new frontier.

References

Berg, Bruce (1998), *Qualitative Research Methods for the Social Sciences*. Boston: Allyn and Bacon.

Bloom, Paul N., George R. Milne, and Robert Adler (1994), "Avoiding Misuse of New Information Technologies: Legal and Societal Considerations," *Journal of Marketing*, 58 (January), 98–110.

Boehlefeld, S. P. (1996), "Doing the Right Thing: Ethical Cyberspace Research," *Information Society*, 12 (2), 141–52.

Bulmer, Martin (1982a), "Ethical Problems in Social Research: The Case of Covert Participant Observation," in *Social Research Ethics*, Martin Bulmer, ed. New York: Homes and Meier Publishers, 3–12.

——— (1982b), "The Merits and Demerits of Covert Participant Observation," in *Social Research Ethics*, Martin Bulmer, ed. New York: Homes and Meier Publishers, 217–51.

Cassell, Joan (1982), "Harm, Benefits, Wrongs, and Rights in Fieldwork," in *The Ethics of Social Research: Fieldwork, Regulation, and Publication*, Joan E. Sieber, ed. New York: Springer-Verlag, 7–31.

Castleberry, Stephen B., Warren French, and Barbara A. Carlin (1993), "The Ethical Framework of Advertising and Marketing Research Practitioners: A Moral Development Perspective," *Journal of Advertising*, 22 (2), 46.

Clapper, Danial L. and Anne P. Massey (1996), "Electronic Focus Groups: A Framework for Exploration," *Information and Management*, 30 (1), 43–50.

Crowley, Aileen (1996), "Looking for Data in All the Right Places," *PC Week*, (October 21), 51.

DeLorme, Denise, Elizabeth Luckey, George M. Zinkhan, and Warren French (1996), "Toward an Advertising Research Code of Ethics," in *Proceedings of the 1996 Conference of the American Academy of Advertising*, Gary B. Wilcox, ed. Austin, TX: University of Texas at Austin, 149–58.

Denzin, Norman K. (1989), *The Research Act: A Theoretical Introduction to Sociological Methods*. Englewood Cliffs, NJ: Prentice Hall.

Eisenberg, Anne (1996), "Privacy and Data Collection on the Net," *Scientific American*, 274 (March), 120.

Eisner, Elliot W. (1991), *The Enlightened Eye: Qualitative Inquiry and the Enhancement of Educational Practice*. New York: Macmillan Publishing Company.

Foxman, Ellen R. and Paula Kilcoyne (1993), "Information Technology, Marketing Practice, and Consumer Privacy: Ethical Issues," *Journal of Public Policy & Marketing*, 12 (1), 106–19.

French, Warren and John Granrose (1995), *Practical Business Ethics*. Englewood Cliffs, NJ: Prentice-Hall.

Giese, Mark and Bette Kauffman (1998), "Being There: Using Ethnographic Methodology in the Study of Electronic Communities," paper presented at the Association for Education in Journalism and Mass Communication Conference, Baltimore, Maryland (August 5–8).

Goode, Erich (1996), "The Ethics of Deception in Social Research: A Case Study," *Qualitative Sociology*, 19 (1), 11–33.

Granitz, Neil A. and James C. Ward (1996), "Virtual Community: A Sociocognitive Analysis," in *Advances in Consumer Research*, Vol. 23, Kim Corfman and John Lynch, eds. Provo, UT: Association for Consumer Research, 161-66.

Greenbaum, Thomas L. (1996), "Focus Group by Video Next Trend of the '90s," *Marketing News*, (July 29), 4.

Harris, Cheryl (1997), "Theorizing Interactivity: Models and Cases to Consider in Developing Online Market Research Methods and Tools," paper presented at ESOMAR Conference, Lisbon (July).

Harris, Leslie M. (1995), "Technology, Techniques Drive Focus Group Trends," *Marketing News*, (February 27), 8.

Hoffman, Donna L., Thomas P. Novak, and Marcos A. Peralta (1999), "Information Privacy in the Marketplace: Implications for the Commercial Uses of Anonymity on the Web," *The Information Society*, 15 (2), 129–39.

Holbrook, Morris B. (1994), "Ethics in Consumer Research: An Overview and Prospectus," in *Advances in Consumer Research*, Vol. 21, Chris Allen and Deborah Roedder John, eds. Provo, UT: Association for Consumer Research, 566–71.

Huff, Charles W. and Jonathon Rosenberg (1989), "The Online Voyeur: Promises and Pitfalls of Observing Electronic Interaction," *Behavior, Research Methods, Instruments, & Computers*, 21 (2), 166–72.

Hunt, Shelby D., Lawrence B. Chonko, and James B. Wilcox (1984), "Ethical Problems of Marketing Researchers," *Journal of Marketing Research*, 221 (August), 309–24.

Jacoby, Jacob (1994), "Ethics, Morality, and the Dark Side of Academia and ACR: Implications for ACR's Future," in *Advances in Consumer Research*, Vol. 22, Chris Allen and Deborah Roedder John, eds. Provo, UT: Association for Consumer Research, 21–47.

Jones, Robert Alun (1994), "The Ethics of Research in Cyberspace," *Internet Research*, 4 (3), 30–35.

Kimmel, Allan J. (1999), "Ethical Trends in Marketing Research," paper presented at the Annual Convention of the American Psychological Association, Boston, Massachusetts (August).

King, Storm A. (1996), "Researching Internet Communities: Proposed Ethical Guidelines for the Reporting of Results," *The Information Society*, 12 (2), 119–27.

Kolko, Beth E. (1999), "Representing Bodies in Virtual Space: The Rhetoric of Avatar Design," *The Information Society*, 15 (3), 177–86.

Lindloff, Thomas R. and Milton J. Shatzer (1998), "Media Ethnography in Virtual Space: Strategies, Limits, and Possibilities," *Journal of Broadcasting and Electronic Media*, 42 (2), 170–89.

Lynch, Tom (1996), "Internet: A Strategic Product Introduction Tool," *Marketing News*, (April 22), 15.

Maddox, Kate (1997), "Online Market Research Helps Web Advertisers," *Advertising Age*, (October 13), 36.

May, William F. (1980), "Doing Ethics: The Bearing of Ethical Theories on Fieldwork," *Social Problems*, 27 (3), 358–70.

McMellon, Charles A. (1997), "Virtual Interviewing," in *Marketing Theory and Applications*, Vol. 8, Michael D. Hartline and Debbie Thorne, eds. Chicago: American Marketing Association, 3.

McQuarrie, Fiona (1995), "Collecting Data From Electronic Communication: Accepted Ethical Rules Should Be Followed," *QS News*, (Winter), 5.

Miller, Cyndee (1994), "Focus Groups Go Where None Has Been Before," *Marketing News*, (July 4), 2.

Morris, Linda and Steven Pharr (1992), "Invasion of Privacy: A Dilemma for Marketing Research and Database Technology," *Journal of Systems Management*, 43 (10), 10–11, 30–31, 42–44.

Morris, Merrill and Christine Ogan (1996), "The Internet as Mass Medium," *Journal of Communication*, 46 (1), 39–50.

Murphy, Ian P. (1997), "Interactive Research," *Marketing News*, (January 20), 1.

Myers, David (1987), "Anonymity Is Part of the Magic: Individual Manipulation of Computer-Mediated Communication Contexts," *Qualitative Sociology*, 10 (3), 251–66.

Newhagen, John E. and Sheizaf Rafaeli (1996), "Why Communication Researchers Should Study the Internet: A Dialogue," *Journal of Communication*, 46 (1), 4–13.

Nissenbaum, Helen (1999), "The Meaning of Anonymity in an Information Age," *The Information Society*, 15 (2), 141–44.

Parks, Alexia (1997), "Online Focus Groups Reshape Market Research Industry," *Marketing News*, (May 12), 28.

Patton, Michael Q. (1990), *Qualitative Evaluation and Research Methods*. Newbury Park, CA: Sage Publications.

Peebles, John (1996), "Online Technology Creates Research Tools," *Marketing News*, (March 11), 5.

Punch, Maurice (1986), *The Politics and Ethics of Fieldwork*. Newbury Park, CA: Sage Publications.

Raman, Niranjan V. (1996), "Wandering on the Web," in *Proceedings of the 1996 Conference of the American Academy of Advertising*, Gary B. Wilcox, ed. Austin, TX: University of Texas at Austin, 224–28.

Reece, Robert D. and Harvey A. Siegal (1986), *Studying People: A Primer in the Ethics of Social Research*. Macon, GA: Mercer University Press.

Richardson, Laurel (1996a), "Ethnographic Trouble," *Qualitative Inquiry*, 2 (2), 227–29.

——— (1996b), "Trash on the Corner: Ethics and Technography," *Journal of Contemporary Ethnography*, 21(1), 103–119.

Roller, Margaret R. (1996), "Virtual Research Exists, but How Real Is It?" *Marketing News*, (June 30), H32.

Schrum, L. (1995), "Framing the Debate: Ethical Research in the Information Age," *Qualitative Inquiry*, 1(3), 311–26.

Sheehan, Kim Bartel and Mariea Grubbs Hoy (1997), "Warning Signs on the Information Highway: An Assessment of Privacy Concerns of Online Consumers," paper presented at The Association for Education in Journalism and Mass Communication Conference, Chicago, Illinois (July 30–August 2).

Smith, Mikey W. (1995), "Ethics in Focus Groups: A Few Concerns," *Qualitative Health Research*, 5 (4), 478–87.

Solomon, Mary Beth (1996), "Targeting Trendsetters," *Marketing Research: A Magazine of Management and Applications*, 8 (2), 9–11.

Taylor, Steven J. (1987), "Observing Abuse: Professional Ethics and Personal Morality in Field Research," *Qualitative Sociology*, 10 (3), 288–302.

van Maanen, John (1988), "The Moral Fix: On the Ethics of Fieldwork," in *Contemporary Field Research: A Collection of Readings*, Robert M. Emerson, ed. Boston: Little, Brown and Company, 269–87.

Waskul, Dennis and Mark Douglass (1996), "Considering the Electronic Participant: Some Polemical Observations on the Ethics of Online Research," *The Information Society*, 12 (2), 129–39.

Wax, Murray (1982), "Research Reciprocity Rather than Informed Consent in Fieldwork," in *The Ethics of Social Research: Fieldwork, Regulation, and Publication*, Joan E. Sieber, ed. New York: Springer-Verlag, 33–48.

——— (1988), "On Fieldwork and Those Exposed to Fieldwork: Federal Regulations and Moral Issues," in *Contemporary Field Research: A Collection of Readings*, Robert M. Emerson, ed. Boston: Little, Brown and Company, 288–99.

Workman, John P., Jr. (1992), "Use of Electronic Media in a Participant Observation Study," *Qualitative Sociology*, 15 (4), 419–25.

Zinkhan, George M., Michael Bisesi, and Mary Jane Saxton (1989), "MBA's Changing Attitudes Toward Marketing Dilemmas: 1981–1987," *Journal of Business Ethics*, 8 (12), 963–74.

17

Advertising Ethics: More Than Avoiding Deception and Protecting Children

Michael R. Hyman
New Mexico State University

Research on business ethics falls into two categories: positive (what is) and normative (what should be). Positive studies serve several purposes. First, they can satisfy scientific curiosity (i.e., knowledge for knowledge sake) by answering questions such as "Do the ethical beliefs of managers and business students differ?" (Harris and Sutton 1995; Robin and Babin 1997). Second, understanding alternative ethical beliefs can enhance communication among businesspeople with differing ethical viewpoints (Hyman and Tansey 1991). Third, discovering ethical norms through surveys about prevailing practices informs the ethical prescriptions of some researchers (Verschoor 1993), who nonetheless commit an is/ought fallacy—what is and what should be are conflated—in this regard (Mackie 1977). Fourth, the obverse of such survey research identifies ethical lapses remediable through education or benchmarking (Boyd 1996; Smith 1995). Fifth, empirical studies can serve as a test bed for developing new ethics-related research tools, such as a new ethics scale (Hyman 1996), or as a context for testing generic research tools, such as a way to reduce social desirability bias in surveys. Finally, positive studies can provide evidence for policy decisions, such as the decision to ban cigarette advertisements from radio and television.

Normative studies are conducted for other reasons; the goals, and often the methods, are far different. The goals of normative studies are both economic (the creation of a more efficient and/or more self-sustaining world) and societal (the creation of a more aesthetically-pleasing and/or fairer world). Furthermore, such studies often are philosophical and rely on arguments grounded in ethical theories (e.g., deontology, virtue ethics).

The types and goals of advertising ethics studies are similarly classifiable. Positive studies typically describe the preponderance of (un)ethical advertising practices (Cameron and Haley 1992) or consumers' beliefs about the ethicality of advertising (Calfee and Ringold 1994; Ong, Ho, and Clow 1997; Treise et al. 1994). Normative studies often involve judging borderline cases—for example, advertising for radar detectors, gambling, contraceptives, alcoholic beverages, firearms, and cigarettes (Abernethy and Wicks 1998; Spain 1997; Wilson and West 1992)—or setting the general limits of commercial speech (Boedecker, Morgan, and Wright 1995; Glantz 1997; Petty 1993).

The goal of this article is to show that advertising ethics is more than avoiding deception and protecting children. This brief yet inclusive survey of the normative and positive literature on advertising ethics proceeds as follows. First, several classic arguments against advertising are introduced and then shown to be either (1) fallacious reasoning or (2) economic or social arguments masquerading as ethical arguments. Second, several advertising practices, such as subliminal advertising and the use of psychoactive advertisements (Hyman and Tansey 1990), are shown to pose either an insubstantial or a real ethical threat. Finally, selected borderline cases involving advertising to sensitive audiences, the use of stereotypes in advertisements, and advertisements for controversial products, are broached.

Although important and interesting, many issues are societal rather than ethical, such as puffery (Preston 1996), advertisers' fracturing of U.S. society into a plethora of small, alienated subgroups incapable of meaningful political and social dialogue (Turow 1997), the selling of brand mythologies rather than product functionality (Randazzo 1995), advertising as "social pollution" (Hackley and Kitchen 1999), advertising as the glorifier and encourager of crass popular culture over high culture (Fowles 1996; McAllister 1996; Twitchell 1996), commercialization of the Internet (Abrahamson 1998), sexual explicitness in advertising (LaTour and Henthorne 1994; Reichert et al. 1999), growing consumer dislike of advertising as distasteful and meaningless (Mittal 1994), and the like. Thus, these issues are beyond the purview of this article.

Economic Criticisms Masquerading as Ethical Arguments

Advertising Encourages Economic Waste and Causes Higher Prices

Advertising is expensive; advertising in the United States cost roughly $200 billion in 1998 (Ruskin 1999) and is projected to cost $212 billion in 1999 (O'Connell 1998). Was this money wasted? Economists such as John Kenneth Galbraith (1956, 1967) argue that advertising is wasteful because

1. it creates demand for unnecessary consumer goods;
2. it encourages irrational purchasing by consumers; and
3. it fosters consumer loyalty to trivially different brands, and this loyalty enables advertisers to earn excess profits by charging higher prices.

The first argument pertains to the value of life in an industrialized society rather than the ethics of advertising. As Berman (1981, p. 20) notes, "the criticism of advertising is about the nature of industrial life. In the view of social rationalism we are in fact not better off under an unlimited, unregulated, and unsanctified form of productivity. Whatever promotes that system is morally suspect." This argument suggests that in striving for economic progress, Western society squanders its scarce natural resources, needlessly pollutes its environment, and corrupts people's values and lifestyles. However, an argument against economic progress is an argument against capitalism rather than an ethical argument against advertising (B.J. Phillips 1997; Twitchell 1996); furthermore, it is equally valid to argue that such progress came at an acceptable cost.

The second argument contends that an advertisement designed to infuse a brand with a desirable image enhances only the brand's perceived value rather than its real value. Yet, Levitt (1970), Fisher and McGowan (1979), and others argue against

Galbraith's ideal of advertisements in the rational (political) state; these advertising scholars and economists contend that symbolism in advertisements is desirable because it instills the fantasies that enrich consumer life. As Berman (1981, p. 62) suggests, "a good deal of argument condemning advertising and productivity is based upon the insubstantial assumption that human desires are or should be rational. It tends not to consider the realities of material life or the reasons for social change." Levitt (1970, p. 90) also argues that advertisements "are symbols of man's aspirations" and that art and advertising share several characteristics:

> [B]oth are rhetorical, and both literally false; both expound an emotional reality deeper than the "real"; both pretend to "higher" purposes, although different ones; and the excellence of each is judged by its effect on its audience—its persuasiveness, in short ... both represent a pervasive, and I believe *universal*, characteristic of human nature—the human audience *demands* symbolic interpretation in everything it sees and knows (Levitt 1970, p. 89, emphasis in original).

Although the third argument appears reasonable, it rests on two heroic assumptions: (1) Only a brand's advertising, and not its characteristics or performance, differentiates it from similar brands (i.e., brand differences are meaningless and fail to provide consumers with additional satisfaction), and (2) the time and effort consumers save when they buy advertised brands are worthless. The first assumption implies that consumers should share a uniform, rational set of preferences, such as a preference for identically colored cars. Henry Ford made such an assumption in the 1920s; he offered car buyers a car in whatever color they wanted, so long as that color was black. Of course, car buyers revolted and bought nonblack cars from General Motors (Levitt 1986).

Consumers and producers benefit from market segmentation; consumers benefit from the increased enjoyment they receive from better-tailored products, and producers benefit from the increased prices they charge for more highly valued products. Thus, product differences are real, because consumer preferences differ, and catering to consumer preferences is profitable (Dickson and Ginter 1987).

The second assumption ignores the information that consumers gain through branding. Branding enables consumers to research the quality and performance of the products they buy; as a result of this information, they make better and easier purchase decisions (Ambler 1997).

The issue of whether advertisements cause higher prices remains unresolved. Although advertising is positively correlated with brand prices for manufactured food products (after controlling for product quality and cost differences) (Wills and Mueller 1989), the following suggest a negative correlation between advertising and prices:

1. Lower prices are associated with higher advertisement expenditures in interregional studies for eyeglasses, toys, soap, chocolate, and ready-to-eat cereals (Brozen 1974).
2. "If the minimum efficient scale is reasonably large, retail prices tend to be lower in heavily advertised industries than in unadvertised industries" (Steiner 1998, p. 322).
3. The use of price advertising generally leads to lower prices (Kaul and Wittink 1995).
4. The ban on cigarette advertising raised prices by reducing competition (Tremblay and Tremblay 1999).

Therefore, it cannot be concluded that advertising encourages economic waste or causes higher prices.

Advertising Reduces Competitiveness and Creates a Barrier to Market Entry

Because total industry advertising is higher in industries with several large competitors, some economists conclude that advertising reduces competitiveness (i.e., fewer competitors means higher prices, lower quality, and fewer new products) and creates a barrier for new competitors (i.e., new competitors cannot afford the large advertising budgets required to overcome consumer loyalty to existing brands). However, other economists argue that advertising increases competitiveness and encourages market entry. According to this view, consumers buy the best value, and advertising makes consumers more price sensitive. Advertising permits new firms to enter established markets; as a result, competition increases (the more efficient firms survive), and pressure increases on firms to lower prices and improve quality (see Leahy 1997).

Regarding the relationship between advertising and concentration (i.e., the combined market share of the leading competitors), a recent review of econometric studies published from 1964 to 1991 suggests that only "television advertising has a significant positive effect on concentration" (Leahy 1997, p. 48). Other evidence for the notion that advertising promotes market entry includes the following:

1. After cigarette advertisements were banned from radio and television, the rate of new brand introductions remained unchanged, but no new brands were successful (Brozen 1974), which suggests that banning cigarette advertisements from radio and television created a barrier to entry for new cigarette brands (Holak and Reddy 1986).
2. Because producers spend more on advertisements for new brands than on those for old brands, advertisements obtain, rather than hold, markets (Brozen 1974); that is, advertising often facilitates market entry (Pass, Sturgess, and Wilson 1994).
3. Because producers spend more on advertisements for experience goods (i.e., goods for which usage information supersedes advertisement information, for example automobiles) than on advertisements for search goods (e.g., refrigerators), advertisements do not induce brand loyalty (Brozen 1974).

Therefore, it cannot be concluded that advertising reduces competitiveness or creates a barrier to market entry.

Advertisements Are Uninformative

Consumer activists prefer advertisements that are objective, informative, and neutral; instead, they find advertisements that are partial, incomplete (e.g., lack carefully reasoned arguments and information about alternatives), and colored (i.e., obscure reality in a mist of subjective desire). Are they justified in their preference?

Partiality is not immoral. Advertisers who advocate products are as ethical as lawyers who defend clients. However, as a friend of the court (i.e., consumers), the advertiser's "proper freedom does not extend to deceiving the court with false representations, nor telling lies to the judge" (Bishop 1949, p. 85).

Running advertisements that deceive consumers intentionally is wrong, because "Truth telling, after all, is a fundamental moral rule.... [T]he liar and the cheat corrupt language and destroy confidence" (Leiser 1978, p. 183). Similarly, "Advertising which arouses disbelief and contempt reflects upon all other advertising, and makes all advertising less effective" (Bishop 1949, p. 100).

Past societies followed the Code of Hammurabi, the Old Testament, Greek and Roman law, and English common law; all stipulated that sellers inform buyers completely. In the nineteenth century, U.S. and British courts switched the presumed philosophy to the rule of caveat emptor, which rid sellers of their duty to inform buyers completely (Preston 1996). Through their current policies, the courts and the Federal Trade Commission (FTC) are reverting the presumed philosophy to one of complete disclosure (Benson 1982).

Although the courts and the FTC penalize advertisers that are found guilty of deceptive practices and the ill-gotten gains of deceptive advertisers are short lived (because consumers wise up quickly), isolated advertisers will run intentionally deceptive ads. However, because currently accepted advertising practices and regulations discourage deception by either omission or commission, today's advertisements are rarely deceptive by design.

Furthermore, Nelson (1974) and Telser (1974) argue that consumers find advertisements informative. As evidence, Telser offers the following:

1. All successful newspapers run advertisements.
2. Newspapers try to boost circulation by running more local advertisements, which stress the price information consumers want.
3. Consumers buy catalogs.

In the closed-ended world of many traditional economists, perfectly informed consumers decide among a limited number of well-known and well-defined alternatives; in the open-ended world of some modern economists, imperfectly informed consumers use fuzzy criteria to decide among an unlimited number of ever-changing alternatives. In a closed-ended world, advertisements are unethical and inefficient because they engineer trivial changes in preferences; in an open-ended world, advertisements are "a welfare-enhancing tool of the economic process providing market information, lower search costs, access to competitive markets, and foundations of the free political system" (Ekelund and Saurman 1988, p. xxiii). Therefore, it cannot be concluded that advocacy in advertisements is immoral or that advertisements are uninformative.

Societal Criticisms Masquerading as Ethical Arguments

Advertisements Corrupt Society's Values

To corrupt society's values, advertisements must influence society's values. However, most advertising scholars assume the reverse—that society's values influence advertising (e.g., Belk and Pollay 1985; B.J. Phillips 1997). According to Petit and Zakon (1962, p. 16), "Sociologically speaking it would be impossible for advertising to be in conflict with the value system. It is the value system which determines the nature and significance of social institutions like advertising, not the other way around." Advertisements in the United States often portray the values and lifestyles of the middle class, the largest market for most mass-market goods. Even if it is assumed, contrary to the beliefs of most advertising scholars, that advertisements influence values, then U.S. advertisements influence values toward middle-class norms. Such influence is not immoral, though it might be of questionable social desirability.

Some critics argue that materialism is bad and that advertising encourages materialism; therefore, advertising is bad (see B.J. Phillips 1997; Twitchell 1996). According to this view, materialism encourages snobbery, vanity, envy, greed, false sentiment, false ideas of culture, and fear. Because materialism encourages the excessive and frivolous consumption of status-granting goods, it leads to waste (Ruskin 1999). By teaching that luxuries are necessities, materialism degrades the quality of human life (Ruskin 1999). By emphasizing consumption over production, materialism corrupts the work ethic. As Lasch (1979, pp. 137–39) writes,

> Advertising serves not so much to advertise products as to promote consumption as a way of life.... It upholds consumption as the answer to the age-old discontents of loneliness, sickness, weariness, lack of sexual satisfaction; at the same time it creates new forms of discontent peculiar to the modern age.... Advertising institutionalizes envy and its attendant anxieties.

Some advocates argue that materialism is good because it fuels economic progress; the alternative, contentment with current economic conditions, leads to economic stagnation. Others argue that the fine line between elevated tastes and hedonistic self-indulgence makes identifying materialism difficult; yesterday's luxuries, such as automobiles, refrigerators, and personal computers, are today's necessities. Still others argue that "advertising serves capitalism, suggesting that a capitalist agenda [rather than advertising] is the underlying cause of increasing materialism in our society" (B.J. Phillips 1997, p. 133).

Although not immoral, presenting advertisements that some viewers find tasteless is bad business: Offended customers often change brands; sponsors who offend noncustomers by speaking to the wrong audience waste advertising dollars. Advertisers try to avoid causing such offense; however mistakes occur when they misunderstand the attitudes and beliefs of their audiences. Two examples of such mistakes are as follows:

1. In the late 1980s, America Petrofina was surprised that spokesman Mel Tillis's tag line, "They're my kind of f-f-folks at Fina," offended stutterers.
2. In early 1997, the Church of England offended many Christians by trivializing Christmas with a holiday campaign poster that read, "Bad hair day?! You're a virgin, you've just given birth and now three kings have shown up. Find out the happy ending at a church near you" (Miller 1998). Seemingly, the Church did not learn from offensive radio and television advertisements it sponsored in 1994. In those, a fictitious vicar claimed, "The money is *diabolical*. The hours are *ungodly*. It's a *miracle* anybody does it. The Church of England clergy; it's a *hell* of a job" (Steyn 1997, emphasis in original).

Therefore, it cannot be concluded that advertising corrupts society's values or that advertisers intentionally show tasteless advertisements.

Advertisements Influence Media Content

The late Howard Gossage, an advertising practitioner known for his criticism of advertisers' abuses, argued that advertising distorts the content of mass media: If advertising revenues rather than user fees cover most of the production costs, attracting mass audiences becomes more important than program quality or written content. He argued convincingly that the economics of mass media was analogous to allowing hot dog vendors to dictate the rules of professional football games by extending halftime to one hour to sell more hot dogs (Hinkle 1974).

Potter (1954) argues that these same economic conditions preclude the mass media from elevating public taste. Potter's argument runs as follows:

1. Elevating public taste requires exposing the public to the best writers.
2. The best writers require good pay.
3. Good pay requires high advertising revenues.

4. High advertising revenues require mass circulation.
5. Mass circulation requires material that appeals to the masses.
6. Mass appeal requires writing to the lowest common denominator.

Therefore, mass media's dependence on advertising revenues discourages, rather than encourages, efforts to elevate public taste. However, failure to elevate public taste is not immoral.

Problematic Practices: Insubstantial and Real Threats

Motivation Research

Vance Packard, in *The Hidden Persuaders* (1958), tried to warn the public about powerful wizards, also known as "ad men," who used the results of motivation research to exploit defenseless consumers' hidden motives for buying goods. In fact, during the heyday of depth psychology in the 1950s, the period about which Packard wrote, many large advertising agencies created separate motivation research departments. However, after academicians in the 1960s declared motivation research unscientific and irrelevant, only isolated practitioners continued to preach its Freudian-based power (Dichter 1964). Therefore, few, if any, advertisers attempt to exploit consumers' hidden motives in the ways suggested by Packard.

Subliminal Advertising

Wilson Bryan Key, in *Subliminal Seduction* (1972) and several related works (Key 1976, 1980, 1989), warned of the pervasive use of subliminal appeals in advertisements—appeals designed to make consumers respond unknowingly to hidden content (i.e., brief visual stimuli in video advertisements, accelerated speech in audio advertisements, embedded images or words in print advertisements). Regardless of the advertiser's purpose, running advertisements that violate consumers' autonomy is unethical (Nebenzahl and Jaffe 1998). Because subliminal appeals always violate consumers' autonomy, such advertisements are always unethical. For example, embedding the phrase "Don't shoplift" in a store's background music is unethical regardless of the store's socially desirable goal of reducing criminal activity (DeGeorge 1982).

Fortunately, there is little evidence for the efficacy and use of subliminal advertisements. James Vicary, the father of subliminal advertising, fabricated his original report to stimulate business for his failing marketing research firm (Clark 1989). In summarizing several empirical studies on subliminal advertising, Michael J. Phillips (1997, p. 119) concludes that "[t]here apparently is no convincing theoretical argument for its effectiveness. In addition, researchers have adduced theoretical reasons why its impact should be slight... [N]o research concludes that subliminal advertising boosts sales." In addition, a national survey of American Advertising Federation members reveals that "despite popular belief to the contrary, subliminal advertising is not used by American advertising practitioners" (Rogers and Seiler 1994, p. 43).

Disguised and Obtrusive Advertisements

More troublesome than the specter of subliminal advertisements are disguised and obtrusive advertisements (Nebenzahl and Jaffe 1998). Disguised advertisements, such as product placements in movies or advertisements presented as editorial content, hide "the fact of sponsorship to give the impression of publicity rather than a commercial message" (Nebenzahl and Jaffe 1998, p. 806). Obtrusive advertisements are "messages secondary to the main stimulus perceived by an audience ... [such as] sideboard advertisements in sports arenas" (Nebenzahl and Jaffe 1998, p. 806). Although obtrusive advertisements are supraliminal, they "escape the attention of the viewer and may, not unlike subliminal communications, impact the consumer's buying behavior while s/he is not aware of it" (Nebenzahl and Jaffe 1998, p. 808). Unfortunately, both disguised and obtrusive advertisements are ethically problematic because they violate consumers' autonomy and right to privacy (i.e., right to avoid involuntary exposure), and disguised advertisements violate consumers' right to know if a message is sponsored.

Associative Advertisements

An advertising campaign that appeals to the hidden motives of consumers is unethical only if it is coercive or manipulative. In Kantian terms, both coercion and manipulation treat people as a means to an end and deny respect for their freedom. Coercion involves force or the threat of force, either physical or psychological. Manipulation does not use force but involves playing on a person's will by trickery or by devious, unfair, or insidious means. Both coercion and manipulation take unfair advantage of a person, and the use of either renders a transaction between the two parties unfair and unjust (DeGeorge 1982, p. 192). The accepted use of associative advertisements is occasionally coercive or manipulative.

Waide (1987, p. 73) defines associative advertisements as those that "induce people to buy (or buy more of) a product by associating that market product with such deep-seated non-market goods as friendship, acceptance and esteem of others, excitement and power, even though the market good seldom satisfies or has any connection with the non-market good." Waide criticizes associative advertisements because (1) they reduce the sensitivity of advertisers to the well-being of others, and (2) they reduce the satisfaction of consumers, because products cannot fulfill the associated promise. Fortunately, Waide's ethical criticisms are avoidable; advertisers can limit promises to the benefits that a product brings most consumers. For example, because whiter teeth and fresher breath increase a person's sex appeal, associating toothpaste with sex appeal is ethical.

Psychoactive Advertisements

Hyman and Tansey (1990, p. 106) define psychoactive advertisements as "emotion-arousing ad[s] that can cause a meaningful, well-defined group of viewers to feel extremely anxious, to feel hostile toward others, or to feel a loss of self-esteem." Sponsors often design such advertisements to serve noble purposes, such as to stimulate contributions to charitable causes or to discourage dangerous behaviors such as driving while intoxicated. Although most consumers believe that a strong fear appeal (i.e., psychoactive) advertisement is ethical if the recommended product can be used to eliminate the advertisement-posed threat (Snipes, LaTour, and Bliss 1999), such messages can also evoke extreme, unintended emotional responses; for example, an antidrug advertisement might drive the hopelessly addicted viewer to suicide.

Although psychoactive advertisements are inherently ethical, deploying them without warning is unethical. Fortunately, the problem is remedied easily by warning viewers before showing them the advertisements. Advertisers use such warning now; for example, some television advertisements for African relief efforts warn that the impending images might disturb some viewers.

Unresolved Borderline Cases

Sensitive Audiences

Advertising to a sensitive audience often poses an ethical dilemma (Rittenburg and Parthasarathy 1997). In this context, a sensitive audience is a consumer segment composed of people who often are unable to evaluate critically a product and/or associated advertising claims. These segments are typically defined by either limited education or extreme age (i.e., very young or very old). For example, the belief that neither African Americans nor young, working-class women could properly assess the health risks of smoking prompted an outcry against firms that planned to market new cigarette brands (e.g., Dakota, Uptown) to these segments (Davidson 1996). American Family Publishers and other publisher's clearinghouses are criticized for sweepstakes mailings that continue to fool many elderly consumers (Rosenfield 1998, 1999). Advertising to children, however, may be the most problematic.

Children represent a huge market; in 1997, "children 14 and younger accounted for $20 billion of direct spending ... and influenced another $200 billion" (Davidson 1998). Arguments against advertising to children include the following:

1. Advertisements interfere with parents' ability to influence their children's values and encourage resistance to parental authority (Baritz 1989; Goldberg and Gorn 1978; Lasch 1979; National Science Foundation 1977; Ruskin 1999).
2. Young children might not discount advertisements as persuasive, because they often confuse advertising with programming (Adler et al. 1980; Cavanagh and McGovern 1988; National Science Foundation 1977).
3. Cumulative exposure to advertisements might warp children's values, attitudes, and behaviors (Adler et al. 1980; Goldberg and Gorn 1978; Higham 1999).
4. Learned cynicism about the veracity of advertisements encourages "preadolescent children to think about socially accepted hypocrisy ... [and brings] an increased tolerance of shady deals, cutting corners, and being dishonest with other people" (Cavanagh and McGovern 1988, p. 103; see also National Science Foundation 1977).
5. Advertisements should be aimed at parents if parents are the intended purchasers.
6. Children are exposed to television advertisements for products or product categories that can be hazardous if misused, for example, ethical drugs (Adler et al. 1980; National Science Foundation 1977).
7. Selling techniques used in some television advertisements might be deceptive or misleading to some children (Adler et al. 1980).
8. "TV advertising might be linked to increased unhappiness in children whose [product] requests were denied" (Goldberg and Gorn 1978, p. 27).

Arguments in favor of advertising to children include the following:

1. Advertisements finance and maintain children's programming; without them, the quality of children's programming would drop (Higham 1999; Maren and Walmsley 1999).
2. Exposure to advertising is part of a child's development (Heubusch 1997; Higham 1999).

Many countries restrict advertising to children. Belgium, Denmark, Norway, and Sweden ban television and radio advertising to children (Dignam 1999). Quebec outlaws television and radio advertising to children less than thirteen years of age. Ronald McDonald is banned from television advertisements in Sweden (Higham 1999). Some countries prohibit children from appearing in food advertisements and cartoon characters from endorsing brands (Clark 1989).

Stereotypes in Advertising

Do stereotypes in advertising—whether the positive portrayal of Asian Americans as affluent, highly educated, and professionally employed (Taylor and Stern 1997) or the negative portrayals of older adults as helpless, unknowledgeable, and disoriented (Carrigan and Szmigin 1999; Peterson and Ross 1997), women as sex objects limited to traditional gender roles (Lavine, Sweeney, and Wagner 1999; Stern 1999), and Gen-X consumers as irreverent slackers (Turow 1997)—present an ethical problem? Because advertisements must communicate quickly and because communication depends on common understanding, advertisements often contain subtle and blatant stereotypes, such as the bumbling husband, the all-knowing mother, and the nosy neighbor. The problem with such stereotypes is connected to the debate about whether advertisements reflect or shape society's values (Lantos 1987; Pollay 1986). If advertisements shape society's values, then can they portray every group conscientiously? If advertisements reflect society's values, then can they represent large, sensitive groups accurately?

Controversial Products

Cigarette and Alcoholic Beverages

Should advertisements for cigarettes and alcoholic beverages be banned? In the United States, cigarette advertisements are banned from radio and television, must include tar and nicotine levels, and should not appear in youth media or use themes attractive to juveniles. In the United Kingdom, cigarette advertisements are banned from television, cannot claim or imply that smoking is a sign of manliness or enhances feminine charm (thus neither Camel nor Marlboro men appear in U.K. advertisements), and cannot appear in youth media or feature heroes of the young (Clark 1989).

If encouraging adolescents and young adults to start smoking is unethical, then why do cigarette advertisements appear in questionable outlets? For example,

> Magazines like *Playboy* and *Penthouse*, which are oriented toward young adults, get 25 percent of their advertising revenues from cigarette companies. Movie magazines, aimed at teenagers and young adults, also carry a large number of cigarette ads. By way of contrast, magazines ... such as *Forbes* and *Fortune*, which young people do not generally read, have little or no cigarette advertising (Cavanagh and McGovern 1988, p. 96).

The debate about banning cigarette and alcoholic beverage advertisements centers on the utilitarian argument that "the government should not interfere if the results of the action fall mainly on the self" (Cavanagh and McGovern 1988). According to this view, smokers who prefer a daily pack of cigarettes to five years of additional life are not wrong. Furthermore, the U.S. government's motives in saving smokers from themselves are economic rather than ethical (i.e., society cannot afford medical care for thousands of diseased and dying smokers).

Manufacturers argue that cigarette and alcohol advertisements change brand loyalties rather than encourage nonsmokers to develop a new habit. Furthermore, because cigarettes and alcoholic beverages are legal products, they should be legal to advertise.

The evidence suggests that neither cigarette nor alcoholic beverage advertisements stimulate primary demand (for cigarettes, see Lambin 1976; Parsons and

Schultz 1976; for alcoholic beverages, see Fisher 1993; Fisher and Cook 1995). Since the early 1970s, each additional dollar spent on advertising has produced less than one additional dollar of cigarette sales in the United States (Andrews and Franke 1991) and less than one additional dollar of alcoholic beverage sales in the United Kingdom (Duffy 1990). Crossnational comparisons show that the number of juvenile smokers is unrelated to a government's policy about cigarette advertisements; furthermore, personal and social pressures overwhelm the effect of advertising in determining who becomes a juvenile smoker (Smith 1990). Finally, antismoking advertising seems more effective than an advertising ban (Hoek 1999; Pechmann and Shih 1999; Quester 1999), and entities such as the Tobacco Control Foundation, the American Lung Association, the American Heart Association, and the American Cancer Association have huge budgets for antismoking advertising campaigns funded by tobacco companies as part of recent negotiated settlements (Teinowitz 1999).

Pharmaceuticals

Should pharmaceutical advertisements be prohibited? The pharmaceutical industry is the world's largest advertiser. Presumably, doctors are immune to advertising; yet the evidence suggests otherwise. Although doctors claim that their clinical experience and training dictate what they prescribe, a Harvard study shows that many unknowingly base their prescriptions on the information in advertisements (even if recent journal articles contradict the advertised information) (Clark 1989).

Advertising pharmaceuticals directly to the public is even more problematic. For example, Eli Lilly advertises its offer of university scholarships for schizophrenic patients who switch to its new antipsychotic drug Zyprexa (Josefson 1998). It could easily be argued that the mentally ill are overly vulnerable to the claims made in such advertisements.

Politicians

Should political advertisements be regulated? Because most political advertisements in the United States sell image rather than substance, some argue that such advertisements subvert the democratic process. Others argue that misrepresentation and shallowness have always characterized U.S. politics and advertising causes little additional harm.

The United States is one of few countries in which politicians can buy television air time. In contrast, advertisements for politicians are banned in the United Kingdom; instead, parties receive free air time in proportion to their relative membership.

Although voters' beliefs about the ethicality of a political advertisement are salient to their choice of candidate, "an unethical ad may nevertheless have a positive impact if it taps positive emotional feelings of the hedonic type" (Tinkham and Weaver-Larisey 1994, p. 56). Eliminating image advertising might slow the growth of negative campaigning. These 30- to 60-second advertisements lend themselves to negative messages (e.g., 70% of 1988 presidential campaign advertisements were negative; Clark 1989, p. 305) and might discourage good people from running for office and registered voters from voting.

Issues to Consider About Borderline Cases

When questioning the ethics of borderline cases, advertisers, regulators, and consumers should consider two issues: consumer autonomy and consumer sovereignty. An advertisement fails to respect consumers' autonomy if it is deceptive, manipulative, or coercive: "[S]ince advertising helps achieve the goal of both seller and buyer, it is morally justifiable and permissible, providing it is not deceptive, manipulative, or coercive. It can be abused, but it is not inherently immoral" (DeGeorge 1982, p. 186). Unfortunately, this issue is easier broached than addressed: "Advertising would be immoral if it always and necessarily manipulated and coerced people. But it does not. The difficulty is deciding what is manipulative and what is not, who should be protected from certain kinds of advertising, and who does not need such protection" (DeGeorge 1982, p. 187). Nonetheless, advertisers, regulators, and consumers should strive to address this issue.

Regarding consumer sovereignty, advertisers should protect sensitive audiences and place advertisements for controversial products carefully; regulators and consumers should help advertisers develop their ability to target advertisements safely. For example, to reduce growing criticism of outdoor advertisements, the Outdoor Advertising Association of America adopted five guidelines for billboards about products that cannot be sold to minors. These include limiting the number of such billboards within a given geographic area and establishing no-billboard zones within 500 feet of churches, schools, and hospitals (Slater 1990).

Furthermore, if advertisers can achieve their goals through more innocuous means, they should use those means. For example, advertisements for the United Negro College Fund could solicit donations without sacrificing the self-esteem of some African Americans (Hyman and Tansey 1990). Regulators and consumers should help advertisers find these alternative means.

Conclusion

Despite the borderline cases and occasional problematic practices, advertising remains the most efficient way to inform a free market. Marketers can contend that advertising actually serves a dual benefit to society. First, by voicing society's dominant values, advertisements promote social cohesion. Second, by voicing even the smallest minority's opinion, advertisements offer the opportunity to question those current values—which results in either a synthesis of new ideals or forbearance of old norms. In short, advertising is indispensable because of the paramount role it plays in shaping society's values.

References

Abernethy, Avery M. and Jan LeBlanc Wicks (1998), "Television Station Acceptance of AIDS Prevention PSAs and Condom Advertising," *Journal of Advertising Research*, 38 (September/October), 53–62.

Abrahamson, David (1998), "The Visible Hand: Money, Markets, and Media Evolution," *Journalism and Mass Communication Quarterly*, 75 (Spring), 14–18.

Adler, Richard P., Gerald S. Lesser, Laurene Krasny Meringoff, Thomas S. Robertson, John R. Rossiter, and Scott Ward (1980), *The Effects of Television Advertising on Children*. Lexington, MA: Lexington Books.

Ambler, Tim (1997), "Do Brands Benefit Consumers?" *International Journal of Advertising*, 16 (3), 167–98.

Andrews, Rick and George R. Franke (1991), "The Determinants of Cigarette Consumption: A Meta-Analysis," *Journal of Public Policy & Marketing*, 10 (1), 81–100.

Baritz, Loren (1989), *The Good Life: The Meaning of Success for the American Middle Class*. New York: Alfred A. Knopf.

Belk, Russell W. and Richard W. Pollay (1985), "Images of Ourselves: The Good Life in Twentieth Century Advertising," *Journal of Consumer Research*, 11 (March), 887–97.

Benson, George C.S. (1982), *Business Ethics in America*. Lexington, MA: Lexington Books.

Berman, Ronald (1981), *Advertising and Social Change*. Beverly Hills, CA: Sage Publications.

Bishop, F.P. (1949), *The Ethics of Advertising*. London: Robert Hale Limited.

Boedecker, Karl A., Fred W. Morgan, and Linda Berns Wright (1995), "The Evolution of First Amendment Protection for Commercial Speech," *Journal of Marketing*, 59 (January), 38–47.

Boyd, Colin (1996), "Ethics and Corporate Governance: The Issues Raised by the Cadbury Report in the United Kingdom," *Journal of Business Ethics*, 15 (February), 167–82.

Brozen, Yale (1974), "Is Advertising a Barrier to Entry?" in *Advertising and Society*, Yale Brozen, ed. New York: New York University Press, 79–109.

Calfee, John E. and Debra Jones Ringold (1994), "The 70% Majority: Enduring Consumer Beliefs About Advertising," *Journal of Public Policy & Marketing*, 13 (Fall), 228–38.

Cameron, Glen T. and John Eric Haley (1992), "Feature Advertising: Policies and Attitudes in Print Media," *Journal of Advertising*, 21 (September), 47–55.

Carrigan, Marylyn and Isabelle Szmigin (1999), "The Representation of Older People in Advertising," *Journal of the Marketing Research Society*, 41 (July), 311–26.

Cavanagh, Gerald F. and Arthur F. McGovern (1988), *Ethical Dilemmas in the Modern Corporation*. Englewood Cliffs, NJ: Prentice Hall.

Clark, Eric (1989), *The Want Makers—The World of Advertising: How They Make You Buy*. New York: Viking.

Davidson, D. Kirk (1996), *Selling Sin: The Marketing of Socially Unacceptable Products*. Westport, CT: Quorum Books.

——— (1998), "Opportunities, Threats When Marketing to Kids," *Marketing News*, (August 17), 10.

DeGeorge, Richard T. (1982), *Business Ethics*. New York: Macmillan Publishing Company.

Dichter, Ernest (1964), *Handbook of Consumer Motivations: The Psychology of the World of Objects*. New York: McGraw-Hill Book Company.

Dickson, Peter R. and James L. Ginter (1987), "Market Segmentation, Product Differentiation, and Marketing Strategy," *Journal of Marketing*, 51 (April), 1–10.

Dignam, Conor (1999), "Ethics Will Be Key in Battling EU-Led Children's Ad Ban," *Marketing*, (April 22), 27.

Duffy, Martyn (1990), "Advertising and Alcoholic Drink Demand in the UK: Some Further Rotterdam Model Estimates," *International Journal of Advertising*, 9 (3), 247–57.

Ekelund, Robert B., Jr., and David S. Saurman (1988), *Advertising and the Market Process: A Modern Economic View*. San Francisco: Pacific Research Institute for Public Policy.

Fisher, Franklin M. and John J. McGowan (1979), "Advertising and Welfare: Comment," *Bell Journal of Economics*, 10 (Autumn), 726–27.

Fisher, Joseph C. (1993), *Advertising, Alcohol Consumption, and Abuse: A Worldwide Survey*. Westport, CT: Greenwood Press.

——— and Peter A. Cook (1995), *Advertising, Alcohol Consumption, and Mortality: An Empirical Investigation*. Westport, CT: Greenwood Press.

Fowles, Jib (1996), *Advertising and Popular Culture*. Thousand Oaks, CA: Sage Publications.

Galbraith, John Kenneth (1956), *American Capitalism: The Concept of Countervailing Power, rev. ed.* Boston: Houghton Mifflin Company.

——— (1967), *The New Industrial State*. New York: Signet Books.

Glantz, Leonard H. (1997), "Controlling Tobacco Advertising: The FDA Regulations and the First Amendment," *American Journal of Public Health*, 87 (March), 446–51.

Goldberg, Marvin E. and Gerald J. Gorn (1978), "Some Unintended Consequences of TV Advertising to Children," *Journal of Consumer Research*, 5 (June), 22–29.

Hackley, Christopher E. and Philip J. Kitchen (1999), "Ethical Perspectives on the Postmodern Communications Leviathan," *Journal of Business Ethics*, 20 (January), 15–26.

Harris, James R. and Charlotte D. Sutton (1995), "Unraveling the Ethical Decision-Making Process: Clues from an Empirical Study Comparing Fortune 1000 Executives and MBA Students," *Journal of Business Ethics*, 14 (October), 805–17.

Heubusch, Kevin (1997), "Is It OK to Sell to Kids?" *American Demographics*, 19 (January), 55.

Higham, Nick (1999), "Industry Divided over Prospect of Ban on Children's Advertising," *Marketing Week*, (July 8), 17.

Hinkle, Warren (1974), "The Adman Who Hated Advertising," *Atlantic Monthly* (March), 67–71.

Hoek, Janet (1999), "Effects of Tobacco Advertising Restrictions: Weak Responses to Strong Measures?" *International Journal of Advertising*, 18 (1), 23–39.

Holak, Susan L. and Srinivas K. Reddy (1986), "Effects of a Television and Radio Advertising Ban: A Study of the Cigarette Industry," *Journal of Marketing*, 50 (October), 219–27.

Hyman, Michael R. (1996), "A Critique and Revision of the Multidimensional Ethics Scale," *Journal of Empirical Generalisations in Marketing Science*, 1, 1–35.

—————— and Richard Tansey (1990), "The Ethics of Psychoactive Ads," *Journal of Business Ethics*, 9 (February), 105–14.

—————— and —————— (1991), "A Rapprochement Between Advertisers and Jungians," *Current Issues and Research in Advertising*, 13, 105–23.

Josefson, Deborah (1998), "Marketing of Antipsychotic Drugs Attacked," *British Medical Journal*, 316 (February), 648.

Kaul, Anil and Dick R. Wittink (1995), "Empirical Generalizations About the Impact of Advertising on Price Sensitivity and Prices," *Marketing Science*, 14 (3), G151–G160

Key, Wilson Bryan (1972), *Subliminal Seduction*. New York: Signet Books.

—————— (1976), *Media Sexploitation*. New York: Signet Books.

—————— (1980), *The Clam-Plate Orgy and Other Subliminal Techniques for Manipulating Your Behavior*. New York: Signet Books.

—————— (1989), *Age of Manipulation: The Con in Confidence and the Sin in Sincere*. New York: Signet Books.

Lambin, J.J. (1976), *Advertising, Competition, and Market Conduct in Oligopoly Over Time*. Amsterdam, Netherlands: North-Holland.

Lantos, Geoffrey P. (1987), "Advertising: Looking Glass or Molder of the Masses?" *Journal of Public Policy & Marketing*, 6 (1), 104–28.

Lasch, Christopher (1979), *The Culture of Narcissism: American Life in An Age of Diminished Expectations*. New York: Warner Books.

LaTour, Michael S. and Tony L. Henthorne (1994), "Ethical Judgements of Sexual Appeals In Print Advertising," *Journal of Advertising*, 23 (September), 81–90.

Lavine, Howard, Donna Sweeney, and Stephen H. Wagner (1999), "Depicting Women as Sex Objects in Television Advertising: Effects on Body Dissatisfaction," *Personality and Social Psychology Bulletin*, 25 (August), 1049–58.

Leahy, Arthur S. (1997), "Advertising and Concentration: A Survey of the Empirical Evidence," *Quarterly Journal of Business and Economics*, 36 (Winter), 35–50.

Leiser, Burton M. (1978), "The Ethics of Advertising," in *Ethics, Free Enterprise, & Public Policy: Original Essays on Moral Issues in Business*, Richard T. De George and Joseph A. Pichler, eds. New York: Oxford University Press, 173–86.

Levitt, Theodore (1970), "The Morality (?) of Advertising," *Harvard Business Review*, 48 (July–August), 84–92.

—————— (1986), "Marketing Myopia," in *The Marketing Imagination*. Theodore Levitt, ed. New York: The Free Press, 141–72.

Mackie, J.L. (1977), *Ethics: Inventing Right and Wrong*. New York: Penguin Books.

Maren, Lars and Nigel Walmsley (1999), "Should We Ban TV Ads for Children?" *Marketing*, (July 15), 8.

McAllister, Matthew P. (1996), *The Commercialization of American Culture: New Advertising, Control and Democracy*. Thousand Oaks, CA: Sage Publications.

Miller, Fiona E.C. (1998), "Bad Hair Day? Blasphemy, Indecency & English Advertising," *International Journal of Advertising*, 17 (3), 381–92.

Mittal, Banwari (1994), "Public Assessment of TV Advertising: Faint Praise and Harsh Criticism," *Journal of Advertising Research*, 34 (January/February), 35–53.

National Science Foundation (1977), *Research on The Effects of Television Advertising on Children*. Washington, DC: U.S. Government Printing Office.

Nebenzahl, Israel D. and Eugene D. Jaffe (1998), "Ethical Dimensions of Advertising Executions," *Journal of Business Ethics*, 17 (May), 805–15.

Nelson, Philip (1974), "The Economic Value of Advertising," in *Advertising and Society*, Yale Brozen, ed. New York: New York University Press, 43–66.

O'Connell, Vanessa (1998), "Ad-Spending Forecast for Next Year Is Cut Slightly, But Growth of 5.5% Is Still Seen," *Wall Street Journal*, (December 8), B13.

Ong, Beng Soo, Foo-Nin Ho, and Kenneth E. Clow (1997), "Ethical Perceptions of Reference Price Advertising," *American Business Review*, 15 (January), 7–14.

Packard, Vance (1958), *The Hidden Persuaders*. New York: Pocket Books.

Parsons, Leonard J. and Randall L. Schultz (1976), *Marketing Models and Econometric Research*. New York: North-Holland Publishing Company.

Pass, Christopher, Brian Sturgess, and Nicholas Wilson (1994), "Advertising, Barriers to Entry and Competition Policy," *Journal of Product and Brand Management*, 3 (3), 51–58.

Pechmann, Cornelia and Chuan-Fong Shih (1999), "Smoking Scenes in Movies and Antismoking Advertisements Before Movies: Effects on Youth," *Journal of Marketing*, 63 (July), 1–13.

Peterson, Robin T. and Douglas T. Ross (1997), "A Content Analysis of the Portrayal of Mature Individuals in Television Commercials," *Journal of Business Ethics*, 16 (May), 425–33.

Petit, Thomas and Alan Zakon (1962), "Advertising and Social Values," *Journal of Marketing*, 26 (October), 15–17.

Petty, Ross D. (1993), "Advertising and the First Amendment: A Practical Test for Distinguishing Commercial Speech from Fully Protected Speech," *Journal of Public Policy & Marketing*, 12 (Fall), 170–77.

Phillips, Barbara J. (1997), "In Defense of Advertising: A Social Perspective," *Journal of Business Ethics*, 16 (January), 109–18.

Phillips, Michael J. (1997), *Ethics and Manipulation in Advertising: Answering a Flawed Indictment*. Westport, CT: Quorum Books.

Pollay, Richard W. (1986), "The Distorted Mirror: Reflections on the Unintended Consequences of Advertising," *Journal of Marketing*, 50 (April), 18–36.

Potter, David M. (1954), *People of Plenty: Economic Abundance and the American Character*. Chicago: The University of Chicago Press.

Preston, Ivan L. (1996), *The Great American Blow-Up: Puffery in Advertising and Selling*, rev. ed. Madison, WI: The University of Wisconsin Press.

Quester, Pascale (1999), "A Cross Cultural Study of Juvenile Response to Anti-smoking Advertisements," *Journal of Euro-Marketing*, 7 (2), 29–46.

Randazzo, Sal (1995), *The Myth Makers: How Advertisers Apply the Power of Classic Myths and Symbols to Create Modern Day Legends*. Chicago: Probus Publishing.

Reichert, Tom, Jacqueline Lambiase, Susan Morgan, Meta Carstarphen, and Susan Zavoina (1999), "Cheesecake and Beefcake: No Matter How You Slice It, Sexual Explicitness in Advertising Continues to Increase," *Journalism and Mass Communication Quarterly*, 76 (Spring), 7–20.

Rittenburg, Terri L. and Madhavan Parthasarathy (1997), "Ethical Implications of Target Market Selection," *Journal of Macromarketing*, 17 (Fall), 49–64.

Robin, Donald and Laurie Babin (1997), "Making Sense of the Research on Gender and Ethics in Business: A Critical Analysis and Extension, *Business Ethics Quarterly*, 7 (October), 61–90.

Rogers, Martha and Christine A. Seiler (1994), "The Answer Is No: A National Survey of the Advertising Industry," *Journal of Advertising Research*, 34 (March/April), 36–45.

Rosenfield, James R. (1998), "American Family Publishers: Strikes Millennial Notes, Creating Ethical Quandaries," *Direct Marketing*, 60 (March), 44–46.

——— (1999), "Sweepstakes 1999: A Look at the Newly Chastened American Family Publishers," *Direct Marketing*, 61 (March), 16–17.

Ruskin, Gary (1999), "The Cost of Commercialism," *Multinational Monitor*, 20 (January/February), 9–15.

Slater, Wayne (1990), "Attack Ads Dominate Campaigns," *The Dallas Morning News*, (June 10), A1, A31, A32.

Smith, Craig (1995), "Marketing Strategies for the Ethics Era," *Sloan Management Review*, 36 (Summer), 85–97.

Smith, Glen (1990), "The Effect of Advertising on Juvenile Smoking Behaviour," *International Journal of Advertising*, 9 (1), 57–79.

Snipes, Robin L., Michael S. LaTour, and Sara J. Bliss (1999), "A Model of the Effects of Self-efficacy on the Perceived Ethicality and Performance of Fear Appeals in Advertising," *Journal of Business Ethics*, 19 (April), 273–85.

Spain, William (1997), "'Unmentionables' Ads Making Their Way onto Cable," *Advertising Age*, (April 14), S6, S10.

Steiner, Robert L. (1998), "Margin and Price Effects of Manufacturers' Brand Advertising," in *How Advertising Works: The Role of Research*, John Philip Jones, ed. Thousand Oaks, CA: Sage Publications, 308–25.

Stern, Barbara B. (1999), "Gender and Multicultural Issues in Advertising: Stages on the Research Highway," *Journal of Advertising*, 28 (Spring), 1–9.

Steyn, Mark (1997), "Flush with Shame," *American Spectator*, 30 (October), 48–50.

Taylor, Charles R. and Barbara B. Stern (1997), "Asian-Americans: Television Advertising and the 'Model Minority' Stereotype," *Journal of Advertising*, 26 (Summer), 47–61.

Telser, Lester (1974), "Advertising and the Consumer," in *Advertising and Society*, Yale Brozen, ed. New York: New York University Press, 25–42.

Teinowitz, Ira (1999), "Tobacco Foes Poised for Huge Campaign," *Advertising Age*, (April 5), 4.

Tinkham, Spenser F. and Ruth Ann Weaver-Larisey (1994), "Ethical Judgments of Political Television Commercials as Predictors of Attitude Towards the Ad," *Journal of Advertising*, 23 (September), 43–57.

Treise, Debbie, Michael F. Weigold, Jenneane Conna, and Heather Garrison (1994), "Ethics in Advertising: Ideological Correlates of Consumer Perceptions," *Journal of Advertising*, 23 (September), 59–69.

Tremblay, Carol Horton and Victor J. Tremblay (1999), "Re-interpreting the Effect of an Advertising Ban on Cigarette Smoking," *International Journal of Advertising*, 18 (1), 41–49.

Turow, Joseph (1997), *Breaking Up America: Advertisers and the New Media World*. Chicago: The University of Chicago Press.

Twitchell, James B. (1996), *ADCULT USA: The Triumph of Advertising in the American Culture*. New York: Columbia University Press.

Verschoor, Curtis C. (1993), "Benchmarking the Audit Committee, " *Journal of Accountancy*, 176 (September), 59–63.

Waide, John (1987), "The Making of Self and World in Advertising," *Journal of Business Ethics*, 6 (February), 73–79.

Wills, Robert L. and Willard F. Mueller (1989), "Brand Pricing and Advertising," *Southern Economic Journal*, 56 (October), 383–95.

Wilson, Aubrey and Christopher West (1992), "Permissive Marketing: The Effect of the AIDS Crisis on Marketing Practices and Messages," *Business Strategy Review*, 3 (Summer), 91–109.

VII

Summary and a Look to the Future

18

Advertising and Societal Trends in the New Millennium

George M. Zinkhan
University of Georgia

I n this final chapter, I discuss several emerging societal trends and their implications for advertising. The emphasis is on identifying trends that might play out over the next 20 years and discussing how these trends may influence advertising and marketing practice. No one can predict the future—not even what will happen tomorrow. As such, it is quite difficult to prognosticate the events that will unfold 20 years from now. Nonetheless, such speculations are offered in this chapter. No doubt, readers in the years 2020 or 2040 will laugh at the absurd ideas put forward here.

To illustrate the difficulties of predicting the future of society and its institutions, consider forecasts that were made in the 1950s. At that time, experts believed that nuclear technology would shape the lives of those living in the late twentieth century. Such prognosticators foresaw a future with nuclear-powered automobiles and nuclear-powered appliances in the home. Very few believed that electronic computing would reshape the landscape of the late twentieth century. Even some of the early computer manufacturers could not imagine that there would be more than five or six buyers for their machines.

The major trends discussed here include the following: the home, the media, and environmentalism. For each area, I extrapolate current trends into the near future and highlight the implications for advertising and marketing.

The Home

Throughout the course of the twentieth century, technology has altered the nature of the American home. Labor-saving devices, including the vacuum cleaner, the electric (or gas) range, the electric (or gas) oven, clean heating systems, electric lights, and so forth are ubiquitous. Although, some of these inventions emerged in the nineteenth century, many were popularized and became widely available in the twentieth century. As mentioned in Chapter one, after we make tools, our tools then proceed to remake us. For example, when the vacuum cleaner became widely available, the standards for cleanliness and the "properly kept home" also changed.

How will the home environment evolve in the twenty-first century? One possibility is the popularization of the "smart house." The smart house is capable of learning the preferences of its occupants. Over time, the house (through a process of trial and error) learns when the occupant turns lights on and off in specific rooms. The house learns when the occupants begin moving around in the morning (and adjusts temperature levels accordingly). It learns when hot water will be in demand so that 100 gallons of hot water do not have to be waiting at all times. Instead, the water can be heated in anticipation of demand, thus saving energy costs (see the following section on environmentalism).

At the present time, most Internet users log on from stationary computers. In the near future, society will enter an era of nomadic computing, in which users will tap into the Internet through hand-held devices. For example, a person might walk into a room and, using a hand-held computer, program a videocassette recorder (VCR). The next phase could be termed "ubiquitous computing," in which many everyday objects will be imbedded with computer chips and communicate with one another constantly. As part of the smart house, there might be the "smart medicine cabinet." This enlightened cabinet will detect when crucial (or even ordinary) pharmaceutical supplies are running low. The cabinet has an online connection, which allows it to contact a pharmacy for refills.

Other appliances might interact in sophisticated ways. The smart refrigerator could take inventory (in the same way as the medicine cabinet) and generate a shopping list. Alternatively, users might type in a dish they wish to prepare for a dinner party. In response, the refrigerator could identify those items that are on hand, begin a defrosting process (if that is required), and contact a store electronically to order the remaining ingredients. At the required time, the refrigerator could communicate with the oven to trigger a preheating sequence.

As another feature, the refrigerator might go online to notify its manufacturer (or distributor) of impending service problems. In other words, appliances might take steps to repair themselves before they are even broken. Such a process exists now for large Dell servers. They contact their manufacturer to correct problems that their owners do not even know exist. At the same time, upgraded software is automatically downloaded from the home base to the server, again without any intervention from the owner.

Some observers shrink away from such descriptions of a ubiquitously wired world. The idea of a home that is constantly communicating with itself about its occupants is slightly scary—even if the ultimate purpose is "to serve humankind." Are people really so lazy and shiftless that everything has to be done for them before they can even think of what they want or lift a finger? Such a future, if it comes to pass, could be fraught with problems.

No technology is successful unless it is adopted and embraced by consumers. In the end, it is consumers who decide which technologies will succeed and which will fail (and in what versions). There is currently a high desire for simplification. Americans believe that they just do not have enough time in the day to do all the things that are expected of them. Thus, ubiquitous computing and the smart house offer a broad appeal in that they promise to simplify life (through complex, behind-the-scenes communications).

The Media

As discussed previously, consumers are looking for ways to simplify their lives and to simplify decision making. The current media environment complicates life. There seems to be too much information that comes too fast in a disorganized way. Once again, technology holds promise for simplification.

Rust and Oliver (1994) describe the concept of the "knowbot." A knowbot is an electronic agent that can simplify commercial communications. For example, consumers could instruct their knowbots to filter all e-mail and web communications they receive. Similarly, consumers could instruct the knowbot to videotape two hours of television programming, starting at 8 P.M. At the same time, the knowbot could edit out the commercials. On a future date, the knowbot's master might request it to search for automobile commercials and tape them in a block for future viewing. In this way, the knowbot serves to simplify the media environment. Consider the implications for advertisers. Currently, advertisers need to find a way to break through the clutter and communicate with a human prospect. In the future, advertisers might have to figure out a way to ensure that their messages can pass through the vigilant filter of the knowbot.

Consider the current trend in product placements: Organizations pay to have their products favorably portrayed in television programs or films. This practice blurs the line between program and commercial. In the future, a consumer might like an outfit that an actor or actress is wearing and be able to order it instantly online. Thus, a television program becomes a kind of direct marketing tool. Such online ordering of products "as seen on television" might not appeal to every consumer, but there might be a segment of buyers who find such an option attractive.

The twentieth century media environment was shaped by a series of technological revolutions. The important technological introductions included radio, wire transfer of photographs for newspapers, magazines that feature photographs (e.g., *Life*), broadcast television, cable television, the VCR, and the Internet. What will come in the future? I explore some possibilities subsequently.

Many U.S. consumers pay for the cable television they watch and are willing to pay extra to watch premium channels (e.g., HBO, Showtime). In the near future, premium channels might offer consumers a discount on their cable bill if they are willing to receive some commercials along with their usual cable fare. These commercials might appear in blocks, much as they do in some European countries.

As discussed previously, the Internet and television have the potential to merge into a new medium. The marketing opportunities created by such a merger are limitless. It is interesting to note how entertainment media have evolved over the course of the twentieth century. For example, the radio was first invented as a way for ships to communicate with one another and with those on shore. Eventually, it became an entertainment medium. However, who was supposed to supply the programming content for this new medium (a similar problem faced by the Internet at the dawn of the twenty-first century)? At first, radio manufacturers resolved to finance the content themselves, so as to stimulate radio sales. This experiment failed. When advertisers adopted the medium and began to sponsor content (e.g., radio programs), radio became a huge success and a true mass medium of communication. Beginning in the 1930s, the death of radio has been predicted frequently. Competing technologies, including talking pictures, broadcast television, cable television, audio tapes, compact disc players, VCRs, and the Internet, seemed to sound the death knell for the radio industry. Each time, radio was able to transform itself into something else and survive. For example, radio's popularity with automobile drivers enabled it to prosper in the late twentieth century. In the twenty-first century, radio is reborn as an attachment to the Internet. Consumers in the United States, for example, enjoy listening to their hometown radio station on the Internet when they find themselves away from home. Similarly, workers who are posted abroad find great pleasure in listening to radio broadcasts from their home countries, through the Internet. Today, advertising revenues from radio are vibrant and fast growing (Krugman 2000).

Environmentalism

Environmentalism is discussed here as an example of an important social trend. This treatment is intended to be illustrative, not exhaustive.

The earth's resources are limited; however consumption in the United States proceeds as if there were no tomorrow. Can this level of production and consumption be maintained into the indefinite future? Marketing and advertising have important roles to play in informing consumers about consumption patterns that are less destructive of the environment (Zinkhan and Carlson 1995). For example, some archeologists now claim that a variety of civilizations (e.g., in Central and South America, in Mesopotamia) failed because their agricultural methods eventually overwhelmed the local environment. In the present day, U.S. agriculture feeds the world, but there might be long-term costs to the land (e.g., due to the use of pesticides and chemical fertilizers) that could end this trend. For every American, it takes 14 acres of land to provide food and raw materials (e.g., clothing, paper products). It takes another 14 acres of land to provide for a distribution system (e.g., the interstate highway system along with local roads, railroads, and airports). If consumers in other countries (e.g., India, China) copied the U.S. pattern of production and consumption, the earth would run out of land and resources.

What is the purpose of consumption? Advertising portrays visions of the good life and stimulates consumption behavior (Zinkhan and Prenshaw 1994). Perhaps advertisers do their job too well. Successful commercials promote materialism, and unchecked materialism contributes to the depletion of the world's resources (Zinkhan 1994). There could be a way out of this trap by distinguishing between "terminal materialism" and "instrumental materialism" (Csikszentmihalyi and Rochberg-Halton 1978). Terminal materialism refers to a runaway habit of possession, and consumption becomes an end in itself. With instrumental materialism, the possession of things serves goals that are independent of greed. For example, a consumer might aim to acquire things so as to cement a closer bond with his or her mother and father or to cement a closer bond with his or her sister, who happens to live in a different state.

Advertising does not necessarily have to serve the role of promoting greed and the possession of things. Advertising is about symbols and values and imagery. That is, commercial messages have the ability to transform the physical world and give new meanings to old things. Thus, advertising plays an important symbolic role within a culture, and it has the potential to bind a society together through the transmission of shared images (Zinkhan 1994).

Summary

Advertising plays an important role in modern life. Advertising can be studied from the point of view of advertisers and their agencies. What makes advertising effective? How can communication effectiveness be enhanced? At the same time, advertising can be studied as an artifact of the culture that produced it. From this perspective, advertising provides a means to track social history.

Advertising can also be viewed through the lens of public policy. What is the best economic system? What role does advertising play in this economic system? At present, proponents of capitalism believe that advertising is part of a system that delivers a high quality of life to many consumers. As advertising evolves and transforms in the twenty-first century, I hope that it continues to play such a positive role within society.

References

Csikszentmihalyi, Mihaly and Eugene Rochberg-Halton (1978), *The Meaning of Things: Domestic Symbols and the Self.* Cambridge: Cambridge University Press.

Krugman, Dean (2000), personal communication (February).

Rust, Roland and Richard W. Oliver (1994), "The Death of Advertising," *Journal of Advertising*, 23 (4), 71–78.

Zinkhan, George M. (1994), "Advertising, Materialism, and Quality of Life," *Journal of Advertising*, 23 (2), 1–4.

—— and Les Carlson (1995), "Green Advertising and the Reluctant Consumer," *Journal of Advertising*, 24 (2), 1–6.

—— and Penelope J. Prenshaw (1994), "Good Life Images and Brand Name Associations: Evidence from Asia, America, and Europe," in *Advances in Consumer Research*, Vol. 21, C. Allen and D. Roedder John, eds. Provo, UT: Association for Consumer Research.

Notes on Contributors

Jon R. Austin is Assistant Professor of Marketing and Research Methods in the School of Hotel Administration at Cornell University. His research examines the effects of low-involvement ad processing on consumers' perceptions of brand symbolism. He is also working on ways of measuring symbolic brand meanings.

Anne L. Balazs is an Associate Professor of Marketing at Mississippi University for Women. Her research interests are in retailing, sales management, and advertising. She was the recipient of the Ethel Olin Corbin Poetry Prize at Smith College and has published her poetry in a variety of outlets.

Subodh Bhat is Associate Professor of Marketing at San Francisco State University, where he teaches marketing strategy and brand management in the MBA program. He has also been Visiting Scholar at the Hong Kong University of Science and Technology and Visiting Associate Professor at Stanford University. His research interests include brands and branding, advertising, entrepreneurship, and high-tech marketing. He has published several articles in journals such as the *Journal of Marketing Research*, *Journal of Advertising*, *Journal of Business Research*, *Journal of Consumer Marketing*, and *Journal of Marketing Theory and Practice*.

Steven P. Brown is Associate Professor of Marketing at the Edwin L. Cox School of Business at Southern Methodist University. He previously taught at the University of Texas at Austin and the University of Georgia. His research has been published in the *Journal of Marketing*, *Journal of Marketing Research*, *Journal of Consumer Research*, *Psychological Bulletin*, *Journal of Applied Psychology*, and other journals. He serves on the editorial review boards of the *Journal of Marketing*, *Journal of the Academy of Marketing Science*, and *Journal of Personal Selling & Sales Management*.

Traci A. Carte is Assistant Professor of Management Information Systems in the Michael F. Price College of Business at the University of Oklahoma. Her research interests include IT implementation, electronic commerce, and change management. Her research has been published in *Information Systems Research*, *Public Productivity and Management Review*, and many national conference proceedings.

Margy Conchar is an Assistant Professor at the University of North Carolina, Charlotte. She is the recipient of four awards for her dissertation research, which considers the financial effects of advertising spending. Her research interests also include advertising and consumer behavior on the Internet; quality-of-life, cross-cultural values; professional services marketing; and the role of risk in consumer behavior. Prior to commencing her doctoral studies, she gained extensive experience as a manager in the fields of advertising and marketing research in South Africa and London.

Ellen Day's research interests include consumer behavior, services marketing, and qualitative research. She has published in various marketing journals.

Denise E. DeLorme is Assistant Professor of Advertising at the University of Central Florida. Her particular research interests are brand placement, integrated marketing communications, qualitative methods, and research ethics. She has published articles in the *Journal of Advertising*, *Journal of Marketing Communications*, and conference proceedings of the American Academy of Advertising.

Alex Gray is currently pursuing a career in business consulting. He is an expert in electronic commerce and web page design.

Cathy L. Hartman is Associate Professor of Marketing at Utah State University, where she teaches buyer behavior and environmental decision making. Her research focuses on environmental NGO-stakeholder collaboration and the development of sustainable marketing relationships. Her work has been published in *Journal of Business Research*, *Journal of Business Ethics*, *Business Horizons*, *Business Strategy and the Environment*, *Long Range Planning*, and various conference proceedings.

Diana L. Haytko is Assistant Professor of Marketing at the M.J. Neeley School of Business at Texas Christian University. Her research includes examining the effects of personal relationships between boundary spanners on interorganizational relationships. In addition, she studies consumer response to retail environments.

Paul J. Hensel is Professor of Marketing and Associate Dean in the College of Business Administration at the University of New Orleans. He has taught previously at the University of Kentucky and Southern Illinois University. He has published more than 50 referred articles and is currently working on Volume III of the *Marketing Scales Handbook* with Dr. Gordon C. Bruner II and Dr. Karen James.

Pamela M. Homer is Professor of Marketing in the College of Business at California State University, Long Beach. Previous to being tenured at CSULB, she was an assistant professor in the Advertising Department at the University of Texas at Austin. Her research interests focus on the general areas of consumer behavior and advertising, including emotion, methodological issues, and structural equation modeling.

Michael R. Hyman is NationsBank Professor of Marketing at New Mexico State University, Las Cruces. During the past two decades, he has taught at University of Illinois at Chicago; University of Houston, University Park; University of Houston, Clear Lake; University of North Texas; Limburgs Universitair Centrum (Belgium); and New Mexico State University. He is co-editor of *Journal of Business and Entrepreneurship*. He has published more than 30 articles in journals such as *Journal of Marketing*, *Journal of the Academy of Marketing Science*, *Journal of Business Research*, *Journal of Retailing*, *Journal of Advertising*, *Journal of Current Issues and Research in Advertising*, and *Journal of Business Ethics*. He has consulted extensively for the hospitality industry; his major clients include Ramada, Hilton, and the Greater Houston Convention and Visitors Bureau. His current research interests include advertising, ethics, knowledge acquisition in academia, and philosophical analyses in marketing.

Jeff Inman has been with the University of Wisconsin since 1994. From 1991–1994, he was on the faculty at the University of Southern California. His research focuses on consumer decision making and consumer interpretation and response to marketing efforts. His work has appeared in the *Journal of Consumer Research, Journal of Marketing Research, Marketing Science, Journal of Retailing,* and *Marketing Letters.*

Karen James is Associate Professor of Marketing at Louisiana State University in Shreveport. Prior to joining the LSUS faculty, she taught at the University of New Orleans for two years as a visiting assistant professor and at Southern Illinois University as an instructor. She has published several referred articles in journals and proceedings, and she is co-author of Volume III of the *Marketing Scales Handbook* with Dr. Gordon C. Bruner II and Dr. Paul J. Hensel.

James H. Leigh is Associate Professor of Marketing at Texas A&M University. Prior to joining Texas A&M University in 1987, he served on the faculty of Eastern Michigan University during the final year of his doctoral program. He has published more than 25 refereed journal articles, and he is co-founder and co-editor of the *Journal of Current Issues and Research in Advertising,* which is now in its 22nd year of publication. His primary research interests are in the areas of advertising measurement and assessment, consumer behavior, marketing research, and public policy.

Erika Matulich is Assistant Professor of Marketing in the College of Business at the University of Tampa. Her areas of expertise include strategic marketing planning, promotional strategies, and educational technologies. She is an active member of the American Marketing Association and serves on the board of her local AMA professional chapter

Gillian Oakenfull is Assistant Professor of Marketing at Miami University, Oxford. Her research focuses on brand meaning and brand equity issues, social and cultural influences on consumers' response to advertising and marketing efforts, and cross-cultural and international marketing issues. Her research has been published in the *Journal of Advertising Research* and the *Journal of Global Marketing.*

Angela Patton is Associate Professor of Art at the University of Houston. Her areas of expertise are foundation design and design theory. She is co-founder of the University of Houston Design Collaborative, an interdisciplinary initiative that introduces design principles and visual processing into other disciplines for the purpose of cultivating intuitive reasoning and integrated thinking skills. She exhibits and publishes her visual and written work in juried exhibitions, museums, academic journals, and the popular press. Her visual work includes environmental projects, products, images, and works on paper. Her written work includes the synthesizing of design theory with other disciplines, the exploration of the interface between design and consumer culture, design history through the context of cultural and social influences, and essays on education.

Misty K. Ritchie is currently employed with Bank of America as the Manager of Balance Building programs in Charlotte, North Carolina. She builds and implements statistical models for the Consumer Credit group.

Edwin R. Stafford is Associate Professor of Marketing at Utah State University, where he teaches marketing strategy. His research centers on the strategy and relationship marketing implications of green alliances and environmental stakeholder collaboration. His work has been published in *Sloan Management Review*, *Journal of Advertising*, *Business Horizons*, *Business Strategy and the Environment*, and *Long Range Planning*, as well as in various conference proceedings.

Miriam B. Stamps is Associate Professor of Marketing at the University of South Florida. Her research focuses on segmentation strategies and marketing to diverse consumer groups. She has published in the *Journal of Leisure Research*, *Journal of Marketing Education*, and the *Journal of Personal Selling & Sales Management*. Her research has also appeared in the proceedings of the Academy of Marketing Science, the Association for Consumer Research, the AMA Winter Educator's Conference, Southern Marketing Association, and the American Institute for Decision Sciences, as well as other conferences. Her teaching interests include consumer behavior and international marketing. She has also lectured overseas and serves as a consultant to several public and private organizations.

Andrea Stanaland is Assistant Professor of Marketing at the National University of Singapore. Her professional experience includes information technology consulting for Andersen Consulting and operational consulting for Arthur Andersen. Her research has been published in the *Journal of Advertising*, *Journal of Personal Selling & Sales Management*, *Journal of Health Care Marketing*, *Marketing Educator*, and *Health Marketing Quarterly*. This research was conducted while the author was a doctoral student at the University of Houston.

Vanitha Swaminathan is Assistant Professor of Marketing at the Isenberg School of Management at the University of Massachusetts, Amherst. Her research interests are in branding strategy and electronic commerce. She has published in the *Journal of Marketing Research*, *Journal of Computer-Mediated Communication*, *Advances in Consumer Research*, and in the proceedings of the American Marketing Association and Association of Management and Relationship Marketing conferences. She has recently written a book chapter on brand alliances in a forthcoming volume titled *Conceptual Foundations in Relationship Marketing*. She received an award from Procter & Gamble's Innovation Research Fund for her dissertation work on brand extensions.

Gail Ayala Taylor is Assistant Professor of Integrated Marketing Communications in the Medill School of Journalism at Northwestern University. She currently teaches graduate courses in marketing management and advertising. In addition to teaching in the Medill School, she has a courtesy appointment at the J.L. Kellogg Graduate School of Management, where she teaches a course on global initiatives in management. Before joining the faculty at Northwestern, Taylor was

Assistant Professor of Marketing in the Terry College of Business at the University of Georgia. Her research interests revolve around examining marketing communications issues as they relate to services marketing and consumer targeting. Her research has appeared in the *International Journal of Retailing and Consumer Services*, *Journal of Services Marketing*, and *Psychology and Marketing*. In addition to publishing in several conference proceedings, she is the lead author of an invited chapter in *Service Quality in Hospitality Organizations*.

Richard Watson is a professor in the Department of Management Information Systems, Terry College, University of Georgia. He has published in leading journals in several fields as well as authored books on data management and electronic commerce. He is a senior editor for *MIS Quarterly*, the MIS field's leading journal, and is the inaugural director of the Terry College's Center for Information Systems Leadership.

Barbara H. Wixom is Assistant Professor of Commerce at the University of Virginia's McIntire School of Commerce. Wixom was made a Fellow of The Data Warehousing Institute for her research in data warehousing, and she has published in journals that include *Information Systems Research*, *Communications of the ACM*, *Journal of Data Warehousing*, *Information Systems Management*, and *End User Computing*. She has presented her work at national and international conferences. She recently published a textbook titled *Systems Analysis and Design: An Applied Approach*.

George M. Zinkhan is the Coca-Cola Company Chair of Marketing and Department Head at the Terry College of Business, University of Georgia. His most recent co-authored book is *Electronic Commerce: The Strategic Perspective*, published in 2000.